T0374204

American Jews with Czechoslovak Roots

Also Authored or Edited by Miloslav Rechcigl, Jr.

Scholarly Publications:

Beyond the Sea of Beer
Encyclopedia of Bohemian and Czech-American Biography 3 vols.
Czech It Out. Czech American Biography Sourcebook
Czech American Timetable. Chronology of Milestones in the History of Czechs in America
Czech American Bibliography. A Comprehensive Listing
Czechmate. From Bohemian Paradise to American Haven. A Personal Memoir
On Behalf of their Homeland: Fifty Years of SVU
Czechs and Slovaks in America
Czech and Slovak American Archival Materials and their Preservation
Czechoslovak American Archivalia 2 vols.
Czech-American Historic Sites, Monuments, and Memorials
US Legislators with Czechoslovak Roots
Educators with Czechoslovak Roots
Deceased Members of the Czechoslovak Society of Arts and Sciences
Czechoslovak Society of Arts and Sciences Directory: 8 editions
The Czechoslovak Contribution to World Culture
Czechoslovakia Past and Present 2 vols.
Studies in Czechoslovak History 2 vols.

Scientific Monographs:

Nutrition and the World Food Problem
Comparative Animal Nutrition. Vol. 1. Carbohydrates, Lipids, and Accessory Growth Factors
Comparative Animal Nutrition. Vol. 2 Nutrient Elements and Toxicants
Comparative Animal Nutrition. Vol. 3. Nitrogen, Electrolytes, Water and Energy Metabolism
Comparative Animal Nutrition. Vol. 4. Physiology of Growth and Nutrition
Man, Food and Nutrition. Strategies and Technological Measures for Alleviating the World Food Problem
World Food Problem: A Selective Bibliography of Reviews
Food, Nutrition and Health. A Multidisciplinary Treatise
Enzyme Synthesis and Degradation in Mammalian Systems
Microbodies and Related Particles

Handbook Series in Nutrition and Food: 18 vols.

Czech Publications:

Tam za tím mořem piva. Naše Amerika jak ji kdo málo zná
Pro Vlast. Padesát let Společnosti pro vědy a umění
Postavy naší Ameriky

American Jews with Czechoslovak Roots

A Bibliography, Bio-Bibliography and Historiography

Miloslav Rechcigl, Jr.

SVU Scholar-in-Residence and Past President
Czechoslovak Society of Arts and Sciences (SVU)

authorHOUSE®

AuthorHouse™
1663 Liberty Drive
Bloomington, IN 47403
www.authorhouse.com
Phone: 1 (800) 839-8640

Published by AuthorHouse 06/15/2018

ISBN: 978-1-5462-3894-2 (sc)
ISBN: 978-1-5462-3895-9 (hc)
ISBN: 978-1-5462-3893-5 (e)

Library of Congress Control Number: 2018904787

Print information available on the last page.

This book is printed on acid-free paper.

In affection to my charming wife Eva,

loving children Jack and Karen,
adorable grandchildren Greg, Kevin, Lindsey, Kristin and Paul,
and dear daughter-in-law Nancy
and
in memory of my beloved parents.

Contents

Listings

FOREWORD

With entries ranging from Paul Desmond to Jerome Kern, Guido Kisch to Bruce A. Gimbel, and Rabbi Isaac M. Wise to Justice Louis D. Brandeis, Miloslav Rechcigl Jr.'s *American Jews with Czechoslovak Roots* is a remarkable reference work, providing vital information on hundreds of individuals who have helped to shape American culture, law, politics, and society over the past three centuries. As such, this book is a crucial resource for anyone wishing to study the ethnic history of the United States and Jewish emigration from Slovakia and the Bohemian lands.

Yet Miloslav Rechcigl aims for much more. American Jews with Czechoslovak Roots combines bio-bibliography with historical bibliography, offering the reader full surveys of scholarly writing on Jewish life in Czechoslovakia: from general histories of Jews in the Czech lands to more focused studies on Jewish-Czech and Jewish-Slovak relations, migration, nationalism and antisemitism, and the Holocaust. It also lists the names and locations of more than one-hundred archival collections in the United States.

With generous and painstaking care, Miloslav Rechcigl invites students, scholars, and interested readers to discover, and add to, a remarkable story.

Hillel J. Kieval, Ph.D.
Goldstein Professor of Jewish History and Thought
Washington University in St. Louis
Department of History
St. Louis, MO 63130

Preface

In one of my essays, I have written that Bohemian or Czech Jews, who have immigrated to America, represent a *terra incognita*. Relatively little is known and relatively little has been written about them, with exception of Guido Kisch's, now classical monograph, *In Search of Freedom*, written in 1949,[1] which dealt primarily with the emigrants from the Czechlands around the year 1848. Some 40 years later, I published an essay,[2] focusing on the earliest arriving Bohemian Jewish pioneers in America. At my suggestion, the Czech Embassy then organized a special conference in 2010 on 'Bohemian and Czech Jews in America,'[3] during which I presented an introductory talk, which was later published.[4]

Both of my studies were also posted on Austria-Czech Sig,[5] and on JewishGen Inc.,[6] respectively, by the foremost Bohemian Jewish genealogist, Randy Schoenberg.[7] In addition, a new project, "Czech (Bohemian) American Jews," encompassing genealogies of noted Bohemian Jews in America was established on GENi.[8]

To complete the picture, I have now prepared a comprehensive bibliography of existing publications on the subject, which, interestingly, has never been attempted. One of the problems, which I also had to tackle in my previous writings, was the question how to identify Bohemian Jews since most of them came to America when the Czechlands were still part of

---

1 Guido Kisch, *In Search of Freedom*. A History of American Jews from Czechoslovakia 1592-1948. London: Edward Goldston, 1948.

2 Miloslav Rechcigl, Jr., "Early Jewish Immigrants in America from the Czech Historic Lands and Slovakia," Review of the Society for the History of Czechoslovak Jews, Vol. 3 (1990-91), pp.157-179.

3 See - https://www.mzv.cz/file/475542/Conference_information.pdf

4 Miloslav Rechcigl, Jr., "Bohemian and Czech Jews in American History," *Kosmas. Czechoslovak and Central European Journal*, 26, No. 1 (Fall 2012), pp.70—112.

5 See: https://www.jewishgen.org/AustriaCzech/early_immig.html

6 See: https://www.jewishgen.org/austriaczech/MilaRechcigl.html

7 His bio is [posted on Wikipedia. See: https://en.wikipedia.org/wiki/E._Randol_Schoenberg

8 See - https://www.geni.com/projects/Czech-Bohemian-American-Jews/14626

the Austro-Hungarian Empire. Because German was the official language of the land, it was thus not surprising that they easily mixed with the German element, and, as such, were *a priori* considered Germans or Austrians, or even Hungarians. This was true even though they had a separate identity and established their own culture. They were not Germans, they were Bohemians Jews. After the Czechoslovak Republic was established, many of them identified themselves as Czech Jews, having learned the Czech language and becoming a part of the Czech cultural milieu.

Even though many Bohemian Jews have had German-sounding names, with some practice, this author has soon developed the skill of 'guessing' whether a given surname might be of Bohemian Jewish origin, which had to be, of course, later verified. As for the selection, as in all my previous work, in my definition of Jews, I have included not only those that have professed in Judaism, but also the descendants of the former Jews who originally lived on the territory of the former Czechoslovakia, regardless of the generation or where they were born.

As for the Bibliography itself, some areas are rather scanty since so little has been written. However, this is not a reflection of the paucity of work done by the American Bohemian/Czech and Slovak Jews in a given area. As the reader will find out, they have been, practically, involved in every field of human endeavor, in numbers that surprise. It is for this reason, why a large space has been devoted to references concerning individuals who distinguished themselves. Consequently, this compendium can also be used as a comprehensive listing of biographical sources relating to American Jews with the Czechoslovak roots.

The biographical information comes mostly from my two recent books,[9] some from the *International Dictionary of Central European Émigrés* [10] and occasionally from Wikipedia. Excellent biographical data can also be found in family papers and collections, held in various archives, as well as on the genealogical GENi websites, to which references have been made,

---

[9] Rechcigl, Miloslav, Jr., *Czech It Out. Czech American Biography Sourcebook*. Bloomington, IN: AuthorHouse, 2015.

Rechcigl, Miloslav, Jr., *Encyclopedia of Bohemian and Czech-American Biography*. Bloomington, IN: AuthorHouse, 2016. 3 vols.

[10] *International Biographical Dictionary of Central European Émigrés 1933-1945*. New York: R. G. Sauer, 1983.

when applicable. As for the GENi websites, they are also excellent sources of geneological information, including family trees on specific families.

As for the sources regarding American Slovak Jews, except for selected listings of prominent individuals in some of my writings,[11] they don't really exist. Consequently, the biographical information on the former, in this publication, is mostly based on my own research.

It is an undisputable fact that the American ethnic literature, generally, if not completely, had ignored history and contributions of American Bohemian and Slovak Jews. The same conclusion can be drawn, even more so, about the few emigration and cultural historians in the former Czechoslovakia, as well as in the present Czech and Slovak Republics. It is the intent of this study to correct such colossal omission. The present publication can thus be viewed as an important addition to the American Bohemian and Slovak historiography.

Image of Justice Brandeis on the cover is courtesy of the Robert D. Farber University Archives & Special Collections Department, Brandeis University.

---

[11] Rechcigl, Miloslav, Jr., "Early Jewish Immigrants in America from the Czech Historic Lands and Slovakia," *op. cit.*; Rechcigl, Miloslav, Jr., "O slovenských velikánech v Americe o nichž se spíše neví. Part 1," *Forum*, October 1995, pp. 8-9; Part 2, Ibid., November 1995, pp. 15-16; Rechcigl, Miloslav, Jr., "Cultural Contributions of Americans with Roots in Slovakia," *Kosmas. Czechoslovak and Central European Journal* 14, No. 1 (Fall 2000), pp. 95-106; Rechcigl, Miloslav, Jr., "Čeští a slovenští lékaři, přírodovědci a technici na americkém kontinentu," in: *Acta Historiae Rerum Naturalium Necnon Technicarum - Prague Studies in the History of Science and Technology*, Vol. 7. Prague: National Technical Museum, 2003, pp. 267-274; Rechcigl, Miloslav, Jr., "Czech and Slovak American Historiography, Kosmas, 24, No. 1 (Fall 2010), pp. 82-124; Rechcigl, Miloslav, Jr., "In Search for Accomplished Young American Professionals of Czech / Slovak Extraction," in: *Young Czech and Slovak Professionals in America.* Selected Papers from the 2011 Regional SVU Conference of the Czechoslovak Society of Arts and Sciences. New York: Publishing House of the Czechoslovak Society of Arts and Sciences, 2012, pp. 164-205.

Listings

I. General References

A. Bibliographies

Kisch, Guido, Bibliography: History of Jews in Czechoslovakia from the Sixteenth to Twentieth Century," in: *In Search of Freedom.* A History of American Jews from Czechoslovakia. London: Edward Goldston and Son Ltd., 1949, pp. 333-365.

Kovtun, George J., "Jews and Jewish Affairs," in: *Czech and Slovak History. An American Bibliography.* Washington, DC: Library of Congress, 1996.

Schoenberg, E. Randol, Austria-Czech Bibliography. Books on Austrian and Bohemian-Moravian Jewry. OnLine: http://www.jewishgen.org/austriaczech/books.html

Muneles, Muneles, *Bibliographical Surveys of Jewish Prague, Jewish Monuments in Bohemia and Moravia.* Edited by Hana Volavková. Prague: Orbis, 1952.

Rechcigl, Miloslav, Jr., *Czech American Bibliography.* A Comprehensive Listing with Focus on the US and with Appendices on Czechs in Canada and Latin America. Bloomington, IN: AuthorHouse, 1011.

B. Archival Material

1. General

Czech Republic Jewish Records. Updated 2014. OnLine: https://familysearch.org/learn/wiki/en/Czech Republic Jewish Records

Czech and Slovak Republics: Jewish Family History Research Guide. OnLine: http://www.cjh.org/pdfs/Czech-Slovak07.pdf

Herman, Jan. "Jewish Community Archives from Bohemia and Moravia; Analytical registers to the catalogues of archive materials from Jewish Communities with the exception of that of Prague." *Judaica Bohemiae.* Vol. 7, No. 1, 1971. YIVO 15/9038

Matusíkova, Lenka, Czech Archival Sources on the History of the Jews in the Czech Lands

Prague: Czech National Archives, First Department. OnLine: http://www.jewishgen.org/austriaczech/Matusikova.htm
Pařik, Arno. *Jewish Prague. The Jewish Museum in Prague.* Czech Republic, 2002.
Petrasova, Marketa, "Collections of the Central Jewish Museum (1942-1945)," *Judaica Bohemiae* 24, No. 1 (1988), pp. 23-38
Rechcigl, Miloslav, Jr., *Czechoslovak American Archivalia.* Olomouc-Ostrava, 2004. 2 vols.

2. Specific Collections

Alfred Adler Papers, in: Library of Congress
Samuel Alschuler Papers, 1893-1940, in: Abraham Lincoln Presidential Library, Springfield, IL
Siegfried Altmann Papers, in: Leo Baeck Institute, NYC
Paul Amann Papers, 1884-1958, in: Leo Baeck Institute, NYC
Karl Arnstein Papers, in: University of Akron, Akron, OK
Leo Ascher Family Collection, in: Leo Baeck Institute, NYC
Leo Baeck Papers, in: Leo Baeck Institute, NYC
Vicki Baum Collection, in: Leo Baeck Institute, NYC
Richard Beer-Hofmann Papers,1705-1998, in: Leo Baeck Institute, NYC
Felix Bloch Papers, 19341-1987, in: Stanford University Archives
Claude Charles Bloch Papers, 1926-1945, in: Library of Congress
Ingram Bloch Collection, Vanderbilt University, Library, Nashville, TN
Brűder Böhm Company Collection, in: Leo Baeck Institute, NYC
Charles and Hana Bruml Family Collection, in: US Holocaust Memorial Museum, Washington, DC
Joseph Hans Bunzel Papers, 1914-1975, in: University of Albany, Albany, NY
Joseph Hans Bunzel Collection, in: Leo Baeck Institute, NYC
Records of the Bunzl Group of Companies, 1857-2008, in: Leo Baeck Institute, NYC
Walter H. Bunzl Family Papers, 1902-1962, MSS 055, in: The Breman Museum, Atlanta, GA
Gerty T. Cori Papers, in: Washington University School of Medicine, St. Louis
Louis Dembitz Brandeis Papers, in: Harvard University Library
Gotthard Deutsch Papers, 1859-1922, in: American Jewish Archives
Hermann Bacher Deutsch Papers, 1827-1970, in: Tulane University Library

Papers of Karl Deutsch, 1939-1990, in: Harvard University

Leopold Eidlitz Papers, 1852—1895, in: Columbia University, Avery Arch. Library

Otto Eisenschiml Papers, in: University of Iowa Libraries, Special Collections, Iowa City

Lorenz Eitner Papers, 1964-1988, in: Stanford University Libraries, Stanford, CA

Paul Elbogen Papers, in: University of California, Davis, Special Collections

Frances Adler Elkis Collection, in: Monterey Peninsula College Library, Archives and Special Collections Department

Papers of Morris Leopold Ernst, in: Harry Ransom Center, University of Texas, Austin

Herbert Feigl Papers, in: University of Pittsburgh, Hillman Library

Abraham Flexner Papers, in: Library of Congress, MS Division

Bernard Flexner Papers, in: Princeton University Library

Simon Flexner Papers, 1891-1946, in: American Philosophical Society

Floersheim Family Papers, 1812-1889, in: American Jewish Archives

Paul Frankl Papers, in: Princeton University Library

Rudolf Friml Collection, in: University of Michigan

Otto Frohlich Collection, 1897, 1956-1969, in: University of Central Florida Libraries

Joswef Herbert Furth Papers, 1932-1981, in: M.E. Grenander Dept. Special Collections & Archives, University of Albany

Edna Gellhorn Papers, 1850-1970, in: Washington Universities Libraries, Special Collections

Joseph Goldberger Papers, 1929-1935, in City University of New York

Goldmark Family Collection, 1832-1959, in: Leo Baeck Institute, NYC

Gratz Family Papers, 1753-1916, in: American Jewish Historical Society, NYC

Rebecca Gratz, 1797-1869, in: American Jewish Archives

Moses J. Gries, 1850-1934, in: American Jewish Archives

Trude Guermonprez Papers, 1947-1976, in: Oakland Museum of California

Trude Guermonprez Papers, 1929-1986, in Smithsonuian Archives of American Art

Thomas H. Guinzburg Reminiscences, in: Columbia University

Martin Harwit Papers, 1957-1987, in: American Jewish Archives

Felix Haurowitz Manuscripts, 1920-1985, in: Indiana University Library

B. Heller & Co. Collection, in: The University of Chicago, Special Collections Research Center

James Gutheim Heller Papers, 1906-1952, in: American Jewish Archives

Maximillian H. Heller Papers, 1871-1929, in: American Jewish Archives

Franziska Porges Hosken Collection, in: Harvard University, Frances Loeb Library

Egon Hostovský Papers, 1934-1970, in: Library of Congress

Bernard Illoway Papers, 1894-1950, in: Yeshiva University Archives

Roman Jakobson Papers, 1908-1982, in: Massachusetts Institute of Technology Libraries

Leo Jung Papers, 193901970, in: Agudath Israel of America, Orthodox Jewish Archives

Erich Kahler, Papers, 1931-1976, in: Princeton University Library

Hugo Kauder Papers, in: University of Chicago Library

Guido Kisch Papers, ca. 1934-1972, in: Cornell University Library, Ithaca, NY

Guido Kisch Papers (1933-1970), in: American Jewish Archives.

Otto Klemperer Collection, in: Library of Congress

Franz Kobler Papers, in: Leo Baeck Institute, NYC

Hans Kohn Collection,1866-1972, in: Leo Baeck Institute

Jacob Kohn Papers, 1913-1968, in: Jewish Theological Seminary of America Library

Walter Kohn Papers, in: University of California, Santa Barbara, Library

Peter Kollisch Collection, 1915-1981, in: Leo Baeck Institute, NYC

Rudolph Kolisch Papers, 1886-1978, Harvard University, Houghton Library

Karl Koller Papers, 18866-1988, in Library of Congress, MS Division

Josef Korbel Papers, University of Denver, Penrose Library

Stella Kramrisch Papers, in: Philadelphia Museum of Art Archives

Norbert Joachim Kreidl Essays and Poetry, 1952-1988, in: American Institute of Physics

Sarah Kussy Papers, 1898—1951, in: American Jewish Historical Society, NYC

Hulda Lashanska Papers,1908-1971, in: New York Public Library for the Performing Arts

Paul Felix Lazarsfeld Reminiscences, in: Columbia University, Butler Library, NYC

Emil Lederer Papers, 1901-1971, in: State University of NY at Albany, Library, NY

David Lef, Jr. Papers, in: American Jewish Archives

David Lefkowitz, Sr. Papers, in: American Jewish Archives, MS Collection No. 195

David Lefkowitz, Jr. Papers, in: American Jewish Archives, Ms Collection No. 650

Louis Edward Levy Family Papers, in: Temple University, University Libraries

David E. Lilienthal Papers, in: Princeton University Library

Records of Ludwig and Erwin Loewy, Lehigh University, Lindernman Library, Bethlehem

Karl Löwner Papers, 1923-1966, in: Stanford University Libraries

Jan Löwenbach Papers, in: San Diego State University, CA

Viktor Lowenfeld Papers, 1880-1955, in: Penn State University Libraries

Mahler-Werfel Papers, in: University of Pennsylvania

Jennie Mannheimer Papers, 1880-1952, in: American Jewish Archives

Lenore Marshall Papers, 1887-1980, in: Columbia University Libraries, Archival Collections

Donald T. McNeill Collection, 1913-1979, in: Marquette University Libraries, Special Collections and University Libraries

Meyer Family Papers, 1850-2008, in: Magnus Collection of Jewish Art and Life, Univ. of California, Berkeley

Nagel Papers, 1930-1988, in: Columbia University, Butler Library

Paul Nettl Papers, in: Indiana University, Lilly Library, Bloomington

Richard Elliot Neustadt, Papers, in: Harry S. Truman Library, Independence, MO

Richard Elliot Neustadt Papers, in: John F. Kennedy Library, Boston, MA

Morris Newfield Papers, 1868-1940, in: American Jewish Archives

William R. Perl Papers, 1925-1998, George Washington University, Gelman Library

Albert Pick and Company Records, 1894-1914, in: Cornell University Library

Albert Pick, Jr. and Family Papers, 1920-1979, in: Chicago History Museum Research Center,

Paul Amadeus Pisk Archive, in: Washington University, St. Louis, Gaylord Musical Library

Jan Popper Papers, in: University of California, Library, Davis

Paul W. Papers, 1858-1972, in: State Historical Society of Missouri

Karl Pribram Papers, 1932-1973, in: State University of New York at Albany, Library

Charles Recht Papers, in: Elmer Holmes Bobst Library, New York, NY

Frederick Ritter Collection, in: Leo Baeck Institute, NYC

Rosewater Family Papers, 1858-1939, in: American Jewish Archives

Adolph J. Sabath Papers, 1903-1952, in: American Jewish Archives

Arnold Franz Schoenberg Collection, in: University of California, Los Angeles, Music Library

Joseph Alois Schumpeter Papers, in: Harvard University Archives

Isidore Singer Papers, 1895-1938, in: American Jewish Archives

Walter Slezak Papers, 1905-1983; in: New York Public Library for the Performing Arts

Walter Sobotka Architectural Records and Papers, in: Avery Architectural & Fine Arts, Columbia University Libraries

Josef Soudek Papers, 1804-1992, in: Leo Baeck Institute, NYC

Robert E. Steiner Records, 1969-1992, in: Alabama Dept. of Archives and History, Montgomery

Moritz Spitz Papers, 1870-1917, in: American Jewish Archives

Clarence Stein Papers, 1905-1983, in: Cornell University Library, Division of Rare and Manuscript Collections

Iphigene Ochs Sulzberger Papers, in: The New York Public Library

Henrietta Szold Papers, 1975-1982, in: Hadassah Archives, NYC

Taussig Family Collection, 1877-1983, in: Leo Baeck Institute

Charles William Taussig Papers, 1928-1948, in: Franklin D. Roosevelt Library, Hyde Park, NY

Edward David Taussig Papers, 1867-1900, in: Library of Congress, MS Division

Frank William Taussig Papers, in: Harvard University, Pusey Library

Helen Brooke Taussig Papers, in Johns Hopkins University Medical Institutions

Joseph Knefler Taussig Papers, 1914-1948, in: Naval War College

Karl Terzaghi Research Collection, in: University of British Columbia, Vancouver

Elizabeth Trahan Papers, 1924-2009, in: Leo Baeck Institute, NYC
Johannes Urzidil Letters, in: University of Albany, SUNY, NY
Sonia Wachstein Papers, in: Leo Baeck Institute, NYC
Harry B. Wehle Papers, 1928-1953, in Smithsonian, Archives of American Art
Louis Brandeis Wehle Papers, in: Franklin D. Roosevelt Library, Hyde Park, NY
Vally Weigl Papers, in: Yale University Library
Caspar Willard Weinberger Papers, 1910-1991, in: Library of Congress, MS Division
Jacob Weinberger Papers, 1906-1960s, in: Norther Arizona University Library, Flagstaff
Hugo Weisgall Papers, 192-1997, in: New York Public Library for the Performing Arts
Hugo Weisgall Collection, in: Library Congress
Max Wertheimer Papers, 1885-1943, in: New York Public Library
Winn Family Collection, 1905-1983, in: Leo Baeck Institute, NYC
Milton Charles Winternitz Papers,1898-1959, in: Yale University Library
Isaac Mayer Wise Papers, 1847-1926, in: American Jewish Archives
Jonah Bondi Wise, in: American Jewish Archives
Stephen Samuel Wise, in: American Jewish Archives
Erich Zeisl Papers, in: University of California, Los Angeles
Stefan Zweig Papers, 1901-1942, in: SU
NY, College at Fredonia, Library

C. Biographical Compendia

International Biographical Dictionary of Central European Émigrés 1933-1945. New York: R. G. Sauer, 1983.
Rechcigl, Miloslav, Jr., *Czech It Out. Czech American Biography Sourcebook.* Bloomington, IN: AuthorHouse, 2015.
Rechcigl, Miloslav, Jr., *Encyclopedia of Bohemian and Czech-American Biography.* Bloomington, IN: AuthorHouse, 2016. 3 vols.

D. Periodicals

Review of the Society for the History of Czechoslovak Jews. An annual. New York: Society for the History of Czechoslovak Jews, 1987-1990-. Vol. 1-3.
Phoenix: Journal of Czech and Slovak Jewish Family and Community. Jamaica, NY: Czech and Slovak Jewish Communities Archive, 1997.

E. Historiography

Donath, Oskar, "K židovskému dějepisectví v Čechách a na Moravě" (On Jewish Historiography in Bohemia and Moravia)," *Židovský kalendář* na rok 5692. Prague, 1931, pp. 53-65.
Kisch, Guido, "Methodological and Bibliographical Remarks," in: *In Search of Freedom. A History of American Jews from Czechoslovakia.* London: Edward Goldston and Son Ltd.,1949, pp. 1-5, 245-50.
Kisch, Guido, "Jewish Historiography in Bohemia, Moravia, Silesia," in: *The Jews of Czechoslovakia.* New York: Society for the History of Czechoslovak Jews, 1968, Vol. 1, pp. 1-11.

F. Conferences

Bohemian and Czech Jews in America. Conference, Embassy of the Czech Republic in Washington, DC, April 14, 2014. OnLine: http://www.czechevents.net/events/details/944-bohemian-and-czech-jews-in-america

II. Czechoslovak Heritage

A. General

Dagan, Avigdor, "The Jewish Contribution to the Cultural Life of Czechoslovakia," in: *Where Cultures Meet: The Story of the Jews of Czechoslovakia, 1990* [Chapter 4, Berger]: 117-25.

The Jews of Czechoslovakia. Historical Studies and Surveys. New York: Society for the History of Czechoslovak Jews, 1961-1984. 3 vols.

Kulka, Erich, "The Jews in Czechoslovakia between 1918 and 1968," in: *Czechoslovakia: Crossroads and Crises, 1918–88.* By Norman Stone and Eduard Strouhal. New York: St. Martins' Press, 1989, pp. 271–279

B. The Czechlands

Fiedler, Jiří, *Jewish Sights of Bohemia and Moravia: Guide* Book. Gegen Books, 1996. 224p.

Fiedler, Jiří, *Old Bohemian and Moravian Jewish Cemeteries.* Prague: Sefer, 1991. 172p.

Gold, Hugo, *Die Juden und Judengemeinden Böhmens in Vergangenheit und Gegenwart* (The Jews and Bohemian Jewish Communities Past and Present). Brno: Jüdischer Buch- und Kunstverlag, 1929. 623p.

Gold, Hugo, *Die Juden und Judengemeinden Mährens in Vergangenheit und Gegenwart* (The Jews and Jewish Communities of Moravia in the Past and Present). Brno, 1929. English translation OnLine: http://www.jewishgen.org/Yizkor/bohemia/bohemia.html

Donath, Oskar, *Židé a židovství v české literatuře XIX. stol.* Brno, 1923, 1930. 2 vols.

Iggers, Wilma Abeles. *The Jews of Bohemia and Moravia. A Historical Reader.* Detroit, MI: Wayne State University Press, 1992. 411 p.

Jewish Communities in Bohemia and Moravia, Czech Republic. OnLine: http://www.geni.com/projects/Jewish-Communities-in-Bohemia-and-Moravia-Czech-Republic/12452

Kestenberg-Gladstein, Ruth, *Neuere Geschichte der Juden in den bömischen Ländern.* Tübingen, 1969.

Kieval, Hillel J., *The Making of Czech Jewry.* National Conflict and Jewish Society in Bohemia, 1870-1918. New York-Oxford, 1988.

Kieval, Hillel J., "Bohemia and Moravia," in: The Yivo Encyclopedia of Jews in Eastern Europe. See - http://www.yivoencyclopedia.org/article.aspx/Bohemia_and_Moravia

Kieval, Hillel J., Languages of Community: The Jewish Experience in the Czech Lands. University of California Press, 2000.

McCagg, William O., Jr., "Bohemian Breakthrough," in: *A History of Habsburg Jews, 1670-1918.* Bloomington: Indiana University Press, c1989.

Miller, Michael Laurence, Rabbis and Revolution: A Study in Nineteenth-Century Moravian Jewry. Ph.D. Dissertation, Columbia University, 2004.

Miller, Michael Laurence, *Rabbis and Revolution: The Jews of Moravia in the Age of Emancipation.* Stanford: Stanford University Press, 2010. 480p.

Miller, Michael, *Rabbis and Revolution: The Jews of Moravia in the Age of Emancipation.* Stanford: Stanford University Press, 2015. 480p.

Pařík, Arno, Jiří Fiedler and Petr Ehl, Old Bohemian and Moravian Jewish Cemeteries. Gefen Books, 1996. 172p.

Pěkný, Tomáš, *Historie židů v Čechách a na Moravě.* Praha: Sefer, 2001. 430p.

The Precious Legacy. Judaic Treasures from the Czechoslovak State Collections. Edited by David Altshuler. New York: Summit Books,1983. 288p.

Alexandr Putík, "Prague Jews and Judah Hasid: A Study on the Social, Political and Religious History of the Late Seventeenth and Early Eighteenth Centuries," pts. 1 and 2, *Judaica Bohemiae* 38 (2002), pp. 72–105 and 39 (2003), pp. 53–92.

Seibt, Ferdinand, Ed., *Die Juden in den böhmischen Ländern.* Munich, 1983.

Veselá-Prudková, Veselá, *Židé a česká společnost v zrcadle literatury od středověku k počátkům emancipace.* Praha: Nakladatelství Lidové noviny, 2003. 153p.

Vobecká, Jana, *Demographic Avant-Garde. Jews in Bohemia between the Enlightenment and the Shoah.* Budapest: Central European University Press, 2013. 250p.

Wein, Martin, *History of the Jews in the Bohemian Lands.* Leiden, The Netherlands: Brill Academic Pub., 2015. 339p.

Wlaschek, Rudolf M., *Juden in Böhmen: Beiträge zur Geschichte des europäischen Judentums im 19. und 20. Jahrhundert.* 2nd ed. München: R. Oldenbourg, 1997. 311p.

B. SLOVAKIA

Buchler, Yehoshua R., "The Jews of Slovakia: Some Historical and Social Aspects," *Review of the Society for the History of Czechoslovak Jews* 1 (1987), pp. 167-76.

Klein-Pejšová, Rebekah, Among the Nationalities: Jewish Refugees, Jewish Nationality, and Czechoslovak State Building, 1914-38. Ph.D. Dissertation, Columbia University, 2006.

III. History

A. General Surveys

Czech (Bohemian) American Jews. By Mila Rechcigl. OnLine: http://www.geni.com/projects/Czech-Bohemian-American-Jews/14626

The Virtual Jewish World, Czech Republic. OnLine: http://www.jewishvirtuallibrary.org/jsource/vjw/Czech.html

Dicker, Herman, *Piety and Perseverance. Jews from the Carpathian Mounta*ins. New York: Sepher-Hermon Press, 1981.226 p.

Kisch, Guido, "Czechoslovak Jews and America," *Historia Judaica,* 6, No. 2 (October 1944), pp. 123-138.

Kisch, Guido, *In Search of Freedom.* A History of American Jews from Czechoslovakia. 1592-1948. London: Edward Goldston, 1947. 366p.

Rechcigl, Miloslav, Jr., "Bohemian and Czech Jews in American History," *Kosmas* 26, No. 1 (Fall 2012), pp. 70-112.

Rechcigl, Miloslav, Jr., *Beyond the Sea of Beer. History of Immigration of Bohemians and Czech-Americans to the New World and their Contributions.* Bloomington, IN: AuthorHouse, 2017.

B. News of Discovery of America in Jewish Bohemia

Kisch, Guido, "News of the Discovery of America in the Ghetto of Prague and the First Emigrants," in: *In Search of Freedom. A History of American Jews from Czechoslovakia.* London: Edward Goldston and Son Ltd., 1949, pp.7-17, 251-57.

C. On to America

Kisch, Guido, "On to America!" in: *In Search of Freedom.* A History of American Jews from Czechoslovakia. London: Edward Goldston and Son Ltd., 1949, pp.45-57.

Kisch, Guido, The Leading Articles and Other Documents Concerning the 'On to America!' Movement of 1848," in: *In Search of Freedom.* A History of American Jews from Czechoslovakia. London: Edward Goldston and Son Ltd., 1949, pp. 215-229.
Kisch, Guido, "The Revolution of 1848 and the Jewish 'On the America' Movement," *Publication of the American Jewish Historical Society,* Vol. 38 (March 1949), pp. 185-208.

D. The Early Colonists and First Settlers in America

1. General

Kisch, Guido, "The First Emigrants," in: In Search of Freedom. A History of American Jews from Czechoslovakia 1592-1948. London: Edward Goldston, 1948, pp.13-17.
Motokoff, Gary and Miloslav Rechcigl, Jr., "Who Were the First Jews in America," *Avotaynu,* 27, No. 2 (Summer 2011), pp. pp. 53-54.
Rechcigl, Miloslav Jr., "Early Jewish Immigrants in America from the Czech Historic Lands and Slovakia," *Rev. Soc. Hist. Czechoslovak Jews* 3 (1990-91), pp. 157-79.
Rechcigl, Miloslav, Jr., "Jewish Pioneer Settlers from the Czechlands and Slovakia in America," *Ročenka. Journal of the Czechoslovak Genealogical Society International* 5 (2002), pp. 18-30.
Rechcigl, Miloslav, Jr., "Bohemian Jewish Pioneers in the Caribbean," in: academia. edu. Ee - https://www.academia.edu/36499091/Bohemian_Jewish_Pioneers_in_the_Caribbean.doc

2. Pioneers

Mathias Bush (1722-1790), b. Prague, Bohemia; pioneer settler, merchant, Philadelphia
Bio: Rechcigl, Miloslav, Jr., "Matthias Bush," in: *Encyclopedia of Bohemian and Czech American Biography.* Bloomington, IN.: AuthorHouse, 2016, Vol. 1, p. 1.

Simon Aaaron Cappé (orig. Benjamin Moses Hönig) (1755-1834); b. Chodová Planá (Kuttenplan), Tachov District, Bohemia; pioneer colonist, St. Thomas, US Virgin Islands
Bio: Rechcigl, Miloslav, Jr., "Bohemian Jewish Pioneers in the Caribbean," in: academia.edu. See - https://www.academia.edu/36499091/Bohemian_Jewish_Pioneers_in_the_Caribbean.doc

Joachim Gans (ca 1560-d.), b. Prague, Bohemia; first Bohemian Jewish colonist in North America
Grassl, Gary S., "Joachim Gans of Prague: America's First Jewish Visitor," *Rev. Soc. History Czechoslovak Jews* 1 (1987), p. 53-90; Rechcigl, Miloslav, Jr., "Joachim Gans," in: *Encyclopedia of Bohemian and Czech American Biography*. Bloomington, IN.: AuthorHouse, 2016, Vol. 1, p. 2.

Bernard Gratz (1738-1801), b. Langendorf, Silesia; early settler, merchant in Philadelphia
Bio: Rechcigl, Miloslav, Jr., "Bernard Gratz," in: *Encyclopedia of Bohemian and Czech American Biography*. Bloomington, IN.: AuthorHouse, 2016, Vol. 1, p. 2.

Michael Gratz (1740-1811), b. Langendorf, Silesia; early settler, merchant, Philadelphia
Bio: Rechcigl, Miloslav, Jr., "Michael Gratz," in: *Encyclopedia of Bohemian and Czech American Biography*. Bloomington, IN.: AuthorHouse, 2016, Vol. 1, p. 2.

Ezekiel Solomon(s) (1735-1808), b. Berlin, Ger., of Bohemian ancestry; first known Jewish resident in Michigan, then moved to Montreal, Canada
Bio: Rechcigl, Miloslav, Jr., "Ezekiel Solomon," in: *Encyclopedia of Bohemian and Czech American Biography*. Bloomington, IN.: AuthorHouse, 2016, Vol. 1, p. 5; First Jewish Settler in Michigan Informational Historical Marker. See - http://detroit1701.org/First%20Jewish%20Settler.html

E. Emigration to America and its Causes

1. General

Kisch, Guido, "Jewish Emigration to America from Bohemia – and its Causes," in: *In Search of Freedom. A History of American Jews from Czechoslovakia.* London: Edward Goldston and Son Ltd., 1949, pp. 21-70; pp. 294-329.
Grosman, Kurt R., "Refugees to and from Czechoslovakia," in: *The Jews of Czechoslovakia.* New York: Society for the History of Czechoslovak Jews, 1968, Vol.2, pp. 565-581.

2. The Revolution of 1848 and the Aftermath

Kisch, Guido, "The Revolution of 1848 and the Jewish 'On the America' Movement," *Publications of the American Jewish Historical Society,* 38 (1949), pp. 185-234.
Goldmark, Josephine, *Pilgrims of '48.* New Haven: Yale University Press, 1930. 311p.
Hahn, Fred, "Jews from the Bohemian Lands in the United States, 1848-1938." In: *Grossbritannien, die USA und die böhmischen Länder 1848-1938.* Ed. Eva Schmidt-Hartmann and Stanley B. Winters. Munich: R. Oldenbourg, 1991, pp. 31-45.
Korn, Betram W., "Jewish 48-ers in America," *American Jewish Archives* 2, No. 1 (June 1949), pp. 11-15.
Rechcigl, Miloslav, Jr., "The Forty-Eighters," in: *Beyond the Sea of Beer. History of Immigration of Bohemians and Czechs to the New World and their Contributions.* Bloomington, IN: AuthorHouse, 2017, pp. 36-40; also, in: academia.edu. See -https://www.academia.edu/11382084/The_Fortunes_of_Bohemian_Forty-Eighters_in_America
Wittke, Carl D Frederick, *Refugees of Revolution: The German Forty-Eighters in America.* Philadelphia: University of Pennsylvania Press, 1952. 284p.

3. Escaping from Nazism

George, Manfred, "Refugees in Prague, 1933-1938," in: *The Jews of Czechoslovakia.* Philadelphia - New York: Jewish Publications Society of

America and Society for the History of Czechoslovak Jews, 1971, Vol. 2, pp. 582-588.

Grossmann, Kurt R., "Refugees to and from Czechoslovakia," in: *The Jews of Czechoslovakia.* Philadelphia - New York: Jewish Publications Society of America and Society for the History of Czechoslovak Jews, 1971, Vol. 2, pp. 565-581.

Rechcigl, Miloslav, Jr., "Czech Intellectual Immigrants in the US from Nazism," in: *Scholars in Exile and Dictatorships of the 20th Century.* Conference Proceedings. Edited by Marco Stella, Soňa Štrbáňová and Antonín Kostlán. Prague, Centre for the History of Sciences and Humanities of the Institute for Contemporary History of the ASCR 2011, pp. 286-308.

Rechcigl, Miloslav, Jr., Czech Intellectual Refugees from Nazism in the US - Natural and Social Sciences," in: *Beyond the Sea of Beer. History of Immigration of Bohemians and Czechs to the New World and their Contributions.* Bloomington, IN: Author House, 2017, pp. 549-578.

Rechcigl, Miloslav, Jr., Czech Intellectual Refugees from Nazism in the US - Humanities and the Arts & Letters," in: *Beyond the Sea of Beer. History of immigration of Bohemians and Czechs to the New World and their Contributions.* Bloomington, IN: Author House, 2017, pp. 578-602.

Wingfield, Nancy M., "Czechoslovak Jewish Immigration to the United States 1938-1945," *Czechoslovak and Central European Journal,*11, No. 2 (Winter 1993), p. 38-48.

F. Regional and Local History

1. California

Rechcigl, Miloslav, Jr., "Bohemian Jews" (California), in: *Beyond the Sea of Beer.* Bloomington, IN: AuthorHouse, 2017, pp. 132-143.

2. Illinois

Rechcigl, Miloslav, Jr., (Chicago), in: *Beyond the Sea of Beer.* Bloomington, IN: AuthorHouse, 2017, pp. 247, 390-391.

3. Kentucky

Rechcigl, Miloslav, Jr., (Kentucky), in: *Beyond the Sea of Beer.* Bloomington, IN: AuthorHouse, 2017, pp. 220-228.

4. Louisiana

Rechcigl, Miloslav, Jr., (Louisiana), in: *Beyond the Sea of Beer.* Bloomington, IN: AuthorHouse, 2017, pp. 114, 115-117, 118, 120-121.

5. Michigan

Aminoff, Helen, "The First Jews of Ann Arbor," *Michigan Jewish History* 23, No. 1 (January 1983), pp. 3-13.
Rechcigl, Miloslav, Jr., "Jewish Bohemian Pioneers," (Michigan), in: *Beyond the Sea of Beer.* Bloomington, IN: AuthorHouse, 2017, pp. 212-214.

6. Missouri

Bush, Isidor, "The Jews in St. Louis," *Bull. Missouri Historical Soc.* 8 (1951), pp. 60-70.
Rechcigl, Miloslav, Jr., "St. Louis - The Frst Bohemian Metropolis in America," in: *Beyond the Sea of Beer.* Bloomington, IN: AuthorHouse, 2017, see especially p. 239-243.

7. New Jersey

Rechcigl, Miloslav, Jr., "New Jersey - Domain of Bohemian Jews," in: *Beyond the Sea of Beer.* Bloomington, IN: AuthorHouse, 2017, pp. 148-156.

8. New York

Rechcigl, Miloslav, Jr., (New York), in: *Beyond the Sea of Beer.* Bloomington, IN: AuthorHouse, 2017, pp. 34-35, 45-48, 126, 359-360, 389.

9. Ohio

Rechcigl, Miloslav, Jr., (Cleveland), in: *Beyond the Sea of Beer.* Bloomington, IN: AuthorHouse, 2017, p. 391.

6. Pennsylvania

Rechcigl, Miloslav, Jr., (Philadelphia), in: *Beyond the Sea of Beer.* Bloomington, IN: AuthorHouse, 2017, pp. 34-35, 45-48, 126, 359-360, 389.

10. Wisconsin

Rechcigl, Miloslav, Jr., "Jewish Bohemian Immigrants" (Milwaukee), in: *Beyond the Sea of Beer.* Bloomington, IN: AuthorHouse, 2017, pp. 231-234.

G. Aiding Czechoslovakia

Kisch, Guido, "Woodrow Wilson and the Independence of Small Nations in Central Europe," *Journal of Modern History,* 19 (19476), pp. 235-238.
Kisch, Guido, "Part in Czechoslovakia's Liberation," in: *In Search of Freedom. A History of American Jews from Czechoslovakia. 1592-1948.* London: Edward Goldston, 1947, pp. 127-135.
Rechcigl, Miloslav, Jr. "Forgotten Gratitude," in: academia.edu. See - https://www.academia.edu/34990926/Forgotten_Gratitude

IV. The Holocaust

A. General

1. Czechoslovakia as a Whole

Heitlinger, Alena, *In the Shadows of the Holocaust and Communism: Czech and Slovak Jews since 1945.* New Brunswick: Transaction Publishers, 2006. 238p.
Kulka, Erich, "The Annihilation of Czechoslovak Jewry," in: *The Jews of Czechoslovakia.* Philadelphia - New York: Jewish Publications Society of America and Society for the History of Czechoslovak Jews, 1984, Vol.3, pp. 262-328.
Sniegon, Tomas, *Vanished History: The Holocaust in Czech and Slovak Culture* (Making Sense History). Oxford, New York: Berghahn Books, 2014.

2. The Czechlands

Adler, H.G., *Theresienstadt 1941-1945: The Face of a Coerced Community.* Cambridge University Press, 2017. 882p.
Brecher, Elinor J., *Schindler's Legacy: True Stories of the List Survivors.* New York: Plume, 1994. 480p.
Hájková, Anna, "To Terezín and Back Again: Czech Jews and their Bonds of Belonging from
Deportations to the Postwar," *Studies on the Holocaust*, Vol. 28, No. 1 (2014), pp. 38-55.
"The Holocaust in Bohemia and Moravia," in: Holocaust Encyclopedia - See: https://www.ushmm.org/wlc/en/article.php?ModuleId=10007323
Křížková, Marie Rut, Jiří Kotouč, Zdeněk Ornest, *We are Children just the Same: Vedem, the Secret Magazine by the Boys of Terezín.* The Jewish Publication Society, 2013. 208p.
Lederer, Zdeněk, "Terezin," in: *The Jews of Czechoslovakia.* Philadelphia - New York: Jewish Publications Society of America and Society for the History of Czechoslovak Jews, 1984, Vol. 3, pp. 104-164.

Rothkirchen, Livia, “The Jews of Bohemia and Moravia: 1938-1945,” in: *The Jews of Czechoslovakia.* Philadelphia - New York: Jewish Publications Society of America and Society for the History of Czechoslovak Jews, 1971, Vol. 3, pp. 3-74.

Rothkirchen, Livia, *The Jews of Bohemia and Moravia: Facing the Holocaust.* Lincoln: University of Nebraska Press, 2012. 464p.

Thomson, Ruth, *Terezin: Voices from the Holocaust.* Sommerville, MA: Candlewick, 2013. 64p.

Troller, Norbert, Theresienstadt: Hitler’s Gift to the Jews. Chapel Hill: University of North Carolina Press, 2004. 224p.

3. Slovakia

Buchler, Yehoshua, “The Deportation of Slovakian Jews to the Lublin District of Poland in 1942,” *Holocaust and Genocide Studies,* 6, No. 2 (1991), pp. 151-66.

Długoborski, Wacław, Desider Tóth, Teresa Świebocki, Jarek Mensfelt, Eds., *The Tragedy of the Jews of Slovakia.* Oświęcim–Banská Bistrica: Auschwitz-Birkenau State Museum, Museum of the Slovak National Uprising.2002.

“The Holocaust in Slovakia,” in: Holocaust Encyclopedia - See: https://www.ushmm.org/wlc/en/article.php?ModuleId=10007324

“The Holocaust in Subcarpathian Rus and southern Slovakia,” in: Holocaust Encyclopedia - See: https://www.ushmm.org/wlc/en/article.php?ModuleId=10007325

Jelinek, Yeshayahu, “The ‘Final Solution’ – The Slovak Version,” *East European Quarterly,* No. 4 (1971), pp. 431-441.

Jelinek, Yeshayahu, “The Holocaust of the Slovak Jewry,” *East Central Europe* 10, No. 1-2 (1983), pp. 14-23.

Jelinek, Yeshayahu A. (1989), “Slovaks and the Holocaust: Attempts at Reconciliation,” Soviet Jewish Affairs, 19, No. 1 (1989), pp.: 57–68.

Lipscher, Ladislav, The Jews of Slovakia: 1939-1945,” in: *The Jews of Czechoslovakia.* Philadelphia - New York: Jewish Publications Society of America and Society for the History of Czechoslovak Jews, 1971, Vol. 3, pp. 165-261.

Reitlinger, Gerald, "Slovakia," in: The Final Solution: The Attempt to Exterminate the Jews of Europe, 1939-1945. New York: Beechhurst Press, 1953, pp. 385-394.

B. The Holocaust Survivor Stories

Albright, Madeleine, *Prague Winter: A Personal Story of Remembrance and War, 1937-1948.* Harper, 2012. 480p.
Backer, Ivan A., *My Train to Freedom: A Jewish Boy's Journey from Nazi Europe to a Life of Activism.* New York: Skyhorse Publishing, 2016. 208p.
Barak-Ressler, Aliza, Cry Lttle Girl: A Tale of the Survival of a Family in Slovakia. Yad Vashem Publications, 2003. 241p.
Bitton-Jackson, Livia, *Saving what Remains: A Holocaust Survivor's Journey Home to Reclaim Her Ancestry.* Lyons Press, 2009. 208p.
Brady, Lara Hana, The Hanas's Story. See - http://www.hanassuitcase.ca
Breznitz, Shlomo, *Memory Fields.* New York: Knopf, 1992. 179p.
Eisen, Max, *By Chance Alone: A Remarkable True Story of Courage and Survival at Auschwitz.* New York: Harper Collins Publishers, 2017. 304p.
Elias, Ruth, *Triumph of Hope: From Theresienstadt and Auschwitz to Israel.* Wiley, 1999. 288p.
Epstein, Helen, Where *She Came From: A Daughter's Search for Her Mother's History.* Routledge, 2017. 253p.
Fantlová, Zdenka, *The Tin Ring: Love and Survival in the Holocaust.* Aswarby: McNidder & Grace, 2013. 240p.
Friesová. Jana Renee, *Fortress of My Youth: Memoir of a Terezín Survivor.* University of Wisconsin Press, 2002. 200p.
Gardella, Lorrie, The Life and Thought of Louis Lowy: Social Work Through the Holocaust. Syracuse, NY: Syracuse University Press, 2011. 213p.
Giesecke, Ulla, *From Prague to the Promised Land. A Jewish Family's Odyssey from Czechoslovakia to Israel.* WestBowPress, 2013. 290p.
Greenfield, Martin, *Measure of a Man: From Auschwitz Survivor to Presidents' Tailor.* Regnery Publishing, 2014. 250p.
Gruenbaum, Michael, *Somewhere There Is Still a Sun: A Memoir of the Holocaust.* New York: Aladdin, 2015. 385p.

Heller, Caroline, *Reading Claudius: A Memoir.* In two parts. The Dial Press, 2015 320p.

Kacer, Katy*: The Underground Reporters* (Holocaust Remembrance Series). Toronto: Second Story Press, 2003. 168p.

Kohner, Nancy, *My Father's Roses: A Family's Journey from World War I to Treblinka.* Pegasus, 2009. 272p.

Kovaly, Heda Margolius, *Under a Cruel Star: A life in Prague 1941-1968.* Teaneck, NJ: Holmes & Meier Publishers, 1997. 192p.

Kraus, Michael, *Drawing the Holocaust: A Teenager's Memory of Terezin, Birkenau, and Mauthausen.* Cincinnati, OH: Hebrew Union College Press, 2016. 144p.

Lewis, Helen, *Time to Speak.* Belfast: Blackstaff Press, 2011. 118p.

Malkin, Lisl, *An Interrupted Lifer. A Holocaust Survivor's Journey to Independence.* Englewood Cliffs, NJ: Full Court Press, 2014. 364p.

Margolius, Ivan, Reflections of Prague: Journeys through the 20th century. New York: Wiley, 2006). 318p.

Meissner, Margit, *Margit's Story.* Schreiber Publishing, 2003. 319p.

Muller, Melissa, *A Garden of Eden in Hell: The Life of Alice Herz-Sommer.* London: Macmillan, 2008. 362p.

Nessy-Perlberg, Anna, T*he House in Prague: How a Stolen House Helped an Immigrant Girl Find Her Way Home.* Golden Alley Press, 2016. 214p.

Pickus, Keith H., and Zev Garber, *Our Only Hope: Eddie's Holocaust Story and the Weisz Family Correspondence.* University Press of America, 2008. 112p.

Pollak, Klaus, *In Spite of Auschwitz.* Bloomington, IN: Xlibris, 2006. 416p.

Polt, Renata, *Thousand Kisses: A Grandmother's Holocaust Letters* (Judaic Studies Series). Tuscaloosa, AL: University Alabama Press, 1998. 216p.

Rubin, Susan Goldman, *Fireflies in the Dark: The Story of Friedl Dicker-Brandeis and the Children of Terezin.* Baltimore, MD: Holiday House, 2000. 48p.

Schapiro, Raya Czerner and Helga Czerner Weinberg, *One Family's Letters from Prague.* Academy Chicago Publishers, 1996. 254p.

Schimmel, Betty, *To See You Again: A True Story of Love in a Time of War.* Dutton Adult, 1999. 279p.

Stoessinger, Caroline, *A Century of Wisdom: Lessons from the Life of Alice Herz-Sommer, the World's Oldest Living Holocaust Survivor.* New York: Spiegel & Grau, 2012. 256p.

Weinberg, Felix, *Boy 30529: A Memoir* Paperback. Brooklyn, NY: Verso, 2014. 192 pages

Weiss, Helga, *Helga's Diary: A Young Girl's Account of Life in a Concentration Camp.*
W. W. Norton & Company, 2013. 256p.
Wilkes, Helen Waldstein, *Letters from the Lost: A Memoir of Discovery.* Vancouver, BC, Canada: UB Press, 2010. 210p.

V. People

A. General

Blau, Bruno, "Nationality among Czechoslovak Jewry," *Historia Judaica* 10, N. 2 (October 1948), pp. 147-54.

Brűgel, J.W., "Jews in Political Life," in: *The Jews of Czechoslovakia.* Philadelphia - New York: Jewish Publications Society of America and Society for the History of Czechoslovak Jews, 1971, Vol. 2, pp.243-252.

Ehrenwald, Jan, "On the so-called Jewish Spirit," in: *The Jews of Czechoslovakia.* Philadelphia - New York: Jewish Publications Society of America and Society for the History of Czechoslovak Jews, 1971, Vol. 2, pp. 455-468.

Kieval, Hillel J., "Negotiating Czechoslovakia: The Challenges of Jewish Citizenship in a Multiethnic Nation-State," in: *Insiders and Outsiders: Dilemmas of East European Jewry.* Edited by Richard I. Cohen, Jonathan Frankel and Stefani Hoffman. Oxford: Littman Library of Jewish Civilization, 2010, pp. 103-119.

Kisch, Guido, "Linguistic Conditions among Czechoslovak Jewry: in: *Czechoslovakia Past and Present.* Edited by Miloslav Rechcigl, Jr. The Hague - Paris: Mouton, 1968, Vol. 2, pp. 1451-1462.

Láníček, Jan, *Czechs, Slovaks and the Jews, 1938-48: Beyond Idealization and Condemnation.* New York: Palgrave Macmilllan, 2013. 265p.

Lichtenstein, Tatjana, *Zionists in Interwar Czechoslovakia: Minority Nationalism and the Politics of Belonging.* Bloomington, IN : 2016. 473p.

Rabinowicz, Oscar K., Czechoslovak Zionism: Analecta to a History," in: *The Jews of Czechoslovakia.* Philadelphia - New York: Jewish Publications Society of America and Society for the History of Czechoslovak Jews, 1971, Vol. 2, pp. 19- 136.

B. Bohemians and Czechs

Čapková, Kateřina, *Czechs, Germans, Jews? National Identity and the Jews of Bohemia.* New York: Berghahn Books, 2014. 298p.

Hahn, Fred, "The Dilemma of the Jews in the Historic Lands of Czechoslovakia, 1918-38," *East Central Europe,* 10, No. 1-2 (1983), pp. 24-39.

Hostovsky, Egon, "The Czech-Jewish Movement," in: *The Jews of Czechoslovakia.* Philadelphia - New York: Jewish Publications Society of America and Society for the History of Czechoslovak Jews, 1971, Vol. 2, pp. 148-152.

Iggers, Wilma A., "The Flexible National Identities of Bohemian Jewry," *East Central Europe,* 7, No. 1 (1980), pp. 39-48.

Iggers, Wilma A., "The Jews of Bohemia and Moravia during the 18th and 19th Centuries: Their Daily Life in Memoirs and Documents," *Review of the Society for the History of Czechoslovak Jews,* 2 (1988-89), pp. 33-52.

Kestenberg-Gladstein, Ruth, "The Jews between Czechs and Germans in the Historic Lands," in: *The Jews of Czechoslovakia.* Philadelphia - New York: Jewish Publications Society of America and Society for the History of Czechoslovak Jews, 1968, Vol. 1, pp. 21-71.

Kieval, Hillel J., Nationalism and the Jews of Prague: Transformation of Jewish Culture in Central Europe, 1880-1918. Ph.D. dissertation, Harvard University, 1981.

Kieval, Hillel J., "Education and National Conflict in Bohemia: Germans, Czechs and Jews," *Studies in Contemporary Jewry,* 3 (1987), pp. 49-71.

Kieval, Hillel J., *The Making of Czech Jewry: National Conflict and Jewish Society in Bohemia, 1870-1918.* New York: Oxford University Press, 1988. 279p.

Kieval, Hillel J., "The Social Vision of Bohemian Jews: Intellectuals and Community in the 1840s," in: *Assimilation and Community: The Jews in Nineteenth-Century Europe.* Edited by Jonathan Frankel and Steven J. Zipperstein. Cambridge, England and New York: Cambridge University Press, 1992, pp. 245-283.

Kieval, Hillel J., *Languages of Community: The Jewish Experience in the Czech Lands.* Berkeley, 2000.

Kieval, Hillel J., choosing Bridge: Revisiting the Phenomenon of Jewish Cultural Mediation," *Bohemia: A Journal of History and Civilization in East Central Europe*, 46, No.1 (2005), pp. 15-27.

Kieval, Hillel J., "Jewish Prague, Christian Prague, and the Castle in the City's 'Golden Age,' *Jewish Studies Quarterly*, 18 (2011), pp. 202-215.

Kieval, Hillel J., "Imperial Embraces and Ethnic Challenges: The Politics of Jewish Identity in the Bohemian Lands," *Shofar: An Interdisciplinary Journal of Jewish Studies*, 30. No. 4 (Summer 2012), pp. 108-123.

Kieval, Hillel J., "The Unforseen Consequences of Cultural Resistance: Haskalah and State-Mandated Reform in the Bohemian Lands," *Jewish Culture and History*, 13, Nos. 2-3 (2012), pp. 108-123.

Kieval, Hillel J., "Polna's Shadow: The Hilsner Affair and the Problem of Jewish Integration in the Bohemian Lands," in: *Jewish Studies in the 21st Century: Prague - Europe - World.* Edited by Marcela Zoufalá. Wiesbaden: Harrassowitz, 2014, pp. 131-141.

Kisch, Guido, "Character and Achievement of Czech Jews in America," in: *In Search of Freedom.* A History of American Jews from Czechoslovakia. London: Edward Goldston and Son Ltd., 1949, pp. 73-82.

Labendz, Jacob Ari, Re-Negotiating Czechoslovakia. The State and the Jews in Communist Central Europe: The Czech Lands, 1945-1989. (Ph.D. Dissertation, Washington University in St. Louis, August 2014.

Lichtenstein, Tatjana, Making Jews at Home. Jewish Nationalism in the Bohemian Lands, 1918-1938. Ph.D. Dissertation, University of Toronto, Toronto, 2009.

Spector, Scott, *Prague Territories: National Conflict and Cultural Innovation in Franz Kafka's Fin de Siècle.* Los Angeles, CA: University of California Press, 2000. 331p.

Stránský, Hugo," The Religious Life in the Historic Lands," in: *The Jews of Czechoslovakia.* Philadelphia - New York: Jewish Publications Society of America and Society for the History of Czechoslovak Jews, 1968, Vol. 1, pp.330-357.

Vobecká, Jana, *Demographic Avant-Garde: Jews in Bohemia between the Enlightenment and the Shoah.* Budapest: Central European University Press, 2013. 250p.

Yahil, Chaim, "Social Work in the Historic Lands," in: *The Jews of Czechoslovakia.* Philadelphia - New York: Jewish Publications Society of America and Society for the History of Czechoslovak Jews, 1971, Vol. 2, pp. 393-400.

Weltsch, Felix, "Realism and Romanticism: Observation on the Jewish Intelligentsia of Bohemia and Moravia," in: *The Jews of Czechoslovakia.* Philadelphia - New York: Jewish Publications Society of America and Society for the History of Czechoslovak Jews, 1971, Vol. 2, pp. 440-454.

C. Slovaks

Buchler, Yehoshua R., "The Jews of Slovakia: Some Historical and Social Aspects," *Review of the Society for the History of Czechoslovak Jews*, 1 (1987), pp. 167-76.

Jelinek, Yeshayahu A., "In Search of Identity: Slovakian Jewry and Nationalism (1918-1938)," in: *A Social and Economic History of Central European Jewry.* New Brunswick: Transaction Publishers, c1990, pp. 207-227.

Klein- Pejšová, Rebekah, *Mapping Jewish Loyalties in Interwar Slovakia.* Bloomington, IN: Indiana University press, 2015. 216p.

VI. The Society

A. Education

1. General

Kisch, Guido, "Contribution to Secular Culture: Education," in: *In Search of Freedom.* A History of American Jews from Czechoslovakia, 1592-1948. London: Edward Goldston, 1947, pp. 145-150.

2. Pioneer Teachers

Siegfried Altmann (1887-1963); b. Mikulov, Moravia; director of Austrian Institute for Science, Arts and Economy in New York
Bio: "Siegfried Altmann," in: Wikipedia. See - https://de.wikipedia.org/wiki/Siegfried_Altmann_(Pädagoge)

Abraham Flexner (1866-1959), b. Louisville, KY, of Bohemian ancestry; b. New York City, of Bohemian ancestry;
Bio:_Flexner, Abraham, *I Remember. The Autobiography of Abraham Flexner.* New York: Simon & Schuster, 1940; Bonner, Thomas Neville, *Iconoclast: Abraham Flexner and a Life in Learning.* Baltimore: Johns Hopkins Univ. Press, 2002; Rechcigl, Miloslav, J., "Abraham Flexner," in: *Beyond the Sea of Beer.* History of Immigration of Bohemians and Czechs to the New World and their Contributions. Bloomington, IN: AuthorHouse, 2017, pp. 503-504.

Rudolph S. Fried (1886-1951), b. Czech.; principal of Florence Nightingale School for Backward Children, Katonah, NY
Bio: Rechcigl, Miloslav, Jr., "Rudolph S. Fried," in: *Encyclopedia of Bohemian and Czech American Biography.* Bloomington, IN.: AuthorHouse, 2016, Vol. 2, p. 1049; "R. S. Fried, 59, Dies; School Principal; Headed Bailey Hall in Katonah for Retarded Boys, Which He Helped Found in 1912," *The New York Times,* June 19, 1951.

Henry Harold Goldberger (1878-1969), b. Moravia; educator, author of textbooks
Bio: Rechcigl, Miloslav, Jr., "Henry Harold Goldberger," in: *Encyclopedia of Bohemian and Czech-American Biography.* Bloomington, IN: AuthorHouse, 2016, Vol. 2, p. 1065; "Henry Harold Goldberger," in: Wikipedia. See - https://de.wikipedia.org/wiki/Henry_Harold_Goldberger

Jennie Mannheimer (1872-1943), b. New York City, of Bohemian ancestry; teacher, elocutionist, acting coach, teacher of speech and drama
Bio: "Mannheimer, Jennie," in: *European Immigrant Women in the United States: A Biographical Dictionary.* Edited by Judy Barrett Litoff and Judith McDonnell. Taylor & Francis, 1994, p. 186; "Jennie Mannheimer," in: Wikipedia. See - https://en.wikipedia.org/wiki/Jennie_Mannheimer

Louise Mannheimer (1845-1920), b. Prague, Bohemia; Sabbath teacher, founder of boy's Industrial School, Cincinnati
Bio: Rechcigl, Miloslav, Jr., "Louise Mannheimer," in: *Encyclopedia of Bohemian and Czech American Biography.* Bloomington, IN.: AuthorHouse, 2016, Vol. 2, p. 1047.

Carrie T. Pollitzer (1881-1974), b. Charleston, SC, of Czech ancestry; innovative teacher
Bio: Rechcigl, Miloslav, Jr., "Carrie T. Pollitzer," in: *Beyond the Sea of Beer.* Bloomington, IN: AuthorHouse, 2017, p. 127, 504; "Carrie Pollitzer," in: The Pollitzer Family of South Carolina. See - http://ldhi.library.cofc.edu/exhibits/show/pollitzer_family_sc/carrie_pollitzer

Mabel L. Pollitzer (1885-1979); b. Charleston, SC, of Czech ancestry; innovative teacher
Bio: Rechcigl, Miloslav, Jr., "Mabel L. Pollitzer," in: *Beyond the Sea of Beer.* Bloomington, IN: AuthorHouse, 2017, pp. 127-128; "Mabel Pollitzer," in: The Pollitzer Family of South Carolina. See - http://ldhi.library.cofc.edu/exhibits/show/pollitzer_family_sc/mabel_pollitzer

Julia Richman (1855-1912), b. New York City, of Bohemian ancestry; teacher, district superintendent of schools in NYC

Bio: Altman, Addie R., and Bertha R. Proskauer, *Julia Richman: An Appreciation of a Great Educator* (1916); Berrol, Selma C., "Superintendent Julia Richman: A Social Progressive in the Public Schools," *The Elementary School Journal,* 72, No. 8 (May 1972), pp. 402-411; Berrol, Selma Cantor, *Julia Richman, A Notable Woman.* Philadelphia: Balch Institute Press, 1993; Jewish Women in America: An Historical Encyclopedia. Edited by Paula E. Hyman and Deborah Dash Moore. New York: Routledge, 1997, pp. 1148-1149; Rechcigl, Miloslav, J., "Julia Richman," in: *Beyond the Sea of Beer.* History of Immigration of Bohemians and Czechs to the New World and their Contributions. Bloomington, IN: AuthorHouse, 2017, p. 503; Obituary, *New York Times,* June 26, 1912, 13:5.

Louis Schnabel (1824-1897), b. Prostějov, Moravia, superintendent of Hebrew Orphan Asylum of NY, principal of preparatory school for Hebrew Union College
Bio: Rechcigl, Miloslav, Jr., "Louis Schnabel," in: *Encyclopedia of Bohemian and Czech American Biography.* Bloomington, IN.: AuthorHouse, 2016, Vol. 2, p. 1048.

3. Later and Contemporary Teachers

Alice Gollan (ca. 1963-), b. US, of Moravian ancestry; music educator, songwriter, founder and director of 'Family Music Makers' - a unique music program for children aged infants through 5 years, Parkinson's patient
Bio: "Songs by Alice." See - https://songsbyalice.wordpress.com/about/

Berthold Lowenfeld (1901-1994), b. Linz, of Bohemian ancestry; psychologist, specialist on education programs for the blind
Bio: "Berthold Lowenfeld," in: *Encyclopedia of Bohemian and Czech-American Biography.* Bloomington, IN: AuthorHouse, 2016, Vol. 2, p. 1072.

Victor Lowenfeld (1903-1960), b. Linz, of Bohemian ancestry; artist, psychologist, professor of art education and therapy
Bio: Rechcigl, Miloslav, Jr., "Victor Lowenfeld," in: *Encyclopedia of Bohemian and Czech-American Biography.* Bloomington, IN: AuthorHouse, 2016, Vol. 2, p. 1072.

Margit Meissner (1922-), b. Innsbruck, Aust., of Czech parents; program planner and admimistrator in education of children with disabilities. Montgomary Co., MD schools
Bio: Rechcigl, Miloslav, Jr., "Margit Meissner," in: *Encyclopedia of Bohemian and Czech American Biography*. Bloomington, IN.: AuthorHouse, 2016, Vol. 2, p. 1057.

Emma N. Plank (née Spira) (1905-1990), b. Vienna, of Czech parents; educator, specialist on child development
Bio: Rechcigl, Miloslav, Jr., "Emma N. Plank," in: *Encyclopedia of Bohemian and Czech-American Biography*. Bloomington, IN: AuthorHouse, 2016, Vol. 2, pp. 1076-1077. "Emma (Nuschi) Plank," in: Transatlantic Perspectives. See - http://www.transatlanticperspectives.org/entry.php?rec=82

Helen Steiner (1927-), b. Prague, Czech.; elementary school teacher, Scotia, NY
Bio: Rechcigl, Miloslav, Jr., "Helen Steiner," in: *Encyclopedia of Bohemian and Czech-American Biography*. Bloomington, IN: AuthorHouse, 2016, Vol. 2, p. 1055.

Karen Worth (née Weisskopf) (1942-), b. New York City, of Bohemian ancestry; specialist on science education
Bio: Rechcigl, Miloslav, Jr., "Karen Worth," in: *Encyclopedia of Bohemian and Czech-American Biography*. Bloomington, IN: AuthorHouse, 2016, Vol. 2, p. 1084; Wheelock College - Directory: Experts Database. See - https://web.wheelock.edu/experts/expert/worth-karen

4. University-Based Educators

Peter George Braunfeld (1930-), **b**. Vienna, of Moravian ancestry; specialist on mathematical education and educational technology, professor with University of Illinois
Bio: Rechcigl, Miloslav, Jr., "Peter George Braunfeld," in: *Encyclopedia of Bohemian and Czech American Biography*. Bloomington, IN.: AuthorHouse, 2016, Vol. 2, p. 1060.

Emil Jacoby (1923-1998), b. Bustina, Czech.; director of education at Valley Jewish Community Center, Los Angeles, executive director of the Bureau of Jewish Education of Greater Los Angeles
Bio: Rechcigl, Miloslav, Jr., "Emil Jacoby," in: *Encyclopedia of Bohemian and Czech American Biography*. Bloomington, IN.: AuthorHouse, 2016, Vol. 2, p. 1068; Ulman, Jane, "Survivor: Emil Jacoby," Jewish Journal. See - http://jewishjournal.com/culture/lifestyle/126790/

Sylvia Schmelkes (1948-), b. Mexico City, of Bohemian father; sociologist, specialist on intercultural education, rural and and adult education, with Iberoamerican University, Mexico City
Bio: "Sylvia Schmelkes," in: Wikipedia. See - https://en.wikipedia.org/wiki/Sylvia Schmelkes;
Rechcigl, Miloslav, Jr., "Sylvia Schmelkes," in: *Encyclopedia of Bohemian and Czech-American Biography*. Bloomington, IN: AuthorHouse, 2016, Vol. 2, pp. 1079-1080.

Stephen S. Winter (1926-), b. Vienna, of Bohemian mother; chemist, specialist on science education, education policy and multi-modal teaching, with SUNY Buffalo and then with Tufts University
Bio: Rechcigl, Miloslav, Jr., "Stephen S. Winter," in: *Encyclopedia of Bohemian and Czech-American Biography*. Bloomington, IN: AuthorHouse, 2016, Vol. 2, p. 1084.

B. Law

1. General

Kisch, Guido, "Law," in: *In Search of Freedom.* A History of American Jews from Czechoslovakia. 1592-1948. London: Edward Goldston, 1947, pp. 113- 122.

2. Pioneer Attorneys

Alfred Abraham Benesch (1879-1973), b. Cleveland, OH, of Bohemian ancestry; sr. partner with one of Cleveland's prestigious law firms

Bio: Rechcigl, Miloslav, Jr., "Alfred Abraham Benesch," in: *Encyclopedia of Bohemian and Czech American Biography.* Bloomington, IN.: AuthorHouse, 2016, Vol. 1, p. 433.

Marianne Beth (née Weisl) (1889-1984), b. Vienna, of Bohemian father; lawyer and feminist, first woman to earn doctorate in law in Austria, taught sociology at Reed College
Bio: "Maranne Beth," in: Wikipedia. See - https://en.wikipedia.org/wiki/Marianne_Beth

Leon Edwin Bloch, Sr. (1881-1976), b. Minneapolis, KS, of Bohemian ancestry; attorney, Minneapolis
Bio: Rechcigl, Miloslav, Jr., "Leon Edwin Bloch, Sr.," in: *Encyclopedia of Bohemian and Czech American Biography.* Bloomington, IN.: AuthorHouse, 2016, Vol. 1, p. 434.

Eleazer Block (1797-1885), b. Williamsburg, VA, of Bohemian ancestry; attorney, St. Louis, MO
Bio:_Rosenwaike, Ira, "Eleazer Block - His Family and Career," *American Jewish Archives,* 31 (1979), pp. 142-149.

August Bondi (1833-1907), b. Vienna, of Bohemian father; after his advanterous career with John Brown, he practiced law in Saline, KS and held everal municipal offices
Bio: Rechcigl, Miloslav, Jr. "August Bondi," in: *Encyclopedia of Bohemian and Czech American Biography.* Bloomington, IN.: AuthorHouse, 2016, Vol. 1, p. 419.

Albert Simon Brandeis (1858-1879), b. Louisville, KY, of Bohemian ancestry; attorney, Louisville, KY
Bio: Rechcigl, Miloslav, Jr., "Albert Simon Brandeis," in: *Encyclopedia of Bohemian and Czech American Biography.* Bloomington, IN.: AuthorHouse, 2016, Vol. 1, pp. 419-420.

Emilie M. Bullowa (1869-1942), b. New York, NY, of Bohemian ancestry; attorney, NYC

Bio: Rechcigl, Miloslav, Jr., "Emilie M. Bullowa," in: *Encyclopedia of Bohemian and Czech American Biography*. Bloomington, IN.: AuthorHouse, 2016, Vol. 1, p. 436.

Ferdinand Ezra Bullowa (1872-1919), b. Newport, RI, of Bohemian ancestry; attorney, NYC
Bio: Rechcigl, Miloslav, Jr., "Ferdinand Ezra Bullowa," in: *Encyclopedia of Bohemian and Czech American Biography*. Bloomington, IN.: AuthorHouse, 2016, Vol. 1, p. 436.

Ralph James Bullowa (1881-d.), b. New York, NY, of Bohemian ancestry; attorney, NYC
Bio: Rechcigl, Miloslav, Jr., "Ralph James Bullowa," in: *Encyclopedia of Bohemian and Czech American Biography*. Bloomington, IN.: AuthorHouse, 2016, Vol. 1, p. 437.

Lewis N. Dembitz (1833-1907), b. Zirke, Posen, Prussia, of Bohemian mother; attorney, Louisville, KY
Bio: Kleber, John E., "Dembitz, Lewis Naphtali," *The Kentucky Encyclopedia*. University Press of Kentucky, 1992, pp. 247–248; "Lewis Naphtali Dembitz," in: Wikipedia, See - https://en.wikipedia.org/wiki/Lewis Naphtali Dembitz;

Ernest Frederick Eidlitz (1879-d.), b. New York, NY, of Bohemian ancestry; attorney, NYC
Bio: Rechcigl, Miloslav, Jr., "Ernest Frederick Eidlitz," in: *Encyclopedia of Bohemian and Czech American Biography*. Bloomington, IN.: AuthorHouse, 2016, Vol. 1, p. 444.

Bernard M. Ernst (1879-1938), b. Uniontown, AL, of Bohemian ancestry; attorney, magician
Bio: "Ernst, Bernard M.L.," in: *Who's Who in American Jewry*. New York: Jewish Biographical Bureau, 1926, Vol. 1, p. 145.

Morris Leopold Ernst (1888-1976), b. Uniontown, AL; attorney, advocate of civil rights

Bio: Rechcigl, Miloslav, Jr., "Morris Leopold Ernst," *Encyclopedia of Bohemian and Czech-American Biography*. Bloomington, IN: AuthorHouse, 2016, Vol. 1, p. 445.

Bernard Flexner (1865-1945), b. Louisville, KY, of Bohemian ancestry; attorney, Louisville, Chicago, New York City
Bio: Rechcigl, Miloslav, Jr., "Bernard Flexner," in: *Encyclopedia of Bohemian and Czech-American Biography*. Bloomington, IN: AuthorHouse, 2016, Vol. 1, p. 421 and Vol. 2., p. 1129; Bernard Flexner Papers, Princeton University Library, Dept. of Rare Books and Special Collections, Seeley G. Mudd Manuscript Library. Princeton, NJ.

Frank C. Friend (1863-d.), b. Bohemia; attorney, Cleveland, OH
Bio: Rechcigl, Miloslav, Jr., "Frank C. Friend," in: *Encyclopedia of Bohemian and Czech-American Biography*. Bloomington, IN: AuthorHouse, 2016, Vol. 1, p. 421.

Henry Hyman Furth (1871-d.), b. St. Louis, MO, of Bohemian ancestry; attorney, St. Louis
Bio: *The Book of St. Louisans*. St. Louis, MO: The St. Louis Republic, 1906, p. P. 210.

David Gerber (1861-1923), b. New York, NY, of Bohemian parents; attorney,
Bio: Rechcigl, Miloslav, Jr., "David Gerber," in: *Encyclopedia of Bohemian and Czech-American Biography*. Bloomington, IN: AuthorHouse, 2016, Vol. 1, p. 421.

Godfrey Goldmark (1881-1968), b. New York, NY, of Bohemian ancestry; attorney, with New York Public Service Commission
Bio: Rechcigl, Miloslav, Jr., "Godfrey Goldmark," in: *Encyclopedia of Bohemian and Czech-American Biography*. Bloomington, IN: AuthorHouse, 2016, Vol. 1, p. 448.

Edgar Aaron Hahn (1882-1970), b. Cleveland, OH, of Bohemian ancestry; attorney, Cleveland

Bio: Rechcigl, Miloslav, Jr., "Edgar A. Hahn," in: *Encyclopedia of Bohemian and Czech-American Biography*. Bloomington, IN: AuthorHouse, 2016, Vol. 1, p. 450.

Emanuel Hertz (1870-1940), b. Rebrény, Slovakia; pioneer lawyer, historian, collector of Lincolniana
Bio: Hertz, Emanuel. Collection, 1921-1937, University of Illinois at Urbana-Champaign, Library; "Hertz, Emanuel," in: Jewish Virtual Library. See - http://www.jewishvirtuallibrary.org/hertz-emanuel

David Hirshfield (1867-d.), b. Slovakia; attorney, jurist, magistrate of NYC
Bio: *Who's Who in American Jewry*. New York: Jewish Biographical Bureau, 1926, Vol.1, p.272.

Benjamin Franklin Jonas (1801-1864), b. Williamsport, KY, of Bohemian ancestry; practiced law before becoming politician, later returned to law practice again
Bio: Rechcigl, Miloslav, Jr., "Benjamin Franklin Jonas," in: *Encyclopedia of Bohemian and Czech-American Biography*. Bloomington, IN: AuthorHouse, 2016, Vol. 1, p. 422.

Melvin Koestler (180-1960), b. Elizabeth, NJ, of Bohemian ancestry; attorney, Elizabeth, NJ
Bio: Rechcigl, Miloslav, Jr., "Melvin Koestler," in: *Encyclopedia of Bohemian and Czech-American Biography*. Bloomington, IN: AuthorHouse, 2016, Vol. 1, p. 462.

Samuel Koestler (1880-1960), b. Elizabeth, NJ, of Bohemian ancestry; attorney, Elizabeth, NJ
Bio: Rechcigl, Miloslav, Jr., "Samuel Koestler," in: *Encyclopedia of Bohemian and Czech-American Biography*. Bloomington, IN: AuthorHouse, 2016, Vol. 1, p. 462.

Adolf Kraus (1850-1928), b. Blovice, Bohemia; attorney, Chicago, IL
Bio: Kraus, Adolf, *Reminiscences and Comments. The Immigrant, the Citizen, a Public Office Jew*. Chicago: Author, 1925. 244p.

Nathan Kussy (1872-1956), b. Newark, NJ, of Bohemian ancestry; attorney, Newark, NJ
Bio: Rechcigl, Miloslav, jr., "Nathan Kussy," in: *Encyclopedia of Bohemian and Czech-American Biography*. Bloomington, IN: AuthorHouse, 2016, Vol. 1, p. 469.

William Liebermann (1872-d.), b. Plešany, Slovakia; lawyer, Brooklyn, NY
Bio: "Lieberamann, William," in: *Wo's Who in American Jewry*. New York: Jewish Biographical Bureau, 1926, Vol. 1, p. 389.

Jacob L. Lorie (1873-1963), b. Natchez, MS, of Bohemian ancestry; attorney, Kansas City, MO
Bio: Rechcigl, Miloslav, Jr., "Jacob L. Lorie," in: *Encyclopedia of Bohemian and Czech-American Biography*. Bloomington, IN: AuthorHouse, 2016, Vol. 1, pp. 471-472.

Charles F. Lowy (1874-d.), b. Bohemia; attorney, Chicago
Bio: Rechcigl, Miloslav, Jr., "Charles F. Lowy," in: *Encyclopedia of Bohemian and Czech-American Biography*. Bloomington, IN: AuthorHouse, 2016, Vol. 1, p. 472.

Max Benjamin May (1866-1929), b. Cincinnati, OH, of Bohemian mother; attorney, Cincinnati
Bio: Rechcigl, Miloslav, Jr., "Max Benjamin May," in: *Encyclopedia of Bohemian and Czech-American Biography*. Bloomington, IN: AuthorHouse, 2016, Vol. 1, p. 474.

Victor Morawetz (1859-1938), b. Baltimore, MD, of Bohemian ancestry; attorney, jurist, Baltimore
Bio: "Victor Morawetz," in: Wikipedia. See - https://de.wikipedia.org/wiki/Victor Morawetz' "Victor Morawetz, noted Lawyer, 79," *The Brooklyn Daily Eagle*, May 18, 1938.

Anthony Neustadt (1825-1901), b. Mladá Boleslav, Bohemia; attorney, Collinsville, IL

Rechcigl, Miloslav, Jr., "Anthony Neustadt," in: *Encyclopedia of Bohemian and Czech-American Biography*. Bloomington, IN: AuthorHouse, 2016, Vo. 1, p. 425.

Max Pam (1865-1925), b. Karlovy Vary, Bohemia; attorney, Chicago, IL
Bio: Rechcigl, Miloslav, Jr., "Max Pam," in: *Encyclopedia of Bohemian and Czech-American Biography*. Bloomington, IN: AuthorHouse, 2016, Vo. 1, p. 426.

James Madison Pereles (1852-1910), b. Milwaukee, WI, of Bohemian ancestry; attorney, school commissioner, county court judge, Milwaukee
Bio: Annual Report of American Bar Association. Baltimore: Lord Baltimore Press, 1911, p. 543.

Nathan Pereles, Jr. (1882-1967), b. Milwaukee, WI, of Bohemian ancestry; attorney, Milwaukee
Bio: Rechcigl, Miloslav, Jr., "Nathan Pereles, Jr.," in: *Encyclopedia of Bohemian and Czech-American Biography*. Bloomington, IN: AuthorHouse, 2016, Vo. 1, p. 483.

Thomas J. Pereles (1853-1913), b. Milwaukee, WI, of Bohemian mother; attorney, Milwaukee
Bio: Rechcigl, Miloslav, Jr., "Thomas J. Pereles," in: *Encyclopedia of Bohemian and Czech-American Biography*. Bloomington, IN: AuthorHouse, 2016, Vo. 1, p. 483.

Henry Mayer Phillips (1811-1884), b. Philadelphia, PA, of Bohemian ancestry; attorney, Philadelphia, US Congressman - Jewish Encyclopedia, 1906; "Henry Meyer Phillip (1811-1884). Served 1857-1859," in: *The Jews of Capitol Hill*. By Kurt F. Stone. Scarecrow Press, 2011, pp. 22-23.

Francis Deak Pollak (1876-1916), b. New York, NY, of Moravian ancestry; attorney, NYC
Bio: Rechcigl, Miloslav, Jr., "Francis deak Pollak," in: *Encyclopedia of Bohemian and Czech-American Biography*. Bloomington, IN: AuthorHouse, 2016, Vo. 1, p. 485.

Walter Heilprin Pollak (1887-1940), b. Summit, NY, of Moravian ancestry; attorney, NYC
Bio: Rechcigl, Miloslav, Jr. "Walter Heilprin Pollak," in: *Encyclopedia of Bohemian and Czech-American Biography*. Bloomington, IN: AuthorHouse, 2016, Vo. 1, p. 485.

Charles C. Recht (1887-1965), b. Bohemia; attorney, counsel for the NY Bureau of Legal Advice, also a writer
Bio: Rechcigl, Miloslav, Jr., "Charles C. Recht," in: *Encyclopedia of Bohemian and Czech-American Biography*. Bloomington, IN: AuthorHouse, 2016, Vo. 1, pp. 486-487.

Stanley Meinrath Rosewater (1885-1951), b. Omaha, NE, of Bohemian ancestry; attorney, Omaha, NE
Bio: Rechcigl, Miloslav, Jr., "Stanley Meinrath Rosewater," in: *Encyclopedia of Bohemian and Czech-American Biography*. Bloomington, IN: AuthorHouse, 2016, Vo. 1, p. 488.

Louis B. Schram (1856-1921), b. Milwaukee, WI; attorney and counselor at law, NYC
Bio: Rechcigl, Miloslav, Jr., "Louis B. Schram," in: *Encyclopedia of Bohemian and Czech-American Biography*. Bloomington, IN: AuthorHouse, 2016, Vo. 1, 427.

Robert Eugene Steiner (1862-1955), b. Greenville, AL, of Bohemian ancestry, attorney, Greenville, AL
Bio: Rechcigl, Miloslav, Jr., "Robert Eugene Steiner," in: *Encyclopedia of Bohemian and Czech-American Biography*. Bloomington, IN: AuthorHouse, 2016, Vo. 1, 428-429.

Max Steinkopf (1881-1935), b. Prague, Bohemia; attorney, first Jewish lawyer in Manitoba,
Bio: Rechcigl, Miloslav, Jr., "Max Steinkopf," in: *Encyclopedia of Bohemian and Czech-American Biography*. Bloomington, IN: AuthorHouse, 2016, Vo. 1, 499; Memorable Manitobans: Max Steinkopf (1881-1935) -http://www.mhs.mb.ca/docs/people/steinkopf_m.shtml

Laurence Arnold Tanzer (1874-1963), b. New York, NY, of Bohemian ancestry; attorney, NYC
Bio: Rechcigl, Miloslav, Jr., "Laurence Arnold Tanzer," in: *Encyclopedia of Bohemian and Czech-American Biography.* Bloomington, IN: AuthorHouse, 2016, Vo. 1, p. 502.

James Taussig (1827-1916), b. Prague, Bohemia; attorney, St. Louis, MO
Bio: Rechcigl, Miloslav, Jr., "James Taussig," in: *Encyclopedia of Bohemian and Czech-American Biography.* Bloomington, IN: AuthorHouse, 2016, Vo. 1, 429.

John Clarence Taussig (1872-), b. St. Louis, MO; of Bohemian ancestry; attorney, St. Louis
Bio: "Taussig Clarence Taussig," in: *The Book of St. Louisans.* 2nd ed. Chicago: A. N. Marquis & Co., 1912, p. 587.

Charles Wehle (1827-1900), b. Hungary, of Bohemian ancestry, attorney
Bio: Rechcigl, Miloslav, Jr., "Charles Wehle," in: *Encyclopedia of Bohemian and Czech-American Biography.* Bloomington, IN: AuthorHouse, 2016, Vo. 1, 430.

Louis Brandeis Wehle (1880-1959), b. Louisville, KY, of Bohemian ancestry; attorney, NYC
Bio: *Encyclopedia of Bohemian and Czech-American Biography.* Bloomington, IN: AuthorHouse, 2016, Vol. 1, p. 510.

Jonas Weil (1873-1933), b. Chicago, IL, of Bohemian ancestry; attorney, Minneapolis
Bio: Rechcigl, Miloslav, Jr., "Jonas Weil," in: *Encyclopedia of Bohemian and Czech-American Biography.* Bloomington, IN: AuthorHouse, 2016, Vol. 1, p. 510.

Edmond Eli Wise (1865-1932), b. Cassel, Germany, of Bohemian ancestry; attorney, NYC
Bio: Rechcigl, Miloslav, Jr., "Charles Wehle," in: *Encyclopedia of Bohemian and Czech-American Biography.* Bloomington, IN: AuthorHouse, 2016, Vol. 1, p. 511.

Otto Irving Wise (1871-1919), b. Vienna, of Moravian ancestry; attorney, spevializing in civil law, editor
Bio: Rechcigl, Miloslav, Jr., "Otto Irving Wise," in: *Encyclopedia of Bohemian and Czech-American Biography*. Bloomington, IN: AuthorHouse, 2016, Vol. 2, p. 1005; "Otto Orving Wise," *The University Magazine*, Vol. 8 (July 1898), pp. 721-722.

Sigmund Zeisler (1832-1898), b. Bilsko, on Silesia-Moravian border; attorney, Chicago
Bio: "Sigmund Zeisler" in: Wikipedia. See - https://en.wikipedia.org/wiki/Sigmund_Zeisler

3. Later and Contemporary Attorneys

Charles Taussig Abeles (1891-1980), b. St. Louis, of Bohemian ancestry; general solicitor, S.A.L. Railway Co.
Bio: Rechcigl, Miloslav, Jr., "Charles Taussig Abeles," in: *Encyclopedia of Bohemian and Czech-American Biography*. Bloomington, IN: AuthorHouse, 2016, Vol. 1, p. 431.

Leon E. Bloch, Jr. (1921-2012), b. Kansas City, MO, of Bohemian ancestry; attorney, Kansas City, 'known as 'Senator'
Bio: Rechcigl, Miloslav, Jr., "Leon E. Bloch, Jr.," in: *Encyclopedia of Bohemian and Czech-American Biography*. Bloomington, IN: AuthorHouse, 2016, Vol. 1, p. 434.

William Joseph Boehm (1919-2001), b. Baltimore, MD, of Bohemian ancestry; attorney, Annapolis, MD
Bio: Rechcigl, Miloslav, Jr., "William Joseph Boehm," in: *Encyclopedia of Bohemian and Czech-American Biography*. Bloomington, IN: AuthorHouse, 2016, Vol. 1, p. 435.

Susan Brandeis (1892-1975), b. Boston, MA, of Bohemian ancestry; daughter of Justice Louis D. Brandeis; attorney, NYC
Bio: Rechcigl, Miloslav, Jr., "Susan Brandeis," in: *Encyclopedia of Bohemian and Czech-American Biography*. Bloomington, IN: AuthorHouse, 2016, Vol. 1, pp. 435-436.

Eberhard Paul Deutsch (1897-1980), b. Cincinnati, OH, of Bohemian ancestry; attorney, New Orleans, authority on international law
Bio: Rechcigl, Miloslav, Jr., "Eberhard Paul Deutsch," in: *Encyclopedia of Bohemian and Czech-American Biography*. Bloomington, IN: AuthorHouse, 2016, Vol. 1, p. 441; "Eberhard Paul Deutsch," in: Prabook. See - https://prabook.com/web/eberhard paul.deutsch/1072747

J. Lester Eisner, Jr. (1913-1987), b. Red Bank, NJ, of Bohemian ancestry; attorney, regional admnisyrator of the Federal Housing and Home Finance Agency
Bio: Rechcigl, Miloslav, Jr., "Lester Eisner, Jr.," in: *Encyclopedia of Bohemian and Czech-American Biography*. Bloomington, IN: AuthorHouse, 2016, Vol. 1, p. 444; "Lester Eisner Jr. Dies at 73; Former U.S. Housing Official," *The New York, Times*, June 19, 1987.

George Goodman Ernst (1894-1944), b. New York, NY, of Bohemian ancestry; attorney, NYC
Bio: "Rechcigl, Miloslav, Jr., "George Goodman Ernst," in: *Encyclopedia of Bohemian and Czech-American Biography*. Bloomington, IN: AuthorHouse, 2016, Vol. 1, p. 445.

Richard C. Ernst (1915-1984), b. of Bohemian ancestry; attorney
Bio: Rechcigl, Miloslav, Jr., "Richard C. Ernst," in: *Encyclopedia of Bohemian and Czech-American Biography*. Bloomington, IN: AuthorHouse, 2016, Vol. 1, p. 446.

Arthur Jerome Freund (1892-1975), b. St. Louis, MO, of Bohemian ancestry; attorney, St. Louis
Bio: Rechcigl, Miloslav, Jr., "Arthur J. Freund," in: *Encyclopedia of Bohemian and Czech-American Biography*. Bloomington, IN: AuthorHouse, 2016, Vol. 1, p. 447.

Jane Ginsburg, b. San Francisco, CA, of Czech ancestry; public relations marketer and then attorney, with her own firm, Referral and Infiormation Service, San Francisco
Bio: Rechcigl, Miloslav, Jr., "Jane Ginsburg," in: *Encyclopedia of Bohemian and Czech-American Biography*. Bloomington, IN: AuthorHouse, 2016, Vol. 1, p. 448.

Edward M. Heller (1926-2013), b. New Orleans, LA, of Moravian ancestry; attorney, New Orleans
Bio: Rechcigl, Miloslav, Jr., "Edward M. Heller," in: *Encyclopedia of Bohemian and Czech-American Biography.* Bloomington, IN: AuthorHouse, 2016, Vol. 1, p. 453; "In Memoriam: Edward M. Heller," in: /heller, draper, Patrick, horn & Manthey, LLC Attorneys at Law. See - http://hellerdraper.com/in-memoriam/

Daniel P. Iggers (1953-), b. US, of Czech mother; attorney, Toronto, Canada, with Ontario Securities Commission
Bio: Rechcigl, Miloslav, Jr., "Daniel P. Iggers," in: *Encyclopedia of Bohemian and Czech-American Biography.* Bloomington, IN: AuthorHouse, 2016, Vol. 1, p. 455.

William Ralph Joseph (1946-2012), b. Cleveland, OH, of Bohemian ancestry; attorney, specialist in nonprofit law, community activist, Cleveland
Bio: Rechcigl, Miloslav, Jr., "William Ralph Joseph," in: *Encyclopedia of Bohemian and Czech-American Biography.* Bloomington, IN: AuthorHouse, 2016, Vol. 1, p. 76; "Obituaries: William Joseph," *Cleveland Jewish News*, Novemver 1, 2012.

Cameron Forbes Kerry (1950-), b. Boston, MA, of Moravian ancestry; brother of Senator John F. Kerry; attorney, legal officer in US Dept. of Commerce
Bio: Rechcigl, Miloslav, Jr., "Cameron Forbes Kerry," in: *Encyclopedia of Bohemian and Czech-American Biography.* Bloomington, IN: AuthorHouse, 2016, Vol. 1, pp. 459-460.

Jacob Mortimer Klein (1889-d.), b. New York, NY, of Bohemian father; attorney, Perth Amboy, NJ
Bio: Rechcigl, Miloslav, Jr., "Jacob Mortimer Klein," in: *Encyclopedia of Bohemian and Czech-American Biography.* Bloomington, IN: AuthorHouse, 2016, Vol. 1, p. 461; "Jacob Mortimer Klein," in: *History of Middlesex County, New Jersey.* Vol. 2, pp. 128-129.

Franz Sigmund Leichter (1930-), b. Vienna, of Czech ancestry; attorney, NY State legislator

Bio: Rechcigl, Miloslav, Jr., "Franz Sigmund Leichter," in: *Encyclopedia of Bohemian and Czech-American Biography*. Bloomington, IN: AuthorHouse, 2016, Vol. 1, p. 470.

Henry O. Leichter (1924-2010), b, Vienna, of Czech ancestry; attorney
Bio: Rechcigl, Miloslav, Jr., "Henry O. Leichter," in: *Encyclopedia of Bohemian and Czech-American Biography*. Bloomington, IN: AuthorHouse, 2016, Vol. 1, p. 470.

John G. Lexa (1914-1977), b. Ústí nad Labem, Bohemia; attorney, with Waldes Kohinoor, NYC
Bio: Rechcigl, Miloslav, Jr., "John G. Lexa," in: *Encyclopedia of Bohemian and Czech-American Biography*. Bloomington, IN: AuthorHouse, 2016, Vol. 1, pp. 470-471.

Sydney Prerau (1900-1968), b. New York, NY, of Moravian ancestry; attorney, authority on Federal tax, founder of J. K. Lasser Tax Institute
Bio: Rechcigl, Miloslav, Jr., "Sydney Prerau," in: *Encyclopedia of Bohemian and Czech-American Biography*. Bloomington, IN: AuthorHouse, 2016, Vol. 1, p. 486.

Andrew Schapiro (1963-), b. Chicago, of Bohemian ancestry; attorney, US Ambassador to Czech Republic
Bio: Rechcigl, Miloslav, Jr., "Andrew Schapiro," in: *Encyclopedia of Bohemian and Czech-American Biography*. Bloomington, IN: AuthorHouse, 2016, Vol. 1, pp. 490-491; "Andrew Schapiro," in: Wikipedia. See - https://en.wikipedia.org/wiki/Andrew_H._Schapiro

Randol Schoenberg (1966-), b. Santa Monica, CA, of Czech ancestry; grandson of composer Arnold Schoenberg; attorney
Bio: Rechcigl, Miloslav, Jr., "Randol Schoenberg," in: *Encyclopedia of Bohemian and Czech-American Biography*. Bloomington, IN: AuthorHouse, 2016, Vo. 1, p. 492.

S. Sidney Stein (1886-1945), b. Chicago, IL, of Bohemian ancestry; attorney, Chicago

Bio: Rechcigl, Miloslav, Jr., "S. Sidney Stein," in: *Encyclopedia of Bohemian and Czech-American Biography*. Bloomington, IN: AuthorHouse, 2016, Vol. 1, p. 498.

Keith James Steiner (ca 1928-), b. Hawaii, of Czech ancestry; attorney, Hawaii
Bio: Rechcigl, Miloslav, Jr., "Keith James Steiner," in: *Encyclopedia of Bohemian and Czech-American Biography*. Bloomington, IN: AuthorHouse, 2016, Vol. 1, p. 498.

Robert Eugene Steiner, 3rd (1924-1999), b. Montgomery, AL, of Bohemian ancestry; attorney, Montgomery, AL
Bio: *Encyclopedia of Bohemian and Czech-American Biography*. Bloomington, IN: AuthorHouse, 2016, Vol. 1, pp. 498-499.

Michaela 'Kai' Kunc Sternstein (1970-), b. Berwyn, IL, of Bohemian ancestry; attorney, vice president of the AMA Advocacy Resource Center, Chicago
Bio: Rechcigl, Miloslav, Jr., "Michaela 'Kai' Kunc Sternstein," in: *Encyclopedia of Bohemian and Czech-American Biography*. Bloomington, IN: AuthorHouse, 2016, Vol. 1, p. 500.

Alfred Laurence Steuer (1892-d.), b. Cleveland, OH, of Czech mother; attorney, Cleveland
Bio: Rechcigl, Miloslav, Jr., "Alfred Laurence Steuer," in: *Encyclopedia of Bohemian and Czech-American Biography*. Bloomington, IN: AuthorHouse, 2016, Vol. 1, pp. 500-501; "Alfred L. Steuer," in: *Cleveland and its Environs*, Chicago-New York: The Lewis Publishing Company, 1918, Vol. 2, p. 289.

David Brandeis Tachau (ca 1956-), b. Louisville, KY, of Bohemian ancestry; attorney, Lousiville
Bio: Rechcigl, Miloslav, Jr., "David Brandeis Tachau," in: *Encyclopedia of Bohemian and Czech-American Biography*. Bloomington, IN: AuthorHouse, 2016, Vol. 1, p. 502.

Eric Weinmann (1913-2007), b. Teplice-Sanov, Bohemia; attorney, Counsel with the Small Business Administration

Bio: Rechcigl, Miloslav, Jr., "Eric Weineman," in: *Encyclopedia of Bohemian and Czech-American Biography*. Bloomington, IN: AuthorHouse, 2016, Vol. 1, p. 510; Schudel, Matt, "Eric Weinmann, 94; Lawyer, Benefactor to D.C. Arts Groups," *Washington Post*, August 20, 2007.

David Harold Weiss (1905-1979), b. Czech.; lawyer, PA State legislator, county judge
Bio: Rechcigl, Miloslav, Jr., "David Harold Weiss," in: *Encyclopedia of Bohemian and Czech-American Biography*. Bloomington, IN: AuthorHouse, 2016, Vol. 1, pp. 510-511.

C. MEDICINE

1. General

Kisch, Guido, "Medicine," in: *In Search for Freedom*. A History of American Jews from Czechoslovakia 1592-1948. London: Edward Goldston, 1948, pp. 135-145.

2. Pioneer Physicians

Franz J. Arzt (1844-1923), b. Česká Třebová, Bohemia; physician, St. Louis
Bio: Rechcigl, Miloslav, Jr., "Franz J. Arzt," in: *Encyclopedia of Bohemian and Czech-American Biography*. Bloomington, IN: AuthorHouse, 2016, Vo. 3, p. 1893.

Samuel Siegfried Karl Ritter von Basch (1837-1905), b. Prague, Bohemia; personal physician of emperor Maximilian of Mexico
Bio: Rechcigl, Miloslav, Jr., "Samuel Siegfried Karl Ritter von Basch," *Encyclopedia of Bohemian and Czech American Biography*. Bloomington, IN.: AuthorHouse, 2016, Vol. 3, p. 1893-1894; Singer, Isidore and Edgar Mels, "Basch, Samuel Siegfried Karl Ritter von," in: JewishEncyclopedia.com. See - http://www.jewishencyclopedia.com/articles/2606-basch-samuel-siegfried-karl-ritter-von; "Samuel Siegfried Karl von Basch," in: Wikipedia. See - https://en.wikipedia.org/wiki/Samuel Siegfried Karl von Basch

Benjamin Berger (1884-1968), b. Hrabovec, Slovakia; physician, dermatologist, urologist, NYC
Bio: *Who's Who in American Jewry*. New York: Jewish Biographical Bureau, 1926, Vol. 1., p. 45.

Emil Bories (1852-1907), b. Úvaly, Bohemia; family physician, pharmacist, one of first Jewish physicians in Portland, OR
Bio: Rechcigl, Miloslav, Jr., "Emil Bories," in: *Encyclopedia of Bohemian and Czech-American Biography*. Bloomington, IN: AuthorHouse, 2016, Vol. 3, p. 1934.

Samuel 'Semmi' Brandeis (1819-1899), b. Prague; physician, Madison, IN and Louisville, KY
Bio: Rechcigl, Miloslav, Jr., "Samuel 'Semmi' Brandeis," in: *Encyclopedia of Bohemian and Czech American Biography*. Bloomington, IN.: AuthorHouse, 2016, Vol., p. 1894.

Jacob George Bruckman (1800-1885), b. Lostice, Moravia; physician, PA
Bio: Rechcigl, Miloslav, Jr., "Jacob George Bruckman," in: *Encyclopedia of Bohemian and Czech American Biography*. Bloomington, IN.: AuthorHouse, 2016, Vol. 3, p. 1894.

Philip Bruckman (1797-1874), b. Plzeň, Bohemia, physician, New York City
Bio: Rechcigl, Miloslav, Jr., "Philip Bruckman," in: *Encyclopedia of Bohemian and Czech American Biography*. Bloomington, IN.: AuthorHouse, 2016, Vol. 3, p. 1894.

Washington Emil Fischel (1850-1914), b. St. Louis, MO, of Bohemian ancestry
Bio: "Washington Emil Fischel," in: *Encyclopedia of Bohemian and Czech American Biography*. Bloomington, IN.: AuthorHouse, 2016, Vol. 3, p. 1895.

Arpad G. C. Gerster (1848-1923), b. Košice, Slovakia; physician, surgeon
Bio: Gerster, Arpad G., *Recollections of a New York Surgeon*. New York: P. B. Hoeber, 1917.

Henry Illoway (1848-1937), b. Kolín, Bohemia; physician, Cincinnati, New York City
Bio: Rechcigl, Miloslav, Jr., "Henry Illoway," in: *Encyclopedia of Bohemian and Czech American Biography*. Bloomington, IN.: AuthorHouse, 2016, Vol. 3, p. 1896 and 2015.

Moses Seligman Kakeles (ca 1820-1903), b. Prague, Bohemia; physician, NYC
Bio: Rechcigl, Miloslav, Jr., "Moses Seligman Kakeles," in: *Encyclopedia of Bohemian and Czech American Biography*. Bloomington, IN.: AuthorHouse, 2016, Vol. 3, p. 1893.

Simon R. Karpeles (ca. 1880-d.), b. Washington, DC, of Bohemian ancestry, physician, Washington, DC

Joseph Kornitzer (1824-1906), b. Nové Město nad Váhom, of Moravian parents; physician, New York City, Topeka, KS, then Cincinnati, OH, New Mexico
Bio: Rechcigl, Miloslav, Jr., "Joseph Kornitzer," in: *Encyclopedia of Bohemian and Czech-American Biography*. Bloomington, IN: AuthorHouse, 2016, Vol. 3, p.1896.

Joseph Lewi (1820-1897), b. Radnice, Bohemia; physician, Albany, NY
Bio: "Lewi, Joseph," in: 1901–1906 Jewish Encyclopedia.com; Rechcigl, Miloslav, Jr., "Joseph Lewi," in: *Encyclopedia of Bohemian and Czech American Biography*. Bloomington, IN.: AuthorHouse, 2016, Vol. 1, p. 46 and Vol. 3, p. 1896.

Leopold Franz Morawetz (1818-1892), b. Roudnice nad Labem; physician, Baltimore, MD
Bio: Rechcigl, Miloslav, Jr., "Leopold F. Morawetz," in: *Beyond the Sea of Beer*. Bloomington, IN: Author House, 2017, p.471.

Simon Pollak (1814-1903), born in Domažlice, Bohemia; physician, St. Louis, MO
Bio: Pollak, S., *The Autobiography and Reminiscences of S. Pollak, M.D.* Edited by Frank J. Lutz. St. Louis, 1904. 331p.; Rechcigl, Miloslav, Jr., "Průkopník

oftalmologie" (Pioneer of Ophthalmology), in: *Postavy naší Ameriky*. Praha: Pražská edice, 2000, pp. 318-319.

Morris Popper (1869-1940), b. Mlasov, Bohemia; physician, St. Louis
Bio: Rechcigl, Miloslav, Jr., "Morris Popper," in: *Encyclopedia of Bohemian and Czech-American Biography*. Bloomington, IN: AuthorHouse, 2016, Vol. 3, p. 1944.

Marcus Rosenwasser (1846-1910), b. Bukovany, Bohemia; physician, Cleveland, OH
Bio: Rechcigl, Miloslav, Jr., "Marcus Rosenwasser," in: *Encyclopedia of Bohemian and Czech American Biography*. Bloomington, IN.: AuthorHouse, 2016, Vol. 3, p. 1899.

Henry Roth (1872-), b. Smoľinské, Slovakia; physician, surgeon, NYC
Bio: *Who's who in American Jewry*. New York: Jewish Biographical Bureau, 1926, Vol. 1., p. 523.

Ernst Saxl (1868-d.), b. Strakonice, Bohemia; physician, specialist on eye disorders, St. Louis
Bio: *The Book of St. Louisans*. St. Louis: St. Louis Republic, 1906, p. 506

Lewis W. Steinbach (1851-1913), b. Vysoká, Bohemia; physician, Philadelphia, PA
Bio: Rechcigl, Miloslav, Jr., "Lewis W. Steinbach," in: *Encyclopedia of Bohemian and Czech American Biography*. Bloomington, IN.: AuthorHouse, 2016, Vol. 3, p. 1898.

William Taussig (1826-1913), b. Prague, Bohemia; physician, St. Louis, MD
Bio: Irving Dilliard, "Taussig, William," *Dictionary of American Biography*. New York: Charles Scribner's Sons, 1936; Rechcigl, Miloslav, Jr., "William Taussig," in: *Encyclopedia of Bohemian and Czech American Biography*. Bloomington, IN.: AuthorHouse, 2016, Vol. 1, p. 194.

Leopold Wedeles (1861-1928), b. Rokycany, Bohemia; physician, Chicago
Bio: "Dr. Leopold Wedeles," in: GENi. See - https://www.geni.com/people/Dr-Leopold-Wedeles/6000000016902398719

Bio:

Charles Winternitz (1843-1959), b. Bohemia; physician, Baltimore, MD
Bio: Rechcigl, Miloslav, Jr., "Charles Winternitz," in: *Encyclopedia of Bohemian and Czech American Biography*. Bloomington, IN.: AuthorHouse, 2016, vol. 3, p. 1900.

Elias Wollin (aft 1710-d.), b. Bohemia; 'chirugeon,' NYC
Bio: Rechcigl, Miloslav, Jr., "Elias Wollin," in: *Encyclopedia of Bohemian and Czech American Biography*. Bloomington, IN.: AuthorHouse, 2016, Vol. 3, p. 1900.

Joseph Zeisler (1858-1919), b. Bilsko, on Silesian-Moravian border, physician, professor of dermatology, Northwestern University
Bio: "Joseph Zeisler, M.D., 1858-1919)," *Arch. Syphilol.*, 1, No. 1 (1920), pp. 61-62.

D. WOMEN

1. General

Rechcigl, Miloslav, Jr., "Czech (Bohemian) Women in US History: Independent Spirit and their Nonconforming Role," *Kosmas* 25, No.1 (Fall 2011), pp.102-139.

2. Pioneer Women

Henrietta Bruckman (1810–1888), b. Bohemia; founder of the Independent Order of True Sisters, NYC
Bio: Rechcigl, Miloslav, Jr., "Henrietta Bruckman," in: *Encyclopedia of Bohemian and Czech American Biography*. Bloomington, IN.: AuthorHouse, 2016, Vol. 1, pp. 66-67.

Josephine Clara Goldmark (1877-1950), b. Brooklyn, NY, of Bohemian ancestry, labor law reformer

Bio: Bremner, Robert H., "Goldmark, Josephine Clara," in: *Notable American Women 1607-1950: A Biographical Dictionary*. 1. Cambridge, MA: Harvard University Press, 1971, pp. 60–61.

Pauline Dorothea Goldmark (1886-1962), b. Brooklyn, NY, of Bohemian ancestry; social worker and activist
Bio: *American Women in 1935–1940*. Edited by Durwood Howes (1981); *Biographical Dictionary of Social Welfare in America*. Edited by Walter Trattner (1986); Obituary, *The New York Times*, October 20, 1962, p. 25.

Rebecca Gratz (1781-1869), b. Philadelphia, PA, of Silesian ancestry; educator, philanthropist, and promoter of religious, educational, and charitable institutions
Bio: Biskin, Miriam, *Pattern for a Heroine: The Life Story of Rebecca Gratz*. New York: Union of American Hebrew Congregations, 1967; Ashton, Dianne, *Rebecca Gratz: Women's Judaism in Antebellum America*. Detroit: Wayne State University Press, 1997; Burlingame, Dwight F., ed., *Philanthropy in America: A Comprehensive Historical Encyclop*edia. Santa Barbara: ABC-CLIO, 2006, Vol. 1, pp. 215-216. Rechcigl, Miloslav, Jr., "Rebecca Gratz," in: *Beyond the Sea of Beer*. Bloomington, IN: AuthorHouse, 2017, 378-379.

Theresa Grotta (1841-1922), b. Krásný Les, Bohemia; tireless social worker, Newark, NJ, after whom the Theresa Gretta Center for Rehabilitation was named
Bio: Rechcigl, Miloslav, Jr., Theresa Grotta," in: *Encyclopedia of Bohemian and Czech-American Biography*. Bloomington, IN: AuthorHouse, 2016, 83-84.

Emma B. Mandl (1842-1928), b. Pilsen, Bohemia; social reformer, clubwoman
Bio: "The Chicago Jewess," *Reform Advocate*, January 30, 1909, pp. 725–729; "Emma B. Mandl, Charity Worker, Dead," *The New York Times*, August 1, 1928, p. 21.

Louise Mannheimer (née Herschman) (1845-1920), b. Prague, Bohemia; writer, poet, school teacher, inventor
Bio: Rechcigl, Miloslav, Jr., "Louise Mannheimer," in: *Encyclopedia of Bohemian and Czech-American Biography*. Bloomington, IN, 2016, Vol. 2,

p. 1047, 1144; "Louise Herschman Mannheimer," in: Wikipedia - See - https://en.wikipedia.org/wiki/Louise Herschman Mannheimer

Jean Wise May (1881-1972), b. Cincinnati, OH, of Bohemian ancestry; Jewish religious leader
Bio: Rechcigl, Miloslav, Jr., "Jean Wise May," in: *Encyclopedia of Bohemian and Czech-American Biography*. Bloomington, IN, 2016, Vol. 1, p. 70;

Rose (Levy) Newberger (1855-1917), b. Bohemia; Jewish religious leader
Bio: Rechcigl, Miloslav, Jr., "Rose (Levy) Newberger," in: *Encyclopedia of Bohemian and Czech-American Biography*. Bloomington, IN, 2016, Vol. 1, p. 86-87.

3. Later and Contemporary Women

Sara Blum (1910-1986), b. Newark, NJ, of Bohemian ancestry; Jewish religious leader, activist
Bio: "Sara Blum, Camping Innovator, Committed Zionist," Jewish Women's Archive.

Lotte Hitschmannova (1909-1990), b. Prague, Bohemia; Canadian journalist, humanitarian, activist
Bio: Lotta Hitschmannova," in: in: the Canadian Encyclopedia. See - https://www.thecanadianencyclopedia.ca/en/article/lotta-hitschmanova/; Lotta Hitschmannova," in: the Canadian Encyclopedia. See - https://www.thecanadianencyclopedia.ca/en/article/lotta-hitschmanova/; Rechcigl, Miloslav, Jr., "Lotte Hittschmannová," in: *Encyclopedia of Bohemian and Czech-American Biography*. Bloomington, IN: AuthorHouse, 2016, Vol. 1, pp. 84-85; "Lotta Hittschmannova," in Wikipedia. See - https://en.wikipedia.org/wiki/Lotta Hitschmanova.

Franziska Hosken (née Porges) (1919-2006), b. Vienna, of Bohemian ancestry; designer, feminist, social activist, writer
Bio: Rechcigl, Miloslav, Jr., "Franziska 'Fran' Hosken," in: *Encyclopedia of Bohemian and Czech-American Biography*. Bloomington, IN: AuthorHouse, 2016, Vol. 2, p. 95 and 1113.

Anita Pollitzer (1894-1975), b. Charleston, SC, of Czech ancestry; photographer, suffragette
Bio: Rechcigl, Miloslav, Jr. "Anita Lily Pollitzer," in: *Beyond the Sea of Beer.* Bloomington, IN: AuthorHouse, 2017, p. 128, 684; Rechcigl, Miloslav, Jr., "Anita Lily Pollitzer," in: *Encyclopedia of Bohemian and Czech-American Biography.* Bloomington, IN, 2016, Vol. 2, p. 874, 1114; "Anita Pollitzer," in: Wikipedia. See- https://en.wikipedia.org/wiki/Anita Pollitzer; "Anita Pollitzer," in: The Pollitzer Family of South Carolina. See - http://ldhi.library.cofc.edu/exhibits/show/pollitzer_family_sc/anita_pollitzer

Elizabeth Brandeis Raushenbush (1896-1980), b. Boston, MA, of Bohemian ancestry; economist
Bio: "Elizabeth Raushenbush, 88. Daughter of Justice Brandeis," *New York Times,* May 3, 1984; Hyman, Paula L., *Jewish Women in America: A Historical Encyclopedia.* New York: Routledge, 1997; Raushenbush, Elizabeth Brandeis. Papers, 1920–1967. Schlesinger Library, Radcliffe College; Raushenbush, Elizabeth Brandeis, and Paul Raushenbush. Papers. State Historical Society of Wisconsin; *Jewish Women in America,* pp. 1129-1130; Rechcigl, Miloslav, Jr., "Elizabeth Brandeis Raushenbush," in: *Beyond the Sea of Beer.* Bloomington, IN: AuthorHouse, 2017, pp. 224, 711-712.

Sonia (Sophie) Wachstein (1907-2001), b. Vienna, of Czech mother; teacher, social worker, psychoanalyst
Bio: Papers of Sonia Wachstein (1907-2001), 1915-1996, in: Leo Baeck Institute, NYC

VII. Religion

A. General

Kisch, Guido, "Contributions to American Judaism," in: *In Search of Freedom.* A History of American Jews from Czechoslovakia. London: Edward Goldston and Son Ltd., 1949, pp. 83-102.

1. Pioneer Rabbis

Leo Baerwald (1883-1970), b. Žatec, Bohemia; Rabbi
Bio: Rechcigl, Miloslav, Jr., "Leo Baerwald," in: *Encyclopedia of Bohemian and Czech-American Biography.* Bloomington, IN: AuthorHouse, 2016, p. 289.

Solomon Baum (1868-d.), b. Šebeš, Slovakia; Rabbi, Cantor
Bio: *American Jewish Year Book.* Philadelphia: Jewish Publication Society of America, 1903, Vol.5, p. 44.

Aaron Albert Siegfried Bettelheim (1830-1890), b. Hlohovec, Slovakia; Rabbi
Bio: Albert Siegfried Bettelheim," in: *The Jewish Encyclopedia.* New York - London: Funk and Wagnalls Company, 1916, Vol. 3, pp. 129-130.

Jacob Bloch (1846-1916), b. Bohemia; Rabbi
Bio: Rechcigl, Miloslav, Jr., "Jacob Bloch," in: *Encyclopedia of Bohemian and Czech-American Biography.* Bloomington, IN: AuthorHouse, 2016, p. 289.

Jonas Bondi (1804-1874), b. Dresden Germany, of Bohemian ancestry; Rabbi
Bio: Rechcigl, Miloslav, Jr., "Jonas Bondi," in: *Encyclopedia of Bohemian and Czech American Biography.* Bloomington, IN.: AuthorHouse, 2016, Vol. 1, p. 290.

Herman Bories (1820-1901), b. Bohemia; Rabbi, Portland, OR

Bio: Rechcigl, Miloslav, Jr., "Herman Bories," in: *Encyclopedia of Bohemian and Czech American Biography*. Bloomington, IN.: AuthorHouse, 2016, Vol. 1, p. 290.

Sigmund Drechsler (1843-), b. Brezová, Slovakia; Rabbi, Cleveland, OH
Bio: *American Jewish Yearbook*, Vol. 5, p. 51.

Shmuel Ehrenfeld 1891-1980), b. Mattersdorf, Austria, of Slovak ancestry; Rabbi, Torah leader
Bio: "Shmuel Ehrenfeld," in: Wikipedia. See - https://en.wikipedia.org/wiki/Shmuel Ehrenfeld

Menahem M. Eichler (1870-d.); b. Budkovce, Slovakia; Rabbi
Bio: *American Jewish Year Book*, 5664 (Sept. 22 to Sept. 1904), p. 51.

Henry Englander (1877-1951), b. Prešov, Slovakia; Rabbi
Bio: *American Jewish Year Book*, 5664 (Sept. 22 to Sept. 1904), p. 52; "Funeral Rites in Texas for Pioneer Rabbi," Jewish Telegraph Agency, September 27, 1934

.

Maurice Faber (1854-1934), b. Široké, Slovakia; Rabbi
Bio: *American Jewish Year Book*. Philadelphia: Jewish Publication Society of America, 1903, Vol.5, p. 53.

Sigmund Frey (1852-1930), b. Nový Rousínov, Moravia; Rabbi
Bio: Rechcigl, Miloslav, Jr., "Sigmund Frey," in: *Encyclopedia of Bohemian and Czech American Biography*. Bloomington, IN.: AuthorHouse, 2016, Vol. 1, p. 290.

Henry R. Goldberger (1899-1946), b. Zemplín, Slovakia; Rabbi, Erie, PA
Bio: *Who's Who in American Jewry*. New York: Jewish Bibliographical Bureau, 1926, Vol. 1, p. 206

Samuel Greenfield (1870-d.), b. Košice, Slovakia; Rabbi
Bio: *American Jewish Year Book*. Philadelphia: Jewish Publication Society of America, 1903, Vol.5, p. 50.

Moses J. Gries (1868-1918), b. Newark, NJ, of Bohemian ancestry; Rabbi
Bio: Rechcigl, Miloslav, Jr., "Moses J. Gries," in: *Encyclopedia of Bohemian and Czech American Biography*. Bloomington, IN.: AuthorHouse, 2016, Vol. 1, p. 291.

Aaron Guinzburg (1813-173), b. Prague, Bohemia; Rabbi
Bio: Rechcigl, Miloslav, Jr., "Aaron Guinzburg," in: *Encyclopedia of Bohemian and Czech American Biography*. Bloomington, IN.: AuthorHouse, 2016, Vol. 1, p. 291.

Adolph Guttman (1854-1927), b. Lipník, Moravia; Rabbi
Bio: Rechcigl, Miloslav, Jr., "Adolph Gutman," in: *Encyclopedia of Bohemian and Czech American Biography*. Bloomington, IN.: AuthorHouse, 2016, Vol. 1, p. 291.

Aaron Hahn (1846-1932); b. Bohemia; Rabbi
Bio: Rechcigl, Miloslav, Jr., "Aaron Hahn," in: *Encyclopedia of Bohemian and Czech American Biography*. Bloomington, IN.: AuthorHouse, 2016, Vol. 1, p. 291

Sigmund Hecht (1849-d.), b. Hliník nad Hronom, Slovakia; Rabbi
Bio: *American Jewish Year Book*. Philadelphia: Jewish Publication Society of America, 1903, Vol.5, p. 62.

James Gutheim Heller (1892-1971), b New Orleans, LA, of Bohemian father; Rabbi, composer
Bio: Heller, James. G., *As Yesterday when It is Past. A History of the Isaac M. Wise Temple.*

Maximilian Heller (1860-1929), b. Prague, Bohemia; Rabbi, New Orleans
Bio: Malone, Barbara S., *Rabbi Max Heller. Reformer, Zionist, Southerner, 1860-1929*: Tuscaloosa, AL: The University of Alabama Press, 1997. 296p.

Adolph Huebsch (1830-1884), b. Sv. Mikuláš, Slovakia, Rabbi
Bio: Rechcigl, Miloslav, Jr., "Adolph Huebsch," in: *Encyclopedia of Bohemian and Czech American Biography*. Bloomington, IN.: AuthorHouse, 2016, Vol. 1, p. 292

Bernard Illowy (1812-1871), b. Kolín, Bohemia; Orthodox Rabbi
Bio: Kisch, Guido, A Pioneer of Orthodox Judaism," in*: In Search of Freedom. A History of American Jews from Czechoslovakia 1592-1948.* London: Edward Goldston, 1948, pp. 85-86

Leo Jung (1892-1987), b. Uherský Brod, Moravia; Orthodox Rabbi
Bio: Jung, Leo, *The Path of Pioneer. Autobiography of Leo Jung.* The Jewish Library, Vol. 8. London and New York: Soncino Press, 1980; Konvitz, Milton R., "Leo Jung-Rabbi for All Jews." *Midstream,* 39.6 (Aug/Sept 1993); Menachem, Mendel Kasher, Norman Lamm, Leonard Rosenfeld. *Leo Jung Jubilee Volume Essays in Honor on the Occasion of his Seventieth Birthday.* New York: The Jewish Center Synagogue, 1962; Schacter, Jacob J., Ed., *Reverence Righteousness and Rahamanut: Essays in Memory of Rabbi Dr. Leo Jung.* Northdale, NJ and London: Jason Aronson Inc., 1992; Schacter, Jacob J., "Rabbi Dr. Leo Jung: Reflections on the Centennial of His Birth," *Jewish Action,* 53, No. 2 (Winter 1992-1993), pp. 20-24.

Alois Kaiser (1840-1908), b Sobotište, Slovakia; American chazzan and composer, founder of American cantorate
Bio: "Alois Kaiser," in Wikipedia. See - https://en.wikipedia.org/wiki/Alois_Kaiser; "Kaiser, Alois," in: JewishEncyclopedia.com. See - http://jewishencyclopedia.com/articles/9137-kaiser-alois

Alexander Kaufman (1886-d.), b. Bardejov, Slovakia; editor, publisher
Bio: *Who's Who in American Jewry.* New York: Jewish Biographical Bureau, 1927, Vol. 1, p. 312.

David Klein (1868-d.), b. Lipany, Slovakia; Rabbi
Bio: *American Jewish Year Book*, 5664 (Sept. 22 to Sept. 1904), p. 68.

Henry Klein (1859-d.), b. Lipany, Slovakia; Rabbi
Bio: *American Jewish Year Book.* Philadelphia: Jewish Publication Society of America, 1903, Vol. 5, pp. 68-69.

Jacob Klein (1870-d.), b. Veľká Ida, Slovakia; Rabbi
Bio: *American Jewish Year Book.* Philadelphia: Jewish Publication Society of America, 1903, Vol.5, p. 69.

Philip Klein (1849-d.), b. Bardoňovo, Slovakia; Rabbi
Bio: *American Jewish Year Book*. Philadelphia: Jewish Publication Society of America, 1903, Vol.5, p. 69.

Eugene Kohn (1887-1977), b. Newark, NJ, of Bohemian ancestry; American Reconstructionist Rabbi, writer, editor
Bio: "Eugene Kohn," in Wikipedia. See - https://en.wikipedia.org/wiki/Eugene Kohn; Rechcigl, Miloslav, Jr., "Eugene Kohn," in: *Beyond the Sea of Beer*. Bloomington, IN: Author House, 2017, p. 151-152.

Jacob Kohn (1881-1968), b. Newark, NJ, of Bohemian ancestry; conservative Rabbi
Bio: Rechcigl, Miloslav, Jr., "Jacob Kohn," in: *Encyclopedia of Bohemian and Czech American Biography*. Bloomington, IN.: AuthorHouse, 2016, Vol. 1, p.292.

Mayer Kopfstein (1866-d.), b. Bratislava, Slovakia; Rabbi
Bio: *American Jewish Year Book*. Philadelphia: Jewish Publication Society of America, 1903, Vol. 5, p. 70.

Joseph Saul Kornfeld (1876-), b. Zlaté Moravce, Slovakia; Rabbi, Pine Bluff, AR
Bio: *American Jewish Year Book*. Philadelphia: Jewish Publication Society of America, 1903, Vol. 5, p. 70

Marcus Krauskopf (1848-1936), b. Merklin, Bohemia; Rabbi
Bio: Rechcigl, Miloslav, Jr., "Marcus Krauskopf," in: *Encyclopedia of Bohemian and Czech American Biography*. Bloomington, IN.: AuthorHouse, 2016, Vol. 1, pp. 292-293.

David Lefkowitz (1875-1955), b. Prešov, Slovakia; Rabbi, Dallas, TX
Bio: "David Fekowitz," in: Wikipedia. See - https://en.wikipedia.org/wiki/David Lefkowitz; *American Jewish Year Book*. Philadelphia: Jewish Publication Society of America, 1903, Vol. 5, p. 72; Weiss, Marshall, "The Federation Founder," *The Dayton Jewish Observer*, November 1, 2010.

Eugene Max Mannheimer (1880-1952), b. Rochester, NY, of Bohemian ancestry; Rabbi
Bio: Rechcigl, Miloslav, Jr., "Eugene Max Mannheimer," in: *Encyclopedia of Bohemian and Czech American Biography*. Bloomington, IN.: AuthorHouse, 2016, Vol. 1, p. 293.

Leo Mannheimer (1878-1954), b. Rochester, NY, of Bohemian ancestry; Rabbi
Bio: Rechcigl, Miloslav, Jr., "Leo Mannheimer," in: *Encyclopedia of Bohemian and Czech American Biography*. Bloomington, IN.: AuthorHouse, 2016, Vol. 1, p. 293.

Ignatius Mueller (1857-d.), b. Prešov, Slovakia; Rabbi
Bio: *American Jewish Year Book*. Philadelphia: Jewish Publication Society of America, 1903, Vol. 5, p. 84.

Morris Newfield (1869-d.), b. Humenné, Slovakia; Rabbi
Bio: *American Jewish Year Book*. *American Jewish Year Book*. Philadelphia: Jewish Publication Society of America, 1903, Vol. 5, p. 85.; "Newfield, Morris," in: *Who's Who in American Jewry*, New York: Jewish Biographical Bureau, 1926, vol. 1, p. 458.

Siegmund Moses Reich (1873-d.), b. Bohemia; Rabbi
Bio: Rechcigl, Miloslav, Jr., "Siegmund Moses Reich," in: *Encyclopedia of Bohemian and Czech American Biography*. Bloomington, IN.: AuthorHouse, 2016, Vol. 1, p. 294.

Bernard Sadler (1854-1917), b. Kostelní Bříza, Bohemia; Rabbi
Bio: Rechcigl, Miloslav, Jr., "Bernard Sadler," in: *Encyclopedia of Bohemian and Czech American Biography*. Bloomington, IN.: AuthorHouse, 2016, Vol. 1, p. 294.

Emanuel Schoenbrun (1859-), b. Veľké Kapušany, Slovakia; Rabbi, Cleveland, OH
Bio: "Schoenbrun, Emanuel," *American Jewish Year Book*. Philadelphia: Jewish Publication Society of America, 1903, Vol. 5, p. 96.

Emanuel Schreiber (1852-1932), b. Lipník, Moravia; Rabbi
Bio: "Emanuel Schreiber," in: Wikipedia. See - https://en.wikipedia.org/wiki/Emanuel Schreiber; Rechcigl, Miloslav, Jr., "Emanuel Schreiber," in: *Encyclopedia of Bohemian and Czech American Biography*. Bloomington, IN.: AuthorHouse, 2016, Vol. 1, p. 294

Solomon H. Sonneschein (1839-1908), b. Svatý Martin, Slovakia, educated in Moravia; Rabbi
Bio: "Rabbi Sonneschein Resigns; He was brilliant and popular, but had many enemies," *The New York Times*, September 10, 1891; *The American Jewish Year Book*, 1903-1904, p. 101.

Hugo Stránský (1905-1983), b. Prague, Bohemia; Rabbi
Bio: Rechcigl, Miloslav, Jr., "Hugo Stránský," in: *Encyclopedia of Bohemian and Czech American Biography*. Bloomington, IN.: AuthorHouse, 2016, Vol. 1, p. 294.

Benjamin Szold (1829-1902), b. Zemianske Sady, Slovakia, Rabbi and scholar
Bio: "Benjamin Szold," in: Wikipedia. See - https://en.wikipedia.org/wiki/Benjamin_Szold;
"Szold, Benjamin," in: JewishEncyclopedia.com. See - http://jewishencyclopedia.com/articles/14180-szold-benjamin

Benjamin Abner Tintner (1884- d.), b. Newark, NJ, of Moravian, ancestry; Rabbi
Bio: Rechcigl, Miloslav, Jr., "Benjamin Abner Tintner," in: *Encyclopedia of Bohemian and Czech American Biography*. Bloomington, IN.: AuthorHouse, 2016, Vol. 1, p. 295.

Moritz Tintner (1843-1906), b. Slavkov, Moravia; Rabbi
Bio: Rechcigl, Miloslav, Jr., "Moritz Tintner," in: *Encyclopedia of Bohemian and Czech American Biography*. Bloomington, IN.: AuthorHouse, 2016, Vol. 1, p. 295; *The American Jewish Year Book*, Vol. 5 (1903), p. 103.

Hermann Vogelstein (1870-1942), b. Pilsen, Bohemia; Rabbi
Bio: Rechcigl, Miloslav, Jr., "Hermann Vogelstein," in: *Encyclopedia of Bohemian and Czech American Biography.* Bloomington, IN.: AuthorHouse, 2016, Vol. 1, p. 295; "Hermann Vogelstein," in: Wikipedia. See - https://de.wikipedia.org/wiki/Hermann Vogelstein; "Dr. Herman Vogelstein, Scholar and Former Rabbi of Breslau, Dies in New York," in: Jewish Telegraphic Agency, October 1, 1942.

Morris Wechsler (1849-d.), b. Michalovce, Slovakia; Rabbi
Bio: *American Jewish Year Book.* Philadelphia: Jewish Publication Society of America, 1903, Vol. 5, p. 104.

Mayer Winkler (1882-1944), b. Veľpolie, Slovakia; Rabbi, Los Angeles
Bio: Who's Who in American Jewry. New York: Jewish Biographical Bureau, 1927, Vol. 1, p. 650.

Aaron Wise (1844-1896), b. Eger, Hungary, of Moravian ancestry; Rabbi
Bio: "Aaron Wise," in: Wikipedia. See - https://en.wikipedia.org/wiki/Aaron_Wise

Isaac Mayer Wise (1819-1900), b. Lomnička, Bohemia; Reform, Rabbi, founder of Reform Judaism
Bio: Heller, James G., Isaac M. Wise, His Life, Work and Thought. The Union of American Hebrew Congregations, 1965; Kisch, Guido, "The Founder and Organizer of Reform Judaism in America," in: *In Search of Freedom.* A History of American Jews from Czechoslovakia 1592-1948. London: Edward Goldston, 1948, pp. 87-89; May, Max B., *Isaac Mayer Wise. The Founder of American Judaism.* New York and London: G. P. Putnam & Sons, 1916; Wise, Isaac Mayer, *Reminiscences.* Cincinnati: Leo Wise & Co., 1901. 361p.

Jonah Bondi Wise (1881-1959), b. Cincinnati, OH, of Bohemian ancestry; Rabbi
Bio: Rechcigl, Miloslav, Jr., "Jonah Bondi Wise," *Encyclopedia of Bohemian and Czech American Biography.* Bloomington, IN.: AuthorHouse, 2016, Vol. 1, p. 296.

Stephen S. Wise 1874-1949), b. Budapest, of Slovak ancestry; Rabbi
Bio: Voss, Carl H., Rabbi *and Minister: The Friendship of Stephen S. Wise and John Haynes Holmes.* New York: Prometheus, 1980; Wise, Stephen S., *The Challenging Years.* New York: Putnam, 1949.

Samuel Wolfenstein (1841-1921), b. Moravia; Rabbi, superintendent of orphan home
Bio: Rechcigl, Miloslav, Jr., "Samuel Wolfenstein," in: *Beyond the Sea of Beer.* Bloomington, IN: AuthorHouse, 2016, p. 392.

2. Later and Contemporary Rabbis

Zvi Dershowitz (1928-), b. Brno, Czech.; Rabbi
Bio: "Zvi Dershowitz," in: Wikipedia. See - https://en.wikipedia.org/wiki/Zvi Dershowitz

Moses M. Landau (1907-d.), b. Austria, descendant of Rabbi Ezekiel Landau of Prague; Rabbi
Bio: Rechcigl, Miloslav, Jr., "Moses M. Landau," in: *Encyclopedia of Bohemian and Czech American Biography.* Bloomington, IN.: AuthorHouse, 2016, Vol. 1, p. 293.

David Lefkowitz, Jr. (1911-1999), b. Dayton, OH, of Slovak ancestry; Rabbi, Shreveport, LA
Bio: "Davis Lefkowitz, Jr. Papers," in: American Jewish Archives, MS collection No. 650

Joshua Loth Liebman (1907-1948), b. Hamilton, OH, of Bohemian ancestry; Rabbi
Bio: Rechcigl, Miloslav, Jr., "Joshua Loth Liebman," in: *Encyclopedia of Bohemian and Czech American Biography.* Bloomington, IN.: AuthorHouse, 2016, Vol. 1, p. 293.

Samuel Rosenblatt (1902-1983), b. Bratislava, Slovakia; Rabbi, Trenton, NJ, lecturer
Bio: Who's Who in American Jewry. New York: Jewish Biographical Bureau, 1927, Vol. 1, p. 514.

Max Vogelstein (1901-1984) b. Bohemia; Rabbi
Bio: Rechcigl, Miloslav, Jr., "Max Vogelstein," in: *Encyclopedia of Bohemian and Czech American Biography*. Bloomington, IN.: AuthorHouse, 2016, Vol. 1, p. 295.

Norbert Weinberg (1948-), b. Frankfurt, Germany, of Bohemian ancestry; Rabbi
Bio: Rechcigl, Miloslav, Jr., "Norbert Weinberg," in: *Encyclopedia of Bohemian and Czech American Biography*. Bloomington, IN.: AuthorHouse, 2016, Vol. 1, p. 295.

William (Wilhelm) Weinberg (1901-1976), b. Dolina, Galicia, of Bohemian ancestry; Rabbi
Bio: Rechcigl, Miloslav, Jr., "William (Wilhelm) Weinberg," in: *Encyclopedia of Bohemian and Czech American Biography*. Bloomington, IN.: AuthorHouse, 2016, Vol. 1, p5. 295-296.

David Wirtschauer (ca 1969-), b. Lexington, KY, of Slovak ancestry; Rabbi at Amos Jewish Congregation in IA and then at Temple Adath Israel in Lexington
Bio: "Rabbi David Wirtschafter," in Gravatar Profile. See - http://en.gravatar.com/rabbidavidw; Miller, Jonathan, "Temple Adath Israel Welcomes Rabbi David Wirtschafter Home," *Shalom. Newspaper of the Jewish Federation of the Bluegrass*, 14, No. 5 (June/July 2015), pp. 1-2.

VIII. Economy

A. General

Kisch, Guido, "Contributions to Secular Culture: Commerce and Industry," in: *In Search of Freedom.* A History of American Jews from Czechoslovakia. 1592-1948. London: Edward Goldston, 1947, pp. 150-166.

B. Merchants

1. Pioneer Merchants

Adolph Abeles (1817-1855), b. Bečov, Bohemia; co-owner of a general store in St. Louis, known as 'Jew Store"
Bio: Rechcigl, Miloslav, Jr., "Adolph Abeles," in: *Encyclopedia of Bohemian and Czech-American Biography.* Bloomington, IN: AuthorHouse, 2016, Vol. 1, p. 107.

Julius David Abeles (1848-1920), b. St. Louis, MO, of Bohemian ancestry; merchant, Philadelphia and St. Louis
Bio: Rechcigl, Miloslav, Jr., "Julius David Adler," *Encyclopedia of Bohemian and Czech-American Biography.* Bloomington, IN: AuthorHouse, 2016, Vol. 1, p. 104.

David Adler (1821-1905), b. Bohemia; wholesale clothing business
Bio: "David Adler," in: *History of Milwaukee, City and County.* By William George Bruce. Chicago-Milwaukee: The S. J. Clarke Publishing Co., 1922, Vol. 3, pp. 8-11; "David Adler," in: *The Columbian Biographical Dictionary and Portrait Gallery of the Representative Men of the US. Wisconsin Volume.* Chicago: The Lewis Publishing Co., 1895, Part 2, pp. 854-856.

Leopold Adler (1861-1928), b. Volyně, Bohemia; founder of Leopold Adler Department stores, Savannah, GA

Bio: Rechcigl, Miloslav, Jr. "Leopold Adler," in: *Encyclopedia of Bohemian and Czech-American Biography*. Bloomington, IN: AuthorHouse, 2016, Vol. 1, p. 105.

Louis J. Adler (1856-d.), b. Milwaukee, WI, of Bohemian ancestry; merchant, Uniontown, AL
Bio: "Louis J. Adler,", in: *Memorial Record of Alabama*. Madison, WI: Brant & Fuller, 1893, Vol. 2, p. 777.

Solomon Adler (1816-1890), b. Bohemia; retail clothing merchant, Milwaukee, WI
Bio: Rechcigl, Miloslav, Jr., "Solomon Adler," in: *Encyclopedia of Bohemian and Czech-American Biography*. Bloomington, IN: AuthorHouse, 2016, Vol. 1, p. 105.

Isidor Auer (1872-1919), b. Tachov, Bohemia; wholesale jeweler, St. Louis
Bio: *The Book of St. Louisans*. St. Louis: St. Louis Republic, 1906, p. 29

Abraham Block (1781-1857), b. Bohemia; pioneer merchant, Arkansas, soldier
Bio: Kwas, Mary L., *Digging for History at Old Washington*. Fayetteville: University of Arkansas Press, 2009; Kwas, Mary L., "Two Generations of the Abraham and Fanny Block Family: Internal Migration, Economics, Family and the Jewish Frontier," *Southern Jewish History*, 12 (2009), pp. 39–114; Rechcigl, Miloslav, Jr., "Abraham Block," *Beyond the Sea of Beer*. Bloomington, IN: AuthorHouse, 2016, p. 28, 85, 115, 198, 391, 443, 511, 783.

Abram Block (1830-1906), b. Švihov, Bohemia; founder of A. Block Fruit Co., Santa Clara, CA, then considered the largest business with fruit in the world
Bio: Rechcigl, Miloslav, Jr., "Abram Block," in: *Encyclopedia of Bohemian and Czech-American Biography*. Bloomington, IN: AuthorHouse, 2016, Vol. 1, p. 107.

Phineas Block (1795-1871), b. Bohemia; grocer, co-owner of Steamship Co. Bio: Rechcigl, Miloslav, Jr., "Phineas Block," in: *Encyclopedia of Bohemian and Czech-American Biography*. Bloomington, IN: AuthorHouse, 2016, Vol. 1, p. 102.

Alfred Brandeis (1854-1928), b. Louisville, KY; president of A. Brandeis & Son, a Cincinnati grain company
Bio: Rechcigl, Miloslav, Jr., "Alfred Brandeis," in: *Encyclopedia of Bohemian and Czech-American Biography*. Bloomington, IN: AuthorHouse, 2016, Vol. 1, p. 107.

Arthur D. Brandeis (1862-1916), b. Manitowoc, WI, of Bohemian ancestry; businessman, president of J. H. Brandeis Co., Omaha, NE and other businesses
Bio: Rechcigl, Miloslav, Jr., "Arthur D. Brandeis," in: *Encyclopedia of Bohemian and Czech-American Biography*. Bloomington, IN: AuthorHouse, 2016, Vol. 1, p. 107.

George Brandeis (1869-1913), b. Libeň, Bohemia; president of J. L. Brandeis & Sons, retail dry goods, Omaha, NE
Bio: Rechcigl, Miloslav, Jr., "George Brandeis," in: *Encyclopedia of Bohemian and Czech-American Biography*. Bloomington, IN: AuthorHouse, 2016, Vol. 1, p. 108.

Jonas L. Brandeis (1836-1903), founder of the J. L. Brandeis Stores, Omaha, NE
Bio: Rechcigl, Miloslav, Jr., "Jonas L. Brandeis," in: *Encyclopedia of Bohemian and Czech-American Biography*. Bloomington, IN: AuthorHouse, 2016, p. 108; Rechcigl, Miloslav, Jr., "Jonas L. Brandeis," in: *Beyond the Sea of Beer*. Bloomington, IN: AuthorHouse, 2016, pp. 744-745; "J. L. Brandeis and Sons," in: Wikipedia. See - https://en.wikipedia.org/wiki/J. L. Brandeis and Sons

Julius Bunzl (1830-1887), b. Prague, Bohemia; wholesale tobacco merchant, NYC
Bio: Rechcigl, Miloslav, Jr., "Julius Bunzl," in: *Encyclopedia of Bohemian and Czech-American Biography*. Bloomington, IN: AuthorHouse, 2016, p. 108.

Mathias Bush (1722-1790), b. Prague, Bohemia; pioneer merchant, Philadelphia, PA
Bio: Rechcigl, Miloslav, Jr., "Mathias Bush," in: *Encyclopedia of Bohemian and Czech-American Biography.* Bloomington, IN: AuthorHouse, 2016, Vol. 1, p.102.

Henry Dormitzer (1827-1911), b. Prague, Bohemia; wholesale tobacco merchant, partner of the firm Bunzl & Dormitzer, NYC
Bio: Rechcigl, Miloslav, Jr., "Henry Dormitzer," in: *Encyclopedia of Bohemian and Czech-American Biography.* Bloomington, IN: AuthorHouse, 2016, pp. 108-109.

Alfred Fantl (1866-1928), b. Karlovy Vary, Bohemia; founder of the firm Alfred Fantl, resident buyers, NYC
Bio: Rechcigl, Miloslav, Jr., "Alfred Fantl," in: *Encyclopedia of Bohemian and Czech-American Biography.* Bloomington, IN: AuthorHouse, 2016, p. 109.

Frederico Figner (1866- 1947), b. Milevsko, Bohemia; Brazilian entrepreneur, founder of the first commercial recording company in Brazil
Bio: "Fred Figner," in: Wikipedia. See - https://en.wikipedia.org/wiki/Fred_Figner

Isaac Newton Fleischner (1859-1927), b. Albany, OR, of Bohemian ancestry; wholesale merchant, partner of Fleischner, Mayer & Co., Portland, OR
Bio: "Isaac Newton Fleischner," in: *Portland, Oregon. Its History and Builders.* Chicago-Portland: S.J. Clarke Publishing Co., 1911, Vol. 2, pp. 665-666.

Jacob Fleischner (1833-1910), b. Bohemia; pioneer merchant in Albany and then Portland, OR
Bio: Rechcigl, Miloslav, Jr., "Jacob Fleischner," in: *Encyclopedia of Bohemian and Czech-American Biography.* Bloomington, IN: AuthorHouse, 2016, Vol. 1, p.110.

Louis Fleischner (1827-1896), b. Vogelsang, Bohemia; owner of a wholesale dry-goods house, Portland
Bio: Gaston, Joseph, *Portland, Oregon. Its History and Builders.* Chicago-Portland: S.J. Clarke Publishing Co., 1911, Vol. 2, pp. 258-262.

Bernard Flesher (1831-1909), b. Klatovy, Bohemia; merchant, KS
Bio: "Bernard Flesher," in: William Elsey Connelley, *A Standard History of Kansas and Kansans.* Chicago – New York: Lewis Publishing Co., 1915, Vol. 5, pp. 2514-15.

Harry Freund (1874-1949), b. St. Louis, of Bohemian ancestry; president of S. E. Freund's Sons Shoe and Clothing Co.
Bio: Rechcigl, Miloslav, Jr. "Harry Freund," in: *Encyclopedia of Bohemian and Czech-American Biography.* Bloomington, IN: AuthorHouse, 2016, Vol. 1, p.110.

Emil Fuerth (1857-1944), b. Sušice, Bohemia; trained as a dentist, president of Ludwig Baumann & Co., and general house furnishings
Bio: Rechcigl, Miloslav, Jr., "Emil Fuerth," in: *Encyclopedia of Bohemian and Czech-American Biography.* Bloomington, IN: AuthorHouse, 2016, Vol. 1, pp.110-111.

Jacob Furth (1840-1914), b. Švihov, Bohemia; merchant, entrepreneur responsible for developing Seattle's public transportation system
Bio: Rechcigl, Miloslav, Jr. "Jacob Furth," in: *Encyclopedia of Bohemian and Czech-American Biography.* Bloomington, IN: AuthorHouse, 2016, Vol. 1, p.111.

Jacob Furth (1844-1918), b. Bohemia; whole-sale grocer, St. Louis
Bio: "Jacob Furth," in: *The Book of St. Louisans.* 2nd ed. Chicago: A. N. Marquis & Co., 1912, pp. 215-216.

Herman Gans (1851-1901), b. Bohemia; head of the firm Gans & Klein Co., Montana
Bio: Rechcigl, Miloslav, Jr., "Herman Gans," in: *Encyclopedia of Bohemian and Czech-American Biography.* Bloomington, IN: AuthorHouse, 2016, Vol. 1, p.111.

Joseph Gans (1838-1917), b. Neustadt, Bohemia; pioneer merchanting Montana, president of Gans & Klein Co.
Bio: "Joseph Gans," in: *A History of Montana*, Vol. 2., p. 994.

Zdeněk Ginsburg (1890-1971), b. Poděbrady, Bohemia; co-owner of the Leader Stores, Chicago
Bio: Rechcigl, Miloslav, Jr., "Zdeněk Ginsburg," in: *Encyclopedia of Bohemian and Czech-American Biography*. Bloomington, IN: AuthorHouse, 2016, Vol. 1, p.112.

Adolph Glaser (1854-d.), b. Terešov, Bohemia; importer of lace, embroideries and handkerchiefs, St. Louis, MO
Bio: "Glaser, Adolph," in: *The Book of St. Louisans*. St. Louis: St. Louis Republic, 1906, p. 225.

Julius Glaser (1862-d.), b. Bohemia; merchant, wholesale dry goods commission merchant, St. Louis, MO
Bio: "Glaser, Julius," in: *The Book of St. Louisiana*. St. Louis: St. Louis Republic, 1906, p. 225.

Sigmund Glaser (1863-1950), b. Bohemia; merchant in laces and embroideries, St. Louis, MO
Bio: "Glaser, Sigmund," in: *The Book of St. Louisiana*. St. Louis: St. Louis Republic, 1906, p. 225.

Otto Herman Goldstein (1883-1937), b. Rokycany, Bohemia; wholesale grocer, Chicago, US Army officer, with the rank of Major Lt. Colonel,
Bio: Rechcigl, Miloslav, Jr., "Otto Herman Goldstein," in: *Encyclopedia of Bohemian and Czech-American Biography*. Bloomington, IN: AuthorHouse, 2016, Vol. 2, p. 2189; Marcosson, Isaac F., "Feeding the Yankees in France," *Saturday Evening Post*, December 14, 1918, pp. 12-13, 98, 101-102, 105-106, 109.

Barnard Gratz (1738-1801), b. Langendorf, Silesia; merchant, Philadelphia, PA
Bio: *B. and M. Gratz. Merchants in Philadelphia, 1754-1798*. Edited by William Vincent Byers. Jefferson City, MO: Hugh Stephens Printing Co., 1916;

"Barnard Gratz," in: JewishEncyclopedia.com. See - http://www.jewishencyclopedia.com/articles/6860-gratz

Hyman Gratz (1776-1857), b. Philadelphia, of Silesian ancestry; merchant and philanthropist
Bio: "Hyman Gratz," in: JewishEncyclopedia.com. See - http://www.jewishencyclopedia.com/articles/6860-gratz

Jacob Gratz (1790-1856), b, Philadelphia, PA, of Silesian ancestry; merchant, PA State legislator
Bio: "Jacob Gratz,", in: JewishEncyclopedia.com. See - http://www.jewishencyclopedia.com/articles/6860-gratz

Michael Gratz (1740-1811), b. Langendorf, Silesia; trader and merchant, Philadelphia, PA
Bio: *B. and M. Gratz. Merchants in Philadelphia, 1754-1798.* Edited by William Vincent Byers. Jefferson City, MO: Hugh Stephens Printing Co., 1916; "Michael Gratz," in: JewishEncyclopedia.com. See - http://www.jewishencyclopedia.com/articles/6860-gratz

Jacob Greil (1839-1900), b. Bohemia; wholesale grocer, Montgomery, AL
Bio: "Jacob Greil," in: *Memorial Record of Alabama.* Madison, WI: Brant & Fuller, 1893, Vol. 2, p. 676.

Frank Guinzburg (1863-1908), b. Annapolis, MD, of Bohemian father; merchant, PA
Bio: Rechcigl, Miloslav, Jr. "Frank Guinzburg," in: *Encyclopedia of Bohemian and Czech-American Biography.* Bloomington, IN: AuthorHouse, 2016, Vol. 1, p. 113.

Emil Gutwillig (1866-d.), b. Plzeň, Bohemia; jobber and importer of woolens, owner of E. Gutwillig & Co., Chicago
Bio: Rechcigl, Miloslav, Jr., "Emil Gutwillig," in: *Encyclopedia of Bohemian and Czech-American Biography.* Bloomington, IN: AuthorHouse, 2016, Vol. 1, p. 113.

Ignatz Hartmann (1841-1902), b. Bohemia; clothing merchant, St. Louis, Union Army veteran
Bio: *Zion in the Valley: The Jewish Community of St. Louis.* Columbia and London: University of Missouri Press, 1997, Vol. 1, p. 169.

Victor H. Heller (1886-1967), b. Czech.; together with his brother George, co-founder of the Vita Food Products, Inc., NYC
Bio: Rechcigl, Miloslav, Jr., "Victor h. Heller," in: *Encyclopedia of Bohemian and Czech-American Biography.* Bloomington, IN: AuthorHouse, 2016, Vol. 1, p. 183; "The Herring Maven: Some Herring History." See - http://herringmaven.blogspot.com/2011/02/some-herring-history.html

John D. Hertz (orig. Schandor Herz) (1879-1961), b. Sklabiňa, Slovakia; founder of Yellow Cab Co. and of Rent-a-Car
Bio: "John D. Hertz," in: Wikipedia. See - https://en.wikipedia.org/wiki/John D. Hertz

Samuel Hirsch (1852-1916), b. České Budějovice, Bohemia; importer of laces and embroideries, known as 'King of Lace Importers'
Bio: Rechcigl, Miloslav, Jr., "Samuel Hirsch," in: *Encyclopedia of Bohemian and Czech-American Biography.* Bloomington, IN: AuthorHouse, 2016, Vol. 1, p. 114.

Henry Horner (1818-1878), b. Čkyně, Bohemia; wholesale grocer, Chicago
Bio: Rechcigl, Miloslav, Jr., "Henry Horner," in: *Encyclopedia of Bohemian and Czech-American Biography.* Bloomington, IN: AuthorHouse, 2016, Vol. 1, p. 115.

Maurice Horner, Jr. (1892-1965), b. Chicago, IL, of Bohemian ancestry; president of Durand-McNeil Horner wholesale groceries
Bio: Rechcigl, Miloslav, Jr., "Maurice Horner, Jr.," in: *Encyclopedia of Bohemian and Czech-American Biography.* Bloomington, IN: AuthorHouse, 2016, Vol. 1, p. 115.

Maurice J. Karpeles (1878-1973), b. Washington, DC, of Bohemian ancestry; merchant dealing with precious stones, Providence, RI
Bio: Miloslav Rechcigl, Jr., "Maurice J. Karpeles," in: *Encyclopedia of Bohemian and Czech-American Biography*. Bloomington, IN: AuthorHouse, 2016, Vol. 1, p. 116; "Karpeles, Maurice J.," in: *American Biography: A New Cyclopedia*, New York: American Historical Society, 1920, Vol. 7, pp. 129-130.

Abraham Klauber (1831-1911), b. Zdeslav, Bohemia; pioneer merchant in California and Nevada
Bio: "Abraham Klauber," in: Wikipedia. See - https://en.wikipedia.org/wiki/Abraham Klauber

Samuel Klauber (1823-1911), b. Mutěnín, Bohemia; dealer in dry-goods
Bio: Rechcigl, Miloslav, Jr., "Samuel Klauber," in: *Encyclopedia of Bohemian and Czech-American Biography*. Bloomington, IN: AuthorHouse, 2016, Vol. 1, pp. 116-117.

Solomon Kohn (1838-1918), b. Bohemia; pioneer furniture dealer, Cleveland, OH
Bio: "Solomon Kohn," *The Grand Rapids Furniture Record,* 37 (September 1918), p. 121; "Solomon Kohn," in: *Cleveland and its Environs*. Chicago-New York: Lewis Publishing Co., 1918, Vol. 3, pp. 459-460.

Henry Kositchek (1851-1925), b. Bohemia; founder of men's clothing store, Lansing, MI
Bio: Rechcigl, Miloslav, Jr., "Henry Kositchek," in: *Encyclopedia of Bohemian and Czech-American Biography*. Bloomington, IN: AuthorHouse, 2016, Vol. 1, p. 117.

Emanuel S. Kuh (1832-1917), b. Bohemia; produce exporter and importer, NYC
Bio: Rechcigl, Miloslav, Jr., "Emanuel S. Kuh," in: *Encyclopedia of Bohemian and Czech-American Biography*. Bloomington, IN: AuthorHouse, 2016, Vol. 1, p. 118.

Gustav Kussy (1825-1907), b. Prašný Újezd, Bohemia; meat dealer, Newark, NJ
Bio: Rechcigl, Miloslav, Jr., "Gustav Kussy," in: *Encyclopedia of Bohemian and Czech-American Biography.* Bloomington, IN: AuthorHouse, 2016, Vol. 1, p. 118.

Simon Levi (1850-1918), b. Dlouhý Újezd, Bohemia; wholesale grocer, San Diego, CA
Bio: Rechcigl, Miloslav, Jr., "Simon Levi," in: *Encyclopedia of Bohemian and Czech-American Biography.* Bloomington, IN: AuthorHouse, 2016, Vol. 1, p. 119.

Solomon Levy (1839-), b. near Karlovy Vary, Bohemia; commission merchant, San Francisco, CA
Bio: Rechcigl, Miloslav, Jr. *Beyond the Sea of Beer.* Bloomington, IN: AuthorHouse, IN, 2017, p. 138.

Max Lurie (1867-1935), b. Petrovice, Bohemia; founder of Lurie Brothers Department Store, Lawndale, Chicago
Bio: Rechcigl, Miloslav, Jr., "Max Lurie," in: *Encyclopedia of Bohemian and Czech-American Biography.* Bloomington, IN: AuthorHouse, 2016, Vol. 1, p. 120.

Jacob Morawetz (1821-1891), b. Bohemia; wholesale grocer, Milwaukee, WI
Bio: Rechcigl, Miloslav, Jr., "Morawetz Family," in: *Beyond the Sea of Beer.* Bloomington, IN: AuthorHouse, 2017, p. 233.

Edward Oplatka (1881-1945), b. Odolená Voda, Bohemia; businessman, founder of the Leader Department Store, Chicago
Bio: Rechcigl, Miloslav, Jr., "Edward Oplatka," in: *Encyclopedia of Bohemian and Czech-American Biography.* Bloomington, IN: AuthorHouse, 2016, Vol. 1, p. 122.

Nathan Pereles (1824-1879), b. Sobotište, Slovakia; pioneer Jewish grocery merchant in Milwaukee, attorney specializing in commercial and real estate law
Bio: "Nathan Pereles," in: *The Columbian Biographical Dictionary and Portrait Gallery of the Representative Men of the US. Wisconsin Volume.* Chicago: The Lewis Publishing Co., 1895, Part 2, pp. 437-442.

Albert Pick (1869-1955), b. Chicago, of Bohemian ancestry; merchant, owner of a large hotel chain
Bio: Barnard, Judith, *The Indestructible Crown: The Life of Albert Pick, Jr.* Chicago: Nelson Hall, 1980.

Morris Rich (orig. Mauritius Reich) (1847-1928), b. Košice, Slovakia; the founder of what would become Rich's Department Store retail chain, Atlanta, GA
Bio: Rich's. A Southern Institution. Charleston, SC: The History Press, 2012

Jacob Salz (1832-1909), b. Pilsen, Bohemia; early merchant, Centerville, CA., later tanner
Bio: Rechcigl, Miloslav, Jr., "Jacob Salz," in: *Encyclopedia of Bohemian and Czech-American Biography.* Bloomington, IN: AuthorHouse, 2016, Vol. 1, p. 124.

David E. Sicher (1827-1914), b. Bohemia; pioneer white goods merchant, NYC
Bio: *Encyclopedia of Bohemian and Czech-American Biography.* Bloomington, IN: AuthorHouse, 2016, Vol. 1, p. 124.

William Sicher (1827-1914), b. Bohemia; the earliest dry goods merchant in St. Louis
Bio: "Sicher, William," in: *The Book of St. Louisiana.* 2nd ed. Chicago: A. N. Marquis & Co., 1912, p. 552.

Jacob Sichl (1847-1909), b. Cheb, Bohemia; merchant, Nebraska City, NE
Bio: "Jacob Sichl," in: GENi

Ezekiel Solomon (1735-1808), b. Berlin, Ger., of Bohemian ancestry; early Jewish merchant, Montreal, Canada
Bio: Rechcigl, Miloslav, Jr., "Ezekiel Solomon," in: *Encyclopedia of Bohemian and Czech-American Biography*. Bloomington, IN: AuthorHouse, 2016, Vol. 1, p.104.

Henry Bernard Steele (1863-1909), b. Chicago, IL, of Bohemian ancestry; merchant, president of Steele-Wedeles Co., wholesale groceries, Chicago
Bio: Rechcigl, Miloslav, Jr., "Henry Bernard Steele," in: *Encyclopedia of Bohemian and Czech-American Biography*. Bloomington, IN: AuthorHouse, 2016, Vol. 1, pp. 124-125.

Samuel Bernard Steele (1866-d.) b. Chicago, IL, of Bohemian ancestry; merchant, president of Steele-Wedeles Co., wholesale groceries, Chicago
Bio: *Encyclopedia of Bohemian and Czech-American Biography*. Bloomington, IN: AuthorHouse, 2016, Vol. 1, p. 125.

Jacob Steinbach, Sr. (1847-1933), b. Bohemia; founder of one of the oldest department stores of the North Jersey coast
Bio: Rechcigl, Miloslav, Jr., "Jacob Steinbach, Sr.," in: *Encyclopedia of Bohemian and Czech-American Biography*. Bloomington, IN: AuthorHouse, 2016, Vol. 1, 125.

James Steiner (1860-1939), b. Miřkov, Bohemia; capitalist, merchant, 'Ice Cream and Candy King,' also in real estate, Hawaii
Bio: Rechcigl, Miloslav, Jr. "James Steiner," in: *Encyclopedia of Bohemian and Czech-American Biography*. Bloomington, IN: AuthorHouse, 2016, Vol. 1, p. 126; "Steiner, James," in: *Men of Hawaii*. Honolulu: Honolulu Star-Bulletin, 1921, Vol. 2, p. 373.

Sig Steiner (1865-1945), b. Auburn, CA, of Bohemian ancestry; merchant, partner in general merchandise business, Escondido, CA
Bio: "Grape Day Park is Sig Steiner's Legacy," San Diego Jewish World. See - http://www.sdjewishworld.com/2014/07/08/grape-day-park-sig-steiners-legacy/; Rechcigl, Miloslav, Jr., "Sig Steiner," in: *Encyclopedia of Bohemian and Czech-American Biography*. Bloomington, IN: AuthorHouse, 2016, Vol. 1, pp. 125-126.

Louis Taussig (1837-1890), b. Bohemia; founder of The Taussig Co., San Francisco, one of the largest liquor establishments in the West
Bio: Rechcigl, Miloslav, Jr., "Louis Taussig," in: *Encyclopedia of Bohemian and Czech-American Biography*. Bloomington, IN: AuthorHouse, 2016, Vol. 1, p. 126.

Rudolph Julius Taussig (1861-1922), b. New York, NY, of Bohemian ancestry; merchant
Rechcigl, Miloslav, Jr., "Rudolph Julius Taussig," in: Beyond the Sea of Beer. Bloomington, IN: AuthorHouse, 2016, p. 142.

Samuel Taussig (1854-1926), b. Bohemia; wholesale tobacco merchant, president of St. Louis Leaf Tobacco Co.
Bio: Rechcigl, Miloslav, Jr. "Samuel Taussig," in: *Encyclopedia of Bohemian and Czech-American Biography*. Bloomington, IN: AuthorHouse, 2016, Vol. 1, pp. 126-127.

David Treichlinger (1852-d.), b. Strakonice, Bohemia; commission merchant, St. louis
Bio: "Treichlinger, David," in: *The Bok of St. Louisans*. St. Louis: St. Louis Republic, 1906, p. 579; "David Treichlinger," in: *Prominent Jews of America*. Toledo, OH: American Hebrew Publishing Company, 1918, p. 304.

Edward Leopold Wedeles (1855-1937), b. Bohemia; a wholesale grocer, Chicago
Bio: Rechcigl, Miloslav, Jr., "Edward Leopold Wedeles," in: *Encyclopedia of Bohemian and Czech-American Biography*. Bloomington, IN: AuthorHouse, 2016, Vol. 1, p.127.

Emil Wedeles (1861-1928), b. Pilsen, Bohemia; leaf tobacco merchant, organized with his brother Joseph the firm Wedeles Brothers, dealers and packers of leaf tobacco
Bio: Rechcigl, Miloslav, Jr., "Emil Wedeles," *Encyclopedia of Bohemian and Czech-American Biography*. Bloomington, IN: AuthorHouse, 2016, Vol. 1, p. 127.

Josef Wedeles (1868-1945), b. Pilsen, Bohemia; associated with his brother in the Wedeles Brothers Co., dealers and packers of leaf tobacco
Bio: Rechcigl, Miloslav, Jr., "Emil Wedeles," *Encyclopedia of Bohemian and Czech-American Biography.* Bloomington, IN: AuthorHouse, 2016, Vol. 1, p. 127.

Max Wedeles (1870-1917), b. Osek, Bohemia; tobacco packer and dealer, owner of Max Wedeles Tobacco Co., Gadson County, Florida

Gottlieb Wehle (1802-1881), b. Prague, Bohemia; merchant, Madison IN, then NYC
Bio: Rechcigl, Miloslav, Jr., "Gottlieb Wehle," in: *Encyclopedia of Bohemian and Czech-American Biography.* Bloomington, IN: AuthorHouse, 2016, Vol. 1, p. 127.

Charles Winternitz (1815-1891), b. Deštná, Bohemia; dealer in iron of all kinds, Baltimore
Bio: Rechcigl, Miloslav, Jr., "Charles Winternitz," in: *Encyclopedia of Bohemian and Czech-American Biography.* Bloomington, IN: AuthorHouse, 2016, p. 128.

2. Later and Contemporary Merchants

Coleman E. Adler, 2nd (ca 1946-), b. Los Angeles, CA; president of Adler's, five stores in New Orleans, LA.
Bio: Rechcigl, Miloslav, Jr., "Coleman E. Adler, 2nd in: *Beyond the Sea of Beer.* Bloomington, IN: AuthorHouse, 2016, p. 745.

Samuel G. Adler (1892-1979), b. Savannah, GA, of Bohemian ancestry; partner and then president of Leopold Adler Co., Savannah, GA, also a banker
Bio: Rechcigl, Miloslav, Jr., "Samuel G. Adler," in: *Encyclopedia of Bohemian and Czech-American Biography.* Bloomington, IN: AuthorHouse, 2016, p. 105.

Maria Altmann (née Bloch-Bauer) (1916-2011), b. Vienna, of Bohemian father; Jewish refugee, established cashmere sweater business in California,

after immigrating to the US; known for her successful legal battle to recover the family portraits painted by Gustav Klimt
Bio: "Maria Altmann," in: Wikipedia. See - https://en.wikipedia.org/wiki/Maria Altmann; Grimes, William, "Maria Altmann, Pursuer of Family's Stolen Paintings, Dies at 94," *The New York Times,* February 9, 2011.

Alan A. Brandeis Baer (1923-2002), b. San Francisco, CA, of Bohemian ancestry; businessman, heir to the J. L. Brandeis Department chain
Bio: Rechcigl, Miloslav, Jr., "Alan Baer," in: *Encyclopedia of Bohemian and Czech-American Biography.* Bloomington, IN: AuthorHouse, 2016, p. 106.

E. John Brandeis (1895-1974), b. of Bohemian ancestry; merchant, president of the Brandeis Department Store, Omaha, NE
Bio: Rechcigl, Miloslav, Jr., "E. John Brandeis," in: *Encyclopedia of Bohemian and Czech-American Biography.* Bloomington, IN: AuthorHouse, 2016, p. 108; "E. John Brandeis Fund established by Alan and Marcia Baer Foundation," *Nebraska Jewish Historical Society News Letter,* Vol. 6, No. 1 (January 1988), p. 1.

Leslie Buck (1922-2010), b. Chust, Czech.; business executive, designer of Anthora coffee cup
Bio: "Leslie Buck," in: Wikipedia. See - https://en.wikipedia.org/wiki/Leslie_Buck

Bruce A. Gimbel (1913-1980), of Bohemian ancestry; head of the Gimbel's Department Store chain
Bio: Bruce A. Gimbel's Obituary, Milestones, *Time Magazine,* October 20, 1980.

Bruce Alva Gimbel (1913-1980), b. New York, NY, of Bohemian ancestry; chairman and chief executive officer of Gimbel Brothers, Inc
Bio: Bender, Marylin, "Gimbel Retires as Stores Head," The New York Times, August 15, 1975; "Bruce A. Gimbel's Obituary," *Time Magazine,* October 20, 1980.

Huntington Hartford (1911-2008), b. New York, NY, of Bohemian ancestry; businessman, philanthropist, stage and film producer and art collector, heir to A&P supermarket chain
Bio: Rechcigl, Miloslav, Jr., "Huntington Hartford," in: *Encyclopedia of Bohemian and Czech-American Biography.* Bloomington, IN: AuthorHouse, 2016, Vol. 1, p. 113.; "Huntington Hartford," in: Wikipedia. See - https://en.wikipedia.org/wiki/Huntington Hartford

Aerin Lauder (Lauder (1970-), b. NYC, of Czechoslovak ancestry; heiress and businesswomen
Bio: "Aerin Rebecca Lauder Zinterhofer," in: Wikipedia. See - https://en.wikipedia.org/wiki/Aerin_Laude

Jane Lauder (1973-), b. Manhattan, NY, of Czechoslovak ancestry; heiress and businesswoman
Bio: "Jane Lauder Warsh," in: Wikipedia. See - https://en.wikipedia.org/wiki/Jane Lauder

Douglas Pokorny Levey (1926-2016), b. New Orleans, LA, of Moravian ancestry; merchant, owner of retail shoe store, New Orleans
Bio: "Douglas Pokorny Levey," in Prabook. See: https://prabook.com/web/douglas_pokorny.levey/1107033

Ralph Pokorny Levey (1890-1958), b. New Orleans, LA, of Moravian ancestry; merchant, president of the retail shoe business, organizer of Better Business Bureau and Retail Merchants Credit Bureau, New Orleans
Bio: "Levey Funeral Rites are Held: St. Charles St., Businessman was 67," *New Orleans Times-Picayune,* September 23, 1958.

Frank S. Pohanka (1891-1959), b. New York, NY, of Moravian ancestry; founder of the Pohanka Automotive Group, one of the oldest car dealerships
Bio: Rechcigl, Miloslav, Jr., "Frank S. Pohanka," in: *Encyclopedia of Bohemian and Czech-American Biography.* Bloomington, IN: AuthorHouse, 2016, Vol. 1, p. 122.

Edwin l. Popper (1910-2003), b. NYC, of Bohemian ancestry; the last president of Leo Popper & Sons Glass, NYC, importers of sheet glass and other glass items.
Bio: Rechcigl, Miloslav, Jr., "Edwin L. Popper," in: *Encyclopedia of Bohemian and Czech-American Biography*. Bloomington, IN: AuthorHouse, 2016, Vol. 1, p. 157.

Elmer L. Winter (1912-2009), b. Milwaukee, WI, of Bohemian ancestry; attorney, businessman, entrepreneur, philanthropist, artist, author
Bio: Rechcigl, Miloslav, Jr., "Elmer L. Winter," in: *Encyclopedia of Bohemian and Czech-American Biography*. Bloomington, IN: AuthorHouse, 2016, Vol. 1, p. 196; "Manpower co-founder Winter dies at 97," Milwaukee *Journal Sentinel*, October 25, 2009; Oster, Marcy, "Elmer Winter, ex-AJC president, dies," Jewish Telegraphic Agency, October 27, 2009.

Robert Haws Wuensch (1908-1964), b. Newark, NJ., of Bohemian ancestry; druggist, owner of surgical appliance store, East Orange, NJ
Bio: Rechcigl, Miloslav, Jr., "Robert Haws Wuensch," in: *Encyclopedia of Bohemian and Czech-American Biography*. Bloomington, IN: AuthorHouse, 2016, Vol. 1, p. 128.

Henry Walter Wyman (1919-1995), b. Ústí nad Labem, Bohemia; businessman, president of Pantasote Co., Passaic, NJ
Bio: Henry Walter Wyman," in: *Encyclopedia of Bohemian and Czech-American Biography*. Bloomington, IN: AuthorHouse, 2016, Vol. 1, p. 196

Ralph Mark Wyman (1926-), b. Ústí nad Labem, Bohemia; businessman, entrepreneur
Bio: "Ralph Mark Wyman," in: *Encyclopedia of Bohemian and Czech-American Biography*. Bloomington, IN: AuthorHouse, 2016, Vol. 1, p. 19

C. Agribusinessmen

Abram Block (1830-1906), b. Švihov, Bohemia; wholesale fruit merchant, Santa Clara, CA

Bio: Rechcigl, Miloslav Jr., "Abram Block" in: *Encyclopedia of Bohemian and Czech-American Biography*. Bloomington, IN: AuthorHouse, 2016, Vol. 1, p. 107.

Adolph Brandeis (1824-1906), b. Prague, Bohemia; grain merchant, Louisville, KY
Bio: Rechcigl, Miloslav, Jr., "Adolph Brandeis," in: *Encyclopedia of Bohemian and Czech-American Biography*. Bloomington, IN: AuthorHouse, 2016, Vol. 1, p. 197.

Alfred F. Brandeis (1854-1928), b. Louisville, KY, of Bohemian ancestry; businessman, president of A. Brandeis & Son, Cincinnati grain firm
Bio: Rechcigl, Miloslav, Jr., "Alfred Brandeis," in: *Encyclopedia of Bohemian and Czech-American Biography*. Bloomington, IN: AuthorHouse, 2016, Vol. 1, p. 107.

Julius Bunzl (1830-1887), b. Prague, Bohemia; wholesale tobacco merchant, NYC
Bio: Rechcigl, Miloslav, Jr., "Julius Bunzl," in: *Encyclopedia of Bohemian and Czech-American Biography*. Bloomington, IN: AuthorHouse, 2016, p. 108.

Isidor Bush (orig. Busch) (1822-1898), b. Prague, Bohemia; viticulturist, owner of Bushberg
Bio: Rechcigl, Miloslav, Jr. "Isidor Bush," in: *Encyclopedia of Bohemian and Czech-American Biography*. Bloomington, IN: AuthorHouse, 2016, Vol. 1, p. 198.

Daniel Nathan Friesleben (1832-1897), b. Mariánské Lázně, Bohemia; merchant, rancher, CA
Bio: Rechcigl, Miloslav, Jr., "Daniel S. Friesleben," in: *Encyclopedia of Bohemian and Czech-American Biography*. Bloomington, IN: AuthorHouse, 2016, Vol. 1, p. 200.

Adolph Heller (1846-1910), b. Křivnice, Bohemia; owner of the Milwaukee Sausage Works
Bio: *Encyclopedia of Bohemian and Czech-American Biography*. Bloomington, IN: AuthorHouse, 2016, Vol. 1, pp. 201-202.

Bernard Heller (ca 1898-1891), b. Citov, Bohemia; founder of the butcher store, Milwaukee Sausage Works
Bio: Rechcigl, Miloslav, Jr., "Heller Family," in: *Beyond the Sea of Beer.* Bloomington, IN: AuthorHouse, 2017, pp. 232-233.

Sam Kane (1920-2010), b. Spišské Podhradie, Czech.; founder of meatpacking company, Corpus Christi, TX
Bio: Rechcigl, Miloslav, Jr., "Sam Kane," in: *Encyclopedia of Bohemian and Czech-American Biography.* Bloomington, IN: AuthorHouse, 2016, Vol. 1., p. 144.; "Sam Kane of Corpus Christi - Holocaust Survivor," in: TexAg, January 4, 2010. See - https://texags.com/forums/49/topics/1561812

Jerry Kane (1947-), b. Prague, Czech.; president of Sam Kane Beef Processors, Inc., Corpus Christi, TX
Bio: Rechcigl, Miloslav, Jr., "Jerry Kane," in: *Encyclopedia of Bohemian and Czech-American Biography.* Bloomington, IN: AuthorHouse, 2016, Vol. 1., pp. 143-144.

Charles Kohn (1848-d.), b. Vlachové, Březí, Bohemia; wholesale wine liquor merchant, CA
Bio: "Charles Kohn," *Pacific Jewish Journal,* Vol. 2 (1898), pp. 162-163

Max M. Lededer (1862-1926), b. Elizabethtown, NJ, of Bohemian ancestry; dealer in leather, hide and fertilizer, New Brunswick, NJ
Bio: Rechcigl, Miloslav, Jr. "Max M. Lederer," in: *Encyclopedia of Bohemian and Czech-American Biography.* Bloomington, IN: AuthorHouse, 2016, Vol. 1., 204.

Adolph Levi (1858-1943), b. Dlouhý Újezd, Bohemia; owner of ranches and dairy farms, San Diego, CA
Bio: Harrison, Donald H., "The Levis' personal Jewish history of San Diego," *San Diego Jewish World,* September 24, 1011 - See - ww.sdjewishworld.com/2011/09/24/the-levis-personal-jewish-history-of-san-diego/; Rechcigl, Miloslav, Jr. "Adolph Lewi," in: *Encyclopedia of Bohemian and Czech-American Biography.* Bloomington, IN: AuthorHouse, 2016, Vol. 1., 204.

Nathan Levy (1889-1967), b. Vicskburg, MS, of Bohemian ancestry; cotton businessman, also owner of insurance agency
Bio: Rechcigl, Miloslav, Jr., "Nathan Levy," in: *Encyclopedia of Bohemian and Czech-American Biography.* Bloomington, IN: AuthorHouse, 2016, Vol. 1, pp. 119-120.

Solomon Levy (1839-d.), b. Karlovy Vary, Bohemia; general commission merchant and dealer in poultry, eggs, fruit, potatoes, butter, hide
Bio: Rechcigl, Miloslav, Jr., "Solomon Levy," in: *Encyclopedia of Bohemian and Czech-American Biography.* Bloomington, IN: AuthorHouse, 2016, Vol. 1., 204-205.

Arthur Nohel (1884-1973), b. nr. Chomutov, Bohemia; grower of onion seed, sugar beet, tomatoes, etc. in CA
Bio: Rechcigl, Miloslav, Jr., "Arthur Nohel," in: *Encyclopedia of Bohemian and Czech-American Biography.* Bloomington, IN: AuthorHouse, 2016, Vol. 1., 205.

Gustave M. Pollitzer (1853-1909), b. New York, NY, of Moravian ancestry; a cotton exporter
Bio: Rechcigl, Miloslav, Jr., "Gustave M. Pollitzer," in: *Encyclopedia of Bohemian and Czech-American Biography.* Bloomington, IN: AuthorHouse, 2016, Vol. 1, pp. 205-206.

Moritz Pollitzer (1819-1902), b. Mikulov, Moravia; cotton merchant and agent for cotton gin, Beaufort, SC
Bio: Rechcigl, Miloslav, Jr., "Moritz Pollitzer", in *Encyclopedia of Bohemian and Czech-American Biography.* Bloomington, IN: AuthorHouse, 2016, Vol. 1, p. 206.

Maximillian Schling (1874-1943), b. Horní Cerekev, Bohemia; noted horticulturist and a retail florist, NYC
Bio: Rechcigl, Miloslav, Jr. "Maximillian Schling," in: *Encyclopedia of Bohemian and Czech-American Biography.* Bloomington, IN: AuthorHouse, 2016, Vol. 1, p. 207

Max Schling, Jr. (1914-1971), b. Yonkers, NY, of Bohemian ancestry; florist, NYC
Bio: Rechcigl, Miloslav, Jr. "Max Schling, Jr.," in: *Encyclopedia of Bohemian and Czech-American Biography*. Bloomington, IN: AuthorHouse, 2016, Vol. 1, p. 207

Adolf Stein (1853-1919), b. Bohemia; merchant, in liquor business, Chicago
Bio: Rechcigl, Miloslav, Jr., "Adolf Stein," in: *Encyclopedia of Bohemian and Czech-American Biography*. Bloomington, IN: AuthorHouse, 2016, Vol. 1, p. 125.

Louis Taussig (1837-1890), founder of the Taussig Co., the largest wholesale liquor establishment in the West
Bio: Rechcigl, Miloslav, Jr., "The Taussig Family," in: *Beyond the Sea of Beer*. Bloomington, IN: AuthorHouse, 2016, pp. 141-142.

Samuel Taussig (1854-1926), b. Bohemia; president of St. Louis Leaf Tobacco Co.
Bio: "Taussig, Samuel," in: *The Book of St. Louisans*. 2nd ed. Chicago: A. N. Marquis & Co., 1912, p. 588.

Emil Wedeles (1861-1928), b. Rokycany, Bohemia; merchant, dealer and packer of leaf tobacco, Chicago.
Bio: Rechcigl, Miloslav, Jr., "Emil Wedeles," in: *Encyclopedia of Bohemian and Czech-American Biography*. Bloomington, IN: AuthorHouse, 2016, Vol. 1, 127.

D. Manufacturers

1. Pioneer Manufacturers

Joseph Biederman (1856-1904), b. Bohemia; cofounder and co-owner of Prinz-Biederman Co., Cleveland, OH, one of the oldest US manufacturers of women's apparel

Bio: Rechcigl, Miloslav, Jr., "Joseph Biederman," in: *Encyclopedia of Bohemian and Czech-American Biography*. Bloomington, IN: AuthorHouse, 2016, Vol. 1, o. 130.

Roy Block (1879-1955), b. CA, of Bohemian ancestry; co-owner of Manasse-Block Tannery, Berkley, Oakland and San Francisco, CA
Bio: Rechcigl, Miloslav, Jr., *Beyond the Sea of Beer.* Bloomington, IN: AuthorHouse, 2017, pp. 132-133.

Victor Charles Bohm (Böhm) (1889-1955), b. Vienna, of Moravian ancestry; hat manufacturer, textile chemist
Bio: Rechcigl, Miloslav, Jr., "Victor C. Boehm," in: *Encyclopedia of Bohemian and Czech-American Biography*. Bloomington, IN: AuthorHouse, 2016, Vol. 1, p. 131.

Arde Bulova (1889-1958), b. New York, NY, of Bohemian ancestry; innovative watchmaker, credited for establishing numerous manufacturing processes, standardization of parts and movements and designer of a number of special tools, gauges and complicated machines required to produce parts
Bio: Rechcigl, Miloslav, Jr., "Arde Bulova," in: *Encyclopedia of Bohemian and Czech-American Biography*. Bloomington, IN: AuthorHouse, 2016, Vol. 1, pp. 132-133; "Bulova, Arde," in: *Biographical Dictionary of American Business Leader.* Edited by John N. Ingham. Westport, CT: Greenwood Press, Vol.1, pp. 112-114.

Joseph Bulova (1851-1935), b. Louny, Bohemia; jeweler, watchmaker, founder of Bulova Watch Co., NYC
Bio: Rechcigl, Miloslav, Jr., "Joseph Bulova," in: *Encyclopedia of Bohemian and Czech-American Biography*. Bloomington, IN: AuthorHouse, 2016, Vol. 1, p. 133; *The Bulova Watches – About Us.* See: http://www.allamericanwatches.com/site/626101/page/45030

Henry Raymond Eisner (1886-1948), b. Red Bank, NJ, of Bohemian ancestry; clothing manufacturer, partner and then president of Sigmund Eisner Co., NJ

Bio: Rechcigl, Miloslav, Jr., "Henry Raymond Eisner," in: *Encyclopedia of Bohemian and Czech-American Biography*. Bloomington, IN: AuthorHouse, 2016, Vol. 1, p. 135.

Sigmund Eisner (1859-1925), b. Horažďovice, Bohemia; large clothing manufacturer, NJ
Bio: *History of Monmouth County, New Jersey 1664-1920*. Chicago: Lewis Historical Publishing Company, 1922, Vol. 2, pp. 99-101.

Albert Epstein (1879-1947), b. St. Louis, MO, of Bohemian ancestry; manufacturer of boys' and children's clothing, St. Louis
Bio: "Epstein, Albert," in: *The Book of St. Louisans*. 2nd ed. Chicago: A. N. Marquis & Co., 1912, p. 182.

Ignatz Epstein (1848-d.), b. Bohemia; clothing manufacture, St. Louis
Bio: "Epstein, Ignatz," in: *The Bok of St. Louisans*. Chicago: A. N. Marquis & Co., 1912, p. 182.

Charles Louis Fleischmann (1835-1897), b. Krnov, Moravia; innovative yeast manufacturer
Bio: Klieger, P. Christian, *The Fleischmann Yeast Family*. Chicago: Arcadia Books. 2004

Carl Freschl (1842-1911), b. Prague, Bohemia; pioneer manufacturer of knit goods, Milwaukee
Bio: Rechcigl, Miloslav, Jr., "Carl Freschl," in: *Encyclopedia of Bohemian and Czech-American Biography*. Bloomington, IN: AuthorHouse, 2016, Vol. 1, p. 137.

Edward Freschl (1877-1930), b. Kalamazoo, MI, of Bohemian ancestry; manufacturer, president of Holeproof Hosiery Co., Milwaukee
Bio: Rechcigl, Miloslav, Jr., "Edward Freschl," in: *Encyclopedia of Bohemian and Czech-American Biography*. Bloomington, IN: AuthorHouse, 2016, Vol. 1, p. 137.

Moritz Freund (1810-1872), b. Bohemia; together with his wife Jetta, they were pioneer bakers in St. Louis, famous for their rye bread

Bio: Rechcigl, Miloslav, Jr., "Moritz Freund," in: *Encyclopedia of Bohemian and Czech-American Biography*. Bloomington, IN: AuthorHouse, 2016, Vol. 1, p. 138.

Benedict J. Greenhut (1872-1932), b. Chicago, IL, of Bohemian ancestry; owner of Greenhut-Siegel-Cooper Department Store in Manhattan, director of Tudor Foundation
Bio: Rechcigl, Miloslav, Jr., "Benedict J. Greenhut," in: *Encyclopedia of Bohemian and Czech-American Biography*. Bloomington, IN: AuthorHouse, 2016, Vol. 1, pp. 181-182.

Joseph Benedict Greenhut (1843-1918), b. Horšovský Týn, Bohemia; founder of the Great Western Distillery in Peoria, IL
Bio: *Publications Amer. Jew. Hist. Soc.* 3, p. 32; Wolf, Simon, *The American Jew as Patriot, Soldier, and Citizen*, op. cit., p. 43.

Henry Aaron Guinzburg (1856-1927), b. Baltimore, MD, of Bohemian ancestry; rubber manufacturer, treasurer and vice president of I. B. Kleinert Rubber Co., NYC
Bio: Rechcigl, Miloslav, Jr., "Henry Aaron Guinzburg," in: *Encyclopedia of Bohemian and Czech-American Biography*. Bloomington, IN: AuthorHouse, 2016, Vol. 1, p. 139.

Victor Guinzburg (1863-1934), b. New York, NY, of Bohemian ancestry; president of Kleinert Rubber Co., inventor
Bio: Rechcigl, Miloslav, Jr., "Victor Guinzburg," in: *Encyclopedia of Bohemian and Czech-American Biography*. Bloomington, IN: AuthorHouse, 2016, Vol. 1, p. 139.

Joseph S. Hartman (1846-1925), b. Břeskovice, Bohemia; trunk manufacturer in Chicago, then in Racine, WI
Bio: Rechcigl, Miloslav, Jr., "Adolph Abeles," in: *Encyclopedia of Bohemian and Czech-American Biography*. Bloomington, IN: AuthorHouse, 2016, Vol. 1, p. 140; "The Hartmann Trunk Company," *Racine, Belle City of the Lakes and Racine County, Wisconsin*. Chicago: S. J. Clarke Publishing co., 1916, p. 1216.

Walter R. Herschman (1883-1932), b. New York, NY, of Bohemian ancestry; in bakery business, president of Purity Bakeries corp., operating 100 stores in NYC, Philadelphia and Chicago
Bio: Rechcigl, Miloslav, Jr., "Walter Herschmann," in: *Encyclopedia of Bohemian and Czech-American Biography.* Bloomington, IN: AuthorHouse, 2016, Vol. 1, p. 141.

Walter Kidde (1877-1943), b. Hoboken, NJ, of Bohemian parents; owner of the Kidde C, manufacturers of fire extinguishers
Bio: Rechcigl, Miloslav, Jr., "Walter Kidde," in: *Encyclopedia of Bohemian and Czech American Biography.* Bloomington, IN: Author house, 2016, Vol. 1, p. 145; "Walter Kidde," in: Wikipedia. See - https://en.wikipedia.org/wiki/Walter_Kidde

D. Emil Klein (1868-1956), b. Vodňany, Bohemia; cigar manufacturer
Bio: Rechcigl, Miloslav, Jr. "D. Emil Klein," in: *Encyclopedia of Bohemian and Czech American Biography.* Bloomington, IN: author house, 2016, Vol. 1, p. 146.

Tobias Kohn (1817-1898), b. Prague, Bohemia; founder of the silk industry un the US
Bio: Rechcigl, Miloslav, Jr., "Tobias Kohn," in: *Encyclopedia of Bohemian and Czech American Biography.* Bloomington, IN: author house, 2016, Vol. 1, p. 147; "Kohn, Tobias," in: JewishEncyclopedia.com. See - http://www.jewishencyclopedia.com/articles/9432-kohn-tobias

Emil Kolben (1862-1943), b. Strančice, Bohemia; engineer, industrialist and entrepreneur, in US with Edison Labs
Bio: Rechcigl, Miloslav, Jr., "Emil Kolben," in: *Encyclopedia of Bohemian and Czech-American Biography.* Bloomington, IN: AuthorHouse, 2016, Vol. 1., p. 148-149.

Andrew Kuenzel (1854-d.), b. Aš, Bohemia; manufacturer, owner of a mill, St. Louis
Bio: "A Kuenzel," in: *The Book of St. Louisans.* St. Louis: St. Louis Republic, 1906, p. 342

David Able Lederer (1886-1943), b. Red Bank, NJ, of Bohemian ancestry; manufacturer of soap and cosmetics, NJ, he then moved to New Haven, where he became president of the Bauman Rubber Co.
Bio: Rechcigl, Miloslav, Jr., "David Able Lederer," in: *Encyclopedia of Bohemian and Czech American Biography.* Bloomington, IN: author house, 2016, Vol. 1, p. 152.

Julius Yehuda Lederer (1859-1922), b. New York, NY, of Bohemian ancestry; manufacturer and merchant, New Haven, CT
Bio: Rechcigl, Miloslav, Jr., "Julius Yehuda Lederer," in: *Encyclopedia of Bohemian and Czech-American Biography.* Bloomington, IN: AuthorHouse, 2016, Vol. 1., p. 152.

Samuel Lederer (1824-1916), b. Doudleby, Bohemia; pioneer merchant and manufacturer in New Jersey
Bio: Rechcigl, Miloslav, r., "Samuel Lederer," in: *Encyclopedia of Bohemian and Czech-American Biography.* Bloomington, IN: AuthorHouse, 2016, Vol. 1., p. 152.

Harold Alvin Levey (1889-1967), b. New Orleans, LA, of Moravian ancestry; manufacturer, pioneer in the field of plastics, New Orleans
Bio: Rechcigl, Miloslav, Jr., "Harold Alvin Levey," in: *Encyclopedia of Bohemian and Czech-American Biography.* Bloomington, IN: AuthorHouse, 2016, Vol. 1, p. 119.

Louis Levy (1850-1951), b. Bohemia; tie manufacturer, NYC
Bio: Rechcigl, Miloslav, Jr. "Louis Levy," in: *Encyclopedia of Bohemian and Czech-American Biography.* Bloomington, IN: AuthorHouse, 2016, Vol. 1, p. 153.

Ignatz Neumann (1852-1920), b. Opozdice, Bohemia; brewer, with Best Brewing Co., Chicago
Bio: Rechcigl, Miloslav, Jr., "Ignatz Neumann," in: *Encyclopedia of Bohemian and Czech-American Biography.* Bloomington, IN: AuthorHouse, 2016, Vol. 1., pp. 154-155.

Edward Andrew Oberweiser (1879-1954), b. Menaha, WI, of Bohemian father; president of the Fox River Paper Corp., Appleton, WI, also bank president
Bio: Rechcigl, Miloslav, Jr., "Edward Andrew Oberweiser," in: *Encyclopedia of Bohemian and Czech-American Biography.* Bloomington, IN: AuthorHouse, 2016, Vol. 1, pp. 121-122.

Charles Pick (1845-1927), b. Karlovy Vary, Bohemia; founder of the large concern Albert Pick & Co., in Chicago, manufacturer of equipment for hospitals, hotels and clubs
Bio: Rechcigl, Miloslav, Jr., "Charles Pick," in: *Encyclopedia of Bohemian and Czech-American Biography.* Bloomington, IN: AuthorHouse, 2016, Vol. 1., p. 157.

Michael Pokorny (1829-1902), b. Puklice, Moravia; shoemaker, New Orleans
Bio: Rechcigl, Miloslav, Jr., "Michael Pokorny," in: *Encyclopedia of Bohemian and Czech-American Biography.* Bloomington, IN: AuthorHouse, 2016, Vol. 1, p. 123.

Leo Popper (1831-1910), b. Terešov, Bohemia; founder of Popper Glass Company, known for its fine glass beads, NYC
Bio: Rechcigl, Miloslav, Jr., "Leo Popper," in: *Encyclopedia of Bohemian and Czech-American Biography.* Bloomington, IN: AuthorHouse, 2016, Vol. 1, p. 157

Morris Printz (1843-1931), b. Košice, Slovakia; pioneer in establishing cloak industry, Cleveland, OH
Bio: *A History of Cleveland and its Environs.* Chicago: Lewis Publishing Co., 1918, Vol. 3, pp. 502-503

Alexander Printz (1869-d.), b. Košice, Slovakia; president of Prinze-Biederman Co., NYC, extensive manufacturers of ladies' garments.
Bio: "Alexander Printz," in: *A History of Cleveland and its Environs.* Chicago: Lewis Publishing Co., 1918, Vol. 3, pp. 502-503

Ansley Kullman Salz (1880-1967), b. Stocton, CA, of Bohemian ancestry; tannery owner, Santa Crus, CA
Bio: Rechcigl, Miloslav, Jr., "Salz Family," in: *Beyond the Sea of Beer*: History of Immigration of Bohemians and Czechs to the New World and their Contributions. Bloomington, IN: AuthorHouse, 2017, pp. 139-140.

Ernest Schoen (1876-d.), b. St. Louis, MO, of Bohemian ancestry; organizer of the Standard Syrup Co., of which he became secretary, veteran of the war with Spain
Bio: Rechcigl, Miloslav, Jr., "Ernest Schoen," in: *Encyclopedia of Bohemian and Czech-American Biography*. Bloomington, IN: AuthorHouse, 2016, Vol. 1, p. 159.

Jacob Schoen (1845-d.), b. Bohemia; syrup refiner, St. Louis, MO
Bio: "Jacob Schoen," in: *The Bok of St. Louisans*. St. Louis: St. Louis Republic, 1906, p. 182.

Arthur Schwarz (1868-1939), b. Brno, Moravia; president of Princeton Worsted Mills, manufacturers of fine woolens, Trenton, NJ

Paul Schwarzkopf (1886-1970), b. Prague, Bohemia; powder metallurgist, co-founder of Am. Electro Metal Corp.., Yonkers, NY
Bio: Rechcigl, Miloslav, Jr., "Paul Schwarzkopf," in: *Encyclopedia of Bohemian and Czech-American Biography*. Bloomington, IN: AuthorHouse, 2016, Vol. 1, p. 160.

Louis A. Shakman (1843-1883), b. Kynžvart, Moravia; partner with his father-in-law, Emmanuel E. Silverman, in E. Silverman & Co., later renamed to L.A. Shakman Co.
Bio: Rechcigl, Miloslav, Jr., "Louis A. Shakman," in: *Encyclopedia of Bohemian and Czech-American Biography*. Bloomington, IN: AuthorHouse, 2016, Vol. 1, p. 160.

William Taussig (1821-1875), b. Prague, Bohemia; founder of William Taussig & Co., NYC, specializing in manufacture of rock candy and rock candy syrup.
Bio: Rechcigl, Miloslav, Jr., "William Taussig," in: Rechcigl, Miloslav, Jr., "William Taussig," in: *Encyclopedia of Bohemian and Czech-American Biography*. Bloomington, IN: AuthorHouse, 2016, Vol. 1., p. 163.

Ludwig Vogelstein (1871-1934), b. Pilsen, Bohemia; founder of the metal firm Ludwig Vogelstein, which was amalgamated in the American Metal. Co., becoming its chairman of the Board
Bio: Rechcigl, Miloslav, Jr., "Ludwig Vogelstein," in: *Encyclopedia of Bohemian and Czech-American Biography*. Bloomington, IN: AuthorHouse, 2016, Vol. 1, p. 166; "Ludwig Vogelstein," in: Wikipedia. See - https://en.wikipedia.org/wiki/Ludwig_Vogelstein

Henry Waldes (1886-1960), b. Prague, Bohemia; industrialist, snap fasteners manufacturer
Bio: Rechcigl, Miloslav, Jr., "Henry Waldes," in: *Beyond the Sea of Beer.* Bloomington, IN: AuthorHouse, 2016, p. 746.

Jacob Weil (1827-1912), b. Čkyně, Bohemia; co-founder, with his brothers, of a tannery in Ann Arbor, MI
Bio: Rechcigl, Miloslav, Jr., "Jacob Weil," in: *Encyclopedia of Bohemian and Czech-American Biography*. Bloomington, IN: AuthorHouse, 2016, Vol. 1, pp. 166-167.

Charles Weiner (1885-1966), b. Pardubice, Bohemia; tape manufacturer, owner of the Chicago Printed String Co.
Bio: Rechcigl, Miloslav, Jr., "Charles Weiner," in: *Encyclopedia of Bohemian and Czech-American Biography*. Bloomington, IN: AuthorHouse, 2016, Vol. 1, p. 167.

Henry Weiskopf (1850—1923), b. Bohemia; pioneer paint manufacturer, Minneapolis, MN
Bio: Rechcigl, Miloslav, Jr., "Henry Weiskopf," in: *Encyclopedia of Bohemian and Czech-American Biography*. Bloomington, IN: AuthorHouse, 2016, Vol. 1, p. 167.

David Philip Wohl (1886-1960), of Bohemian ancestry; giant in the shoe industry
Bio: Boxerman, Burton, "David P. Wohl - Shoe Merchant," *Gateway Heritage,* 9, No. 2 (Fall 1988), pp. 24–33.

Hans Wyman (orig. Weinman) (1885-1960), b. Ústí nad Labem, Bohemia; president of Pantasote Leather Co., Passaic, NJ and then H. O. Canfield C., Bridgeport, CT
Bio: Rechcigl, Miloslav, Jr., "Hans Wyman," in: *Encyclopedia of Bohemian and Czech-American Biography*. Bloomington, IN: AuthorHouse, 2016, Vol. 1, p. 168.

2. Later and Contemporary Manufacturers

Leopold Lionel Garrick Bentley (orig. Bloch-Bauer), (1905-1986), b. Vienna, of Bohemian ancestry; Canadian manufacturer, co-founder of Pacific Veneer and Plywood Co.
Bio: *A History of the Austrian Migration to Canada*. By Frederick C. Engelmann, Manfred Prokop and Franz A. J. Szabo. Carleton University Press, 1996, p. 181.

Peter John Gerald Bentley (1930-), b. Vienna, of Bohemian ancestry; Canadian businessman, manufacturer
Bio: "Peter Bentley," in Wikipedia. See - https://en.wikipedia.org/wiki/Peter Bentley (businessman)

Karl David Bloch-Bauer (1901-1968), b. Vienna, of Bohemian father; associated with his brother Leopold's Canadian firm Pacific Veneer and Plywood Co.
Bio: Rechcigl, Miloslav, Jr. "Karl Bloch-Bauer," in: *Encyclopedia of Bohemian and Czech-American Biography*. Bloomington, IN: AuthorHouse, 2016, Vol. 1, p. 106.

Peter H. Blum (1924-2002), b. Czech.; chemical engineer, developer of formula for several beers, with Stroh Brewery Co., beer historian and archivist, expert on brewery collectibles

Bio: Rechcigl, Miloslav, Jr., "Peter Blum," in: *Encyclopedia of Bohemian and Czech-American Biography*. Bloomington, IN: AuthorHouse, 2016, Vol. 1, p. 131; "Peter Blum, of the Stroh Brewery Co., dead at 78," in: The Free Library. 2002 Business Journals, Inc., 28 Mar. 2018

George Brady (1928-), b. Nové Mesto na Moravě; Holocaust survivor, founder of plumbing business, Toronto, Canada
Bio: Rechcigl, Miloslav, Jr., "George Brady," in: *Encyclopedia of Bohemian and Czech-American Biography*. Bloomington, IN: AuthorHouse, 2016, Vol. 2, p. 1116.

Rudolph Hans Bunzl (1922-2016), b. Vienna, of Slovak ancestry; manufacturer, founder of American Filtrona Corp.
Bio: Robertson, Ellen, "Rudolph H. Bunzl, retired president of America Filtrona Corp., dies at 94," *Richmond Times-Dispatch*, October 18, 2016; "Rudolph Hans Bunzl," in: GENi. See - https://www.geni.com/people/Rudolph-Bunzl/6000000014958397072

Walter Henry Bunzl (1913-1988), b. Vienna, of Slovak ancestry; manufacturer, Textile & Paper Supply Corp., Atlanta, GA

Monroe Eisner (1893-1972), b. Red Bank, NJ, of Bohemian ancestry; president of Sigmund Eisner Co.
Bio; Rechcigl, Miloslav, Jr., "Monroe Eisner," in: *Encyclopedia of Bohemian and Czech-American Biography*. Bloomington, IN: AuthorHouse, 2016, Vol. 1, p. 135.

Ralph Kleinert Guinzburg (1891-1957), b. New York, NY of Bohemian ancestry; president and director of the I. B. Kleinert Rubber Co., NYC
Bio: *National Cyclopedia of American Biography*. New York: James T. White, 1961, Vol. 43, p. 192.

Emmett Heitler (1909-2005), b. Denver, CO, of Bohemian ancestry; trained as electrical engineer, with Schwader Bros., Inc., a manufacturer of Samsonite Luggage, where he advanced to general manager and then to Executive Vice President. He was instrumental in building Samsonite from a small local business into the world's largest luggage manufacturer.

Bio: Rechcigl, Miloslav, Jr., "Emmett Heitler," in: *Encyclopedia of Bohemian and Czech-American Biography*. Bloomington, IN: AuthorHouse, 2016, Vol. 1, pp. 140-141; Hon. Scott McInnis," Paying Tribute to Emmett Heitler," in: *Congressional Record*, Vol. 148, Part 1, January 23, 2002; "Emmett Heitler," Colorado Business Hall of Fame. See - http://www.coloradobusinesshalloffame.org/emmett-heitler.html

Benjamin Heller (1893-1933), b. Milwaukee, WI, of Bohemian ancestry; wholesale manufacturer of dry powders used in the preparation of meat products, variety of other food ingredients, as well as insecticides, cleaning agents and range of kitchen and office supplies
Bio: Rechcigl, Miloslav, Jr., "Benjamin Heller," in: *Encyclopedia of Bohemian and Czech-American Biography*. Bloomington, IN: AuthorHouse, 2016, Vol. 1, p. 114.

Harry B. Henshel (1919-2007), b. New York, NY, b. New York, of Bohemian ancestry; a watch manufacturer, the last member of the Bulova family to run the Bulova Watch Company
Bio: Rechcigl, Miloslav, Jr., "Harry Henshel," in: *Encyclopedia of Bohemian and Czech-American Biography*. Bloomington, IN: AuthorHouse, 2016, Vol. 1, p. 141; Miller, Stephen, "Harry Henshel, 88, Bulova CEO in Tumultuous Times," *New York Sun*, July 5, 2007.

Frank H. Jellinek (1920-2008), b. Buffalo, NY, of Bohemian ancestry; founder of the Erie Scientific Co., the largest manufacturer of microscope slides and related products, La Jolla, CA
Bio: "Frank H. Jellinek Obituary," in: Seacoastonline, January 12-16, 2008.

Georgette Klinger (née Eckstein) (1915-2004), b. Brno, Moravia; skin-care innovator, who revolutionized the field of cosmetics and skin care by developing products and techniques to treat the skin rather than simply cover it with makeup
Bio: Rechcigl, Miloslav, Jr., "Georgette Klinger," in: *Encyclopedia of Bohemian and Czech-American Biography*. Bloomington, IN: AuthorHouse, 2016, Vol. 1, p. 147; Martin, Douglas, "Georgette Klinger, of Facials Fame, Dies at 88," The New York Times, January14, 2004.

Leo Koerner (1892-1972), b. Moravia; Canadian businessman and philanthropist
Bio: Rechcigl, Miloslav, Jr., "Leo Koerner,", in: *Encyclopedia of Bohemian and Czech-American Biography.* Bloomington, IN: AuthorHouse, 2016, Vol. 1, p. 117.

Walter Charles Koerner (1898-1995), b. Nový Hrozenkov, Moravia; Canadian businessman and philanthropist, founder of the Alaska Pine and Cellulose Company
Bio: "Walter Koerner," in: Wikipedia. See - https://en.wikipedia.org/wiki/Walter Koerner; Rechcigl, Miloslav, Jr., "Walter Charles Koerner,", in: *Encyclopedia of Bohemian and Czech-American Biography.* Bloomington, IN: AuthorHouse, 2016, Vol. 1, p. 117.

Paul Kohner (1900-1965), b. Tachov Bohemia; founder of the firm Kohner Bros., a wooden bead company, making pull toys, puppets, latter made in plastic, and manufactured games
Bio: Rechcigl, Miloslav, Jr., "Paul Kohner," in: *Encyclopedia of Bohemian and Czech-American Biography.* Bloomington, IN: AuthorHouse, 2016, Vol. 1., pp. 147-148.

Esther Lauder (née Mentzer) (1906-2004), b. Corona, NY, of Bohemian Jewish ancestry; founder of Estee Lauder Cos., her eponymous cosmetic company
Bio: Alpern, Sara, "Estee Lauder," in: *Jewish Women: A Comprehensive Historical Encyclopedia.* Shalvi Publishing, Ltd., 2006; Kent, Jacqueline C., *Business Builders in Cosmetics.* Minneapolis, MN: The Oliver Press, 2003.

Leonard, Lauder (1933-), b. Manhattan, NY; billionaire businessman
Bio: "Leonard Lauder," in: Wikipedia. See - https://en.wikipedia.org/wiki/Leonard_Lauder

Ronald Lauder (1944-), businessman, art collector, philanthropist, US Ambassador to Austria
Bio: "Ronald Lauder," in: Wikipedia. See - https://en.wikipedia.org/wiki/Ronald Lauder

Henry B. Lederer (1920-2013), b. Bridgeport, CT., of Bohemian ancestry; founder of Lederer Brothers in 1946, a jewelry manufacturer, known for 'Lady Ellen' pearls and patents for magnetically interchangeable jewelry.
Bio: Rechcigl, Miloslav, Jr., "Henry B. Lederer," in: *Encyclopedia of Bohemian and Czech-American Biography*. Bloomington, IN: AuthorHouse, 2016, Vol. 3, p. 2193; "Obituary: Henry B. Lederer," in: Dignity Memorial. See - https://www.dignitymemorial.com/obituaries/hewlett-ny/henry-lederer-5675957

Erwin Loewy (1897-1959), b. Bečov nad Teplou, Bohemia; hydraulic engineer, founder and president of Loewy-Hydropress, Inc., NYC
Bio: Rechcigl, Miloslav, Jr., "Erwin Loewy," in: *Encyclopedia of Bohemian and Czech-American Biography*. Bloomington, IN: AuthorHouse, 2016, Vol. 1., p. 153.

Friedrich Mandl (1900-1977), b. Vienna, of Bohemian ancestry; founder of new airplane manufacturing firm, Industria Metalúrgica y Plástica Argentina
Bio: Rechcigl, Miloslav, Jr., "Friedrich Mandl," in: *Encyclopedia of Bohemian and Czech-American Biography*. Bloomington, IN: AuthorHouse, 2016, Vol. 1, p. 154.

Albert Osterreicher (1895-d.), b. Karlovy Vary, Bohemia; manufacturer of infants' wear, Puerto Rico, then in Wilkes Barre, PA
Bio: Rechcigl, Miloslav, Jr., "Albert Osterreicher," in: *Encyclopedia of Bohemian and Czech-American Biography*. Bloomington, IN: AuthorHouse, 2016, Vol. 1, p. 156.

John Prentice (orig. Pick) (1907-d.-), b. Vienna, of Bohemian ancestry; trained as a lawyer, co-founder of Pacific Veneer manufacturing company in Canada.
Bio: "John Prentice," in: Business Laureates of British Columbia Hall of Fame. See - http://www.businesslaureatesbc.org/laureate/john-prentice/

Charles William Taussig (1896-1948), b. New York, NY, of Bohemian ancestry; president of the American Molasses Co.
Bio: *National Cyclopedia of American Biography*. New York: James T. White, 1951, vol. 36, 78-79.

Charles Alfred Wyman (orig. Weimann) (1914-1971), b. Ústí nad Labem. Bohemia; manufacturer of rubber goods, Bridgeport, CT
Bio: Rechcigl, Miloslav, Jr., "Charles Alfred Wyman," in: *Encyclopedia of Bohemian and Czech-American Biography.* Bloomington, IN: AuthorHouse, 2016, Vol. 1., p. 168; "Charles Wyman; Led Pantasote," *The New York Times,* December 25, 1971.

E. Builders and Realtors

Frederick Brown (1870-1960), b. Plzeň Bohemia; largest real estate operator in the US
Bio: *National Cyclopedia of American Biography,* 1953, vol. 1, p. 141.

Marc Eidlitz (1826-1892), b. Prague, Bohemia; prominent builder, NYC
Bio: Rechcigl, Miloslav, Jr., "Marc Eidlitz," in: *Encyclopedia of Bohemian and Czech-American Biography.* Bloomington, IN: AuthorHouse, 2016, Vol. 1., p. 169.

Otto Marc Eidlitz (1860-1928), b. New York City, of Bohemian ancestry; building contractor, NYC
Bio: Rechcigl, Miloslav, Jr., "Otto Marc Eidlitz," in: *Encyclopedia of Bohemian and Czech-American Biography.* Bloomington, IN: AuthorHouse, 2016, Vol. 1., p. 169.

Louis R. Lurie (1888-1972), b. Chicago, of Bohemian ancestry; president of the real estate Lurie Company, San Francisco
Bio: Byington, Lewis Francis, *History of San Francisco.* Chicago: S. J. Clarke Publishing Co., 1931, vol. 2, pp. 326-328.

Robert Alfred Lurie (1929-), b. San Francisco, CA, of Bohemian ancestry; real estate magnate, philanthropist, San Francisco
Bio: Rechcigl, Miloslav, Jt., "Robert Alfred Lurie," in: *Encyclopedia of Bohemian and Czech-American Biography.* Bloomington, IN: AuthorHouse, 2016, Vol. 1., p. 174.

F. Corporate Executives

Roland E. Arnall (1939-2008), b. Paris, France, of Czech ancestry; mortgage innovator, American millionaire and diplomat
Bio: Rechcigl, Miloslav, Jr., "Roland E. Arnall," in: *Encyclopedia of Bohemian and Czech-American Biography*. Bloomington, IN: AuthorHouse, 2016, Vol. 1., p. 176; "Roland Arnall, Mortgage Innovator, Dies at 68," *The New York Times,* March 19, 2008; Reckard, E. Scott, "Roland Arnall, 68; founder of subprime specialist Ameriquest," *Los Angeles Times*, March 18, 2008.

Henry W. Bloch (1922-), b. Kansas City, MO, of Bohemian ancestry; co-founder of H.&R Block Co. a tax preparation company
Bio: Rechcigl, Miloslav, Jr., "Henry W. Bloch," in: *Encyclopedia of Bohemian and Czech-American Biography*. Bloomington, IN: AuthorHouse, 2016, Vol. 1., p. 177.

Richard Adolf Bloch (1926-2004), b. Kansas City, MO, of Bohemian ancestry; co-founder of H.&R Block Co. a tax preparation company
Bio: Rechcigl, Miloslav, Jr., "Richard Bloch," in: *Encyclopedia of Bohemian and Czech-American Biography*. Bloomington, IN: AuthorHouse, 2016, Vol. 1., p. 177; Tavernise, Sabrina, "Richard Bloch, 78, Businessman Who Helped Create H&R Block," *The New York Times*, July 22, 2004.

Charles Leo Eidlitz (1866-1951), b. New York, NY, of Bohemian ancestry; electrical engineer, president of Charles L. Eidlitz Co. and other corporations
Bio: Rechcigl, Miloslav, Jr., "Charles Leo Eidlitz," in: *Encyclopedia of Bohemian and Czech-American Biography*. Bloomington, IN: AuthorHouse, 2016, Vol. 1., p. 180

J. Lester Eisner (1889-), b, Red Bank, NJ, vice president of Sigmund Eisner Co., and director of other corporations
Bio: *Prominent Families of New Jersey*. Edited by William Starr Myers. New York-Chicago: Lewis Historical Publishing Co., 1945, Vol. 1, p. 638.p. 638

Michael D. Eisner (1942-), b. Mount Kisco, NY, of Bohemian ancestry; chairman and chief executive officer of the Walt Disney Co.
Bio: "Michael," in: Wikipedia. See - https://en.wikipedia.org/wiki/Michael Eisner; Rechcigl, Miloslav, Jr., "Michael Eisner," in: *Encyclopedia of Bohemian and Czech-American Biography*. Bloomington, IN: AuthorHouse, 2016, Vol. 1., p. 180; *Current Biography*, November 1987, pp. 13-17.

John L. Ernst (1941-), b. of Bohemian ancestry; chairman and president of Bloomingdale Properties Inc., etc.
Bio: Rechcigl, Miloslav, Jr., "John L. Ernst," in: *Encyclopedia of Bohemian and Czech-American Biography*. Bloomington, IN: AuthorHouse, 2016, Vol. 1., pp. 180-181.

Charles Otta Heller (1936-), b. Prague, Czech; aerospace engineer, co-founder of CADCOM, Inc., one of the earliest software companies
Bio: Rechcigl, Miloslav, Jr. "Charles Otta Heller," in: *Encyclopedia of Bohemian and Czech-American Biography*. Bloomington, IN: AuthorHouse, 2016, Vol. 1., p2. 182-183.

David Hirschhorn (1918-2006), Prague, Bohemia; president of American Trading and Production Corp. and executive of many other corporations, Jewish communal worker
Bio: Rechcigl, Miloslav, Jr. "David Hirschhorn," in: *Encyclopedia of Bohemian and Czech-American Biography*. Bloomington, IN: AuthorHouse, 2016, Vol. 1., p. 183; "David Hirschhorn Obituary," *The Baltimore Sun*, September 7, 2006

Brett Icahn (1979-), b. New York, NY, of Czech mother; businessman, investor, and philanthropist
Bio: "Brett Icahn," in: Wikipedia. See - tps://en.wikipedia.org/wiki/Brett_Icahn; Rechcigl, Miloslav, Jr. "Brett Icahn," in: *Encyclopedia of Bohemian and Czech-American Biography*. Bloomington, IN: AuthorHouse, 2016, Vol. 1., p. 184.

Eric Kauders (1907-1995), b. Prague, Bohemia; president of Craig Machine, Inc., Lawrence, MA, Craig Vending Machine Co., etc.
Bio: Rechcigl, Miloslav, Jr., "Eric Kauders," in: *Encyclopedia of Bohemian and Czech-American Biography*. Bloomington, IN: AuthorHouse, 2016, Vol. 1., p. 145.

Frederick Kauders (1919-2014), b. Prague, Czech.; co-founder of Craig Systems Co. and director of several manufacturing and service corporations
Bio: Rechcigl, Miloslav, Jr., "Frederick Kauders," in: *Encyclopedia of Bohemian and Czech-American Biography*. Bloomington, IN: AuthorHouse, 2016, Vol. 1., pp. 185-186; "Frederick Kauders 1919-2914 Obituary," *The Boston Globe*, October 25-27, 2014.

Aerin Lauder (1970-), b. New York, NY, of Czechoslovak ancestry; billionaire heiress and cosmetics executive, style and image director for the Estee Lauder companies
Bio: "Aerin Rebecca Lauder Zinterhofer," in: Wikipedia. See - https://en.wikipedia.org/wiki/Aerin_Lauder

Jane Lauder (1973-), b. Manhattan, NY, of Czechoslovak ancestry; heiress and businesswoman, executive with Estee Lauder Companies
Bio: "Jane Lauder," in: Wikipedia. See - https://en.wikipedia.org/wiki/Jane_Lauder

Leonard A. Lauder (1933-), b. US, of Czechoslovak ancestry; billionaire businessman, art collector, humanitarian
Bio: "Leonard Lauder," in: Wikipedia. See - https://en.wikipedia.org/wiki/Leonard_Lauder

Ronald Lauder (1944-), b. New York, NY, of Czechoslovak ancestry; billionaire businessman, art collector, philanthropist, heir of Estée Lauder Companies, diplomat
Bio: "Ronald Lauder," in: Wikipedia. See - https://en.wikipedia.org/wiki/Ronald_Lauder

Jon Ledecky (195-8), b. New York, NY, of Czech immigrant father; businessman, founder of US Office Products
Bio: Rechcigl, Miloslav, Jr. "Jonathan Joseph Ledecky," in: *Encyclopedia of Bohemian and Czech-American Biography.* Bloomington, IN: AuthorHouse, 2016, Vol. 1., p. 187; "Jon Ledecky, in: Wikipedia. See - https://en.wikipedia.org/wiki/Jon_Ledecky.

Nathan Levy (1889-1967), b. Vicksburg, MS, of Bohemian father; founder Nathan Levy & Co., a cotton business, head if insurance agency, etc.
Bio: Rechcigl, Miloslav, Jr., "Nathan Levy," in: *Encyclopedia of Bohemian and Czech-American Biography.* Bloomington, IN: AuthorHouse, 2016, Vol. 1., p. 188.

Albert Pick, Jr. (1895-1966), b, Chicago, IL, of Bohemian ancestry; a hotel chain magnate
Bio: "Albert Pick, Jr." in: Accuracy Project. See - https://www.accuracyproject.org/cbe-Pick,Albert.html; Barnard, Judith, *The Indestructible Crown: The Life of Albert Pick, Jr.* Chicago: Nelson-Hall, 1980.

Albert Pick, 3rd (1935-2009), b. Chicago, of Bohemian ancestry; philanthropist and investment executive
Bio: Jensen, Trevor, "Albert Pick III, 1934-2009: Philanthropist and investment executive," *Chicago Tribune*, Aril 20, 20009

Pedro J. Pick (1935-2004), b. Prague, Czech.; businessman, corporate executive in Venezuela, US and in Prague
Bio: Rechcigl, Miloslav, Jr., "Pedro J. Pick," in: *Encyclopedia of Bohemian and Czech-American Biography.* Bloomington, IN: AuthorHouse, 2016, Vol. 1., p. 190.

Milan Platovský Stein (1922-2012), b. Prague, Czech.; Holocaust survivor, entrepreneur, owner of some 10 technology-geared companies
Bio: Rechcigl, Miloslav, Jr., "Milan Platovský Stein," in: *Encyclopedia of Bohemian and Czech-American Biography.* Bloomington, IN: AuthorHouse, 2016, Vol. 1., p. 192; "Milan Platovsky," in: Wikipedia. See - https://en.wikipedia.org/wiki/Milan Platovsky

Joanna Popper (1977-), b. Chicago, of Bohemian ancestry; a Hollywood and Silicon Valley media executive
Bio: Rechcigl, Miloslav, Jr., "Joanna Popper," in: *Encyclopedia of Bohemian and Czech-American Biography*. Bloomington, IN: AuthorHouse, 2016, Vol. 1., p. 190

Edward Holmes Taussig (1892-1983), b. Wheeling, WV, of Bohemian ancestry; founder of Towles Taussig cotton brokers and executive of other corporations
Bio: Rechcigl, Miloslav, Jr., "Edward Holmes Taussig," in: *Encyclopedia of Bohemian and Czech-American Biography*. Bloomington, IN: AuthorHouse, 2016, Vol. 1., p. 193

James Edward Taussig (1865-1941), b. St. Louis, MO, of Bohemian ancestry; railroad president, Wabash Ry., etc.
Bio: Rechcigl, Miloslav, Jr., "James Edward Taussig," in: *Encyclopedia of Bohemian and Czech-American Biography*. Bloomington, IN: AuthorHouse, 2016, Vol. 1., p. 193

John J. Taussig (1843-1943), b. Prague, Bohemia; president of Pacific Railroad of Missouri and corporate executive of other corporations
Bio: Rechcigl, Miloslav, Jr., "John J. Taussig," in: *Encyclopedia of Bohemian and Czech-American Biography*. Bloomington, IN: AuthorHouse, 2016, Vol. 1., p. 193

Richard S. Taussig (1903-1992), b. New York, NY, of Bohemian ancestry; corporate executive of the American Molasses Co., etc.
Bio: Rechcigl, Miloslav, Jr., "Richard S. Taussig," in: *Encyclopedia of Bohemian and Czech-American Biography*. Bloomington, IN: AuthorHouse, 2016, Vol. 1., p. 193

William Taussig (1826-1913), b. Prague, Bohemia; orig. physician, then president of The Bridge Co., Terminal Railroad Assn., etc.
Bio: Rechcigl, Miloslav, Jr., "William Taussig," in: *Encyclopedia of Bohemian and Czech-American Biography*. Bloomington, IN: AuthorHouse, 2016, Vol. 1., p. 194.

Elmer L. Winter (1912-2009), b. Milwaukee, of Bohemian ancestry; attorney, president of Manpower, Inc., a worldwide temporary help agency, Milwaukee and communal worker
Bio: Rechcigl, Miloslav, Jr., "Elmer L. Winter," in: *Encyclopedia of Bohemian and Czech-American Biography*. Bloomington, IN: AuthorHouse, 2016, Vol. 1., p. 196.

Henry Walter Wyman (1919-1995), b. Ústí nad Labem, Czech.; president of Pantasote Co., Passaic, NJ, and other corporations
Bio: Rechcigl, Miloslav, Jr., "Henry Walter Wyman," in: *Encyclopedia of Bohemian and Czech-American Biography*. Bloomington, IN: AuthorHouse, 2016, Vol. 1., p. 196

Ralph Mark Wyman (1926-), b. Ústí nad Labem, Czech.; president of Veritas, Inc., and other corporations
Bio: Rechcigl, Miloslav, Jr., "Ralph Mark Wyman," *Encyclopedia of Bohemian and Czech-American Biography*. Bloomington, IN: AuthorHouse, 2016, Vol. 1., p. 193

G. Bankers & Financiers

Leopold Adler (1861-1948), b. Volyně, Bohemia; banker, founder of department store, Savannah, GA
Bio: "Adler, Leopold," *Who's Who in American Jewry*, Vol. 1, p. 15; "Leopold Adler,", in Prabook. See - https://prabook.com/web/leopold.adler/1042950

Jacob Furth (1840-1914), b. Švihov, Bohemia; businessman, founder of Seattle National Bank
Bio: Bagley, Clarence, *De Luxe Supplement to the History of Seattle*. Chicago-Seattle: The S.J. Clarke Publishing Co., 1916; Speidel, Bill, *Through the Eye of the Needle*. Seattle: Nettle Creek Publishing Co., 1989.

Lee A. Klauber (-1919), b. Bohemia; merchant and banker, St. George, SC
Bio: South Carolina Genealogy Trails. See- http://genealogytrails.com/scar/dorchester/biographies.htm

Robert Lee Klauber (1884-1954), b. St. George, SC, of Bohemian ancestry; banker, merchant, St. George, SC
Bio: South Carolina Genealogy Trails. See- http://genealogytrails.com/scar/dorchester/biographies.htm

William Adolph Klauber (1882-1952), b. St. George, SC; banker and merchant, Bamberg, SC
Bio: South Carolina Genealogy Trails. See- http://genealogytrails.com/scar/dorchester/biographies.htm

Carl Kohn (1814-1895), b. Hořany, Bohemia; banker, financier, New Orleans
Bio: Rechcigl, Miloslav, Jr., "Carl Kohn," in: *Encyclopedia of Bohemian and Czech-American Biography*. Bloomington, IN: AuthorHouse, 2016, Vol. 1, p. 218.

Samuel Kohn (1782-1853), b. Hořany, Bohemia; pioneer financier, investor, realtor, New Orleans
Bio: Rechcigl, Miloslav, Jr., "Samuel Kohn," in: *Beyond the Sea of Beer.* Bloomington, IN: AuthorHouse, 2016, pp. 29-30, 114, 443.

Moritz O. Kopperl (1826-1883), b. Moravia; president of Texas National Bank
Bio: Ornish, Natalie, *Pioneer Jewish Texans*. Dallas: Texas Heritage, 1989.

Daniel Meyer (1824 -1911), b. Salzburg, of Bohemian ancestry; pioneer banker, philanthropist, San Francisco
Bio: Rechcigl, Miloslav, Jr., "Daniel Meyer," in: *Encyclopedia of Bohemian and Czech-American Biography*. Bloomington, IN: AuthorHouse, 2016, Vol. 1, p. 222.

Julian J. Meyer (1889-d.), b. San Francisco, CA, of Bohemian ancestry; businessman, banker, San Francisco
Bio: "Julian J. Meyer," in: *Encyclopedia of Bohemian and Czech-American Biography.* Bloomington, IN: AuthorHouse, 2016, Vol. 1, p. 222.

Matthias Meyer (1829-1908), b. Furth, Bavaria, of Bohemian ancestry; banker, stock broker, merchant, San Francisco
Bio: Rechcigl, Miloslav, Jr., "Matthias Meyer," in: *Encyclopedia of Bohemian and Czech-American Biography.* Bloomington, IN: AuthorHouse, 2016, Vol. 1, pp. 222-223.

William Michelstetter (1851-d.) b. Milwaukee, of Bohemian father; banker, Seymour, WI
Bio: Rechcigl, Miloslav, Jr., "William Michelstetter," in: *Encyclopedia of Bohemian and Czech-American Biography.* Bloomington, IN: AuthorHouse, 2016, Vol. 1, p. 223.

Walter Mintz (1929-2004), b. Vienna, of Moravian ancestry; investor, co-founder of one of first hedge funds
Bio: Rechcigl, Miloslav, Jr. "Walter Mintz," in: *Encyclopedia of Bohemian and Czech-American Biography.* Bloomington, IN: AuthorHouse, 2016, Vol. 1, p. 223; "Walter Mintz, 75, Investor and Hedge Fund Co-founder, is Dead," *The New York Times*, November 21, 2004.

Walter Wehle Naumburg (1867-1956), b. New York, NY, of Bohemian ancestry; commercial banker, NYC
Bio: Rechcigl, Miloslav, Jr., "Walter Wehle Naumburg," in: *Encyclopedia of Bohemian and Czech-American Biography.* Bloomington, IN: AuthorHouse, 2016, Vol. 1, p. 224.

Michael N. Robert de Rothschild (1946-), b. Paris, of Bohemian ancestry; American banker
Bio: Rechcigl, Miloslav, Jr., "Michael N. Robert de Rothschild," in: *Beyond the Sea of Beer*. Bloomington, IN: AuthorHouse, 2017, p.748

Karl Schenk (1874-1947), b. Slabce, Bohemia; banker, with Trade Bank of NY
Bio: "Schenk, Karl," *Who's Who in American Jewry*, Vol. 1, p. 545.

Burghard Steiner (1857-1923), b. Pilsen, Bohemia; banker, financier, Uniontown, Hamburg, AL
Bio: "Burghard Steiner," in: *History of Alabama and Dictionary of Alabama Biography*. Chicago: S. J. Clarke Publishing company, 1921, Vol. 4, p. 1619

Herbert E. Steiner (1890-1970), b. Birmingham, AL, banker, Birmingham and NYC
Bio: Rechcigl, Miloslav, Jr., "Herbert E. Steiner," in: *Encyclopedia of Bohemian and Czech-American Biography*. Bloomington, IN: AuthorHouse, 2016, Vol. 1, p. 228.

Leo K. Steiner (1870-1944), Kořen, Bohemia; banker, Birmingham, AL
Bio: "Leo K. Steiner," in: *History of Alabama and Dictionary of Alabama Biography*. Chicago: S. J. Clarke Publishing company, 1921, Vol. 4, p. 16.

Peter Richard Steiner (1920-), b. Prague, Bohemia; bank investment officer
Bio: Rechcigl, Miloslav, Jr., "Peter Richard Steiner," in: *Encyclopedia of Bohemian and Czech-American Biography*. Bloomington, IN: AuthorHouse, 2016, Vol. 1, p. 229.

Sigfried Steiner (1859-1902), b. Bohemia; banker, Uniontown, Hamburg, AL
Bio: "Sigfried Steiner," in: *History of Alabama and Dictionary of Alabama Biography*. Chicago: S. J. Clarke Publishing company, 1921, Vol. 4, p. 1619.

Garfield Joseph Taussig (1881-1968), b. St. Louis, of Bohemian ancestry; investment dealer, St. Louis
Bio: Rechcigl, Miloslav, Jr., "Garfield Joseph Taussig," in: *Encyclopedia of Bohemian and Czech-American Biography*. Bloomington, IN: AuthorHouse, 2016, Vol. 1, p. 230.

John Joseph Taussig (1843-1943), b. Prague, Bohemia; banker and broker, St. Louis
Bio: "Taussig, John J.," in: *The Book of St. Louisans*. S. Louis: St. Louis Republic, 1906, p. 565

Joseph Seligman Taussig (1832-1911), b. of Bohemian ancestry; banker and broker, St. Louis
Bio: "Taussig, Joseph Seligman," in: *The Book of St. Louisans*. S. Louis: St. Louis Republic, 1906, p. 566

Ralph J. Taussig (1922-2007), b. Elkins Park, PA, of Bohemian ancestry; investment banker
Bio: Rechcigl, Miloslav, Jr., "Ralph J. Taussig," in: *Encyclopedia of Bohemian and Czech-American Biography*. Bloomington, IN: AuthorHouse, 2016, Vol. 1, p. 230.

H. Stock and Bond Brokers

Philip Barth (1852-1897), b. Lochouň, Bohemia; stock broker, San Francisco
Bio: Rechcigl, Miloslav, Jr., *Beyond the Sea of Beer*. Bloomington, IN: AuthorHouse, 2017, p. 135.

Jacob Barth (1863- 1913), b. Bohemia; stock broker, San Francisco
Bio: Rechcigl, Miloslav, Jr., *Beyond the Sea of Beer*. Bloomington, IN: AuthorHouse, 2017, p. 135.

Gustav Epstein (1885-1951), b. Turnov, Bohemia; stock and bond broker, president of the San Francisco Stock Exchange
Bio: Rechcigl, Miloslav, Jr., "Gustav Epstein," in: *Encyclopedia of Bohemian and Czech-American Biography*. Bloomington, IN: AuthorHouse, 2016, Vol. 1, p. 233.

Carl Samuel Glaser (1878-), b. St. Louis, MO, of Bohemian ancestry; broker in stocks and bonds; St. Louis, MO
Bio: *The Book of St. Louisans.* St. Louis: St. Louis Republic, 1906, p. 225.

Joseph Glaser (1852-1917), b. Bohemia; broker, St. Louis, MO
Bio: "Glaser, Joseph," in: *The Book of St. Louisans.* 2nd ed. Chicago: A. N. Marquis & Co., 1912, pp. 229; Rechcigl, Miloslav, Jr., "Joseph Glaser," in: *Encyclopedia of Bohemian and Czech-American Biography.* Bloomington, IN: AuthorHouse, 2016, Vol. 1., p. 233.

Henry Simon Glazier (1868-1939), b. San Francisco, CA, of Bohemian ancestry; bond and stock broker, NYC
Bio: Rechcigl, Miloslav, Jr. "Henry Simon Glazier," in: *Encyclopedia of Bohemian and Czech-American Biography.* Bloomington, IN: AuthorHouse, 2016, Vol. 1, p. 233.

Isaac Glazier (1829-1906), b. Bohemia; broker and trader, San Francisco
Bio: "Isaac Glazier," in: *Encyclopedia of Bohemian and Czech-American Biography.* Bloomington, IN: AuthorHouse, 2016, Vol. 1, pp. 233-234.

Simon W. Glazier (1830-d.), b. Bohemia; broker and trader, San Francisco
Bio:" Simon W. Glazier," in: *Encyclopedia of Bohemian and Czech-American Biography.* Bloomington, IN: AuthorHouse, 2016, Vol. 1, p. 233-234.

William Simon Glazier (1907-1962), b. New/York, NY, of Bohemian ancestry; stock and bond broker, NYC
Bio: Rechcigl, Miloslav, Jr., "William Simon Glazier," in: *Encyclopedia of Bohemian and Czech-American Biography.* Bloomington, IN: AuthorHouse, 2016, Vol. 1, p. 234.

Benjamin Franklin Stein (1880-1948), b. Chicago, IL, of Bohemian ancestry; stock broker
Bio: Rechcigl, Miloslav, Jr., "Benjamin Franklin Stein," in: *Encyclopedia of Bohemian and Czech-American Biography.* Bloomington, IN: AuthorHouse, 2016, Vol. 1, p. 235.

L. Montefiore Stein (1884-1956), b. Chicago, IL, of Bohemian ancestry; merchant a later stock and bond broker, Chicago
Bio: Rechcigl, Miloslav, Jr., "L. Montefiore Stein,", in: *Encyclopedia of Bohemian and Czech-American Biography.* Bloomington, IN: AuthorHouse, 2016, Vol. 1, p. 235.

IX. Public Life

A. General

Kisch, Guido, "Public Life," in: `: In Search of Freedom. A History of American Jews from Czechoslovakia 1592-1948. London: Edward Goldston, 1948, pp. 122-127.

B. US Government

1. Executive Branch

a. The Cabinet

Madeleine Albright (1937-); b. Prague, Czech.; political scientist, professor, US Ambassador to the UN, US Secretary of State
Bio: Madeleine Albright, *Madam Secretary: A Memoir.* New York: Miramax, 2003.

John Forbes Kerry (1943-), b. Aurora, CO, of Moravian ancestry; politician, US Senator, US Secretary of State
Bio: *Biographical Directory of the United States Congress, 1774-Present.* Washington, DC: US Government Office, 1998; Rechcigl, Miloslav, Jr., "John Forbes Kerry," in: *Beyond the Sea of Beer.* History of Immigration of bohemians and Czechs to the New Work. Bloomington, IN: AuthorHouse, 2017, p. 741.

Caspar Weinberger (1917-2006), b. San Francisco, CA, of Czech ancestry; attorney, politician, businessman, Chair of Federal Trade Commission, Director of Management and Budget, US Secretary of HEW, US Secretary of Defense
Bio: Weinberger, Caspar, *Fighting for Peace: Seven Critical Years in the Pentagon.* Grand Central Publishing, 1990. 500p.
Weinberger, Caspar W. with Gretchen Roberts, *In the Arena. A Memoir of the Century.* Washington, DC: Regnery Publishing Co., 2001.

b. US Agencies

David Eli Lilienthal (1899-1981), b. Morton, IL, of Slovak ancestry; American attorney, chairman of Tennessee Valley Authority (TVA) and of the Atomic Energy commission.
Bio: Neuse, Steven M., "David E. Lilienthal: Exemplar of public purpose," I*nternational Journal of Public Administration,* 14, No. 6 (1991), pp. 1099-1148. Neuse, Steven M., *David E. Lilienthal: The Journey of an American Liberal.* University of Tennessee Press, 1996.

George Michael Low (1926-1984), b. Vienna, of Czech ancestry; NASA Administrator, President of Rensselaer Polytechnic Institute
Bio: "George Low," in: Wikipedia. See - https://en.wikipedia.org/wiki/George Low; Rechcigl, Miloslav, Jr., "George Michael Low," in: *Encyclopedia of Bohemian and Czech-American Biography.* Bloomington, IN: AuthorHouse, 2016, Vol. 2, p. 1096.

Frank William Taussig (1959-1940), b. St. Louis Mo., of Bohemian ancestry, economist, Chairman of US Tariff Commission (1917-1919)
Bio: Keene, Ann T., "Taussig, Frank William," in: *American National Biography.* New York: Oxford University Press, 1999; "Frank William Taussig," in: Wikipedia. See - https://en.wikipedia.org/wiki/Frank William Taussig

Sanford 'Sandy' J. Ungar (1945-), b. Slovak ancestry; journalist, director of Voice of America
Bio: "Stanford J. Ungar," in: Wikipedia. See - https://en.wikipedia.org/wiki/Sanford_J._Ungar

c. US Diplomats

Roland E. Arnall (1939-2008), b. Paris, of Czech ancestry; US Ambassador to the Netherlands (2006-08)
Bio: "Roland E. Arnall," in: Wikipedia. See- https://en.wikipedia.org/wiki/Roland_Arnall

Norman L. Eisen (1960-), b. Los Angeles, CA, of Czechoslovak ancestry; US Ambassador to the Czech Republic (2011-14)

Bio: "Norman L. Eisen," in: Wikipedia. See - https://en.wikipedia.org/wiki/Norman_L._Eisen

Roger Ernst (1925-2014), b. New York, NY; director of USAID in Ethiopia and Thailand
Bio: "Roger Ernst Obituary," *The New York Times*, December 17, 2014; Rechcigl, Miloslav, Jr., "Roger Ernst," in: *Encyclopedia of Bohemian and Czech-American Biography*. Bloomington, IN: AuthorHouse, 2016, Vol. 1., pp. 315-316.

Richard John Kerry (1915-2000), b. Brookline, MS, of Moravian ancestry; lawyer and US Foreign service officer
Bio: "Richard Kerry," in: Wikipedia. See - https://en.wikipedia.org/wiki/Richard_Kerry

Ronald Lauder (1944-), b. New York, NY, of Czechoslovak ancestry; US Ambassador to Austria (1986-87)
Bio: "Ronald Lauder," in: Wikipedia. See - https://en.wikipedia.org/wiki/Ronald_Lauder

Robert G. Neumann (1916-1999), b. Vienna, of Moravian ancestry; US Ambassador to Afghanistan (1977-73), Morocco (1973-76), Saudi Arabia (1981).
Bio: "Robert G. Neumann," in: Wikipedia. See - https://en.wikipedia.org/wiki/Robert_G._Neumann

Ronald E. Neumann (1944-), b. Washington, DC, of Bohemian ancestry; US Ambassador to Algeria (1994-97), Bahrain (2001-04), Afghanistan (2005-07)
Bio: https://en.wikipedia.org/wiki/Ronald_E._Neumann

Andrew H. Schapiro (1963-), b. Chicago, IL, of Bohemian ancestry; attorney, US Ambassador to the Czech Republic (2014-17)
Bio: Rechcigl, Miloslav, Jr., "Andrew H. Schapiro," in: *Encyclopedia of Bohemian and Czech-American Biography*. Bloomington, IN: AuthorHouse, 2016, Vol. 1. P. 319 and 416; "Andrew H. Schapiro," in: Wikipedia. See - https://en.wikipedia.org/wiki/Andrew_H._Schapiro

2. Legislative Branch

Victor l. Berger (1860-1929), b. Nieder Rebbach, Austria, of Slovak parents; journalist, US Congressman from Wisconsin
Bio: "Victor L. Berger," in: Wikipedia. See - https://en.wikipedia.org/wiki/Victor_L._Berger

Julius Goldzier (1854-1925), b. Vienna, of Bohemian ancestry; attorney, city councilman of Chicago, US Congressman.
Bio: *Biographical Directory of the United States Congress, 1774-Present.* Washington, DC: US Government Office, 1998.

Benjamin Franklin Jonas (1834-1911), b. Williamsport, KY, of Bohemian ancestry; attorney, US Congressman, US Senator
Bio: *Biographical Directory of the United States Congress, 1774-Present.* Washington, DC: US Government Office, 1998.

John Forbes Kerry (1943-), b. Aurora, CO, of Moravian ancestry; politician, US Senator, US Secretary of State
Bio: *Biographical Directory of the United States Congress, 1774-Present.* Washington, DC: US Government Office, 1998; Rechcigl, Miloslav, Jr., "John Forbes Kerry," in: *Beyond the Sea of Beer.* History of Immigration of bohemians and Czechs to the New Work. Bloomington, IN: AuthorHouse, 2017, p. 741.

Henry Myer Phillips (1811-1884), b. Philadelphia, Pa, of Bohemian ancestry; attorney, US Congressman
Bio: Biographical Directory of the United States Congress, 1774-Present. Washington, DC: US Government Office, 1998.

Joseph J. Pulitzer (1847-1911), b. Makó, Hungary, of Moravian ancestry; publisher, journalist, US Congressman
Bio: *Biographical Directory of the United States Congress, 1774-Present.* Washington, DC: US Government Office, 1998; Morris, James McGrath, "The Political Education of Joseph Pulitzer," *Missouri Historical Review*, 104, No. 2 (Jan 2010), pp. 78–94; Morris, James MacGrath, *Pulitzer: A Life in Politics, Print and Power.* Harper Perennial, 2011. 592p.

Adolph Joachim Sabath (1866-1952); b. Záboří, Bohemia; attorney, US Congressman
Bio: *Biographical Directory of the United States Congress, 1774-Present.* Washington, DC: US Government Office, 1998; Boxerman, Barton Alan, "Adolph Joachim Sabath in Congress," *J. Illinois State Historical Society,* 66 (1973), pp. 327-401, 428-443.

Lynn Schenk (1945-), b. Bronx, NY, of Bohemian ancestry; attorney, politician, US Congressman.
Bio: "Lynn Schenk," in: Wikipedia. See - https://en.wikipedia.org/wiki/Lynn_Schenk

3. Judicial Branch

Samuel Alschuler (1859-1939), b. Chicago, IL, of Czech ancestry; Federal Judge, US Court of Appeals for the 7th District
Bio: "Samuel Alschuler," in: Wikipedia. See - https://en.wikipedia.org/wiki/Samuel Alschuler

William Bondy (1870-1964), b. 1870-1964), b. New York, NY, of Bohemian ancestry; a longtime Federal Judge of the US District Court for the Southern District of New York
Bio: "William Bondy," in: Wikipedia. See - https://en.wikipedia.org/wiki/William_Bondy

Louis D. Brandeis (1856-1941), b. Louisville, KY, of Bohemian ancestry; attorney, jurist, Associate Justice of the Supreme Court of the US
Bio: Baker, Leonard, *Brandeis and Frankfurter: A Dual Biography.* Harper & Row, 1984. 567p.; Dawson, Nelson, l. *Brandeis and America.* Lexington, KY: University Press of Kentucky, 1989; Mason, Alpheus Thomas, *Brandeis: A Free Man's Life.* Viking, 1956. 713p.; Paper, Lewis J., *Brandeis: An Intimate Biography of Supreme Court Justice Louis D. Brandeis.* Open Road Media, 2014. 709p.; Rosen, Jeffrey, *Louis D. Brandeis: American Prophet.* New Haven: Yale University Press, 2017. 256p.; Urofsky, Melvin I., *Louis Brandeis: A Life.* Schocken, 2012. 976p.

Thomas Buergenthal (1934-), b. Ľubochňa, Czech.; U.S. judge on the International Court of Justice, professor of comparative law and jurisprudence, George Washington University
Bio: "Life after the Holocaust: Thomas Buergenthal," in: *Holocaust Encyclopedia*. See - https://www.ushmm.org/wlc/en/article.php?ModuleId=10007192; "Thomas Buergenthal," in: Wikipedia. See - https://en.wikipedia.org/wiki/Thomas Buergenthal

Felix Frankfurter (1882-1965), b. Vienna, of Czech and Slovak ancestry; attorney, professor, jurist, Associate Justice of the Supreme Court of the US
Bio: Hirsch, H. N., *The Enigma of Felix Frankfurter.* Quid Pro, LLC, 2014. 230p.; Lash, Joseph P., *From Diaries of Felix Frankfurter.* W.W. Norton & Co., 1975. 366p.; Thomas, Helen Shirley, *Felix Frankfurter: Scholar on the Bench.* Baltimore: The John Hopkins University Press, 1960. 381p.

Louis Heilprin Pollak (1922-2012), b. New York, NY, of Bohemian ancestry; attorney, jurist, educator, Dean, legal scholar
Bio: Rechcigl, Miloslav, Jr., "Louis Heilprin Pollak," in: *Encyclopedia of Bohemian and Czech-American Biography*. Bloomington, IN: AuthorHouse, 2016, Vol. 1, p. 526; "Louis H. Pollak," in: Wikipedia. See - https://en.wikipedia.org/wiki/Louis H. Pollak; Blumenthal, Jeff, "Longtime Philadelphia Federal Judge Pollak Dies," *Philadelphia Business Journal*, May 9, 2012.

Stephen Roy Reinhardt (1931-), b. Los Angeles, CA, of Bohemian ancestry; attorney, Federal Judge of US Court of Appeals for 9th District
Bio: "Stephen Reinhardt," in: Wikipedia, See - https://en.wikipedia.org/wiki/Stephen Reinhardt

Andrew J. Salz (1914-1995), b. CA, of Bohemian ancestry; attorney, Hawaii District Judge
Bio: "Andrew J. Salz," *San Francisco Chronicle*, October 9, 1995.

Frank E. Schwelb (1932-2014), b. Prague, Czech; Judge of the Superior Court of the DC (1979-88), Associate Judge of the DC Court of Appeals (1988-2006), Senior Judge of the DC Court of Appeals (2006-2014)

Bio: "Frank E. Schwelb," in: Wikipedia. See - https://en.wikipedia.org/wiki/Frank_E._Schwelb

Jacob Weinberger (1882-), b. Czech., attorney, city attorney of San Diego, US Federal Judge
Bio: "Jacob Weinberger," in: Wikipedia. See - https://en.wikipedia.org/wiki/Jacob Weinberge' "Weinberger, Jacob," in: Biographical Directory of Federal Judges. See - https://web.archive.org/web/20160730115701/http://www.fjc.gov/public/home.nsf/hisj

Edward Weinfeld (1901-1988), b. Manhattan, NY, of Slovak ancestry; lawyer, Federal Judge of the US District Court for the Southern District of New York
Bio: "Edward Weinfeld," in: Wikipedia. See - https://en.wikipedia.org/wiki/Edward_Weinfeld

4. Military Service

a. General

Kisch, Guido, "Military Service," in: *In Search of Freedom.* A History of American Jews from Czechoslovakia. 1592-1948. London: Edward Goldston, 194, pp. 103-113.

b. American Revolutionary War (1775-1890)

Lewis Bush (1753-1777), b. Philadelphia, Pa, of Bohemian father; veteran of the American Revolutionary War, with the rank as a Major
Bio: Rechcigl, Miloslav, Jr., "Lewis Bush," in: *Encyclopedia of Bohemian and Czech-American Biography.* Bloomington, IN: AuthorHouse, 2016, Vol. 2, pp. 2170-2171.

Solomon Bush (1753-1795), b. Philadelphia, PA, of Bohemian father; officer in the American Revolutionary Army, with the rank as Deputy-Adjutant-General
Bio: Simonhoff, Harry, "Colonel Solomon Bush," in: *Jewish Notables in America, 1776-1865.* New York: Greenberg, 1956, pp. 79-82.

c. War of 1812

Abraham Block (1780-1857), b. Bohemia; veteran of 1812 War, pioneer settler in Washington, AR Bio: Rechcigl, Miloslav, Jr. "Abraham Block," in: *Encyclopedia of Bohemian and Czech-American Biography*. Bloomington, IN: AuthorHouse, 2016, Vol. 2, pp. 2174-2175.

d. War of Texas Independence (1836)

Herman Ehrenberg (1815-1866), b. Steuben, Prussia, possibly of Bohemian ancestry; military volunteer in the New Orleans Greys and fought against Mexico in the Texas Revolution
Bio: "Herman Ehrenberg," in: Wikipedia. See - https://en.wikipedia.org/wiki/Herman Ehrenberg; Rechcigl, Miloslav, Jr., "Herman Ehrenberg," in: *Encyclopedia of Bohemian and Czech-American Biography*. Bloomington, IN: AuthorHouse, 2016, Vol. 2, pp. 2175-2176.

e. Border War (1854-1860)

August Bondi (1833-1907), b. Vienna, of Bohemian ancestry; abolitionist, member of John Brown's group
Bio: Bondi, August, *Autobiography of August Bondi (1833-1907)*. Galesburg, IL: Wagoner, 1910.

f. US Civil War (1861-1865)

Jacob Greil (1839-1900), b. Bohemia; veteran of Civil War, with the rank of Captain
Bio: Rechcigl, Miloslav," in: *Encyclopedia of Bohemian and Czech-American Biography*. Bloomington, IN: AuthorHouse, 2016, Vol. 2, p. 2182.

Joseph Benedict Greenhut (1843-1918), b. Horšovský Týn, Bohemia; veteran of Civil War, with the rank of a Captain, then chief of staff of the Brigade, later founder of the Great Western Distillery in Peoria, IL
Bio: *Publications Amer. Jew. Hist. Soc.* 3, p. 32; Wolf, Simon, *The American Jew as Patriot, Soldier, and Citizen*, op. cit., p. 43; "Joseph B. Greenhut," in: *Historical Encyclopedia of Illinois and History of Peoria County* (1902).

Benjamin Franklin Jonas (1834-1911), b. Williamsport, KY, of Bohemian ancestry; Confederate Army officer, with the rank of Sergeant Major, and then Adjutant
Bio: Rechcigl, Miloslav, Jr., "Benjamin Franklin Jonas," in: *Encyclopedia of Bohemian and Czech-American Biography*. Bloomington, IN: AuthorHouse, 2016, Vol. 2, p. 2183.

Charles J. Jonas (1834-d.), b. US, of Bohemian ancestry; Confederate Army officer, with the rank of Captain
Bio: Rechcigl, Miloslav, Jr., "Charles H. Jonas," in: *Encyclopedia of Bohemian and Czech-American Biography*. Bloomington, IN: AuthorHouse, 2016, Vol. 2, pp. 2183.

Leopold Karpeles (1838-1909), b. Prague, Bohemia; veteran of Civil War, recipient of Congressional Medal of Honor
Bio: Brody, Seymour 'Sy,' "Sergeant Leopold Karpeles: Received the Congressional Medal of Honor," in: *Jewish Heroes and Heroines in America from Colonial Times to 1900*. Hollywood: Lifetime Books, Inc., 1996.

Emanuel Woodic (1836-d.), b. Bohemia; veteran of Civil War, served throughout the War;
Bio: Rechcigl, Miloslav, Jr., "Emanuel Woodic," in: *Encyclopedia of Bohemian and Czech-American Biography*. Bloomington, IN: AuthorHouse, 2016, Vol. 2, p. 2186.

g. Spanish-American War (1898)

Edward David Taussig (1847-1921), b. St. Louis, MO, of Bohemian ancestry; Rear Admiral of US Navy
Bio: "Rites for Admiral Taussig," Special to Washington Post. *The Washington Post*. Washington, D.C., Feb 2, 1921. p. 3; "Rear Admiral Edward D. Taussig, USN, (1847-1921)," Department of the Navy, Naval Historical Center, Washington Navy Yard, Washington, DC.

h. Nicaraguan Campaign

Emile Phillips Moses (1880-d.), b. Sumpter, SC, of Czech ancestry; US Marines Corps officer, with the rank of Major General
Bio: Rechcigl, Miloslav, Jr., "Emile Phillips Moses," in: *Encyclopedia of Bohemian and Czech-American Biography.* Bloomington, IN: AuthorHouse, 2016, Vol. 2, p. 2188.

i. World War I

Otto Herman Goldstein (1883-1937), b. Rokycany, Bohemia; US Army officer, with the rank of Major Lt. Colonel,
Bio: Rechcigl, Miloslav, Jr., "Otto Herman Goldstein," in: *Encyclopedia of Bohemian and Czech-American Biography.* Bloomington, IN: AuthorHouse, 2016, Vol. 2, p. 2189; Marcosson, Isaac F., "Feeding the Yankees in France," *Saturday Evening Post,* December 14, 1918, pp. 12-13, 98, 101-102, 105-106, 109.

Robert Eugene Steiner (1862-1955), of Bohemian ancestry; Brigadier General in US Army
Bio: *History of Alabama and Dictionary of Alabama Biography.* Chicago: S. J. Clarke Publishing Co., 1921, Vol. 4, p. 1619.

Joseph Knefler Taussig (1877-1947), b. Dresden, Germany, of Bohemian ancestry; Vice Admiral of US Navy
Bio: "Joseph K. Taussig," *Dictionary of American Naval Fighting Ships,* Department of the Navy, Naval Historical Center, Washington Navy Yard, Washington, DC; Taussig, Joseph K., *Three Splendid Little Wars. The Diaries of Joseph K. Taussig. 1889-1901.* Naval War College, 2009.

j. Pearl Harbor

Claude C. Bloch (1878-1967), Woodbury, KY, of Bohemian ancestry; Admiral of US Navy
Bio: Prange, Gordon W., *At Dawn We Slept: The Untold Story of Pearl Harbor.* New York: McGraw-Hill Book Co., 1981; Kleber, John E., *The Kentucky Encyclopedia.* Lexington: University Press of Kentucky, 1992, p. 88;

Claude Charles Bloch Papers, Manuscript Division, Library of Congress, Washington, DC; Rechcigl, Miloslav, Jr., "Claude Charles Bloch," in: *Encyclopedia of Bohemian and Czech-American Biography*. Bloomington, IN: AuthorHouse, 2016, Vol. 2, p. 2191.

k. World War II

Henry B. Lederer (1920-2013), b. Bridgeport, CT, of Bohemian ancestry; Lt., fighter pilot, veteran of World War II
Bio: Rechcigl, Miloslav, Jr., "Henry B. Lederer," in: *Encyclopedia of Bohemian and Czech-American Biography*. Bloomington, IN: AuthorHouse, 2016, Vol. 2, p. 2193; Obituary: Henry B. Lederer," in: Dignity Memorial. See - https://www.dignitymemorial.com/obituaries/hewlett-ny/henry-lederer-5675957

l. Canadian Military

William Solomon (1777-1857), b. Montreal, Canada, of Bohemian ancestry; served as Indian interpreter in the War of 1812 between the British and Americans.
Bio: "Solomon, William," in: *Dictionary of Canadian Biography*, Vol. 8 (1851-1860); Rechcigl, Miloslav, Jr., "William Solomon," in: *Encyclopedia of Bohemian and Czech-American Biography*. Bloomington, IN: AuthorHouse, 2016, Vol. 3, p.2205.

C. State and Municipal Government

1. Governors

Henry Horner (1878-1940), b. Chicago, IL, of Bohemian ancestry; attorney, probate judge, Governor of Illinois
Bio: Lewis, Lloyd, *Henry Horner of Illinois. A Tribute*. Chicago: Lakeside Press, 1949; Littlewood, Thomas B., Horner of Illinois. Evanston, IL: Northwestern University Press, 1969. 273p.

2. State Legislators

Adolph Abeles (1817-1855), b. Bečov nad Teplou, Bohemia; pioneer merchant, Missouri State Legislator
Bio: Rechcigl, Miloslav, Jr., "Adolph Abeles," in: *Encyclopedia of Bohemian and Czech-American Biography.* Bloomington, IN: AuthorHouse, 2016, Vol. 1, p. 107, 332.

Samuel Charles Abeles (1875-1907), b. St. Louis, MO, of Bohemian ancestry; stock and bond broker, St. Louis
Bio: Rechcigl, Miloslav, Jr. "Samuel Charles Abeles," in: *Encyclopedia of Bohemian and Czech-American Biography.* Bloomington, IN: AuthorHouse, 2016, Vol. 1, p. 233.

Leopold Fuerth (1845-d.), b. Bohemia; member of the PA State House of Representative
Bio: Rechcigl, Miloslav, Jr., "Leopold Fuerth," in: *Encyclopedia of Bohemian and Czech-American Biography.* Bloomington, IN: AuthorHouse, 2016, Vol. 1, p. 335.

Jacob Gratz (1790-1856), b. Philadelphia, of Silesian ancestry; merchant, PA State Representative and Senator, 1st Senator of Jewish faith
Bio: "Jacob Gratz,", in: JewishEncyclopedia.com. See - http://www.jewishencyclopedia.com/articles/6860-gratz

Frederick L. Hackenburg (1887-1952), b. Prague, Bohemia; member of New York State Assembly (1921-27)
Bio: "Frederick L Hackenburg," in: Political Graveyard.com. See: http://politicalgraveyard.com/geo/NY/lawyer.H.html

Moritz O. Kopperl (1826-1883), b. Moravia; member of TX State in 1876 Legislature
Bio: Rechcigl, Miloslav, Jr., "Moritz O. Kopperl," in: *Encyclopedia of Bohemian and Czech-American Biography.* Bloomington, IN: AuthorHouse, 2016, Vol. 1, p. 339.

Louis J. Korper, b. Willington, CT of Bohemian ancestry; CT State legislator, representing Willington, Tolland Co., CT (1902)

Charles S. Kuh (-1871), b. Prague, Chodová Planá, Bohemia; South Carolina State Legislator
Bio: Rechcigl, Miloslav, Jr., "Charles S. Kuh," in: *Beyond the Sea of Beer*. Bloomington, IN: AuthorHouse, 2017, p. 34, 126; Rechcigl, Miloslav, Jr., "Charles S. Kuh," in: *Encyclopedia of Bohemian and Czech-American Biography*. Bloomington, IN: AuthorHouse, 2016, Vol. 1, pp. 85-86, 341.

Franz S. Leichter (1930-), b. Vienna, of Bohemian ancestry; attorney, member of New York State Legislator (1969-74) and then Senator (1975-98). Bio: Rechcigl, Miloslav, Jr., "Franz S. Leichter," in: *Encyclopedia of Bohemian and Czech-American Biography*. Bloomington, IN: AuthorHouse, 2016, Vol. 1, p. 341 and 470

Altamont Moses (1846-1905), b. Sumpter, SC, of Bohemian ancestry; Confederate soldier, merchant, South Carolina State Legislator
Bio: Rechcigl, Miloslav, Jr., "Altamont Moses," in: *Beyond the Sea of Beer*. Bloomington, IN: AuthorHouse, 2017, p. 129; *History of South Carolina*. Chicago- New York: Lewis Publishing
Co., 1920, Vol. 4, pp. 45-46.

Friedrich Porges (1890-1978), b. Vienna, of Bohemian ancestry; journalist, publicist, playwright, novelist
Bio: "Friedrich Porges," in: Wikipedia. See - https://de.wikipedia.org/wiki/Friedrich Porges; Rechcigl, Miloslav, Jr., "Frederick Porges," in: *Encyclopedia of Bohemian and Czech-American Biography*. Bloomington, IN: AuthorHouse, 2016, Vol. 2, p. 1034.

Edward Rosewater (1841-190), b. Bukovany, Bohemia; journalist, publisher, NE State legislator
Bio: Rechcigl, Miloslav, Jr., "Edward Rosewater," in: *Beyond the Sea of Beer*. Bloomington, IN: AuthorHouse, 2017, p. 294; "Edward Rosewater," in: Wikipedia. See - https://en.wikipedia.org/wiki/Edward Rosewater; Rosewater Family Papers, MS Collection No. 503, American Jewish Archives, Cincinnati, OH.

Edward P. Saltiel (1897-1990), b. Chicago, IL, of Bohemian ancestry; member of Illinois State Legislature and Illinois State Senator
Bio: Rechcigl, Miloslav, Jr., "Edward P. Saltiel," in: *Encyclopedia of Bohemian and Czech-American Biography*. Bloomington, IN: AuthorHouse, 2016, Vol. 1, p. 347.

Robert Eugene Steiner (1862-1953), b. Greenville, AL, of Bohemian ancestry; member of AL State House of Representative and the State Senate
Bio: Rechcigl, Miloslav, Jr., "Robert E. Steiner," in: *Encyclopedia of Bohemian and Czech-American Biography*. Bloomington, IN: AuthorHouse, 2016, Vol.1, p. 394, Vol. 2, p. 2189.

Eric S. Tachau (1924-2002), b. Louisville, KY, of Czech ancestry; member of Ky State Legislature (1975).
Bio: Rechcigl, Miloslav, Jr., "Eric S. Tachau," in: *Encyclopedia of Bohemian and Czech-American Biography*. Bloomington, IN: AuthorHouse, 2016, Vol.1, p. 350.

David Harold Weiss (1905-1979), b. Czech.; attorney, PA State legislator (1937), reelected to 6 more terms, judge, Westmoreland County Common Pleas Court (1957-1977).
Bio: "WEISS, David Harold - PA House of Representatives." See - http://www.house.state.pa.us/BMC/Bios/PDF/2385.PDF

3. Mayors

Julius Fleischman (1871-1925), b. Cincinnati, OH, of Bohemian ancestry; businessman, Mayor of Cincinnati
Bio: "Julius Fleischmann Dies at 68; Stage Producer and Art Patron," *New York Times,* Oct. 24, 1968; Klieger, P. Christiaan, "Julius Fleischmann," in: *The Fleischmann Yeast Family*, Arcadia Publishing, 2004, pp. 31–36.

Isaac William Taussig (1850 -1917), b. Manhattan, NY, of Bohemian ancestry; Mayor of Jersey City, NJ
Bio: "Isaac William Taussig," in: Wikipedia. See - https://en.wikipedia.org/wiki/Isaac_W._Taussig

Walter M. Taussig (1862-1923), b. of Bohemian ancestry; Mayor of Yonkers, NY
Bio: Rechcigl, Miloslav, Jr., "Walter m. Taussig," in: *Encyclopedia of Bohemian and Czech-American Biography*. Bloomington, IN: AuthorHouse, 2016, Vol. 1, pp. 330-331.

William Taussig (1826-1913), b. Prague, Bohemia; physician, businessman, Mayor of Carondelet, MO
Bio: "William Taussig," in: Wikipedia. See - https://en.wikipedia.org/wiki/William Taussig; Dillard, Irving, "Taussig, William," *Dictionary of American Biography*. New York: Charles Scribner's Sons, 1936; Rechcigl, Miloslav, Jr., "William Taussig," in: *Beyond the Sea of Beer*. Bloomington, IN: AuthorHouse, 2017, p. 471; Rechcigl, Miloslav, Jr., "William Taussig," in: *Encyclopedia of Bohemian and Czech-American Biography*. Bloomington, IN: AuthorHouse, 2016, Vol.1, p. 194

4. Judges

Nanette Dembitz (1912-1989), b. Washington, DC, of Bohemian ancestry; Judge of the Family Court of New York
Bio: Anderson, Susan Heller, "Judge Nanette Dembitz, 76, Dies; Served in New York Family Court," *The New York Times*, April 5, 1989.

Joseph Jerome Drucker (1900-1977), b. Chicago, IL, of Czech ancestry; Judge of the Chicago Municipal Court, Judge of the Circuit Court (1958-63) and then the Appellate Court.
Bio: Rechcigl, Miloslav, Jr., "Joseph Jerome Drucker," in: *Encyclopedia of Bohemian and Czech-American Biography*. Bloomington, IN: AuthorHouse, 2016, Vol.1, p. 535.

Hugo Morris Friend (1882-1966), b. Prague, Bohemia; jurist, Judge of the Cook County Circuit Court, IL
Bio: "Hugo Friend," in: Wikipedia. See - https://en.wikipedia.org/wiki/Hugo Friend; Rechcigl, Miloslav, Jr., "Hugo M. Friend," in: *Encyclopedia of Bohemian and Czech-American Biography*. Bloomington, IN: AuthorHouse, 2016, Vol.1, p. 536.

Frederick L. Hackenburg (1887-1952), b. Prague, Bohemia; NY State Legislator, Judge of the Court of Special Sessions (1935-52)
Bio: Rechcigl, Miloslav, Jr., "Frederick Hackenburg," in: *Encyclopedia of Bohemian and Czech-American Biography*. Bloomington, IN: AuthorHouse, 2016, Vol.1, p. 537.

Moses Hartmann (1872-1943), b. St. Louis, MO, of Bohemian father; Judge of the Circuit Court of the 8th Judicial District of Missouri
Bio: Rechcigl, Miloslav, Jr., "Moses Hartmann," in: *Encyclopedia of Bohemian and Czech-American Biography*. Bloomington, IN: AuthorHouse, 2016, Vol.1, p. 537; "Hartmann, Moses," in: *Encyclopedia of American Biography*. New Series. New York: American Historical Society, 1938, Vol. 9, p. 170; "Biography of Hon. Moses Hartmann," in: Access Genealogy. See - https://www.accessgenealogy.com/missouri/biography-of-hon-moses-hartmann.htm

Henry Horner (1878-1940), b. Chicago, IL, of Bohemian ancestry; politician, probate Judge of Cook County, IL (1915-1931)
Bio: "Henry Horner," in: Wikipedia. See - https://en.wikipedia.org/wiki/Henry_Horner

Otto Michael Kaus (1920-1996), b. Vienna, of Slovak ancestry; lawyer, Justice of the Supreme Court of California
Bio: "Otto Kaus," in: Wikipedia. See - https://en.wikipedia.org/wiki/Otto Kaus

Edward Lazansky (1872-1955), b. Brooklyn, NY, of Bohemian ancestry; Secretary of State of New York (1911-12), Justice of the New York State Supreme Court (1917-26), Justice of the Appellate Division (1926-1943)
Bio: "Edward Lazansky," in: Wikipedia. See - https://en.wikipedia.org/wiki/Edward Lazansky

Geoffrey Brian Morawetz (1954-), b. Toronto, Canada, probably of Bohemian ancestry; Justice of Ontario Superior Court of Justice
Bio: Rechcigl, Miloslav, Jr., "Geoffrey Brian Morawetz," in: *Encyclopedia of Bohemian and Czech-American Biography*. Bloomington, IN: AuthorHouse,

2016, Vol.1, p. 541; Golick, Steven, "The Honourable Mr. Justice Geoffrey B. Morawetz," *Emory Bankruptcy Developments Journal*, Vol. 29, Issue 1, pp. 1-3.

Hugo Pam (1870-1930), b. Chicago, IL, of Czech ancestry; Judge of the Superior Court, Chicago
Bio: Rechcigl, Miloslav, Jr., "Hugo Pam," in: *Encyclopedia of Bohemian and Czech-American Biography*. Bloomington, IN: AuthorHouse, 2016, Vol.1, p. 541.

James Madison Pereles (1852-1910), b. Milwaukee, WI, of Bohemian ancestry; Judge of County court, Wisconsin
Bio: Rechcigl, Miloslav, Jr., "James Madison Pereles," in: *Encyclopedia of Bohemian and Czech-American Biography*. Bloomington, IN: AuthorHouse, 2016, Vol.1, pp. 541-542.

Justine Wise Polier (1903-1987), b. Portland, OR, of Moravian ancestry; Judge of the Domestic Relations Court, NY (1935-87)
Bio: "Justine W. Polier," in: Wikipedia. See - https://en.wikipedia.org/wiki/Justine W. Polier;
Rechcigl, Miloslav, Jr., "Justine W. Polier," in: *Encyclopedia of Bohemian and Czech-American Biography*. Bloomington, IN: AuthorHouse, 2016, Vol.1, p. 542.

Joseph Sabath (1870-1956), b. Záboří, Bohemia; Judge of Superior Court, Cook Co., IL
Bio: "Joseph Sabath, 86, Ex-Judge, is Dead; Granted 70,000 Divorces in 36 Years' Service in Chicago Superior Court 'To Bear and to Forbear' Native of Bohemia," *The New York Times*, May 4, 1956.

Jacob Steinbach, Jr. (1881-1954), b. Long Beach, NJ, of Bohemian ancestry; District Court Judge (1913-18), Judge of the County Court (1926-30)
Bio: Rechcigl, Miloslav, Jr., "Jacob Steinbach, Jr.," in: *Encyclopedia of Bohemian and Czech-American Biography*. Bloomington, IN: AuthorHouse, 2016, Vol. 1, p. 544.

George B. Weiss (1894-d.), b. Chicago, IL, of Czech ancestry; Judge of the Municipal Court, Chicago (s. 1934)

Bio: Rechcigl, Miloslav, Jr., "George B. Weiss," in: *Encyclopedia of Bohemian and Czech-American Biography*. Bloomington, IN: AuthorHouse, 2016, Vol.1, p. 545.

5. Other

Lewis Fleischner (1829-1896), b. Vogelsang, Bohemia; businessman, OR State Treasurer
Bio: Joseph Gaston, *Portland, Oregon. Its History and Builders*. Chicago-Portland: S.J. Clarke Publishing Co., 1911, Vol. 3, pp. 258-262.

Adolph Korper (1846-1912), b. Terešov, Bohemia; postmaster, South Wellington, CT, town's first selectman, -10 times re-elected
Bio: "Adolph Korper," *Illustrated Popular Biography of Connecticut*. Hartford, CT: Case, Lockwood & Brainard Company, 1891, p. 233

Harry Sonnenschein (1892-d), b. Chicago, IL, of Czech ancestry; Mayor Cermak's confidential secretary, Alderman
Bio: Rechcigl, Miloslav, Jr., "Henry Sonnenschein," in: *Encyclopedia of Bohemian and Czech-American Biography*. Bloomington, IN: AuthorHouse, 2016, Vol.1, p. 360.

D. Civic and Communal Work

1. Communal and Religious Workers

Solomon G. Adler (1816-1890), b. Bohemia; clothing merchant, organizer of the first Jewish congregation, and the consolidated Congregation Emanu-El B'ne Jeshurun, Milwaukee
Bio: Rechcigl, Miloslav, Jr., "Solomon Adler," in: *Encyclopedia of Bohemian and Czech-American Biography*. Bloomington, IN: AuthorHouse, 2016, Vol. 1, pp. 105; "Solomon Adler, Clothing Merchant and Jewish Serviceman," in: Wisconsin Historical Society. See - https://www.wisconsinhistory.org/Records/Article/CS4717

Ivan A. Backer (1929-), b. Prague, Czech.; theologian, humanitarian, leader of community revitalization
Bio: "2003 Haupert Humanitarian Award - Ivan Backer'49" in: Moravian College Alumni. See - https://www.moravian.edu/alumni/recognition/award-recipients/backer

Alfred Abraham Benesch (1879-1973), b. Cleveland, OH, of Bohemian ancestry; attorney, civic leader, community worker, Cleveland
Bio: Rechcigl, Miloslav, Jr., "Alfred Abraham Benesch," in: *Encyclopedia of Bohemian and Czech-American Biography*. Bloomington, IN: AuthorHouse, 2016, Vol. 1, pp. 58-59.

Sidonia Cyd Bettelheim (1866-1959), b. Hungary, of Slovak ancestry; resident directress of Emanu El Sisterhood, NYC
Bio: "Bettelheim, Cyd," *The American Jewish Yearbook*, 7 (1905-1906), p.43.

Daniel Block (1802-1853), b. Bohemia; Jewish leader, founder of the B'nai B'rith Synagogue, St. Louis
Bio: Rechcigl, Miloslav, Jr. "Daniel Block," in: *Encyclopedia of Bohemian and Czech-American Biography*. Bloomington, IN: AuthorHouse, 2016, Vol. 1, p.65; "Daniel Block," in: Wikipedia. See - https://en.wikipedia.org/wiki/Daniel_Block

Sarah Blum (née Abeles), b. Newark, NJ, of Bohemian ancestry; Jewish community leader
Bio: Rechcigl, Miloslav, Jr., "Sarah (Abeles) Blum," in: *Encyclopedia of Bohemian and Czech-American Biography*. Bloomington, IN: AuthorHouse, 2016, Vol.1, p. 66.

Samuel Bettelheim (1873-1942), b. Bratislava, Slovakia; Zionist, organizer of the Agudath Israel in America
Bio: "Samuel Bettelheim Reported Dead in Hungary" in: Jewish Telegraph Agency, June 25, 1942.

Henrietta Bruckman (née Kahn) (1810-1888), b. Prague, Bohemia; founder of the Independent Order of True Sisters, NYC

Bio: Rechcigl, Miloslav, Jr., "Henrietta (Kahn) Bruckman," in: *Encyclopedia of Bohemian and Czech-American Biography*. Bloomington, IN: AuthorHouse, 2016, Vo. 1, pp. 66-67.

Morris Engelman (1872-), b. Bardejov, Slovakia; insurance agent, communal worker, secretary of Union Orthodox Jewish Congregations, organizer of Ohab Zedek Sisterhood
Bio: *Who's Who in American Jewry*. New York: Jewish Biographical Bureau, 1926, Vol. 1, pp. 141-142; "Morris Engelman," in: *Distinguished Jews of America*. New York, 1917, Vol. 1, pp. 115-116.

Isaac N. Fleischner (1859-1927), b. Albany OR; merchant, president of Concordia Club and B'rith Lodge, vice president of City Board of Charities
Bio: "Fleischner, Isaac N.," *The American Jewish Yearbook*, 7 (1905-1906), p. 56; "Isaac Newton Fleischner," in: *Portland, Its History and Builders*. By Joseph Gaston. Chicago-Portland: S. J. Clarke Publishing Co., 1911, vol. 2, pp. 665-666.

Jacob Furth (1844-1918), b. Bohemia; merchant, treasurer of Independent Order of B'nai B'rith
Bio: "Furth, Jacob," *The American Jewish Yearbook*, 7 (1905-1906), p. 61

Julius Glaser (1862-), b. Bohemia; merchant, director of Jewish Alliance and The United Jewish Educational and Charitable Assn., director of the Jewish Federation of St. Louis
Bio: Rechcigl, Miloslav, Jr., "Julius Glaser," in: *Encyclopedia of Bohemian and Czech-American Biography*. Bloomington, IN: AuthorHouse, 2016, Vol. 1, p. 54. community

Rebecca Gratz (1781-1869), b. Philadelphia, PA, of Silesian ancestry; educator, founder of Hebrew Benevolent Society, philanthropist
Bio: "Rebecca Gratz," in: Wikipedia. See - https://en.wikipedia.org/wiki/Rebecca_Gratz
"Rebecca Gratz," in: Jewish Virtual Library. See - https://www.jewishvirtuallibrary.org/rebecca-gratz

Theresa Grotta (1841-1922), b. Krásný Les, Bohemia; communal worker, founder of the Newark Chapter of the National Jewish Women
Bio: Rechcigl, Miloslav, Jr., "Theresa Grotta," in: *Encyclopedia of Bohemian and Czech-American Biography*. Bloomington, IN: AuthorHouse, 2016, Vol. 1, p. 83

Henry Aaron Guinzburg (1856-1928), b. Baltimore, MD, rubber manufacturer, communal worker, president of the Jewish Burial Society, VP of the United Hebrew Charities, treasurer of the Federation for the Support of Jewish Philanthropic Societies, chairman of the Building Fund Co, etc.
Bio: "Col. H. A. Guinzberg, Philanthropist and Leader, Dies at 73," Jewish Telegraphic Agency, November 19, 1928. See - https://www.jta.org/1928/11/19/archive/col-h-a-guinzberg-philanthropist-and-leader-dies-at-73

Joseph Herbach (1873-d.), b. Slovakia; editor, publisher, communal worker, president of Hebrew Sheltering Home, president of Home for Infants, director of Federation for Jewish Charities, etc. Philadelphia
Bio: *Who's Who in American Jewry*. New York: Jewish Biographical Bureau, 1926, Vol. 1., p. 259

Martha J. Joseph (née Hahn) (1917-2006), b. Cleveland, OH, of Bohemian ancestry; a cultural leader of the Greater Cleveland community
Bio: Rechcigl, Miloslav, Jr., "Martha J. Joseph," in: *Encyclopedia of Bohemian and Czech-American Biography*. Bloomington, IN: AuthorHouse, 2016, Vol. 1, p. 76.

William Ralph Joseph (1946-2012), b. Cleveland, OH, of Bohemian ancestry; attorney, specialist in nonprofit law, community activist, Cleveland
Bio: Rechcigl, Miloslav, Jr., "William Ralph Joseph," in: *Encyclopedia of Bohemian and Czech-American Biography*. Bloomington, IN: AuthorHouse, 2016, Vol. 1, p. 76; "Obituaries: William Joseph," *Cleveland Jewish News*, November 1, 2012.

Leopold Keiser (1826-), b. Bzenec, Moravia; cofounder of the Hebrew Benevolent Society and of Temple Beth Zion

Bio: "Keiser, Leopold," *The American Jewish Yearbook*, 7 (1905-1906), p. 74; Rechcigl, Miloslav, Jr., "Leopold Keiser," in: *Encyclopedia of Bohemian and Czech-American Biography*. Bloomington, IN: AuthorHouse, 2016, Vol. 1, p. 68.

Simon Klauber (1824-1891), b. Prague, Bohemia; manufacturer, president of Die vereinigen Brűder, a Bohemian-Jewish mutual aid society, NYC
Bio: Rechcigl, Miloslav, Jr., "Simon Klauber," in: *Encyclopedia of Bohemian and Czech-American Biography*. Bloomington, IN: AuthorHouse, 2016, Vol. 1, p. 62.

Rebekah Kohut (1864-1951), b. Košice, Slovakia, president of Ahawath Chesed Sisterhood
Bio: Rebekah Bettelheim Kohut,", in: Jewish Women's Archive. Encyclopedia. See - https://jwa.org/encyclopedia/article/kohut-rebecca; Kohut, Rebekah. Papers. AJA, Cincinnati, Ohio, and American Jewish Historical Society, Waltham, MA; "Rebekah Bettelheim Kohut," in: Wikipedia. See - https://en.wikipedia.org/wiki/Rebekah Bettelheim Kohut; "Rebekah Kohut, Noted American Jewish Women's Leader, Dies at age of 86," *The Wisconsin Jewish Chronicle*, August 17, 1951; Wald, Lillian D., "American Jewry's First Lady. Rebekah Kohut on the Golden Jubilee in Public Life," *The Wisconsin Jewish Chronicle*, November 15, 1935; "Kohut, Rebekah," *The American Jewish Yearbook*, 7 (1905), p. 76.

Adolf Kraus (1850-1928), b. Blovice, Bohemia; attorney, president of Isaiah Temple in Chicago and a prominent executive of the Union of American Hebrew Congregations
Bio: Rechcigl, Miloslav, Jr., "Adolf Kraus," in: *Encyclopedia of Bohemian and Czech-American Biography*. Bloomington, IN: AuthorHouse, 2016, Vo. 1, p. 423; "Kraus, Adolf," in: Jewishencyclopedia.com See - http://jewishencyclopedia.com/articles/9499-kraus-adolf

Sarah Kussy (1869-1956), b. Newark, NJ, of Bohemian ancestry; communal worker, one of the founders of Hadassah and the National Women's League of the US Synagogue of America.
Bio: Rechcigl, Miloslav, Jr., "Sarah Kussy," in: *Encyclopedia of Bohemian and Czech-American Biography*. Bloomington, IN: AuthorHouse, 2016, Vo. 1,

p. 69; "Sarah Kussy," in Jewish Women's Archive. See - https://jwa.org/encyclopedia/article/Kussy-Sarah

Moritz Loth (1832-1913), b. Milotice, Moravia; president of Congregation of Bene Jeshurun, founder of the Union of American Hebrew Congregations
Bio: "Loth, Moritz," *The American Jewish Yearbook*, 7 (1905-1906), p.83.

Emma B. Mandl (1842-1928), b. Pilsen, Bohemia; president of Baron Hirsch Ladies' Aid Society
Bio: "Mandl, Emma B.," *The American Jewish Yearbook*, 7 (1905-1906), p. 86; Rechcigl, Miloslav, Jr., "Emma B. Mandl," in: *Encyclopedia of Bohemian and Czech-American Biography*. Bloomington, IN: AuthorHouse, 2016, Vo. 1, p. 86; "Emma B. Mandl," in: Jewish Women's Archive Encyclopedia. See - https://jwa.org/encyclopedia/article/mandl-emma-b

Adolph Robi (1848-1919), b. Popovice, Bohemia; manager of United Jewish Charities
Bio: "Robi, Adolph," *The American Jewish Yearbook*, 7 (1905-1906), p.97.

Edward Rubovitz (1840-), b. Seben, near Prešov, Slovakia; superintendent of the United Hebrew Charities, Zionist
Bio: "Rubovitz, Edward," *The American Jewish Yearbook*, 7 (1905-1906), p. 99.

Henrietta Szold (1860-1945), b. Baltimore, MD, of Slovak ancestry; Jewish Zionist leader and founder of Hadassah
Bio: Kessler, B. (ed.). *Daughter of Zion: Henrietta Szold and American Jewish Woman.* 1995; Lowenthal, Marvin, *Henrietta Szold: Life and Letters.* New York: Viking, 1942; Kessler, B. (ed.). *Daughter of Zion: Henrietta Szold and American Jewish Woman.* 1995; Lowenthal, Marvin. Henrietta Szold: Life and Letters. New York: Viking, 1942; Reinharz, S. and M. Raider (eds.), *American Jewish Women and the Zionist Enterprise* (2005); Shargel, B.R. *Lost Love: The Untold Story of Henrietta Szold* (1997).

David Treichlinger (1852-1925), b. Strakonice, Bohemia; owner of brokerage, president of Jewish Education Alliance, Temple Israel, VP of Jewish Charitable and Education Assn., etc.

Bio: *Prominent Jews of America.* Toledo, OH: American Hebrew Publishing Co., 1918, pp. 804-805.

Elmer L. Winter (1912-2009), b. Milwaukee, WI, of Bohemian ancestry; attorney, businessman, entrepreneur, national president of the American Jewish Committee
Bio: Oster, Marcy, "Elmer Winter, ex AJC president, dies," Jewish Telegraphic Agency, October 27, 2009

Samuel Wolfenstein (1841-1921), b. Velké Meziříčí, Moravia; Rabbi, superintendent of Jewish Orphan Asylum
Bio: "Wolfenstein, Samuel," *The American Jewish Yearbook*, 7 (1905-1906), p. 117; Rechcigl, Miloslav, Jr., "Samuel Wolfenstein," in: *Encyclopedia of Bohemian and Czech-American Biography.* Bloomington, IN: AuthorHouse, 2016, Vo. 1, p. 87.

Samuel Woolner (1846-), b. Senica, Slovakia; distiller, financier, president of Union of American Hebrew Congregations
Bio: "Woolner, Samuel," *The American Jewish Yearbook*, 7 (1905-1906), p. 117; "Samuel Woolner," in: Peoria City and County, Illinois. Chicago: S. J. Clarke Publishing Co., 1912, pp. 807-809.

2. Social Activists and Reformers

Matthias Bush (1722-1790), b. Prague, Bohemia; pioneer merchant, signatory of the Philadelphia Merchants Non-Importation Resolution, first American document of civic rights
Bio: Rechcigl, Miloslav, Jr., "Mathias Bush," in: *Encyclopedia of Bohemian and Czech-American Biography.* Bloomington, IN: AuthorHouse, 2016, Vo. 1, p. 102.

Ernestine Fűrth (née Kisch) (1877-1946), b. Prague, Bohemia; activist, founder and leader of suffrage movement in Austria
Bio: Rechcigl, Miloslav, Jr., "Ernestine Fűrth," in: *Encyclopedia of Bohemian and Czech-American Biography.* Bloomington, IN: AuthorHouse, 2016, Vo. 2, p. 1112.

Edna Fischel Gellhorn (1878-), b. St. Louis, MO, of Bohemian ancestry; reformer, founder of the National League of Women Voters
Bio: Rechcigl, Miloslav, JR., "Edna Fischel Gellhorn," in: *Encyclopedia of Bohemian and Czech-American Biography.* Bloomington, IN: AuthorHouse, 2016, Vo. 2, p. 1112; "Edna Fischel Gellhorn," in: Wikipedia. See - https://en.wikipedia.org/wiki/Edna_Fischel_Gellhorn

Chaviva Milada Hošek (1946-), b. Bohemia; feminist, suffragist, politician
Bio: Rechcigl, Miloslav, Jr., "Chaviva Milada Hošek, in: *Encyclopedia of Bohemian and Czech-American Biography.* Bloomington, IN: AuthorHouse, 2016, Vo. 2, 1113; "Chaviva Hošek," in: Wikipedia. See - https://en.wikipedia.org/wiki/Chaviva_Hošek

Franziska Porges Hosken (1920-2006), b. Vienna, Aust., of Bohemian ancestry; suffragist, social activist, advocate against female genital mutilation
Bio: Rechcigl, Miloslav, Jr., "Fran Hosken," in: *Encyclopedia of Bohemian and Czech-American Biography.* Bloomington, IN: AuthorHouse, 2016, Vo. 2, p. 1113; "Fran Hosken" in: Wikipedia. See - https://en.wikipedia.org/wiki/Fran Hosken; Kahn, Joseph P., "Fran P. Hosken, 86; activist for women's issues," *The Boston Globe*, February 12, 2006.

Anita Pollitzer (1894-1975), b. Charleston, SC, of Czech ancestry; feminist, social activist, suffragette
Bio: "Anita Pollitzer," in: *Encyclopedia of Bohemian and Czech-American Biography.* Bloomington, IN: AuthorHouse, 2016, Vo. 2, pp. 1114.

Clara G. Rabinowitz (née Greenhut) (1893-1984), b. of Bohemian ancestry; active in Jewish social service and philanthropic organizations, director of Tudor Foundation
Bio: "Clara G. Rabinowitz, 91, Dies; Director of Tudor Foundation," *The New York Times,* September 11, 1984.

Elizabeth Brandeis Raushenbush (1896-1984), b. Boston, MA, of Bohemian ancestry; labor economist and social reformer

Bio: "Elizabeth Brandeis Raushenbush," in: *Encyclopedia of Bohemian and Czech-American Biography*. Bloomington, IN: AuthorHouse, 2016, Vo. 2, pp. 1110-1111.

Eric Samuel Tachau (1924-2002), b. Louisville, KY, of Bohemian ancestry; civil rights activist
Bio: Rechcigl, Miloslav, Jr., "Eric S. Tachau," in: *Encyclopedia of Bohemian and Czech-American Biography*. Bloomington, IN: AuthorHouse, 2016, Vo. 2, 1124; The Civil Rights Activist Tachau Dies at 78," *The Enquirer*, November 26, 2002.

Jean Brandeis Tachau (1894-1978), b. Louisville, KY, of Bohemian ancestry; social activist, advocate of birth control
Bio: Rechcigl, Miloslav, Jr., "Jean Brandeis Tachau," in: *Encyclopedia of Bohemian and Czech-American Biography*. Bloomington, IN: AuthorHouse, 2016, Vo. 2, p. 1111 and Vol. 3, p. 2133.

3. Other Activists

Manfred Ackerman (1898-1991), b. Mikulov, Moravia; politician, trade union official
Bio: Rechcigl, Miloslav, Jr., "Manfred Ackerman," in *Encyclopedia of Bohemian and Czech-American Biography*. Bloomington, IN: AuthorHouse, 2016, Vol. 2, pp. 1114-1115; "Manfred Ackerman," in: Wikipedia. See - https://en.wikipedia.org/wiki/Manfred Ackermann

Victor L. Berger (1860-1929), b. Nieder Rebbach, Austria, journalist, founding member of the Social Democratic Party of America, later renamed the Socialist Party of America
Bio: Victor L. Berger," in: Wikipedia. See - https://en.wikipedia.org/wiki/Victor_L._Berger

Alice Goldmark Brandeis (1866-1945), b. Brooklyn, NY, of Bohemian ancestry; advocate of woman suffrage, industrial reform, organized labor, legal rights of children

Bio: Rechcigl, Miloslav, Jr., "Alice Goldmark Brandeis," in: *Encyclopedia of Bohemian and Czech-American Biography*. Bloomington, IN: AuthorHouse, 2016, Vol. 2, pp. 1117-1117;
"Alice Goldmark Brandeis," in: Jewish Women's Archive. Encyclopedia. See - https://jwa.org/encyclopedia/article/brandeis-alice-goldmar

Friedrich Adler (1879-1960), b. Vienna, of Bohemian ancestry; politician, Socialist, activist
Bio: Rechcigl, Miloslav, Jr., "Friedrich Adler," in *Encyclopedia of Bohemian and Czech-American Biography*. Bloomington, IN: AuthorHouse, 2016, Vol. 2, p. 1115; "Friedrich Adler," in: Wikipedia. See - https://en.wikipedia.org/wiki/Friedrich Adler (politician)

Andrei Cherny (1975-), b. Los Angeles, CA, of Czechoslovak parents; lawyer, political 'wunderkind,' Presidents speechwriter, historian, founder of *Democracy: A Journal of Ideas, chair of the Arizona Democratic Party, etc.,*
Bio: Tracy, Marc, "Arizona's Savvy Israel Ally…" in: Tabletmag.com. See - http://www.tabletmag.com/jewish-news-and-politics/100017/arizonas-savvy-israel-ally; Andrei Cherny," in: Wikipedia. See - https://en.wikipedia.org/wiki/Andrei Cherny

Lewis Naphthali Dembitz (1833-1907), b. Zirke, Posen, Prussia, of Bohemian mother; a lawyer, a staunch unionist, frequent antislavery agitator, member of the new Republican Party, member of the Republican Convention that nominated Abraham Lincoln for the Presidency
Bio: Rechcigl, Miloslav, Jr., "Lewis N. Dembitz," in: *Encyclopedia of Bohemian and Czech-American Biography*. Bloomington, IN: AuthorHouse, 2016, Vol. 1, pp. 364-365; Lewis Naphthali Dembitz," in: Wikipedia. See - https://en.wikipedia.org/wiki/Lewis_Naphtali_Dembitz

Jack Halberstam (aka Judith Halberstam) (1961-), b. of Bohemian ancestry; literary scholar, gender and queer theorist and author
Bio: "Jack Halberstam," in: Wikipedia. See - https://en.wikipedia.org/wiki/Jack Halberstam

Michael J. Hirschhorn (1959-), b. US, of Bohemian ancestry; non -profit strategy consultant, president of Jacob & Hilda Blaustein Foundation, ex.

director of the International Human Rights Funders Group and other education and human rights organizations
Bio: Rechcigl, Miloslav, Jr., "Michael J. Hirschhorn," in: *Encyclopedia of Bohemian and Czech-American Biography*. Bloomington, IN: AuthorHouse, 2016, Vol. 1, pp. 183-184.

Jane Lobman Katz (1931-1986), b. Montgomery, AL, of Bohemian ancestry; political activist, advocate for election law reform
Bio: Rechcigl, Miloslav, Jr., "Jane Lobman Katz," in: *Encyclopedia of Bohemian and Czech-American Biography*. Bloomington, IN: AuthorHouse, 2016, Vol. 2, p. 1117; "Jane Lubomir Katz," in: Wikipedia. See - https://en.wikipedia.org/wiki/Jane Lobman Katz

Eva Kollisch (1925-), b. Venna, of Bohemian ancestry; poet, literary scholar, peace activist, anti-Stalinist Marxist Trotskyite
Bio: Rechcigl, Miloslav, Jr., "Eva Kollisch," in: *Encyclopedia of Bohemian and Czech-American Biography*. Bloomington, IN: AuthorHouse, 2016, Vol. 2, p. 1118; Kollisch, Eva, *Girl in Movement*. Glad Day Books, 2000.

Lenore Guinzburg Marshall (1897-1971), b. New York, NY, of Bohemian ancestry; writer, political activist, co-founder of the committee for Nuclear Responsibility
Bio: "Lenore Marshall," in: Wikipedia. See - https://en.wikipedia.org/wiki/Lenore Marshall; Rechcigl, Miloslav, Jr., "Lenore Guinzburg Marshall," in: *Encyclopedia of Bohemian and Czech-American Biography* Bloomington, IN: AuthorHouse, 2016, Vol. 2, p. 974; "Lenore Guinzburg Marshall," in: Jewish Women's Archive. See - https://jwa.org/encyclopedia/article/marshall-lenore-guinzburg

Hanna Newcombe (née Hammerschlag) (1922-2011), Prague, Czech.; chemist, activist, founder of Canadian Peace Research Institute
Bio: "Hanna Newcombe," in: Wikipedia. See - https://en.wikipedia.org/wiki/Hanna Newcombe; Rechcigl, Miloslav, Jr., "Hanna (Hammerschlag) Newcombe," in: *Encyclopedia of Bohemian and Czech-American Biography* Bloomington, IN: AuthorHouse, 2016, Vol. 2, pp. 1119-1120.

William R. Perl (1906-1998), b. Prague, Bohemia; activist, Zionist, rescuer of Jews from annihilation by Nazis
Bio: "William R. Perl," in: Wikipedia. See - https://en.wikipedia.org/wiki/William R. Perl; Rechcigl, Miloslav, Jr., "William R. Perl," in: Encyclopedia of Bohemian and Czech-American Biography Bloomington, IN: AuthorHouse, 2016, Vol. 2, p. 1120-1121.

Fredy Perlman (1934-1985), b. Brno, Czech.; publisher, educator, activist, anarchist, author
Bio: "Fredy Perlman," in: Wikipedia. See - https://en.wikipedia.org/wiki/Fredy Perlman; Rechcigl, Miloslav, Jr., "Fredy Perlman," in: *Encyclopedia of Bohemian and Czech-American Biography.* Bloomington, IN: AuthorHouse, 2016, Vol.2, pp. 1121-1122.

Paul W. Preisler (1902-1971), b. St. Louis, of Bohemian ancestry; biochemist, lawyer, photographer, union organizer, instrumental in getting teachers unionized
Bio: Rechcigl, Miloslav, Jr., "Paul W. Preisler," in: *Encyclopedia of Bohemian and Czech-American Biography.* Bloomington, IN: AuthorHouse, 2016, Vol. 1, pp. 89-90; "Preisler, Paul W.," in: Our Campaigns. See - https://www.ourcampaigns.com/CandidateDetail.html?CandidateID=158585

Daniel 'Dan' Samuel Senor (1971-), b. Utica, NY, of Slovak ancestry; columnist, writer, a Pentagon and White House adviser, foreign policy adviser to US presidential candidate Mit Romney
Bio: "Dan Senor," in: Wikipedia. See - https://en.wikipedia.org/wiki/Dan_Senor

Tom Stonier (1927-1999), b. Hamburg, Germany, of Moravian ancestry; biologist, information philosopher, professor of futurology, humanist
Bio: Rechcigl, Miloslav, Jr., "Tom Stonier," in: *Encyclopedia of Bohemian and Czech-American Biography.* Bloomington, IN: AuthorHouse, 2016, Vo. 2, 1124; "Tom Stonier," in Wikipedia. See - https://en.wikipedia.org/wiki/Tom Stonier

James Taussig (1827-1916), b. Prague, Bohemia; lawyer but also politician, St. Louis, most ardent supporter of the newly found Republican Party; presented to President Lincoln resolution for the abolition of slavery
Bio: Rechcigl, Miloslav, Jr. "James Taussig," in: *Encyclopedia of Bohemian and Czech-American Biography*. Bloomington, IN: AuthorHouse, 2016, Vol. 1, p. 370.

Zvi Weinberg (1935-2006), b. Brekov, Slovakia; politician, Zionist, advocate for peace in Middle East, educator
Bio: "Zvi Weinberg," in: Wikipedia. See - https://en.wikipedia.org/wiki/Zvi Weinberg

E. Canadian Politicians

Louis Marchand (orig. Levi Koopman) (1800-1881), b. Amsterdam, The Netherlands, of Jewish Bohemian ancestry; Canadian businessman and politician, Alderman and acting Mayor, Montreal
Bio: Rechcigl, Miloslav, Jr., "Louis Marchand," in: *Encyclopedia of Bohemian and Czech-American Biography*. Bloomington, IN: AuthorHouse, 2016, Vol. 1, p. 388.

Newman Leopold Steiner (1829-1903); b. Tachov, Bohemia; marble dealer, Alderman in Toronto of many years, Justice of the Peace, Honorary Commissioner of Pan-American Exposition in Buffalo
Bio: "Newman Leopold Steiner, Toronto," in: *The Newspaper Reference Book of Canada,* Toronto: Press Publishing Co., 1903, p. 472.

Maitland Steinkopf (1912-1970), b. Winnipeg, Manitoba, Canada, of Czech ancestry; Progressive conservative member of the Legislative Assembly of Manitoba, Cabinet minister
Bio: "Matland Steinkopf," in: Wikipedia. See - https://en.wikipedia.org/wiki/Maitland Steinkopf

F. Czech Politicians

Rita Klímová (1931-1993), b. Prague, Czech.; economist, politician, dissident, Czechoslovak Ambassador to the US
Bio: "Ria Klímová," in: Wikipedia, See - https://en.wikipedia.org/wiki/Rita Klímová; Rechcigl, Miloslav, Jr., "Rita Klímová," *in: Encyclopedia of Bohemian and Czech-American Biography.* Bloomington, IN: AuthorHouse, 2016, Vol. 1, p. 391.

Hynek Kmoníček (1962-), b. Pardubice, Czech.; diplomat. Czech Ambassador to the US
Bio: Rechcigl, Miloslav, Jr., "Hynek Kmoníček," in: *Encyclopedia of Bohemian and Czech-American Biography.* Bloomington, IN: AuthorHouse, 2016, Vol. 1, p. 407; "Hynek Kmoníček," in: Wikipedia. See - https://en.wikipedia.org/wiki/Hynek_Kmoníček

Michael Žantovský (1949-), b. Prague, Czech.; diplomat, Czech Ambassador to the US
Bio: "Michael Žantovský to lead VHL from September 2015," in: vaclav.havel-library.org. See- http://www.vaclavhavel-library.org/en/index/news/850/knihovnu-vaclava-havla-od-zari-povede-michael-zantovsky; "Michael Žantovský," in: Wikipedia. See - https://en.wikipedia.org/wiki/Michael Žantovský; Rechcigl, Miloslav, Jr., "Michael Žantovský," in: *Encyclopedia of Bohemian and Czech-American Biography.* Bloomington, IN: AuthorHouse, 2016, Vol. 1, pp. 396-397.

X. Cultural Contributions

A. General

Kisch, Guido, "Contributions of Czechoslovak Jews to American Civilization," *In Search of Freedom.* A History of American Jews from Czechoslovakia, 1592-1948. London: Edward Goldston, 1947, pp. 70-186, pp. 330-364.
Rechcigl, Miloslav, "Contributions of Bohemian Jews to America," in: *Beyond the Sea of Beer.* History of Immigration of Bohemians and Czechs to the New World. Bloomington, IN, 2017, pp. 738-767.
Rechcigl, Miloslav, Jr., "Bohemian and Czech American Jewish Hall of Fame.
Notable Individuals Who Made a Difference". Posted: academia.edu. See - https://www.academia.edu/32042292/Bohemian_and_Czech_Jewish_American_Hall_of_Fame.doc

B. Journalism & Publishing

1. General

Kisch, Guido, "Jewish Journalism and Publishing," in: *In Search of Freedom.* A History of American Jews from Czechoslovakia 1592-1948. London: Edward Goldston, 1948, pp. 97-102.
Kisch, Guido, "Israel's Herold: The First Jewish Weekly in New York," *Historia Judaica,* 2 (1940), p. 69.

2. Journalists

Margot Susanna Adler (1946-2014), b. Little Rock, AR, of Slovak ancestry; journalist, New York correspondent for National Public Radio (NPR)
Bio: "Margot Adler," in: Wikipedia. See - https://en.wikipedia.org/wiki/Margot_Adler

Meyer Berger (1898-1959), b. New York City, of Czechoslovak ancestry; journalist, reporter
Bio: Meyer M Berger," in: Wikipedia. See - https://en.wikipedia.org/wiki/Meyer Berger; "Meyer Berger, 60, of times is Dead, Reporter Got Pulitzer Prize in '50," *The New York Times,* February 9, 1959.

Shanik Berman (1959-), b. Mexico City, Mexico, of Slovak ancestry; Showbiz journalist, Mexico
Bio: "Shanik Berman," in: Wikipedia. See - https://en.wikipedia.org/wiki/Shanik Berman

Joseph Bondi (1804-1874), b. Dresden, of Bohemian ancestry; Rabbi, proprietor and editor of the Jewish paper, the *Hebrew Leader*
Bio: Rechcigl, Miloslav, Jr., "Joseph Bondi," in: *Encyclopedia of Bohemian and Czech-American Biography.* Bloomington, IN: AuthorHouse, 2016, Vol. 2, p. 1020.

(Oscar) Henry Brandon (1916-1993), b. Liberec, Bohemia; associate editor of *The Sunday Times,* columnist for the *New York Times* World syndicate
Bio: Rechcigl, Miloslav, Jr. "(Oscar) Henry Brandon," in: *Encyclopedia of Bohemian and Czech-American Biography.* Bloomington, IN: AuthorHouse, 2016, Vol. 2, p. 1021; Pace, Eric, "Henry Brandon, British Correspondent, Dies at 77," *The New York Times,* April 21, 1993.

Stanislav Budín (orig. Bencion Bat) (1903-1979), b. Kamenec Podolský; leftist journalist
Bio: "Stanislav Budin," in: Wikipedia. See - https://cs.wikipedia.org/wiki/Stanislav_ Budín

Isidor Bush (orig. Busch) (1822-1898), b. Prague, Bohemia; pioneer journalist, publisher of *Israel's Herald,* the first Jewish weekly in the US
Bio: Rechcigl, Miloslav, Jr., "Isidor Bush," in: Rechcigl, Miloslav, Jr., "Gustav Frisch," in: *Encyclopedia of Bohemian and Czech-American Biography.* Bloomington, IN: AuthorHouse, 2016, Vol. 2, p. 1020; Ehrlich, Walter, "Bush, Isidor (182-1898)" in: *Dictionary of Missouri Biography.* Ed. By Lawrence O. Christensen et al. Columbia and London: University of Missouri Press, 1999, pp. 138-140.

Hermann Bacher Deutsch (1889-1970), b. Most, Bohemia; journalist
Bio: Rechcigl, Miloslav, Jr., "Hermann Bacher Deutsch," in: *Encyclopedia of Bohemian and Czech-American Biography*. Bloomington, IN: AuthorHouse, 2016, Vol. 2, pp. 1020-1021; Hermann B. Deutsch Collection, Mss 8, Earl Long Library, University of New Orleans

Ignaz Eckstein (1873-1952), b. Pilsen, Bohemia; journalist
Bio: "Eckstein, Ignaz.," in: *Handbuch österreichischer Autorinnen und Autoren jüdischer Herkunft*. München: K. G. Saur, 2002, p. 244.

Julius Epstein (1901-1975), b. Vienna, of Czech ancestry; journalist and scholar, anti-communist researcher and critic of the Soviet Union
Bio: Rechcigl, Miloslav. Jr., "Julius Epstein," in: *Encyclopedia of Bohemian and Czech-American Biography*. Bloomington, IN: AuthorHouse, 2016, Vol. 2, p. 1021; "Julius Epstein," in: Wikipedia. See - https://en.wikipedia.org/wiki/Julius Epstein (author)

Emil Friend (orig. Freund) (1863-1921), b. Prague, Bohemia; journalist, with *Chicago News*, finance editor for *Chicago Examiner*, then *Herald Examiner*.
Bio: Rechcigl, Miloslav, Jr., "Emil Friend," in: *Encyclopedia of Bohemian and Czech-American Biography*. Bloomington, IN: AuthorHouse, 2016, Vol. 2, p. 1021; *The National Cyclopedia of American Biography*. New York: James T. White & Co., 1920, Vol. 17, pp, 64-65.

Gustav Frisch (1860-1941), b. Bohemia; brother of William Frisch; editor of *The Baltimore American*
Bio: Rechcigl, Miloslav, Jr., "Gustav Frisch," in: *Encyclopedia of Bohemian and Czech-American Biography*. Bloomington, IN: AuthorHouse, 2016, Vol. 2, p. 1022.

William Frisch (1854-1021), b. Bohemia; managing editor, *The Baltimore American*
Bio: "William Frisch," *American Jewish Year Book,* 24 (September 1922), pp. 109-218; Rechcigl, Miloslav, Jr., "William Frisch," in: *Encyclopedia of Bohemian and Czech-American Biography*. Bloomington, IN: AuthorHouse, 2016, Vol. 2, p. 1021.

Hana Gartner (1948-), b. Prague, Czech.; Canadian TV journalist
Bio: Rechcigl, Miloslav, Jr., "Hana Gartner," in: *Encyclopedia of Bohemian and Czech-American Biography*. Bloomington, IN: AuthorHouse, 2016, Vol. 2, p. 1036; "Hana Gartner," in: Wikipedia. See - https://en.wikipedia.org/wiki/Hana_Gartner

Francis J. Grund (1798-1863), b. Liberec, Bohemia; journalist
Bio: "Death of Francis J. Grund," *The New York Times*, October 2, 1863.

Jeff Jacoby (1959-), b. Cleveland, OH, of Czech ancestry; conservative journalist and syndicated newspaper columnist; with the *Boston Globe*
Bio: "Jeff Jacoby," in: Wikipedia. See - https://en.wikipedia.org/wiki/Jeff Jacoby (columnist); Rechcigl, Miloslav, Jr., "Jeff Jacoby," in: *Encyclopedia of Bohemian and Czech-American Biography*. Bloomington, IN: AuthorHouse, 2016, Vol. 2, p. 1023.

Robert Jungk (1913-1994), b. Berlin, Ger., of Bohemian ancestry; writer, journalist
Bio: "Robert Jungk," in: Wikipedia. See - https://en.wikipedia.org/wiki/Robert_Jungk; *International Biographical Dictionary of Central European Emigrés 1933-1945*. München: K. G. Saur, 1983, Vol. 2, p. 577.

Egon Kisch (1885-1948), b. Prague, Bohemia; journalist, writer
Bio: "Egon Kisch," in: Wikipedia. See - https://en.wikipedia.org/wiki/Egon Kisch

Edward V. Klauber (1887-1954), b. Louisville, KY, of Bohemian ancestry; reporter and editor, eventually executive V.P. of CBS
Bio: Rechcigl, Miloslav, Jr., "Edward V. Klauber," in: *Encyclopedia of Bohemian and Czech-American Biography*. Bloomington, IN: AuthorHouse, 2016, Vol. 2, p. 1038.

Max Knight (orig. Kuehnel) (1909-1993), b. Plzeň, Bohemia; journalist, writer
Bio: "Max Knight, Writer and Translator, 84," *The New York Times*, September 30, 1993; Rechcigl, Miloslav, Jr., "Max Knight," in: *Encyclopedia*

of Bohemian and Czech-American Biography. Bloomington, IN: AuthorHouse, 2016, Vol. 2, pp. 1024.

Anna Krommer (1924-), Dolný Kubín, Czech., of Moravian father, was a journalist
Bio: "Krommer, Anna," in: *International Biographical Dictionary of Central European Emigrés 1933-1945*. Műnchen: K. G. Saur, 1983, Vol. 2, p. 667.

Anton Kuh (1890-1941), b. Vienna, of Bohemian ancestry; Jewish journalist and essayist
Bio: "Anton Kuh," in: Wikipedia. See - https://de.wikipedia.org/wiki/ Anton Kuh; Rechcigl, Miloslav, Jr. "Anton Kuh" in: *Encyclopedia of Bohemian and Czech-American Biography*. Bloomington, IN: AuthorHouse, 2016, Vol. 2, p. 1033.

Arne Laurin (1889-1945), b. Hrnčíř, nr Prague, Bohemia; journalist, editor-in-chief of *Prager Presse,* head of index dept of the Czechoslovak Information Service, NYC
Bio: Rechcigl, Miloslav, Jr., "Arne Laurin," in: *Encyclopedia of Bohemian and Czech-American Biography*. Bloomington, IN: AuthorHouse, 2016, Vol. 2, p. 1025; "Arne Laurin," in: Wikipedia. See - https://en.wikipedia.org/wiki/ Arne Laurin.

Otto Leichter (1897-173), b. Vienna, of Moravian parents; journalist and essayist, Socialist
Bio: Rechcigl, Miloslav, Jr., "Oto Leichter," in: *Encyclopedia of Bohemian and Czech-American Biography*. Bloomington, IN: AuthorHouse, 2016, Vol. 2, p. 1033; "Otto Leichter," in: Wikipedia. See - https://de.wikipedia.org/ wiki/Otto_Leichter

Isidor Lewi (1850-1939), b. Albany, Ny, of Bohemian ancestry; journalist, with *The New York Tribune*
Bio: Rechcigl, Miloslav, Jr., "Isidor Lewi," in: *Encyclopedia of Bohemian and Czech-American Biography*. Bloomington, IN: AuthorHouse, 2016, Vol. 2, p. 1025; "Isidor Lewi Dead; Long a Journalist; Member of *Herald Tribune* Staff Was 88 and Had Been News Writer Since 1870 Covered the Chicago

fire; also Wrote of Historic River Packet Races—Saw Lincoln on Way to Inaugural," *The New York Times,* January 3, 1939.

David Loth (1899-1988), b. St. Louis, MO, of Moravian ancestry; journalist and author; with The New York World, one of the founders of the *Majorca Sun an Spanish Times*, on staff of The *New York Times*
Bio: Rechcigl, Miloslav, Jr., "David Loth," in: *Encyclopedia of Bohemian and Czech-American Biography.* Bloomington, IN: AuthorHouse, 2016, Vol. 2, p. 1025

Otto Lowy (1921-2002), b. Prague, Czech.; host of CBC Radio, Canada
Bio: "Otto Lowy," in: Wikipedia. See - https://en.wikipedia.org/wiki/Otto_Lowy

Donald T. 'Don' McNeill (1907-1996), b. Galena, Il, of Bohemian ancestry; American radio personality
Bio: Van Gelder, Lawrence, "Don McNeill, 'Breakfast Club' Host, Dies at 88," *The New York Times,* May 8, 1996; "Don McNeill (radio presenter)," in: Wikipedia. See - https://en.wikipedia.org/wiki/Don McNeill (radio presenter); Rechcigl, Miloslav, Jr., "Don McNeil," in: *Encyclopedia of Bohemian and Czech-American Biography.* Bloomington, IN: AuthorHouse, 2016, Vol. 2, p. 1040.

Michael 'Mike' Miller (1962-), b. New York, NY, of Czech mother; senior editor with *Wall Street Journal*, overseeing Features and WSJ Weekend
Bio: Rechcigl, Miloslav, Jr., "Michael 'Mike' Miller," in: *Encyclopedia of Bohemian and Czech-American Biography.* Bloomington, IN: AuthorHouse, 2016, Vol. 2, p. 1026.

Peter C. Newman (orig. Neuman) (1929-), b. Vienna, of Czech ancestry; Canadian journalist and writer
Bio: "Peter Charles Newman," in: The Canadian Encyclopedia. See - http://www.thecanadianencyclopedia.com/en/article/peter-charles-newman/

Oswald Ottendorfer (1826-1900), b. Svitavy, Moravia; co-publisher of *Staatszeitung* New York

Bio: Zeydel, Edwin H., "Ottendorfer, Oswald," in: *Dictionary of American Biography*. New York: Charles Scribner's Sons, 1962, Vol. 7, Part 2, p. 107

Barnet Phillips (1826-1905), b. Philadelphia, PA, of Bohemian ancestry; journalist, with *The New York Times*
Bio: Rechcigl, Miloslav, Jr., "Barnet Phillips," in: *Encyclopedia of Bohemian and Czech-American Biography*. Bloomington, IN: AuthorHouse, 2016, Vol. 2, p. 1028; Barnet Phillips Dies, ending a Busy Life; He Was Soldier, Traveler, Journalist, and Litterateur. Was Gen. Wheeler's Aide. Knew Many Illustrious Frenchmen — Had Been on the Staff of The Times for Thirty Years," The New York times, April 9, 1905.

Walter Rudolf Porges (1931-1999), b. Vienna, of Bohemian ancestry; radio news writer and editor, with ABC
Bio: Rechcigl, Miloslav, Jr., "Walter Rudolf Porges," in: *Encyclopedia of Bohemian and Czech-American Biography*. Bloomington, IN: AuthorHouse, 2016, Vol. 2, p. 1041.

Edward Rosewater (1841-1906), b. Bukovany, Bohemia; founder of the daily newspaper *The Omaha Daily Bee*
Bio: "Rosewater Family Papers, 1853-1940, Nebraska State Historical Society, Omaha, NE; "Edward Rosewater," in: Wikipedia. See - https://en.wikipedia.org/wiki/Edward_Rosewater

Victor S. Rosewater (1871-1940), b. Omaha, NE, of Bohemian ancestry, managing editor, *Omaha Bee,* politician
Bio: "Victor Rosewater," in: Wikipedia. See - https://en.wikipedia.org/wiki/Victor_Rosewater; "Rosewater, Victor," in JewishEncyclopedia.com. See: http://www.jewishencyclopedia.com/articles/12886-rosewater-victor

Joe Schlesinger (1928-), b. Vienna, of Czech ancestry, raised in Czechoslovakia; Canadian TV journalist and author
Bio: "Joe Schlesinger," in: Wikipedia. See - https://en.wikipedia.org/wiki/Joe Schlesinger; Rechcigl, Miloslav, Jr., "Joe Schlesinger," in: *Encyclopedia of Bohemian and Czech-American Biography*. Bloomington, IN: AuthorHouse, 2016, Vol. 2, pp. 1042-1043.

Sonja Sinclair (née Morawetz) (1921-), b. Světlá nad Sázavou, Czech.; Canadian journalist, freelancer for the CBC, *Time* magazine and the *Financial Post*
Bio: Rechcigl, Miloslav, Jr., "Sonja Sinclair," in: *Encyclopedia of Bohemian and Czech-American Biography*. Bloomington, IN: AuthorHouse, 2016, Vol. 2, p. 1029.

Rosa Sonneschein (1847-1932), b. Prostějov, Moravia; editor and publisher of the *American Jewess,* first English language periodical targeted at American Jewish women
Bio: Porter, Jack Nusan, "Rosa Sonneschein and *The American Jewess*: The First Independent English Language Jewish Women's Journal in the United States," *AJH,* 67 (September 1978), pp. 57–63, and "Rosa Sonneschein and *The American Jewess* Revisited: New Historical Information on an Early American Zionist and Jewish Feminist," AJA, 32 (1980), pp. 125–131.

Georg Stefan Troller (1921-), b. Vienna, of Moravian father; journalist, writer
Bio: Rechcigl, Miloslav, Jr., "Georg Stefan Troller," in: *Encyclopedia of Bohemian and Czech-American Biography*. Bloomington, IN: AuthorHouse, 2016, Vol. 2, p. 1034; "Georg Stefan Troller," in: Wikipedia. See - https://de.wikipedia.org/wiki/Georg Stefan Troller

Emil Gregory Steiner (1978-), b. West Philadelphia, Pa, of Czech ancestry; descendant of Holocaust survivors; novelist and journalist, investigative reporter, news blogger
Bio: Rechcigl, Miloslav, Jr., "Emil Gregory Steiner," in: *Encyclopedia of Bohemian and Czech-American Biography*. Bloomington, IN: AuthorHouse, 2016, Vol. 2, p. 1029.

Stanford J. Ungar (1945-), b. of Slovak ancestry; journalist, Dean at American University, President of Goucher College
Bio: "Stanford J. Ungar," in: Wikipedia. See - https://en.wikipedia.org/wiki/Sanford J. Ungar; "Sanford. J. Ungar, Goucher's 10th President," in Goucher College. See: http://www.goucher.edu/explore/who-we-are/history/gouchers-presidents/sanford-ungar

Henry J. Weidenthal (1870-1940), b. Cleveland, OH, of Bohemian ancestry; journalist, with *Cleveland World, the Leader, Plain Dealer*; publisher-editor of the *Jewish Independent*
Bio: Rechcigl, Miloslav, Jr., "Henry Weidenthal," in: *Encyclopedia of Bohemian and Czech-American Biography*. Bloomington, IN: AuthorHouse, 2016, Vol. 2, p. 1031.

Leo Weidenthal (1878-1967), b. Hostice, Bohemia; Editor of *Jewish Independent*
Bio: Rechcigl, Miloslav, Jr., "Leo Weidenthal," in: *Beyond the Sea of Beer.* Bloomington, IN AuthorHouse, 2017, p. 178, 749; Rechcigl, Miloslav, Jr., "Leo Weidenthal," in: *Encyclopedia of Bohemian and Czech-American Bio*graphy. Bloomington, IN: AuthorHouse, 2016, Vol. 1, p. 82 and Vol. 2, p. 1031.

Eric Weiser (1907-1986), b. Vienna, of Moravian father; medical journalist, publicist
Bio: "Eric Weiser,", in: Wikipedia. See - https://de.wikipedia.org/wiki/Eric Weiser

Adolf Wiesner (orig. Wiener) (1807-1867), b. Prague, Bohemia; trained as lawyer but was primarily involved as a journalist and author; editor of *Turn-Zeitung* (in Baltimore) and then *Illinois-Staatszeitung.*
Bio: Rechcigl, Miloslav, Jr., "Adolf Wiesner," in: *Encyclopedia of Bohemian and Czech-American Biography*. Bloomington, IN: AuthorHouse, 2016, Vol. 2, p. 1035; "Wiesner, Adolf," in: JewishEncyclopedia.com. See: http://www.jewishencyclopedia.com/articles/14912-wiesner-adolf

Isidor Wise (1894-1989), b. Cincinnati, OH, of Bohemian ancestry; journalist, associate editor of *American Israelite*
Bio: "Isidor Wise Dead; Writer and Associate Editor of *The American Israelite*," *The New York Times,* November 16, 1929; Rechcigl, Miloslav, Jr., "Isidor Wise," in: *Encyclopedia of Bohemian and Czech-American Bio*graphy. Bloomington, IN: AuthorHouse, 2016, Vol. 2, p. 1031,

3. Publishers

Charles E. Bloch (1861-1940), b. Cincinnati, OH, of Bohemian ancestry; president/owner, Bloch Publishing Co., NYC
Bio: "Deaths: Bloch, Charles E.," *The New York Times*, September 11, 2006.

Edward H. Bloch (1829-1906), b. Bohemia; founder of Bloch & Co., the first Jewish publishing house in the US
Bio: Singerman, Robert, "Bloch & Company: Pioneer Jewish Publishing House in the West," *Jewish Book Annual*, 52, pp. 110-30.

Jonas Bondi (1804-1874), b. Dresden, Ger., of Bohemian ancestry; Rabbi, editor, proprietor of the Jewish paper, *The Hebrew Leader*
Bio: Rechcigl, Miloslav, Jr., "Jonas Bondi," in: *Encyclopedia of Bohemian and Czech-American Biography*. Bloomington, IN: AuthorHouse, 2016, Vol. 2, pp. 996-997.

Steven Cohn (1949-), b. US., of Bohemian ancestry; director of Duke University Press
Bio: Rechcigl, Miloslav, Jt., "Steven Cohn," in: *Encyclopedia of Bohemian and Czech-American Biography*. Bloomington, IN: AuthorHouse, 2016, Vol. 2, p. 998; Mock, Geoffrey, "Cohn reappointed Director of Duke University Press," Working & Duke, April 9, 2014

Richard Charles Ernst (1915-1984), b. of Bohemian ancestry; founding director of the Atheneum Publishers, later also of Scribner Book Companies
Bio: Blair, William G., "Richard Ernst of Bloomingdale Unit is Dead," *The New York Times,* June 20, 1984; Rechcigl, Miloslav, Jr. "Richard C. Ernst," in: *Encyclopedia of Bohemian and Czech-American Biography*. Bloomington, IN: AuthorHouse, 2016, Vol. 1, p. 446.

Peter Fleischmann (1922-1993), b. New York, NY, of Moravian ancestry; president and chairman, of *The New Yorker* magazine
Bio: Lambert, Bruce, "Peter Fleischmann, 71, Who Led The New Yorker into the 1980's," *The New York Times,* April 18, 1993; Rechcigl, Miloslav, Jr., "Peter Fleischmann," in: *Encyclopedia of Bohemian and Czech-American*

Biography. Bloomington, IN: AuthorHouse, 2016, Vol. 2, p. 999; "Peter Fleischmann," in: Wikipedia. See - https://en.wikipedia.org/wiki/Peter_Fleischmann

Harold Kleinert Guinzburg (1899-1961), b. Prague, Bohemia; co-founder and the head of Viking Press
Bio: "Harold K. Guinzburg, 61, Dead; Co-Founder of the Viking Press," *The New York Times,* October 19, 1961; Rechcigl, Miloslav, Jr., "Harold Kleinert Guinzburg," in: *Encyclopedia of Bohemian and Czech-American Biography*. Bloomington, IN: AuthorHouse, 2016, Vol. 2, p. 1000.

Thomas H. Guinzburg (1926-2010), b. Manhattan, NY, of Bohemian ancestry; editor and publisher
Bio: Weber, Bruce, "Thomas Guinzburg, Paris Review Co-Founder, Dies at 84," *The New York Times*, September 10, 2010; "Thomas Guizburg," in: Wikipedia. See - https://en.wikipedia.org/wiki/Thomas Guinzburg

Ruth Sulzberger Holmberg (1921-2017), b. New York, NY, of Bohemian ancestry; publisher of *The Chattanooga Times*
Bio: "Obit: Ruth Holmberg," *Times Free Press,* April 24, 2017; McFadden, Robert D., "Ruth Sulzberger Holmberg, Newspaper Publisher born for the Job, dies at 96," *The New York Times*, April 19, 2017; Rechcigl, Miloslav, Jr., "Ruth Sulzberger Holberg," in: *Encyclopedia of Bohemian and Czech-American Biography*. Bloomington, IN: AuthorHouse, 2016, Vol. 2, p. 1001.

Benjamin W. Huebsch (1875-1964), b. New York, NY, of Slovak ancestry; publisher, NYC
Bio: "B. W. Huebsch," in: Wikipedia. See - https://en.wikipedia.org/wiki/B. W. Huebsch; Rechcigl, Miloslav, Jr., "Benjamin W. Huebsch," in: *Beyond the Sea of Beer*. History of Immigration of Bohemians and Czechs to the New World and their Contributions. Bloomington, IN: AuthorHouse, 2017, p. 776; *Dictionary of American Biography*, Suppl. 7, (1981), pp. 373-375.

Alexander Kaufman (1886-d.), b. Bardejov, Slovakia; Rabbi, editor, publisher, *The Jewish Voice*, St. Louis
Bio: *Who's Who in American Jewry*. New York: The Jewish Biographical Bureau, 1926, Vol. 1, p. 312.

Jonathan Marshall (1924-2008), b. of Bohemian ancestry; journalist, newspaper publisher and philanthropist
Bio: "Jonathan Marshall," in: Wikipedia. See - https://en.wikipedia.org/wiki/Jonathan Marshall; Gabrielson, Ryan, "Ex-Progress publisher Jonathan Marshall dies," *East Valley Tribune*, December 14, 2008; Rechcigl, Miloslav, Jr., "Jonathan Marshall," in: *Encyclopedia of Bohemian and Czech-American Biography*. Bloomington, IN: AuthorHouse, 2016, Vol. 2, p. 1002.

Joseph J. Pulitzer (1847-1911), b. Makó, Hungary, of Moravian ancestry; publisher, journalist, US Congressman
Bio: Morris, James McGrath, "The Political Education of Joseph Pulitzer," *Missouri Historical Review*, 104, No. 2 (Jan 2010), pp. 78–94; Morris, James MacGrath, *Pulitzer: A Life in Politics, Print and Power.* Harper Perennial, 2011. 592p.

Joseph Pulitzer, Jr. (1885-1955), b. New York, NY, of Moravian ancestry; editor and publisher of *St. Louis Post-Dispatch*
Bio: Rechcigl, Miloslav, Jr., "Joseph Pulitzer, Jr.," in: *Encyclopedia of Bohemian and Czech-American Biography*. Bloomington, IN: AuthorHouse, 2016, Vol. 2, p. 1003; "Joseph Pulitzer, Jr.," in: Wikipedia. See - https://en.wikipedia.org/wiki/Joseph Pulitzer Jr.;

Joseph Pulitzer, 3rd (1913-1993), b. St. Louis, MO, of Moravian ancestry; publisher, chairman of the Pulitzer Publishing Company, art collector
Bio: Hevesi, Dennis, Joseph Pulitzer Jr. Is Dead at 80; Publisher Was Avid Art Collector," *The New York Times*, May 27, 1993; Rechcigl, Miloslav, Jr., "Joseph Pulitzer 3rd," in: *Encyclopedia of Bohemian and Czech-American Biography*. Bloomington, IN: AuthorHouse, 2016, Vol. 2, p. 1003.

Ralph Pulitzer (1879-1939), b. St. Louis, MO, of Moravian ancestry; newspaper publisher and author, president of the Press Publishing Company, which published the *New York World* and the *Evening World*.
Bio: "Ralph Pulitzer," in: Wikipedia. See - https://en.wikipedia.org/wiki/Ralph Pulitzer; Rechcigl, Miloslav, Jr., "Ralph Pulitzer," in: *Encyclopedia of Bohemian and Czech-American Biography*. Bloomington, IN: AuthorHouse, 2016, Vol. 2, p. 1003.

Charles Coleman Rosewater (1874-1946), b. Omaha, NE, of Bohemian ancestry; manager, organizer and publisher of newspapers and magazines in Omaha, NE, Los Angeles, CA, Kansas City, KS, Seattle, WA and New York City.
Bio: Rechcigl, Miloslav, Jr., Charles Coleman Rosewater," in: *Encyclopedia of Bohemian and Czech-American Biography*. Bloomington, IN: AuthorHouse, 2016, Vol. 2, p. 1003.

Edward Rosewater (1841-1906), b. Bukovany, Bohemia; founder of the daily *The Omaha Bee*
Bio: Rechcigl, Miloslav, Jr., "Edward Rosewater," in: *Encyclopedia of Bohemian and Czech-American Biography*. Bloomington, IN: AuthorHouse, 2016, Vol. 2, pp. 1003-1004; "Edward Rosewater," in: Wikipedia. See - https://en.wikipedia.org/wiki/Edward_Rosewater

Isidore Singer (1859-1930), b. Hranice, Moravia; editor of twelve-volume authoritative Jewish Encyclopedia
Bio: Isidore Singer Papers, Manuscript Collection No. 42, American Jewish Archives, Cincinnati, OH; Rechcigl, Miloslav, Jr., "Isidore Singer," in: *Encyclopedia of Bohemian and Czech-American Biography*. Bloomington, IN: AuthorHouse, 2016, Vol. 2, p. 1004.

Arthur Gregg Sulzberger (1980-), b. Washington, DC, of Bohemian ancestry; journalist, publisher of *The New York Times*
Bio: "Arthur Gregg Sulzberger," in: Wikipedia, See - https://en.wikipedia.org/wiki/Arthur Gregg Sulzberger; A. G. Sulzberger, 37, to Take over as New York Times Publisher, *The New York T\times,* December 14, 2017

Arthur Ochs Sulzberger (1926-2012), of Bohemian ancestry; publisher of *The New York Times*
Bio: Diamond, Edwin, *Behind the Times: Inside the New York Times.* Villard Books; Jones, Alex S. and Susan E. Tifft, T*he Trust: The Private and Powerful Family Behind The New York Times.* Back Bay Books (2000); "Arthur Ochs Sulzberger," in: Wikipedia. See - https://en.wikipedia.org/wiki/Arthur Ochs Sulzberger

Arthur Ochs Sulzberger, Jr. (1951-), b. Mount Kisco, NY, of Bohemian ancestry; publisher of *The New York Times* and chairman of The New York Times Company
Bio: Rechcigl, Miloslav, Jr., "Arthur Ochs Sulzberger, Jr.," in: *Encyclopedia of Bohemian and Czech-American Biography*. Bloomington, IN: AuthorHouse, 2016, Vol. 2, p. 1004; "Arthur Ochs Sulzberger, Jr.," in: Wikipedia. See - https://en.wikipedia.org/wiki/Arthur_Ochs_Sulzberger_Jr.

Iphigene Ochs Sulzberger (1892-1990), b. Chattanooga, TN, of Bohemian ancestry; *New York Times* heiress, newspaper executive
Bio: Rechcigl, Miloslav, Jr., "Iphigene Ochs Sulzberger," in: *Encyclopedia of Bohemian and Czech-American Biography*. Bloomington, IN: AuthorHouse, 2016, Vol. 2, pp. 1004-1005; "Iphigene Sulzberger; New York Times Heiress," *Los Angeles Times,* February 27, 1990

Francis Brewster Taussig (1900-1970), b. Yonkers, NY, of Bohemian ancestry; publisher, president of Grolier International, Inc., publishers of encyclopedias and textbooks
Bio: Rechcigl, Miloslav, Jr., "Francis Brewster Taussig," in: *Encyclopedia of Bohemian and Czech-American Biography*. Bloomington, IN: AuthorHouse, 2016, Vol. 2, p. 1005; "Francis Taussig of Grolier Dead," *The New York Times,* May 26, 1970.

Maurice Weidenthal (1856-1917), b. Hostice, Bohemia; founder of *Jewish Independent Weekly,* editor of the *Plain Dealer,* Cleveland
Bio: "Maurice Weidenthal," in: A History of *Cleveland and its Environs.* Chicago and New York: Lewis Publishing Company, 1918, Vol. 2, p. 550; Rechcigl, Miloslav, Jr., "Maurice Weidenthal," in: *Encyclopedia of Bohemian and Czech-American Biography*. Bloomington, IN: AuthorHouse, 2016, Vol. 2, p. 1005.

Leo Wise (1849-1933), b. Albany, NY, son of Rabbi Isaac Mayer Wise; editor, publisher of the *Deborah* and of the *American Israelite*
Bio: Rechcigl, Miloslav, Jr., "Leo Wise," in: *Encyclopedia of Bohemian and Czech-American Biography*. Bloomington, IN: AuthorHouse, 2016, Vol. 2, p. 1005

4. Booksellers

Franz Bader (1903-1994), b. Vienna, of Moravian father; art gallery and bookstore owner
Bio: Smith, J. Y., "Franz Bader, Arts Figure in D.C., Dies," *The Washington Post,* September15, 1994; Rechcigl, Miloslav, Jr., "Franz Bader," in: *Encyclopedia of Bohemian and Czech-American Biography.* Bloomington, IN: AuthorHouse, 2016, Vol. 2, p. 1008.

Hans Peter Kraus (1907-1988), b. Vienna, of Bohemian father; a rare book dealer
Bio: Rechcigl, Miloslav, Jr., "Hans Peter Kraus," in: *Encyclopedia of Bohemian and Czech-American Biography.* Bloomington, IN: AuthorHouse, 2016, Vol. 2, p. 942; "Hans P. Kraus," in: Wikipedia. See - https://en.wikipedia.org/wiki/Hans P. Kraus; "H. P. Kraus, Internationally Prominent Rare Book Dealer," *AB Bookman's Weekly* (March 20, 1989), pp. 1284-1285; Saxon, Wolfgang, "Hans Peter Kraus, 81, Book Dealer and Collector," *The New York Times,* November 2, 1988.

Thomas Peter Kraus (1945-), b. Sutton, Surrey, England, of Bohemian ancestry; founder of Ursus Rare Books, Manhattan, NY
Bio: "Thomas Peter Kraus," in: Prabook. See - https://prabook.com/web/thomas_peter.kraus/1361657

5. Printers

Washington Flexner (1869-1942), b. Louisville, KY, of Bohemian father; founder of Lincoln Engraving and Printing Co.
Bio: Rechcigl, Miloslav, Jr., "Washington Flexner," in: *Encyclopedia of Bohemian and Czech-American Biography.* Bloomington, IN: AuthorHouse, 2016, Vol. 2, p. 1006.

6. Literary Agents

John Peter Riva (1950-), b. Manhattan, NY, of Bohemian ancestry; literary agent and producer of TV documentaries, co-founder of International Transactions, Inc.
Bio: "Peter Riva," in: Wikipedia. See - https://en.wikipedia.org/wiki/Peter Riva; Rechcigl, Miloslav, Jr., "John Peter Riva," in: *Encyclopedia of Bohemian and Czech-American Biography*. Bloomington, IN: AuthorHouse, 2016, Vol. 2, p. 800.

C. Librarianship

Pamela Bluh (1942-), b. Birmingham, England, of Moravian father; librarian, the John Hopkins and then University of Maryland Library
Bio: Rechcigl, Miloslav, Jr., "Pamela Bluh Van Oosten," in: *Encyclopedia of Bohemian and Czech-American Biography*. Bloomington, IN: AuthorHouse, 2016, Vol. 2, p. 1342.

Jewel Drickamer (orig. Weidenthal), (1917-20005), b. Cleveland, OH; librarian, pioneer in development of Rhode Islands' State library network
Bio: Rechcigl, Miloslav, Jr., "Jewel Drickamer," in: *Encyclopedia of Bohemian and Czech-American Biography*. Bloomington, IN: AuthorHouse, 2016, Vol. 2, pp. 1347-1348.

Jennie Maas Flexner (1882-1944), b. Louisville, KY, of Bohemian ancestry; pioneer librarian, New York Public Library
Bio: Rechcigl, Miloslav, Jr., Jennie Maas Flexner," in: *Encyclopedia of Bohemian and Czech-American Biography*. Bloomington, IN: AuthorHouse, 2016, Vol. 2, p. 1348.

Paul Horecky (1913-1999), b. Trutnov, Bohemia; librarian, Library of Congress
Bio: "Obituaries: Paul Horecky," *The Washington Post*, November 23, 1999.

Wilhelm Moll (1920-1979), b. Vienna, of Bohemian father; librarian
Bio: Rechcigl, Miloslav, Jr., "Wilhelm moll," in: *Encyclopedia of Bohemian and Czech-American Biography*. Bloomington, IN: AuthorHouse, 2016, Vol. 2, p. 1355.

Zdenka Műnzer (née Roubíčková) (1902-1986), b. Čelakovice, Bohemia; historian of art and architecture, librarian
Bio: Rechcigl, Miloslav, Jr., "Zdenka Műnzer (née Roubíčková," in: *Encyclopedia of Bohemian and Czech-American Biography*. Bloomington, IN: AuthorHouse, 2016, Vol. 2, p. 1356.

Irena Murray-Žantovská (1946-), b. Prague, Czech; architectural historian, curator, librarian, McGill University
Bio: Rechcigl, Miloslav, Jr. "Irena Žantovská-Murray," in: *Encyclopedia of Bohemian and Czech-American Biography*. Bloomington, IN: AuthorHouse, 2016, Vol. 2, p. 1356.

Adolf K. Placzek (1913-2013), b. Vienna, of Moravian ancestry; architectural librarian
Bio: "Adolf K. Placzek, former Avery Librarian, dies at 87," in: Columbia University Libraries, See - http://library.columbia.edu/news/libraries/2000/20000319 placzek.html; McDowell, Edwin, "Adolf K. Placzek, 87, is Dead; Architecture Library Director," *The New York Times*, March 21, 2000; Rechcigl, Miloslav, Jr., "Adolf K. Placzek," in: *Encyclopedia of Bohemian and Czech-American Biography*. Bloomington, IN: AuthorHouse, 2016, Vol. 2, p. 1357.

Felix Pollak (1909-1987), b. Vienna, of Bohemian ancestry; librarian, translator, poet
Bio: "Felix Pollak," in: Wikipedia. See - https://en.wikipedia.org/wiki/Felix_Pollak https://en.wikipedia.org/wiki/Felix Pollak; Rechcigl, Miloslav, Jr., "Felix Pollak," in: *Encyclopedia of Bohemian and Czech-American Biography*. Bloomington, IN: AuthorHouse, 2016, Vol. 2, pp. 1357-1358; Wallace, Ron, "In Memoriam: Felix Pollak," *Wisconsin Academy Review*, 34, No. 2 (March 1988), pp. 24-27.

Ruben Ernest Weltsch (1921-2011), b. Berlin, of Bohemian ancestry; librarian
Bio: Rechcigl, Miloslav, Jr., "Ruben Ernest Weltsch." In: *Encyclopedia of Bohemian and Czech-American Biography*. Bloomington, IN: AuthorHouse, 2016, Vol. 2, p. 1361.

Otto Wierer (1912-2001), b. Prague, Bohemia; librarian
Bio: Rechcigl, Miloslav, Jr., "Otto Wierer," in: *Encyclopedia of Bohemian and Czech-American Biography*. Bloomington, IN: AuthorHouse, 2016, Vol. 2, p. 1361.

D. Creative and Nonfiction Writing

1. General

Kisch, Guido, "Poetry," in: *In Search of Freedom*. A History of American Jews from Czechoslovakia 1592-1948. London: Edward Goldston, 1948, pp. 170-174.

2. Czech Language

Egon Hostovský (1908-1973), b. Hronov, Bohemia; popular Czech novelist
Bio: Vladimir Forst et al., *Lexikon české literatury: Osobnosti, díla, instituce*. Praha: Academia, 1993

Hedviga Margolius Kovály (née Bloch) (1919-2010), b. Prague, Czech.; writer, translator of notable German works to Czech
Bio: Rechcigl, Miloslav, Jr., "Hedviga Margolius Kovály," in: *Encyclopedia of Bohemian and Czech-American Biography*. Bloomington, IN: AuthorHouse, 2016, Vol. 2, pp. 986-987; Brown, Emma, "Heda Kovaly dies; Czech wrote movingly of persecution by Nazis and communists," *Washington Post*, December 12, 2010; "Heda Margolius Kovály," in: Wikipedia. See - https://en.wikipedia.org/wiki/Heda Margolius Kovály

George (Jiří) Kovtun (1927-2014); b. Horinčevo, Czech.; poet, prosaist, translator, publicist, librarian
Bio: Rechcigl Miloslav, Jr., "George Kovtun," in: *Encyclopedia of Bohemian and Czech-American Biography*. Bloomington, IN: AuthorHouse, 2016, Vol. 2, p. 972.

Arnošt Lustig (1926-2011), b. Prague, Bohemia; novelist, Holocaust writer
Bio: "Arnošt Lustig 1925-," *Contemporary Literary Criticism*, 56, pp. 181-190; Haman, Ales, "Man in a Violent World: The Fiction of Arnošt Lustig," *Kosmas,* 11, No. 1 (Summer 1992), pp. 73-80.; "Czech Jewish Writer Dies," *České noviny*, Czech News Agency, February 26, 2011; Tietjen, Jeanie, "Lustig, Arnošt," in: *The Routledge Encyclopedia of Jewish Writers of the Twentieth Century*. Ed. By Sorret Kerbel. New York-London: Fitzroy Dearborn, 2003, pp. 636-639.

Bronislava Volková (1946-); b. Děčín, Czech.; literary scholar, poet
Bio: Rechcigl, Miloslav, Jr., "Bronislava Volková," in: *Encyclopedia of Bohemian ad Czech-American Biography*. Bloomington, IN: AuthorHouse, 2016, Vol. 2, p. 979 and 1264; Rechcigl, Miloslav, Jr., "Bronislava Volková," in: *Beyond the See of Beer.* History of Immigration of Bohemians and Czechs to the New World and their Contributions. Bloomington, IN: AuthorHouse, 2017, p. 611 and 710-711; "Volková, Bronislava," in: encyclopedia.com. See - http://www.encyclopedia.com/arts/educational-magazines/volkova-bronislava-1946-bronislava-volkova

Joseph Winn (-1983), b. Poděbrady, Bohemia; psychiatrist, also Czech writer (pseud.: Alcantara) of short stories, aphorisms and commentaries
Bio: "Joseph Winn," in: Winn Family Collection. Leo Baeck Institute, NYC. See - http://findingaids.cjh.org/?pID=1624995; Rechcigl, Miloslav, Jr., "Joseph Alcantara Winn," in: *Encyclopedia of Bohemian ad Czech-American Biography*. Bloomington, IN: AuthorHouse, 2016, Vol. 3. P. 1992.

3. English Language

Barbara Adler, b. of Czech ancestry; Canadian Team Slam Champion, musician, poet
Bio: "Barbara Adler," in: Wikipedia. See - https://en.wikipedia.org/wiki/Barbara Adler

Richard James Appel (1963-), b. New York, NY, of Bohemian mother; writer, producer, a former attorney
Bio: "Richard Appel," in: https://en.wikipedia.org/wiki/Richard_Appel

Franzi Ascher-Nash (1910-1991), b. Vienna, of Moravian ancestry; freelance writer, poet
Bio: "Franzi Ascher-Nash: in: Prabook. See - https://prabook.com/web/franzi.ascher-nash/359042; Rechcigl, Miloslav, Jr., "Franzi Ascher-Nash," in: *Encyclopedia of Bohemian and Czech-American Biography*. Bloomington, IN: AuthorHouse, 2016, Vol. 2, pp. 946-947.

Vicki Baum (1888-1960), b. Vienna, of Moravian mother; famous novelist
Bio: "Vicki Baum," in: Wikipedia. See - https://en.wikipedia.org/wiki/Vicki_Baum

Anne Bernays (1930-), b. New York, NY, of Moravian ancestry; novelist
Bio: "Anne Bernays," in: *Jewish Women's Archive. Jewish Women: A Comprehensive Historical Encyclopedia.*

Louis James Block (1851-1927), b. Tachov, Bohemia; teacher, writer, poet, and lecturer
Bio: Rechcigl, Miloslav, Jr., "Louis James Bock," in: *Encyclopedia of Bohemian and Czech-American Biography*. Bloomington, IN: AuthorHouse, 2016, Vol. 2, p. 984.

Otto Eisenschiml (1880-1963), b. Vienna, of Bohemian father; chemist, but also Civil War historian and author
Bio: "Otto Eisenschiml," in: Spartacus Educational. See - http://spartacus-educational.com/USAeisenschiml.htm; Hanchett, William, "The Historian as Gamesman: Otto Eisenschiml, 1880-1963," in: Project

Muse. See - https://muse.jhu.edu/article/420534/pdf; Rechcigl, Miloslav, Jr., "Otto Eisenschiml," in: *Encyclopedia of Bohemian and Czech-American Biography*. Bloomington, IN: AuthorHouse, 2016, Vol. 2, p. 985.

Helen Epstein (1947-), b. Prague, Bohemia, author, co-author or translator of ten books of literary non-fiction
Bio: Rechcigl, Miloslav, Jr., "Helen Epstein," in: *Encyclopedia of Bohemian and Czech-American Biography*. Bloomington, IN: AuthorHouse, 2016, Vol. 2, p. 966; "Helen Epstein," in: Wikipedia. See - https://en.wikipedia.org/wiki/Helen_Epstein

Morris Leopold Ernst (1898-1976), b. Uniontown, NJ, of Bohemian ancestry; lawyer but also author
Bio: Rechcigl, Miloslav, Jr., "Morris Leopold Ernst.," in: *Encyclopedia of Bohemian and Czech-American Biography*. Bloomington, IN: AuthorHouse, 2016, Vol. 2, p. 985; "Morris Ernst,", in: Wikipedia. See - https://en.wikipedia.org/wiki/Morris_Ernst.

Joseph Fabry (orig. Epstein) (1909-1999), b. Vienna, of Bohemian father; writer
Bio: Rechcigl, Miloslav, Jr., "Joseph Fabry," in: *Encyclopedia of Bohemian and Czech-American Biography*. Bloomington, IN: AuthorHouse, 2016, Vol. 2, p. 949; "Joseph Fabry," in: Wikipedia. See - https://en.wikipedia.org/wiki/Joseph Fabry

Hortense Flexner (1885-1973), b. Louisville, KY, of Bohemian ancestry, writer, playwright, poet
Bio: Rechcigl, Miloslav, Jr., "Hortense Flexner," in: *Encyclopedia of Bohemian and Czech-American Biography*. Bloomington, IN: AuthorHouse, 2016, p. 981; "Hortense Flexner," in: Wikipedia. See - https://en.wikipedia.org/wiki/Hortense Flexner

James Thomas Flexner (1908-2003), b. New York, NY, of Bohemian ancestry; biographer and historian
Bio: Rechcigl, Miloslav, Jr., "James Thomas Flexner," in: *Encyclopedia of Bohemian and Czech-American Biography*. Bloomington, IN: AuthorHouse,

2016, Vol. 2, p. 966; "James Thomas Flexner," in: Wikipedia. See - https://en.wikipedia.org/wiki/James Thomas Flexner.

Regina 'Gina' Kaus (née Wiener) (1893-1985), b. Vienna, of Slovak ancestry; novelist, screenwriter
Bio: "Gina Kaus," in: Wikipedia. See - https://en.wikipedia.org/wiki/Gina_Kaus

Franz Kobler (1882-1965), b. Mladá Boleslav, Bohemia; attorney, but also a prolific writer
Bio: Rechcigl, Miloslav, Jr., "Franz Kobler," in: *Encyclopedia of Bohemian and Czech-American Biography*. Bloomington, IN: AuthorHouse, 2016, Vol. 2, pp. 985-986.

Frederick Kohner (1905-1986), b. Teplice-Šanov, Bohemia; novelist and screenwriter, best known for the "Gidget" novels
Bio: Rechcigl, Miloslav, Jr., "Frederick Kohner," in: *Encyclopedia of Bohemian and Czech-American Biography*. Bloomington, IN: AuthorHouse, 2016, Vol. 2, p. 982.; "Frederick Kohner," in: Wikipedia. See - https://en.wikipedia.org/wiki/Frederick_Kohner

Maxine Kumin (née Winokur) (1925-2014), b. Philadelphia, NA, of Bohemian ancestry; notable poet, novelist, essayist
Bio: "Kumin, Maxine," in: *American Poets*. Ed. Rosemary M. Canfield Reisman. 4th ed. Vol. 2. Pasadena, CA: Salem Press, 2011, pp. 1073-1083; Philip Schultz: "Postscript: Maxine Kumin (1925-2014)," *The New Yorker*, February 14, 2014; Maxine Kumin, *Inside the Halo and Beyond. The Anatomy of a Recovery*. New York: W. W. Norton & Co., 2000; Meg Schoerke, "On Maxine Kumin's Life and Career." *Modern American Poetry*. 2002. 24 February 2005.
1439 AHC Interview with Erika Ostrovsky.

Nathan Kussy (1872-1956), b. Newark, NJ, of Bohemian ancestry; lawyer, but also a writer
Bio: Rechcigl, Miloslav, Jr., "Nathan Kussy," in: *Encyclopedia of Bohemian and Czech-American Biography*. Bloomington, IN: AuthorHouse, 2016, Vol. 2, p. 953.

David Goldsmith Loth (1899-1988), b. St. Louis, MO, of Bohemian ancestry; author of many books
Bio: "David Loth, Author, 88," *The New York Tim*es, June 3, 1988.

Ernst Lothar (orig. Műller) (1890-1974), b. Brno, Moravia; writer, theatre director/manager and producer
Bio: "Ernst Lothar," in: Wikipedia. See - https://en.wikipedia.org/wiki/Ernst Lothar; Rechcigl, Miloslav, Jr., "Ernst Lothar," in: *Encyclopedia of Bohemian and Czech-American Biography*. Bloomington, IN: AuthorHouse, 2016, Vol. 2, p. 982.

Janet Malcolm (1934-), b. Prague, Czech; writer and journalist, with the *New Yorker* magazine
Bio: Rechcigl, Miloslav, Jr., "Janet Malcolm," in: *Encyclopedia of Bohemian and Czech-American Biography*. Bloomington, IN: AuthorHouse, 2016, Vol. 2, p. 987; "Janet Malcolm," in: Wikipedia. See - https://en.wikipedia.org/wiki/Janet_Malcolm

Lenore Guinzburg Marshall (1899-1971), b. New York City, of Bohemian ancestry; poet, novelist, archivist
Bio: "Lenore Marshall," in: Wikipedia. See - https://en.wikipedia.org/wiki/Lenore Marshall; "Lenore G. Marshall, 72, Dies, Was Poet, Novelist and Editor," *The New York Times*, September 25, 1971.

Sharona Muir (1957-), b. MA, of Slovak ancestry; writer, professor of creative writing at Bowling Green Univ.
Bio: Rechcigl, Miloslav, Jr., "Sharona Muir," in: *Encyclopedia of Bohemian and Czech-American Biography*. Bloomington, IN: AuthorHouse, 2016, Vol. 2, pp. 974-975; "Sharona Bentov Muir," in: Wikipedia. See - https://en.wikipedia.org/wiki/Sharona_Ben-Tov_Muir

Erika Ostrovsky (née Spielberg) (1926-2010), b. Bohemia, of Bohemian ancestry; professor of French, writer
Bio: Rechcigl, Miloslav, Jr., "Erika Ostrovsky," in: *Encyclopedia of Bohemian and Czech-American Biography*. Bloomington, IN: AuthorHouse, 2016, Vol. 2, pp. 987-988.

Ann S. Perlman (1919-2002), b. San Francisco, CA, of Bohemian ancestry, poet, newspaper reporter
Bio: "Anne S. Perlman — S.F. poet, journalist," *San Francisco Chronicle*, June 26, 2002.

Arthur Porges (1915-2006), b. Chicago, IL, of Bohemian ancestry; mystery and science fiction writer
Bio: "Porges, Arthur," in: SFE The Encyclopedia of Science Fiction, April 12, 2017. See: http://www.sf-encyclopedia.com/entry/porges arthur; "Arthur Porges," in: Wikipedia. See: https://en.wikipedia.org/wiki/Arthur Porges

Jonathan Rabb (1964-), b. Boston, MA, of Bohemian ancestry; novelist, essayist, writer and actor
Bio: "Jonathan Rabb," in: Wikipedia. See - https://en.wikipedia.org/wiki/Jonathan Rabb; Rechcigl, Miloslav, Jr., "Jonathan Rabb," in: *Encyclopedia of Bohemian and Czech-American Biography*. Bloomington, IN: AuthorHouse, 2016, Vol. 2, p. 956.

Charles C. Recht (1887-1965), b. Czech., lawyer, and writer
Bio: Rechcigl, Miloslav, Jr., "Charles C. Recht," in: *Encyclopedia of Bohemian and Czech-American Biography*. Bloomington, IN: AuthorHouse, 2016, Vol. 1, pp. 486-487 and Vol. 2, p. 956; "Recht, Charles," in: Who's Who in American Jewry, Vol. 1, p. 491.

Alexander Roda-Roda (orig. Šandor Friedrich Rosenfeld) (1872-1945), b. Drnovice, Moravia; writer
Bio: Rechcigl, Miloslav, Jr., "Alexander Roda-Roda", in: *Encyclopedia of Bohemian and Czech-American Biography*. Bloomington, IN: AuthorHouse, 2016, Vol. 2, p. 964; "Alexander Roda-Roda," in: Wikipedia. See - https://en.wikipedia.org/wiki/Alexander_Roda_Roda

Michael Salcman (1946-), b. Pilsen, Czech.; poet and physician
Bio: "Michael Salcman," in: Wikipedia. See - https://en.wikipedia.org/wiki/Michael Salcman; Rechcigl, Miloslav, Jr., "Michael Salcman," in: *Encyclopedia of Bohemian and Czech-American Biography*. Bloomington, IN: AuthorHouse, 2016, Vol. 2, p. 976.

Roger L. Simon (1943-), b. New York, NY, of Bohemian ancestry; novelist and Academy Award-nominated screenwriter
Bio: Rechcigl, Miloslav, Jr., "Roger L. Simon," in: *Encyclopedia of Bohemian and Czech-American Biography.* Bloomington, IN: AuthorHouse, 2016, Vol. 2, p. 983; "Roger l. Simon," in: Wikipedia. See - https://en.wikipedia.org/wiki/Roger L. Simon

Mark Strand (orig. Stransky) (1934-2014), b. Summerside, Prince Edward Island, Canada, of Czech ancestry; poet, essayist, translator
Bio: "Mark Strand," in: Wikipedia. See - https://en.wikipedia.org/wiki/Mark Strand' Rechcigl, Miloslav, Jr., "Mark strand," in: *Encyclopedia of Bohemian and Czech-American Biography.* Bloomington, IN: AuthorHouse, 2016, Vol. 2, p. 977.

Joseph Wechsberg (1907-1983), b. Ostrava, Moravia; free-lance writer
Bio: "Joseph Wechsberg," *Current Biography Yearbook* 1955, pp. 638-640; Wechsberg, Joseph, *Homecoming.* New York: Alfred Knopf, 1946. 117p.; Wechsberg, Joseph, *Looking for a Bluebird.* Westport, CT: Greenwood Press, 1974. 210.

Helen Waldstein Wilkes (1936-), b. Czechoslovakia; professor of French, author of prize-winning *Letters from the Lost: A Memoir of Discovery*
Bio: Rechcigl, Miloslav, Jr., "Helen Waldstein Wilkes," in: *Encyclopedia of Bohemian and Czech-American Biography.* Bloomington, IN: AuthorHouse, 2016, Vol. 2, p. 989.

Lawrence Weschler (1952-), b. Van Nuys, CA, of Moravian ancestry; longtime staffer at *The New Yorker,* author of works of creative nonfiction, distinguished writer in residence at the Carter Journalism Institute
Bio: "Lawrence Weschler," The Transom Review, Vol. 4, Issue 3 (October 2004); "Lawrence Weschler," in: Wikipedia. See - https://en.wikipedia.org/wiki/Lawrence_Weschler

Marie Winn (1936-), b. Prague, Czech; journalist, author, bird-watcher
Bio: "Marie Winn," in: Wikipedia. See - https://en.wikipedia.org/wiki/Marie Winn; Rechcigl, Miloslav, Jr., "Marie Winn," in: *Encyclopedia of*

Bohemian and Czech-American Biography. Bloomington, IN: AuthorHouse, 2016, Vol. 2, pp. 989-990.

James Waterman Wise (1902-1983), b. Portland, OR, of Czechoslovak ancestry; author and art dealer
Bio: "James W. Wise, 81; Author and Lecturer Warned of the Nazis," *The New York Times,* November 30, 1983; Rechcigl, Miloslav, Jr., "James Waterman Wise," in: *Encyclopedia of Bohemian and Czech-American Biography*. Bloomington, IN: AuthorHouse, 2016, Vol. 2, p. 990.

Martha Wolfenstein (1869-1906), b. Insterburg, Prussia, of Moravian ancestry; essayist, short story teller and publicist
Bio: Sarna, Jonathan D, "Martha Wolfenstin," in: Jewish Women's' Archive. See - https://jwa.org/encyclopedia/article/wolfenstein-martha; Rechcigl, Miloslav, Jr., "Martha Wolfenstein," in: *Encyclopedia of Bohemian and Czech-American Biography*. Bloomington, IN: AuthorHouse, 2016, Vol. 2, p. 960.

4. German Language

Paul Amann (1884-1958), b. Prague, Bohemia; poet
Bio: Rechcigl, Miloslav, Jr., "Paul Amann," in: *Encyclopedia of Bohemian and Czech-American Biography*. Bloomington, IN: AuthorHouse, 2016, Vol. 2, p. 968.

Richard Beer-Hofmann (1866-1945), b. Vienna, of Moravian parents; novelist, dramatist, poet
Bio: Rechcigl, Miloslav, Jr., "Richard Beer-Hofmann," in: *Encyclopedia of Bohemian and Czech-American Biography*. Bloomington, IN: AuthorHouse, 2016, Vol. 2, pp. 961-962; Beer-Hofmann, Richard," in: *International Biographical Dictionary of Central European Emigrés 1933-1945*. Műnchen: K. G. Saur, 1983, Vol. 2, p. 69.

Paul Elbogen (1894-1987), b. Vienna, of Bohemian ancestry; writer, Canada
Bio: "Paul Elbogen," in: *Handbuch österreichischer Autorinnen und Autoren jüdischer Herkunft*. Műnchen: K. G. Saur, 2002, p. 272.

Oskar Benjamin Frankl (1881-1955), b. Kroměříž, Moravia; free-lance writer, broadcaster
Bio: Frankl, Oskar Benjamin," in: *International Biographical Dictionary of Central European Emigrés 1933-1945.* Műnchen: K. G. Saur, 1983, Vol. 2, p. 321.

Anna Antoinette Fried (née Politzer), b. Vienna, of Moravian ancestry; writer
Bio: Rechcigl, Miloslav, Jr., "Anna Antoinette Fried," in: *Encyclopedia of Bohemian and Czech-American Biography.* Bloomington, IN: AuthorHouse, 2016, Vol. 2, pp. 949-950.

Heinrich Glűcksmann (1864-1947), b. Rakšice, Moravia; Argentine writer
Bio: "Heinrich Glűcksmann," in: Wikipedia. See - https://en.wikipedia.org/wiki/Heinrich_Gl%C3%BCcksmann

Oskar Jellinek (1886- 1949), b. Brno, Moravia; lawyer, free-lance writer, short story teller
Bio: Rechcigl, Miloslav, Jr., "Oskar Jellinek," in: *Encyclopedia of Bohemian and Czech-American Biography.* Bloomington, IN: AuthorHouse, 2016, Vol. 2, p. 952.

Peter Stephan Jungk (1952-), b. Santa Monica, CA, of Bohemian ancestry; free-lance writer, novelist
Bio: Rechcigl, Miloslav, Jr., "Peter Stephen Jungk," in: *Encyclopedia of Bohemian and Czech-American Biography.* Bloomington, IN: AuthorHouse, 2016, Vol. 2, p. 962; "Peter Stephan Jungk," in: Wikipedia. See - https://en.wikipedia.org/wiki/Peter Stephan Jungk.

Richard Katz (1888-1968), b. Prague, Bohemia; journalist, a travel writer and essayist, Brazil
Bio: Rechcigl, Miloslav, Jr., "Richard Katz," in: *Encyclopedia of Bohemian and Czech-American Biography.* Bloomington, IN: AuthorHouse, 2016, Vol. 2, pp. 962-963; "Richard Katz," in: Wikipedia. See - https://en.wikipedia.org/wiki/Richard_Katz

Gina Kaus (née Regina Wiener) (1893-1985), b. Vienna, of Slovak ancestry; novelist, screenwriter
Bio: "Gina Kaus," in: Wikipedia. See - https://en.wikipedia.org/wiki/Gina Kaus

Margarette Kollisch (née Moller) (1893-1979), b. Vienna, of Bohemian father; writer and poet
Bio: Rechcigl, Miloslav, Jr. "Margarette Kollisch," in: *Encyclopedia of Bohemian and Czech-American Biography*. Bloomington, IN: AuthorHouse, 2016, Vol. 2, pp. 971-972.

Louise Herschmann Mannheimer (1845-1920), b. Prague, Bohemia; writer, poet, teacher, school founder, inventor, Cincinnati
Bio: "Mannheimer, Louise Herschmann," in: *European Immigrant Women in the United States. A Biographical Dictionary*. Edited by Judy Barrett Litoff and Judith McDonnel. New York-London: Garland Publishing, 1994, pp. 185-186; "Louise Herschmann Mannheimer," in: Wikipedia. See - https://en.wikipedia.org/wiki/Louise_Herschman_Mannheimer

Hans Natonek (1892-1963), b. Vinohrady, Prague, Bohemia; writer and journalist
Bio: Natonek, Hans, *In Search of Myself*. New York: G. P. Putnam's Sons, 1943. 261p.

Felix Pollak (1909-1987), b. Vienna, of Moravian ancestry; librarian, translator, poet
Bio: Ron Wallace, "In Memoriam: Felix Pollak," *Wisconsin Academy Review*, Vol. 34, No. 2 (March 1988), pp. 24-27; *International Biographical Dictionary of Central European Emigrés 1933-1945*. Műnchen: K. G. Saur, 1983, Vol. 2, p. 916.

Alexander Roda-Roda (orig. Šandor Friedrich Rosenfeld) (1872-1945), b. Drnovice, Moravia; writer, dramatist and novelist
Bio: Rechcigl, Miloslav, Jr., "Alexander Roda-Roda," in: *Encyclopedia of Bohemian and Czech-American Biography*. Bloomington, IN: AuthorHouse, 2016, Vol. 2, p. 964; "Alexander Roda-Roda," in: Wikipedia. See - https://en.wikipedia.org/wiki/Alexander_Roda_Roda

Alice Rűhle-Gerstel (1894-1943), b. Prague, Bohemia; writer, feminist and psychologist, Mexico
Bio: Rechcigl, Miloslav, Jr., "Alice Rűhle-Gerstel," in: *Encyclopedia of Bohemian and Czech-American Biography*. Bloomington, IN: AuthorHouse, 2016, Vol. 2, p. 964; "Alice Rűhle-Gerstel," in: Wikipedia. See - https://en.wikipedia.org/wiki/Alice_R%C3%BChle-Gerstel

Erich Fritz Schweinburg (1890-1958), b. Mikulov, Moravia; novelist, short story teller, attorney
Bio: Rechcigl, Miloslav, Jr., "Erich Fritz Schweinburg," in: *Encyclopedia of Bohemian and Czech-American Biography*. Bloomington, IN: AuthorHouse, 2016, Vol. 2, pp. 964-965; "Erich Fritz Schweinburg," in: Wikipedia. See - https://en.wikipedia.org/wiki/Erich Fritz Schweinburg

Kurt Singer (orig. Deutsch) (1911-2005), b. Vienna, of Bohemian ancestry; publicist, novelist, biographer, spy
Bio: Rechcigl, Miloslav, Jr., "Kurt Singer," in: *Encyclopedia of Bohemian and Czech-American Biography*. Bloomington, IN: AuthorHouse, 2016, Vol. 2, pp. 966-967; "Kurt D. Singer," in: Wikipedia. See - https://de.wikipedia.org/wiki/Kurt_D._Singer

Peter Spielberg (1929-), b. Bohemia, of Bohemian ancestry; professor of English, writer:
Bio: "Peter Spielberg: in: Rechcigl, Miloslav, Jr., *Encyclopedia of Bohemian and Czech American Biography*. Bloomington, IN: AuthorHouse, 2016, Vol. 2, pp. 958 and p. 1235.

Friedrich Torberg (1908-1979); b. Vienna, of Bohemian ancestry; writer
Bio: Wikipedia. See - https://en.wikipedia.org/wiki/Friedrich Torberg; Rechcigl, Miloslav, Jr., "Friedrich Torberg," in: *Encyclopedia of Bohemian and Czech-American Biography*. Bloomington, IN: AuthorHouse, 2016, Vol. 2, p. 965.

Johannes Urzidil (1896-1970), b. Prague, Bohemia; writer, poet, historian
Bio: Rechcigl, Miloslav, Jr., "Johannes Urzidil," in: *Encyclopedia of Bohemian and Czech-American Biography*. Bloomington, IN: AuthorHouse, 2016, Vol.

2, p. 965; "Johannes Urzidil," in: Wikipedia. See - https://en.wikipedia.org/wiki/Johannes_Urzidil

Franz Weiskopf (1900-1955), b. Prague, Bohemia; writer
Bio: "Weiskopf, Franz," in: *Twentieth Century Authors*, Suppl. 1, pp. 1059-1060; "Franz Werfel," in: Wikipedia. See: https://en.wikipedia.org/wiki/Franz_Carl_Weiskopf

Franz Werfel (1890-1945), b. Prague, Bohemia; novelist, poet, playwright, essayist
Bio: Fox, W. H., "Franz Werfel," in: *German Men of Letters*. Ed Alex Natan. Wolff, 1964, pp. 107-125; Jungk, Peter Stephan, *Franz Werfel: A Life in Prague, Vienna, & Hollywood*." New York: Grove Weidenfeld, 1990. 318p.; *Franz Werfel, 1890-1945*. Ed. Lore Barbara Foltin. Pittsburgh: University of Pittsburgh Press, 1961. 102 p.' "Franz Werfel," in: Wikipedia. See: https://en.wikipedia.org/wiki/Franz Werfel

Otto Zoff (1890-1963), b. Prague, Bohemia; author, script writer, dramaturge, journalist
Bio: Keller, Ulrike, *Otto Zoffs dramatische Werke: vom Theater zum Hörspiel*. München 1988; 'Otto Zoff," in: Wikipedia. See: https://de.wikipedia.org/wiki/Otto_Zoff; *International Biographical Dictionary of Central European Emigrés 1933-1945*. Műnchen: K. G. Saur, 1983, Vol. 2, p. 1281.

Friderike Maria Zweig (1882-1971), b. Vienna, of Bohemian ancestry; writer
Bio: Zohn, Harr, *Liber Amicorum – Friderike Maria Zweig. In Honor of her Seventieth Birthday*. Dahl. Stamford, 1952; "Friderike Maria Zweig," in: Wikipedia. See: https://de.wikipedia.org/wiki/Friderike_Maria_Zweig; *International Biographical Dictionary of Central European Emigrés 1933-1945*. Műnchen: K. G. Saur, 1983, Vol. 2, p. 1287.

Stefan Zweig (1881-1942), b. Vienna, of Bohemian ancestry; biographer, essayist, short story teller, Brazil
Bio: Rechcigl, Miloslav, Jr., "Stefan Zweig," in: *Encyclopedia of Bohemian and Czech-American Biography*. Bloomington, IN: AuthorHouse, 2016, Vol. 2,

pp. 967-968; "Stefan Zweig," in: Wikipedia. See - https://en.wikipedia.org/wiki/Stefan Zweig

5. Spanish Language

Alejandra (Flora) Pizarnik (1936-1972), b. Avellaneda, Argentina, of Slovak ancestry; Argentine poet
Bio; "Alejandra Pizarnik,", in: Wikipedia. See - https://en.wikipedia.org/wiki/Alejandra_Pizarnik

E. Music

1. General

Fischmann, Zdenka, Jewish Musicians with Roots in Czechoslovakia. *Rev. Soc. Hist. Czechoslovak Jews,* 3 (190-91), p. 193-217.
Kisch, Guido, "Music," in: *In Search of Freedom.* A History of American Jews from Czechoslovakia 1592-1948. London: Edward Goldston, 1948, pp. 166-170.
Lowenbach, Jan, "Composers and Musicians in America," *The Musical Quarterly* 29, No. 3 (July 1943), pp. 313-328.

2. Composers

Leo Ascher (1880-1942), b. Vienna, of Moravian ancestry; composer of operettas, popular songs and film scores
Bio: "Leo Ascher," in: Wikipedia. See - https://en.wikipedia.org/wiki/Leo Ascher

Ralph Benatzky (1884-1957), b. Moravské Budějovice, Moravia; composer
Bio: "Ralph Benatzky," in: Wikipedia. See - https://en.wikipedia.org/wiki/Ralph Benatzky; *Handbuch österreichischer Autorinnen und Autoren jüdischer Herkunft.* München: S. G. Saur, 2002, p.92.

Frederick Brandeis (1832-1899), b. Vienna, of Bohemian ancestry; pianist and accompanist, composer
Bio: Rechcigl, Miloslav, Jr., "Frederick Brandeis," in: *Encyclopedia of Bohemian and Czech-American Biography*. Bloomington, IN: AuthorHouse, 2016, Vol 1, p. 549.

Hanns Eisler (1898-1962), b. Leipzig, Saxony, of Bohemian ancestry; composer
Bio: "Hanns Eisler," in: Wikipedia. See - https://en.wikipedia.org/wiki/Hanns_Eisler

Richard Fall (1882-1943), b. Jevíčko, Moravia, was a composer of operettas and popular songs
Bio: Richard Fall," in: Wikipedia. See: https://de.wikipedia.org/wiki/Richard Fall; *International Biographical Dictionary of Central European Emigrés 1933-1945*. Műnchen: K. G. Saur, 1983, Vol. 2, p. 281.

Rudolf Friml (1879-1972), b. Prague, Bohemia; composer of operettas, musicals, songs and piano pieces, as well as a pianist
Bio: Ewen, David, "Friml, Rudolf," in: *Complete Book of the American Musical Theater*. Holt, 1958, pp. 91-97; Paris, Leonard Allen, "Friml, Rudolf," in: *Man and Melodies*. Crowell, 1959, pp. 49-58; Green, Stanley, "Rudolf Friml 1879-1972," in: *World of Musical Comedy*. 3rd ed. New York: Barnes, 1974, pp. 37-47; Everett, William, *Rudolf Friml*. Champaign, IL: University of Illinois Press, 2008. 152p.

William Friml (1921-1973), b. New York, NY; of Bohemian father; composer and writer
Bio: Rechcigl, Miloslav, Jr., "William Friml," in: *Encyclopedia of Bohemian and Czech-American Biography*. Bloomington, IN: AuthorHouse, 2016, Vol 1, p. 553.

Herschel Garfein (1958-), b. New York, NY, of Czech ancestry; Grammy Award-winning composer, librettist, stage director. Teacher
Bio: "Herschel Garfein," in: Wikipedia. See - https://en.wikipedia.org/wiki/Herschel Garfein' Rechcigl, Miloslav, Jr., "Herschel Garfein," in:

Encyclopedia of Bohemian and Czech-American Biography. Bloomington, IN: AuthorHouse, 2016, Vol 1, p. 553.

Marvin Frederick Hamlisch (1944-2012), b. Manhattan, NY, of Bohemian ancestry; composer, conductor
Bio: Hamlisch, Marvin, *The Way I Was*. Scribner, 1992; "Marvin Hamlisch," in: Wikipedia. See- https://en.wikipedia.org/wiki/Marvin Hamlisch

James Gutheim Heller (1892-1971), b. New Orleans, LA, of Bohemian ancestry; Rabbi, composer
Bio: Rechcigl, Miloslav, Jr., "James Gutheim Heller," in: *Encyclopedia of Bohemian and Czech-American Biography*. Bloomington, IN: AuthorHouse, 2016, Vol 1, p. 554.

James Horner (1953-2015), b. Los Angeles, CA, of Bohemian ancestry; composer, conductor, orchestrator
Bio: "James Horner," in: Wikipedia. See - https://en.wikipedia.org/wiki/James Horner; Rechcigl, Miloslav, Jr., "James Roy Horner," in: *Encyclopedia of Bohemian and Czech-American Biography*. Bloomington, IN: AuthorHouse, 2016, Vol 1, p. 5.

Alfred Hugo Kauder (1888-1972), b. Tovačov, Moravia; composer, violin teacher, conductor
Bio: "Hugo Kauder," in: Wikipedia. See: https://en.wikipedia.org/wiki/Hugo_Kauder; *International Biographical Dictionary of Central European Emigrés 1933-1945*. Műnchen: K. G. Saur, 1983, Vol. 2, p. 603-604.

Walter Kaufmann (1907-1984), b. Karlovy Vary, Bohemia; composer, conductor, musicologist, and educator
Bio: "Walter Kaufmann," in: Wikipedia. See - https://en.wikipedia.org/wiki/Walter_Kaufmann_(composer)

Jerome Kern (1885-1945) (1885-1945), b. New York City, of Bohemian ancestry; composer of musical theatre and popular music
Bio: - Banfield, Stephen and Geoffrey Holden Block, *Jerome Kern*, New Haven, Connecticut, Yale University Press, 2006; Bordman, Gerald, *Jerome*

Kern: his Life and Music. New York, 1980; Fordin, Hugh, *Jerome Kern: The Man and his Music.* Santa Monica, CA, 1975;
Freedland, M. *Jerome Kern: A Biography.* London, 1978.

Erich W. Korngold (1897-1957), b. Brno, Moravia; composer, conductor
Bio: Brendan G. Carroll, *The Last Prodigy. A Biography of Erich Wolfgang Korngold.* Portland, OR: Amadeus Press, 1997; Hoffmann, Rudolf Stephan, *Erich Wolfgang Korngold.* Wien: C. Stephenson, 19122. 129p.

Georg Kreisler (1922-2011), b. Vienna, of Slovak ancestry; cabarettist, satirist, composer, songwriter
Bio: "George Kreisler," in: Wikipedia. See - https://en.wikipedia.org/wiki/Georg_Kreisler

Gustav Mahler (1860-1911, b. eastern Bohemia; composer, conductor
Bio: Carr, Jonathan, *Mahler: A Biography.* Woodstock, NY: The Overlook Press, 1998; Fischer, Jens Malte (trans. Stewart Spencer), *Gustav Mahler.* New Haven, Connecticut: Yale University Press, 2011; Mitchell, Donald; Nicholson, Andrew (1999). *The Mahler Companion.* Oxford, England: Oxford University Press, 1999; "Gustav Mahler," in: Wikipedia. See: https://en.wikipedia.org/wiki/Gustav_Mahler

Oskar Morawetz (1917-2007), b. Světlá nad Sázavou, Bohemia, Canadian composer
Bio: "Oskar Morawetz," in: Wikipedia. See: https://en.wikipedia.org/wiki/Oskar Morawetz

Paul Amadeus Pisk (1893-1990), b. Vienna, of Moravian ancestry; composer, musicologist
Bio: "Paul Pisk" in: Wikipedia. See: https://en.wikipedia.org/wiki/Paul_Pisk; *International Biographical Dictionary of Central European Emigrés 1933-1945.* Műnchen: K. G. Saur, 1983, Vol. 2, p. 908-909.

Jan Popper (1907- 1987), b. Liberec, Bohemia; conductor
Folkart, Burt A., "Was Teacher, Lecturer and Conductor: Opera Devotee Jan Popper Dies at 79," *Los Angeles Times*, September 3, 1987

Alfred Eduard Emmerich Rosé (1902-1975), b. Vienna, of Bohemian mother; composer conductor
Bio: Rechcigl, Miloslav, Jr., "Alfred Eduard Emmerich Rosé," in: *Encyclopedia of Bohemian and Czech-American Biography*. Bloomington, IN: AuthorHouse, 2016, Vol 1, p. 561.

Felix Salzer (1904-198), b. Vienna (probably), of Bohemian ancestry; music theorist, musicologist
Bio: "Felix Salzer," in: Wikipedia. See - https://en.wikipedia.org/wiki/Felix_Salzer

Hans A. Schimmerling (1900-1967), b. Brno, Moravia; pianist, composer, teacher, musicologist
Bio: Cooper, Stuart Richard, "Hans Schimmerling: Pianist, Composer, Teacher," *Stammbaum, The Journal of German-Jewish Genealogical Research,* No. 23, Summer 200; "Hans Schimmerling," in Wikipedia. See - https://en.wikipedia.org/wiki/Hans_Schimmerling

Arnold Schoenberg (1874-1951), b. Vienna, of Bohemian ancestry; composer, music theorist, and painter
Bio: Rosen, Charles, *Arnold Schoenberg.* Chicago: University of Chicago Press, 1996. 128p.; Shawn, Allen, *Arnold Schoenberg's Journey.* New York: Farrar Straus and Giroux, 2002; Rechcigl, Miloslav, Jr., "Skladatel, který zvěčnil Švandu dudáka" (Composer who Eternized Schwanda the Piper), in: *Postavy naší Ameriky.* Praha: Pražská edice, 2000, pp. 205-206; "Arnold Schoenberg," in: Wikipedia. See: https://en.wikipedia.org/wiki/Arnold Schoenberg

Frederick William Sternberg (1914-1994), b. Vienna, of Bohemian ancestry; musicologist
Bio: Rechcigl, Miloslav, Jr., "Frederick, William Sternberg," in: *Encyclopedia of Bohemian and Czech-American Biography.* Bloomington, IN: Author.House, 2016, Vol 1, p. 708.

Robert E. Stolz (1880-1975), b. Graz, of Bohemian ancestry; songwriter, conductor, composer of operettas and film music
Bio: Rechcigl, Miloslav, Jr., "Robert E. Stolz," in: *Encyclopedia of Bohemian and Czech-American Biography*. Bloomington, IN: AuthorHouse, 2016, Vol 1, p. 562; "Robert Stolz," in: Wikipedia. See - https://en.wikipedia.org/wiki/Robert_Stolz

Peter Elyakim Taussig (1944-), b. Prague, Bohemia; composer, pianist, video artist, Canada, now US
Bio: Rechcigl, Miloslav, Jr. "Peter Elyakim Taussig," in: *Encyclopedia of Bohemian and Czech-American Biography*. Bloomington, IN: AuthorHouse, 2016, Vol 1, p. 598; "Peter Elyakim Taussig," in: Wikipedia. See - https://en.wikipedia.org/wiki/Peter_Elyakim_Taussig

Ernst Toch (1887-1964), b. Vienna, of Moravian father; composer of classical music and film scores
Bio: "Ernst Toch, in: Wikipedia. See - https://en.wikipedia.org/wiki/Ernst Toch; Weschler, Lawren, "My Grandfather's Last Tale," *The Atlantic*, December 1996 issue.

Vally Weigl (née Pick) (1894-1982), b. Vienna, of Bohemian ancestry; composer, music therapist
Bio: "Weigl, Vally," in: *International Biographical Dictionary of Central European Emigrés 1933-1945*. Műnchen: K. G. Saur, 1983, Vol. 2, p. 1217; "Vally Weigl," in: Wikipedia. See: https://en.wikipedia.org/wiki/Vally_Weiglhttps://en.wikipedia.org/wiki/Vally_Weigl

Jaromír Weinberger (1896-1967), b. Královské Vinohrady, Prague, Bohemia; composer
Bio: Ewen, David, "Weinberger, Jaromir," in: *American Composers Today*. New York: H. W. Wilson, 1949, pp. 285 58-260; Kushner, David Z., "Jaromir Weinberger (1896-1967): From Bohemia to America," *American Music*, 6, no. 3 (Autumn 1998), pp. 293-313; "Jaromír Weinberger," in: Wikipedia. See: https://en.wikipedia.org/wiki/Jaromír_Weinberger

Hugo D. Weisgall (1912-1997), b. Ivančice, Moravia; composer, conductor
Bio: Griffiths, Paul, "Hugo Weisgall, Opera Composer, Dies at 84," *The New York Times*, March 12, 1997; Hugo Weisgall," in: Wikipedia. See - https://en.wikipedia.org/wiki/Hugo_Weisgall

Philip Yosowitz (ca 1950-), b. Cleveland, OH, of Czech immigrant father; a surgeon by day, composer by night
Bio: Rechcigl, Miloslav, Jr., "Philip Yosowitz," in: *Encyclopedia of Bohemian and Czech-American Biography*. Bloomington, IN: AuthorHouse, 2016, Vol 1, p. 565; "World premiere of 'The Gold' here on March 29," *Jewish Herald-Voice,* March 14, 2018.

Erich Zeisl (1905-1959), b. Vienna, of Bohemian and Moravian ancestry; composer
Bio: "Erich Zeisl," in: Wikipedia. See - https://en.wikipedia.org/wiki/Erich Zeisl; Rechcigl, Miloslav, Jr., "Eric Zeisl," in: *Encyclopedia of Bohemian and Czech-American Biography*. Bloomington, IN: AuthorHouse, 2016, Vol 1., pp. 565-566.

3. Conductors

Kurt Adler (1907-1977), b. b. Jindřichův Hradec, Bohemia; classical chorus master, music conductor, author and pianist
Bio: *Baker's Biographical Dictionary of Musicians*, Centennial Edition. New York: Schirmer Reference, 2000, p. 21; Urban, Václav, *Kurt Adler (1907 Neuhaus – 1977 New York)*. 1. vydání, Jindřichův Hradec, Kostelní Radouň, 2007, pp. 11–13; "Kurt Adler, 70, Conductor of 20 Different Operas at Met during 22 Years," *The New York Times*, September 23, 1977; "Kurt Adler," in: Wikipedia. See - https://en.wikipedia.org/wiki/Kurt Adler

Kurt Herbert Adler (1905-1988), b. Vienna, of Slovak ancestry; conductor and opera house director
Bio: Randel, Don Michael, ed. "Adler, Kurt Herbert," in: *The Harvard Biographical Dictionary of Music.* Cambridge, MA: Belknap Press of Harvard

University Press, 1996; "Kurt Herbert Adler," in: Wikipedia. See - https://en.wikipedia.org/wiki/Kurt Herbert Adler

Peter Herman Adler (1899-1990), b. Jablonec, Bohemia; conductor
Bio: Randel, Don Michael, ed. (1996), "Adler, Peter Herman," *The Harvard Biographical Dictionary of Music.* Cambridge, Mass.: Belknap Press of Harvard Univ. Press. p. 5; "Peter Herman Adler," in: Wikipedia. See - https://en.wikipedia.org/wiki/Peter_Herman_Adler

Franz Allers (1905-1995), b. Karlovy Vary, Bohemia; conductor
Bio: Franz Allers, 89, a Conductor and Broadway Musical Director, Obituary" *The New York Times,* January 28, 1995.

Karel Ančerl (1908-1973), b. Tučapy, southern Bohemia; conductor
Bio: "Karel Ančerl," in: Wikipedia. See - **https://en.wikipedia.org/wiki/Karel Ančerl;** Rechcigl, Miloslav, Jr., "Karel Ančerl," in: *Encyclopedia of Bohemian and Czech-American Biography.* Bloomington, IN: AuthorHouse, 2016, Vol 1., p. 566.

Jan Behr (1911-1996), b. Prague, Bohemia; conductor and concert pianist
Bio: Rechcigl, Miloslav, Jr., "Jan Behr," in: *Encyclopedia of Bohemian and Czech-American Biography.* Bloomington, IN: AuthorHouse, 2016, Vol 1., pp. 566-567; "Jan Behr, 85, Conductor at the Met," *The New York Times,* December 2, 1996

Artur Bodanzky (1877-1939), b. Vienna, of Moravian ancestry; conductor
Bio: "Artur Bodanzky," in: Wikipedia. See - https://en.wikipedia.org/wiki/Artur Bodanzky ; Rechcigl, Miloslav, Jr., "Artur Bodanzky," in: *Encyclopedia of Bohemian and Czech-American Biography.* Bloomington, IN: AuthorHouse, 2016, Vol 1., p. 567.

Otto Frohlich (1905-1988), b. Moravská Ostrava, Moravia; conductor, composer
Bio: Rechcigl, Miloslav, Jr., "Otto Frohlich," in: *Encyclopedia of Bohemian and Czech-American Biography.* Bloomington, IN: AuthorHouse, 2016, Vol 1., pp. 568.

Fritz Jahoda (1909-2009), b. Vienna, of Moravian ancestry; conductor, pianist, educator
Bio: Rich Hewitt, "Fritz Jahoda, 99, pianist, teacher, cookie maker dies," bangordailynews.com, January 8, 2009; *International Biographical Dictionary of Central European Emigrés 1933-1945.* Műnchen: K. G. Saur, 1983, Vol. 2, p. 563.

Julian Andreas Kuerti (1976-), b. Toronto, Canada, of Moravian ancestry; Canadian conductor
Bio: "Julian Kuerti," in: Wikipedia. See - https://en.wikipedia.org/wiki/Julian Kuerti; Rechcigl, Miloslav, Jr., "Julian Andreas Kuerti," in: *Encyclopedia of Bohemian and Czech-American Biography.* Bloomington, IN: AuthorHouse, 2016, Vol 1., pp. 570-571.

Jonathan Kuhner, b. Vienna, of Moravian ancestry; music director of Berkleys' West Edge Opera and assistant conductor of major opera companies, i.e., San Francisco, Lyric Opera of Chicago and the Metropolitan Opera.
Bio: "Khuner, Felix - Violinist," in: Berkeley Historical Plaque Project." See - http://berkeleyplaques.org/e-plaque/felix-khuner-violinist/

Otto Klemperer 1885-1973), Breslau, Poland, of Bohemian father; conductor and composer
Bio: Montgomery, Paul L., "Otto Klemperer; Conductor Dead at 88," *The New York Times,* July 8, 1973; Rechcigl, Miloslav, Jr., "Otto Klemperer," in: *Encyclopedia of Bohemian and Czech-American Biography.* Bloomington, IN: AuthorHouse, 2016, p. 570; "Otto Klemperer," in: Wikipedia. See - https://en.wikipedia.org/wiki/Otto Klemperer

Richard Lert (1885-1980), b. Vienna, of Bohemian ancestry; conductor
Bio: "Richard Lert," in: Wikipedia. See - https://en.wikipedia.org/wiki/Richard Lert; Rechcigl, Miloslav, Jr., "Richard Lert," in: *Encyclopedia of Bohemian and Czech-American Biography.* Bloomington, IN: AuthorHouse, 2016, p. 571.

Fritz Mahler (1901-1973), b. Vienna, of Bohemian ancestry; conductor, composer
Bio: "Fritz Mahler," in: Wikipedia. See - https://en.wikipedia.org/wiki/Fritz_Mahler

Egon Pollak (1879-1933), b. Prague, Bohemia; conductor
Bio: Rechcigl, Miloslav, Jr., "Egon Pollak," in: *Encyclopedia of Bohemian and Czech-American Biography.* Bloomington, IN: AuthorHouse, 2016, p. 572; "Egon Pollak (Dirigent), in: Wikipedia. See - https://de.wikipedia.org/wiki/Egon Pollak (Dirigent)

Jan Popper (1907-1987), b. Liberec, Bohemia; conductor, professor at UCLA
Bio: "Conductor JAN POPPER, 79, who fled Adolf Hitler's takeover...," *Orlando Sentinel,* September 4, 1987; Spilsbury, Duane, "Dr. Jan Popper, Conductor, Czech aviator, master's Opera workshop," The Stanford Daily, August 19, 1949; Rechcigl, Miloslav, Jr., "Jan Popper," *Encyclopedia of Bohemian and Czech-American Biography.* Bloomington, IN: AuthorHouse, 2016, Vol. 1, p. 572.

George Schick (1908-1985), b. Prague, Bohemia; conductor, vocal coach, accompanist, and music educator
Bio: "George Schick," in: Wikipedia. See - https://en.wikipedia.org/wiki/George Schick; "George Schick, 76, Is Dead; President of Music School," *The New York Times.* March 8, 1985.

Fritz Stiedry (1883-1968), b. Vienna, of Bohemian ancestry; conductor and composer
Bio: "Fritz Stiedry," in: Wikipedia. See - https://en.wikipedia.org/wiki/Fritz Stiedry; Rechcigl, Miloslav, Jr., "Fritz Stiedry," in: *Encyclopedia of Bohemian and Czech-American Biography.* Bloomington, IN: AuthorHouse, 2016, Vol., p. 574.

Josef Stránský (1872-1936), b. Humpolec, Bohemia; conductor and composer
Bio: Rechcigl, Miloslav, Jr., "Josef Stránský," in: *Encyclopedia of Bohemian and Czech-American Biography.* Bloomington, IN: AuthorHouse, 2016, Vol.

1, p. 574; "Josef Stránský," in: Wikipedia. See - https://en.wikipedia.org/wiki/Josef Stránský

Jan Walter Susskind (1913-1980), b. Prague, Bohemia; conductor
Bio: *Baker's Biographical Dictionary of 20th Century Classical Musicians.* New York: G. Schirmer, 1997.

George Szell (1897-1970), b. Budapest, of Czechoslovak ancestry; conductor and composer
Bio: Michael Charry and Stanley Sadie, "George Szell," in: *The New Grove Dictionary of Music and Musicians,* 2nd ed. London: MacMillan, 2001, vol. 24, pp. 880–881; Rechcigl, Miloslav, Jr., "George Szell," in: *Encyclopedia of Bohemian and Czech-American Biography.* Bloomington, IN: AuthorHouse, 2016, Vol. 1, p. 575.

Walter Taussig (1908-2003), b. Vienna, of Bohemian ancestry, conductor
Bio: "Walter Taussig," in: Wikipedia. See - https://en.wikipedia.org/wiki/Walter Taussig; Rechcigl, Miloslav, Jr., "Walter Taussig," in: *Encyclopedia of Bohemian and Czech-American Biography.* Bloomington, IN: AuthorHouse, 2016, Vol. 1, p. 575.

Georg Tintner (1917-1999), b. Vienna, of Moravian ancestry; Canadian conductor, composer
Bio: "Georg Tintner," in: Wikipedia. See - https://en.wikipedia.org/wiki/Georg_Tintner

Fritz Zweig (1893 1984), b. Olomouc, Moravia, conductor
Bio: "Fritz Zweig," in: Wikipedia. See: https://de.wikipedia.org/wiki/Fritz_Zweig; *International Biographical Dictionary of Central European Emigrés 1933-1945.* Műnchen: K. G. Saur, 1983, Vol. 2, p. 1287.

4. Classical Musicians

a. Pianists

Rudolf Firkušný (1912-1994), b. Napajedla, Bohemia; pianist
Bio: Ewen, David, "Firkušný, Rudolf," in: *Living Musicians*. New York: H. W. Wilson, 1957, Suppl. 1, pp. 54-55; "Firkušný, Rudolf," *Current Biography*, 1979, pp.136-139.

Ernest Goldman (1913-2014), b. Vienna, of Bohemian ancestry; pianist, accompanist
Bio: Rechcigl, Miloslav, Jr., "Ernest Goldman," in: *Encyclopedia of Bohemian and Czech-American Biography*. Bloomington, IN, 2015, Vol. 1, p. 590.

Fritz Jahoda (1908-2008), b. Vienna, of Moravian ancestry; pianist, conductor, teacher
Bio: "Fritz Jahoda, 99, pianist, teacher, cookie maker dies," BDN Hancock. See - http://bangordailynews.com/2009/01/08/news/hancock/fritz-jahoda-99-pianist-teacher-cookie-maker-dies/; "Fritz Jahoda," in: Wikipedia. See - https://de.wikipedia.org/wiki/Fritz_Jahoda

Rafael Joseffy (1852-1915), b. Huncovce, Slovakia; pianist, composer, teacher
Bio: "Rafael Joseffy,", in: Wikipedia. See - https://en.wikipedia.org/wiki/Rafael Joseffy

Catherine Kautsky (1950-), b. St. Louis, MO, of Bohemian ancestry; pianist, chair of Keyboard, Lawrence University
Bio: Rechcigl, Miloslav, Jr., "Catherine C. Kautsky," in: *Encyclopedia of Bohemian and Czech-American Biography*. Bloomington, IN, 2015, Vol. 1, p. 592; Miller, Sarah Bryan, "Q&A: St. Louis native Catherine Kautsky on her love of Debussy's music," St. Louis Post-Dispatch, March 8, 2018.

Lili Kraus (1903-1986), b. Budapest, of Czech father; a noted pianist
Bi: Rechcigl, Miloslav, Jr., "Lili Kraus," in: *Encyclopedia of Bohemian and Czech-American Biography*. Bloomington, IN, 2015, Vol. 1, p. 592

Anton Kuerti (1938-), b. Vienna, of Moravian ancestry; Canadian pianist, composer, conductor
Bio: "Anton Kuerti," in: Wikipedia. See - https://en.wikipedia.org/wiki/Anton_Kuerti

Artur Schnabel (1882-1951), b. Lipnik, Bilsko; classical pianist
Bio: Schnabel, Artur, *My Life and Music.* New York: Dover, 1961; republished 1988. 288p.; Searchinger, Cesar, *Artur Schnabel: A Biography.* Westport, CT: Greenwood Press, 1973; Wolff, Konrad, *The Teaching of Artur Schnabel.* New York: Prager, 1972. 189p.

Kurt Ulrich Schnabel (1909-2001), b. Berlin, Ger., son of Artur Schnabel; pianist
Bio: Rhodes, Richard, T*he Teaching of Karl Ulrich Schnabel. Hofheim*: Wolke, 2013; *International Biographical Dictionary of Central European Emigrés 1933-1945.* Műnchen: K. G. Saur, 1983, Vol. 2, p. 1041.

Peter Serkin (1947-), b. New York, NY, of Bohemian father; pianist
Bio: Rechcigl, Miloslav, Jr., "Peter Serkin," in: *Encyclopedia of Bohemian and Czech-American Biography.* Bloomington, IN, 2015, Vol. 1, p. 596; "Peter Serkin," in: Wikipedia. See - https://en.wikipedia.org/wiki/Peter Serkin

Rudolf Serkin (1903-1991, b. Cheb, Bohemia; pianist
Bio: "Serkin, Rudolf," *Current Biography,* 1940, pp. 725-726; Chasins, Abrams, "Rudolf Serkin," in: *Speaking of Pianists.* New York: Knopf, 1957, pp. 130-135; Kolodin, I., "Complete Musician (Rudolf Serkin)," *Horicon,* 4 (1961), pp. 82-87; Lehman, Stephen and Marion Farber, *Rudolf Serkin. A Life.* New York: Oxford University Press, 2002. 344p.

Paul Wittgenstein (1887-1961), b. Vienna, of Bohemian ancestry; concert pianist
Bio: Rechcigl, Miloslav, Jr., "Paul Wittgenstein", in: *Encyclopedia of Bohemian and Czech-American Biography.* Bloomington, IN, 2015, Vol. 1, p. 601.

Fannie Bloomfield Zeisler (née Bloomfield) (1863-1927), b. Bilsko, on Silesian-Moravian border, pianist

Bio: Rechcigl, Miloslav, Jr., "Fannie Bloomfield Zeisler," in: *Encyclopedia of Bohemian and Czech-American Biography*. Bloomington, IN, 2015, Vol. 1, p. 601; "Fannie Bloomfield Zeisler," in: Wikipedia. See - https://en.wikipedia.org/wiki/Fannie_Bloomfield_Zeisler

b. Violinists

Max Ignatz Fischel (1878-1937), b. Prague, Bohemia; violinist and composer
Bio: Rechcigl, Miloslav, Jr., "Max Ignatz Fischel," in: *Encyclopedia of Bohemian and Czech-American Biography*. Bloomington, IN, 2015, Vol. 1, p. 609.

Felix Khuner (1906-1991), b. Vienna, of Moravian ancestry; second violinist of the Kolisch Quartet
Bio: "Felix Khuner," in: Wikipedia. See - https://en.wikipedia.org/wiki/Felix_Khuner

Paul Kling (1929-2005), b. Opava, Moravia; Canadian violinist
Bio: "Paul Kling," in: Canadian Encyclopedia. See - http://www.thecanadianencyclopedia.ca/en/article/paul-kling-emc/

Franz Kneisel (1865-1926), b. Bucharest, of Moravian father; violinist
Bio: Rechcigl, Miloslav, Jr., "Franz Kneisel," in: *Encyclopedia of Bohemian and Czech-American Biography*. Bloomington, IN, 2015, Vol. 1, p. 615.

Marianne Kneisel (1897-1972), b. violinist
Bio: "Marianne Kneisel, Violinist, 75, Dead," *The New York Times,* March 4, 1972

Rudolf Kolisch (1896-1978), b. Klamm, Austria, of Bohemian ancestry; violinist, leader of string quartets
Bio: "Rudolf Kolisch," in: Wikipedia. See - https://en.wikipedia.org/wiki/Rudolf_Kolisch

Herbert Thomas Mandl (1926-2007), b. Bratislava, of Moravian parents; concert violinist, professor of music, philosopher, writer

Bio: Stirken, Norbert, "Herbert Thomas Mandl," *Rheinische Post,* August 21, 1995; "Herbert Thomas Mandl," in: Wikipedia. See - https://en.wikipedia.org/wiki/Herbert_Thomas_Mandl

Adolph Pick (1870-d.), b. Czech.; violinist, Ithaca College of Music
Bio: Rechcigl, Miloslav, Jr., "Adolph Pick," in: *Encyclopedia of Bohemian and Czech-American Biography.* Bloomington, IN, 2015, Vol. 1, p. 620.

Felix Winternitz (1872-1948), b. Austria, of Czech ancestry; violinist, composer
Bio: Rechcigl, Miloslav, Jr., "Felix Winternitz," in: *Encyclopedia of Bohemian and Czech-American Biography.* Bloomington, IN, 2015, Vol. 1, p. 627.

c. Other Musicians

Gaby Haas (1920-1987), b. Františkovy Lázně, Czech; accordionist, Edmonton, Canada
Bio: Herzog, Lawrence, "Canada's Mr. Polka - Gaby Haas," *People,* September 29, 2015. See - https://citymuseumedmonton.ca/2015/09/29/canadas-mr-polka-gaby-haas/; Rechcigl, Miloslav, Jr., "Gaby Haas," in: *Encyclopedia of Bohemian and Czech-American Biography.* Bloomington, IN, 2015, Vol. 1, pp. 662-663.

5. Jazz Musicians

Barbara Adler, b. Vancouver, BC, of Czech ancestry; Canadian musician, poet, and storyteller
Bio: "Barbara Adler," in: Wikipedia. See - https://en.wikipedia.org/wiki/Barbara_Adler; Rechcigl, Miloslav, Jr., "Barbara Adler," in: *Encyclopedia of Bohemian and Czech-American Biography.* Bloomington, IN, 2015, vol. 1, p. 678.

Paul Desmond (orig. Breitenfeld) (1924-1977), b. San Francisco, CA, of Bohemian ancestry; jazz alto saxophonist and composer
Bio: Ramsey, Doug, *Take Five: The Public and Private Lives of Paul Desmond.* Seattle: Parkside Publications, 2005; "Paul Desmond," in Wikipedia. See - https://en.wikipedia.org/wiki/Paul_Desmond

Jack Gilinsky (1996-), b. Omaha, NE, of Czech ancestry; singer, part of the pop-rap duo Jack & Jack, along with Jack Johnson
Bio: "Jack & Jack," in: Wikipedia. See - https://en.wikipedia.org/wiki/Jack_%26_Jac

Adam Green (1981-), b. Mount Kisco, NY, singer-songwriter, artist and filmmaker
Bio: "Adam Green (Musician), in: Wikipedia. See - https://en.wikipedia.org/wiki/Adam Green (musician)

Lenka Lichtenberg, b. Prague, Czech.; Canadian singer, composer, songwriter, animal rights activist and chazanit
Bio: "Lenka Lichtenberg," in Wikipedia. See - https://en.wikipedia.org/wiki/Lenka Lichtenberg; Rechcigl, Miloslav, Jr., "Lenka Lichtenberg," in: *Encyclopedia of Bohemian and Czech-American, Biography*, Bloomington, IN: AuthorHouse, 2016, Vol. 1, pp. 684-685.

Paul Wittgenstein (1887-1961), b. Vienna, of Bohemian ancestry; concert pianist
Bio: "Paul Wittgenstein," in: Wikipedia. See - https://en.wikipedia.org/wiki/Paul_Wittgenstein

6. Opera Singers

Kurt Baum (1908-1989), b. Prague, Bohemia; operatic tenor
Bio: "Kurt Baum: Ending on A High Note," *Los Angeles Times*, January 24, 1988; Oestreich, James R., "Kurt Baum, Tenor, Is Dead at 81; He Sang at Met in 40's and 50's," *The New York Times,* December 29, 1989; "Kurt Baum," in: Wikipedia. See - https://en.wikipedia.org/wiki/Kurt_Baum.

Rudolf Berger (1874-1915), b. Brno, Moravia; operatic baritone and later tenor
Bio: Rechcigl, Miloslav, JR., "Tenorista s vysokým C," in: *Postavy naší Ameriky*. Praha: Pražská edice, 2000, pp.227-229; "Rudolf Berger (Sänger)," Wikipedia. See - in: https://de.wikipedia.org/wiki/Rudolf_Berger_ (Sänger)

Ernestine Schumann-Heink (1861-1936), b. Prague, Bohemia; operatic contralto

Bio: "Lawton, Mary, *Schumann-Heink: The Last of the Titans*. New York: Macmillan Co., 1928;

Borchard, Beatrix, "Ernestine Schumann-Heink," in: Jewish Women's Archive. See - https://jwa.org/encyclopedia/article/schumann-heink-ernestine; Zwart, Ann Townsend, "Schumann-Heink, Ernestine," *Notable Women*, Vol. 3, pp. 240-242; Amero, Richard W., "Madame Schumann-Heink: A Legend in Her Time," *Southern California Quarterly, Summer*, 1991, pp. 157-182, also at - http://www.balboaparkhistory.net/glimpses/scheink.htm; "Ernestine Schumann-Heink," in: Wikipedia. See - https://en.wikipedia.org/wiki/Ernestine Schumann-Heink; "Schumann-Heink, Great Singer Dead," *The New York Times*, November 18, 1936.

Hans Joachim Heinz (1904-1982), b. Vienna, of Moravian mother; singer, tenor, teacher

Bio: Rechcigl, Miloslav, Jr., "Hans Joachim Heinz," in: *Encyclopedia of Bohemian and Czech- American Biography*. Bloomington, IN: AuthorHouse, 2016, Vol. 1, p. 670.

Hulda Lashanska Rosenbaum (1894-1974), b. New York City, of Czech ancestry; lyric soprano

Bio: "Hulda Lashanska, a New Vocal Star," *New York Post*, January 25, 1918); "Hulda Lashanska," in: Wikipedia. See - https://en.wikipedia.org/wiki/Hulda Lashanska; "Hulda Lashanska Rosenbaum, concert Soprano, Dies at 80," *The New York Times*, January 18, 1974.

Julia Nessy-Backer (1889-1981), b. Prague, Bohemia; harpist, soprano, concert and opera singer

Bio: Rechcigl, Miloslav, Jr., "Julia Nessy-Backer," in: *Encyclopedia of Bohemian and Czech- American Biography*. Bloomington, IN: AuthorHouse, 2016, vol. 1, p. 674.

Leo Slezak (1873-1940), b. Šumperk, Moravia; prominent tenor

Bio: David Hamilton, ed., *The Metropolitan Opera Encyclopedia*. New York: Simon & Schuster, 1984, p. 342; *The International Cyclopedia of Music and Musicians*. 11th ed. New York: Dodd, Mead, 1985, pp. 2084-85; *Baker's*

Biographical Dictionary of Musicians, p. 1726; *Who Was Who in America* (1950), 2, p. 491.

Josef Turnau (1888-1954), b. Bohemia; opera singer, tenor, intendant and stage director
Bio: "Josef Turnau," in: Wikipedia. See: https://de.wikipedia.org/wiki/Josef Turnau; *International Biographical Dictionary of Central European Emigrés 1933-1945*. Műnchen: K. G. Saur, 1983, Vol. 2, p. 1178-1179.

7. Popular Singers and Songwriters

Anabel Englund (1922-), b. New York, Ny, of Bohemian ancestry; singer and songwriter
Bio: "Anabel Englund," in: Wikipedia. See - https://en.wikipedia.org/wiki/Anabel Englund

Jack Gilinsky (1996-), b. Omaha, NE, of Slovak ancestry; singer
Bio: "Jack Gilinsky," in: FANDOM. See - http://madisonbeer.wikia.com/wiki/Jack_Gilinsky

8. Musicologists

Richard Cohn (1955-), b. US, of Bohemian ancestry; music theorist, professor of music theory at Yale
Bio: "Richard Cohn," in: Wikipedia. See -https://en.wikipedia.org/wiki/Richard_Cohn; "Richard Cohn," in: Yale Department of Music. See - https://yalemusic.yale.edu/people/richard-cohn; Rechcigl, Miloslav, Jr. "Richard Cohn," in: *Encyclopedia of Bohemian and Czech-American Biography*, Bloomington, IN: AuthorHouse, 2016, vol. 1, pp. 699-700.

Frederick Dorian (orig. Deutsch) (1902-1991), b. Vienna, of Bohemian ancestry; professor of music
Bio: "Frederick Dorian, 89, A Professor of Music," *New York Times*, January 26, 1991; *International Biographical Dictionary of Central European Emigrés 1933-1945*. Műnchen: K. G. Saur, 1983, Vol. 2, p. 223.

Leoš Firkušný (1905-1950), b. Napajedla, Moravia; musicologist, Buenos Aires, Argentina
Bio: "Leoš Firkušný," in: Wikipedia. See - https://en.wikipedia.org/wiki/Leoš Firkušný; Rechcigl, Miloslav, Jr., "Leoš Firkušný," in: *Encyclopedia of Bohemian and Czech-American Biography*, Bloomington, IN: AuthorHouse, 2016, vol. 1, p. 701.

Hermann Grab (1903-1949), b. Prague, Bohemia; music teacher and music critic
Bio: Rechcigl, Miloslav, Jr., "Hermann Grab," in: *Encyclopedia of Bohemian and Czech-American Biography*, Bloomington, IN: AuthorHouse, 2016, vol. 1, p. 701; "Hermann Grab," in: Wikipedia. See - https://en.wikipedia.org/wiki/Hermann_Grab

Max Graf (1873-1958), b. Vienna, of Bohemian ancestry; musicologist, music critic
Bio: "Max Graf," in: Wikipedia. See - https://en.wikipedia.org/wiki/Max Graf; Rechcigl, Miloslav, Jr., "Max Graf," in: *Encyclopedia of Bohemian and Czech- American Biography*. Bloomington, IN: AuthorHouse, 2016, vol. 1, pp. 701-702.

Heinrich Jalowetz (1882-1946), b. Brno, Moravia; musicologist and conductor
Bio: "Heinrich Jalowetz," in: Wikipedia. See - https://en.wikipedia.org/wiki/Heinrich_Jalowetz

Walter Kaufmann (1907-1984), b. Karlovy Vary, Bohemia; composer, conductor, musicologist, and educator
Bio: "Walter Kaufmann (Composer)," in: Wikipedia. See - https://en.wikipedia.org/wiki/Walter_Kaufmann_(composer)

Julius Korngold (1860-1945), b. Brno, Moravia; a noted music critic
Bio: Carroll, Brendan; G. Pauly, Reinhard G., *The Last Prodigy: A Biography of Erich Wolfgang Korngold.* Amadeus Press, Portland, 1997.

Jan Lowenbach (1880-1972), b. Rychnov nad Kněžnou, Bohemia; lawyer, music critic

Bio: Jan Lowenbach Papers, San Diego State University, Special Collections and University Archives, Urbana-Champaign.

Bruno Nettl (1930-), b. Prague, Czech.; ethnomusicologist and musicologist, University of Illinois, Urabana-Champaign
Bio: Keller, Marcello Sorce, "Intervista con un etnomusicologo: Bruno Nettl," *Nuova Rivista Musicale Italiana,* 1980. No. 4, 567- 576; Bruno Nettl Papers, 1966-1988, University of Illinois Archives, Urbana-Champaign; Rechcigl, Miloslav, Jr., "Bruno Nettl," in: *C*; "Bruno Netttl," in: Wikipedia. See - https://en.wikipedia.org/wiki/Bruno_Nettl

Paul Nettl (1889-1972), b. Vrchlabí, Bohemia; musicologist, professor, Indaiana University
Bio: "Nettl, Paul," in: *Český hudební slovník osob a institucí.* See- http://www.ceskyhudebnislovnik.cz/slovnik/index.php?option=com mdictionary&task=record.record detail&id=2515; Paul Nettl Papers, Indiana University, Special Collections, Music Library, Bloomington, IN; Rechcigl, Miloslav, Jr., "Paul Nettl," in: *Encyclopedia of Bohemian and Czech-American Biography.* Bloomington, IN: AuthorHouse, 2016, Vol. 1, p. 705.

Frederick Neumann (1907-1994), b. Bilsko, on Silesian-Moravian border; professor of music theory, University of Richmond
Bio: Rechcigl, Miloslav, Jr., "Frederick Neumann," in: *Encyclopedia of Bohemian and Czech-American Biography.* Bloomington, IN: AuthorHouse, 2016, Vol. 1, p. 706; Homer, Rudolf, "Frederick Neumann (1907-1994, multi-faceted musician and scholar," *Performance Practice Review,* Vol. 7, No. 2 (Fall 1994), pp. 105-104.

Paul A. Pick (1893-d.), Vienna, of Moravian ancestry, professor of musicology, University of Texas, Austin
Bio: Rechcigl, Miloslav, Jr., "Paul A. Pick," in: *Encyclopedia of Bohemian and Czech-American Biography.* Bloomington, IN: AuthorHouse, 2016, Vol. 1, p. 706.

Felix Salzer (1904-1986), b. Vienna, of Bohemian ancestry; music theorist, musicologist, professor

Bio: Rechcigl, Miloslav, Jr., "Felix Salzer," in: *Encyclopedia of Bohemian and Czech-American Biography*. Bloomington, IN: AuthorHouse, 2016, Vol. 1, pp. 706-707; "Felix Salzer," in: Wikipedia. See - https://en.wikipedia.org/wiki/Felix_Salzer

Hannus A. Schimmerling (1900-1967), b. Brno, Moravia; pianist, composer, teacher, musicologist, and writer
Bio: Stuart Richard Cooper, "Hans Schimmerling: Pianist, Composer, Teacher," *Stammbaum, The Journal of German-Jewish Genealogical Research*, Issue No. 23, Summer 2003; "Hans Schimmerling," in: Wikipedia. See - https://en.wikipedia.org/wiki/Hans_Schimmerling

Paul Stefan (1879-1943), b. Brno, Moravia; music historian and critic
Bio: "Paul Stefan", in: Wikipedia. See - https://en.wikipedia.org/wiki/Paul Stefan

Frederick William Sternfeld (1914-1994), b. Vienna, of Bohemian mother; musicologist
Bio: Rechcigl, Miloslav, Jr., "Frederick William Sternfeld," in: *Encyclopedia of Bohemian and Czech-American Biography*. Bloomington, IN: AuthorHouse, 2016, Vol. 1, p. 708.

Richard Stőhr (orig. Stern) (1874-1967), b. Vienna, of Bohemian ancestry; composer, music author, teacher
Bio: "Richard Stőhr," in: Wikipedia. See - https://en.wikipedia.org/wiki/Richard_Stöhr

Edith Vogl-Garret (1904-1995), b. Nýrsko, Bohemia; pianist and musicologist
Bio: Rechcigl, Miloslav, Jr., "Edith Vogl-Garret," in: *Encyclopedia of Bohemian and Czech-American Biography*. Bloomington, IN: AuthorHouse, 2016, Vol. 1, p. 710.

Arnold Walter (1902-1973), b. Hanušovice, Moravia; musicologist
Bio: "Arnold Walter," in: Wikipedia. See: https://en.wikipedia.org/wiki/Arnold_Walter; *Contemporary Canadian Composers*. Edited by Keith MacMillan, John Beckwith. Oxford University Press, 1975, p. 229.

Emanuel Winternitz (1898-1983), b. Vienna, of Bohemian ancestry; musicologist, curator of musical instruments at Metropolitan Museum of Art
Bio: Rechcigl, Miloslav, Jr., "Emanuel Winternitz," in: *Encyclopedia of Bohemian and Czech-American Biography*. Bloomington, IN: AuthorHouse, 2016, Vol. 1, pp. 710-711; "Emanuel Winternitz," in: Wikipedia. See - https://en.wikipedia.org/wiki/Emanuel_Winternitz

9. Impresarios, Opera Directors

Jack Garfein (1930-), b. Mukačevo, Czech.; director and teacher, the Actors'Studio, writer, producer
Bio: "Jack Garfein," in: Wikipedia. See - https://en.wikipedia.org/wiki/ Jack Garfein; Rechcigl, Miloslav, Jr., "Jack Garfein," in: *Encyclopedia of Bohemian and Czech-American Biography*. Bloomington, IN: AuthorHouse, 2016, Vol. 2, p. 787.

Joseph Glűcksmann (1900-1963), b. Vienna, of Moravian father; stage director, and producer, actor, playwright
Bio: Rechcigl, Miloslav, Jr. "Joseph Glűcksmann," in: *Encyclopedia of Bohemian and Czech-American Biography*. Bloomington, IN: AuthorHouse, 2016, Vol. 2, p. 787.

Herbert Graf (1903-1973), b. Vienna, of Bohemian ancestry, opera producer
Bio: Herbert Graf," in: Wikipedia. See: https://en.wikipedia.org/wiki/ Herbert Graf; *International Biographical Dictionary of Central European Emigrés 1933-1945*. Műnchen: K. G. Saur, 1983, Vol. 2, p. 411.

Erich Juhn (1895-1973), b. Přerov, Moravia; theatre impresario, journalist
Bio: Rechcigl, Miloslav, Jr., "Erich Juhn," in: *Encyclopedia of Bohemian and Czech-American Biography*. Bloomington, IN: AuthorHouse, 2016, Vol. 2, p. 788.

Adolph Klauber (1879-1933), b. Louisville, KY, of Bohemian ancestry; theatrical producer, drama critic

Bio: "Adolph Klauber," in: Wikipedia. See - https://en.wikipedia.org/wiki/Adolph Klauber; Rechcigl, Miloslav, Jr., "Adolph Klauber," in: *Encyclopedia of Bohemian and Czech-American Biography*. Bloomington, IN: AuthorHouse, 2016, Vol. 2, p. 789; Adolph Klauber, Producer, Dies; Husband of Jane Cow) and Former Dramatic Critic, He Began Career as Actor," *The New York Times*, December 8, 1933

Ernst Lert (orig. Levy) (1883-1955), b. Vienna, of Bohemian ancestry; opera and theatre director, writer, composer, librettist, music historian
Bio: "Ernst Lert," in: wikip3edia. See - https://en.wikipedia.org/wiki/Ernst Lert; Rechcigl, Miloslav, Jr., "Ernst Lert," in: *Encyclopedia of Bohemian and Czech-American Biography*. Bloomington, IN: AuthorHouse, 2016, Vol. 2, p. 789.

Max Maretzek (1821-1897), b. Brno, Moravia; composer, conductor, and impresario
Bio: Maretzek, Max, *Crotchets and Quavers or Revelations of an Opera Manager in America*. New York: S. French, 1855. 346p.; Reprinted - New York: De Capo Press, 1966; Maretzek, Max, *Further Revelations of an Opera Manager in the 19th Century America*. The Third Book of Memoirs. Edited by Ruth Henderson. Sterling Heights, MI: Harmonie Park Press, 2006. 165p.; "Max Maretzek," in: Wikipedia. See - https://en.wikipedia.org/wiki/Max Maretzek

Max Reinhardt (orig. Goldmann) (1873-1943), b. Baden, Aust., of Moravian ancestry; theatre and film director, theatrical producer
Bio: "Max Reinhardt,", in: Wikipedia. See - https://en.wikipedia.org/wiki/Max Reinhardt; Rechcigl, Miloslav, Jr., "Max Reinhardt," in: *Encyclopedia of Bohemian and Czech-American Biography*, Bloomington, IN: AuthorHouse, 2016, Vol.2, p. 791.

Kurt Robitschek (aka Ken Robey) (1890-1950), b. Prague, Bohemia; popular cabaret and theatre director
Bio: "Kurt Robitschek," in: Wikipedia. See - https://de.wikipedia.org/wiki/Kurt Robitschek; Rechcigl, Miloslav, Jr., "Kurt Robitschek," in: *Encyclopedia of Bohemian and Czech-American Biography*, Bloomington, IN: AuthorHouse, 2016, Vol. 2, p. 791.

Maurice Strakosch 1825-1887), b. Židlochovice, Moravia; pianist, opera impresario
Bio: "Maurice Strakosch," in: Wikipedia. See - https://en.wikipedia.org/wiki/Maurice Strakosch; Rechcigl, Miloslav, JR., "Maurice Strakosch," in: *Encyclopedia of Bohemian and Czech-American Biography*, Bloomington, IN: AuthorHouse, 2016, Vol. 1, p. 698.

Josef Turnau (1888-1954), b. Bohemia; intendant and stage director, opera producer, head of opera department at New School for Social Research
Bio: Rechcigl, Miloslav, Jr., "Josef Turnau," in: *Encyclopedia of Bohemian and Czech-American Biography*, Bloomington, IN: AuthorHouse, 2016, Vol. 2, p. 784.

Lothar Wallerstein (1882-1949), b. Prague, Bohemia; stage director, opera director
Bio: Götz Klaus Kende, "Zur Erinnerung an Lothar Wallerstein (1882–1949)," in: Richard Strauss-Blätter. 8 (1982), pp. 6–10; "Lothar Wallerstein," in: Wikipedia. See - https://de.wikipedia.org/wiki/Lothar_Wallerstein; *International Biographical Dictionary of Central European Emigrés 1933-1945*. Műnchen: K. G. Saur, 1983, Vol. 2, p. 1204.

William Wymetal (1862-1937), b. Aust., of Bohemian ancestry; producer of operas, NY Meropolitan Opera
Bio: Rechcigl, Miloslav, Jr., "William Wymetal," in: *Encyclopedia of Bohemian and Czech-American Biography*, Bloomington, IN: AuthorHouse, 2016, Vol. 1, p. 699.

William Wymetal, Jr. (1890 - 1970), b. Vienna, of Bohemian ancestry; stage director, director of operas
Bio: Rechcigl, Miloslav, Jr., "William Wymetal, Jr.," in: *Encyclopedia of Bohemian and Czech-American Biography*, Bloomington, IN: AuthorHouse, 2016, Vol. 1, p. 699.

10. Record Producers

George W. Korngold (1928-1987), b. Vienna, of Moravian ancestry; record producer

Bio: "George W. Korngold, Record Producer, Dies," *The New York Times*, November 27, 1987; "George Korngold," in: Wikipedia. See - https://en.wikipedia.org/wiki/George Korngold

F. Drama & Dance

1. General

Kisch, Guido: "Theatre," in: *In Search for Freedom.* A History of American Jews from Czechoslovakia 1592-1948. London: Edward Goldston, 1948, pp. 175-176.

2. Actors[12]

Angélica Aragón (orig Stransky) (1953-), b. Mexico, of Bohemian ancestry; Mexican stage, film and TV actrees and singer
Bio: Rechcigl, Miloslav, Jr., "Angelica Aragon," in: *Encyclopedia of Bohemian and Czech-American Biography*, Bloomington, IN: AuthorHouse, 2016, Vol. 2, p. 719.

[12] I was tempted to include in this listing also the famous Czech duo Voskovec and Werich (V &W), the pioneers of avant-garde theatre and gifted comedians, singers and writers, the enduring symbols of pre-War Czechoslovak culture, whose names were suggestive of Jewish origin. This was particularly indicated in case of George (Jiří) Voskovec, not so much that his original name was Wachsman, but because his mother came from the Pinkas family, having been the daughter of the famous Czech painter Hippolyt (later changed to Soběslav) Pinkas, both names being typically Jewish. In fact, there is plenty of evidence that Jews by the name of Pinkas lived in the early Prague and, beyond that, the second oldest surviving synagogue in Prague, bears the Pinkas name. In case of Jan Werich, claims were also made that he may have been Jewish. Beyond that, Voskovec and his inseparable partner Werich, also sought refuge in America, from the Nazi prosecution, at the onset of World War II. In case of Jan Werich, claims were also made that he may have been Jewish. Nevertheless, no tangible evidence has ever been provided that either of the two were Jewish and neither of them thought that they had any Jewish ancestors. Hopefully, a competent genealogist may figure this out in the future.

Buddy Baer (1915-1986), b. Omaha, NE, of Bohemian ancestry; boxer but later an actor
Bio: Rechcigl, Miloslav, Jr., "Buddy Baer," in: *Encyclopedia of Bohemian and Czech-American Biography*, Bloomington, IN: AuthorHouse, 2016, Vol. 2, p. 729.

Max Baer, Jr. (1937-), b. Oakland, California, of Bohemian ancestry; actor, screenwriter, producer and director
Bio: "Max Baer Jr.," in: Wikipedia. See - ttps://en.wikipedia.org/wiki/Max_Baer_Jr.

Blanche Baker (1956-), b. New York City, of Czech ancestry; actress and filmmaker
Bio; "Blanche Baker," in: Wikipedia. See - https://en.wikipedia.org/wiki/Blanche Baker

Michael Berryman (1948-), b. Los Angeles, CA, of Czech ancestry; actor
Bio: Rechcigl, Miloslav, Jr., "Michael Berryman," in: *Encyclopedia of Bohemian and Czech-American Biography*, Bloomington, IN: AuthorHouse, 2016, Vol. 2, p. 729.

Turhan Bey (1922-2012), Vienna, of Czech ancestry; actor
Bio: "Turhan Bey," in: Wikipedia. See - https://en.wikipedia.org/wiki/Turhan Bey; "Turhan Bey, Actor Dies at 90," The New York Times, October 11, 2012.

Mayim Bialik (1975-), b. San Diego, CA, of Czech ancestry; actress, neuroscientist
Bio: "Mayim Bialik," in: Wikipedia. See - https://en.wikipedia.org/wiki/Mayim Bialik

Karen Blanche Black (née Ziegler) (1939-2013), b. Parke Ridge, IL, of Bohemian ancestry; actress, screenwriter, singer and songwriter
Black,", in: Wikipedia. See - https://en.wikipedia.org/wiki/Karen Black; Rechcigl, Miloslav, Jr., "Karen Blanche Black," in: *Encyclopedia of Bohemian and Czech-American Biography*, Bloomington, IN: AuthorHouse, 2016, Vol. 2, p. 720.

Nikky Blonsky (1988-), b. Great Neck, NY, of Czech ancestry; actress, singer and dancer
Bio: "Nikki Blonsky," in: wuikipedia. See - https://en.wikipedia.org/wiki/Nikki_Blonsky

Melissa Bolona (1989-), b. Greenwich, CT, of Czech mother; actress and model
Bio: "Melisa Bolona," in: Wikipedia. See - https://en.wikipedia.org/wiki/Melissa_Bolona

Egon Brecher (1880-1946), b. Olomouc, Moravia, stage actor, director
Bio: "Egon Brecher," in: Wikipedia. See - https://en.wikipedia.org/wiki/Egon_Brecher

Barbara Brecht-Schall (1930-2015), b. Berlin, Ger., of Moravian ancestry; stage actress
Bio: Rechcigl, Miloslav, Jr., "Barbara Brecht-Schall," in: *Encyclopedia of Bohemian and Czech-American Biography*, Bloomington, IN: AuthorHouse, 2016, Vol. 2, p. 721; "Barbara Brecht-Schall," in: Wikipedia. See - https://en.wikipedia.org/wiki/Barbara_Brecht-Schall

Adrien Brody (1973-), b. Woodhaven, Queens, NY; actor, producer
Bio: "Adrien Brody," in: Wikipedia. See - https://en.wikipedia.org/wiki/Adrien_Brody

Sarah Wayne Callies (1977-), b. La Grange, IL, of Czech father; actress
Bio: Rechcigl, Miloslav, Jr., "Sarah Anne Wayne Callies," in: *Encyclopedia of Bohemian and Czech-American Biography*, Bloomington, IN: AuthorHouse, 2016, Vol. 2, pp. 731-732.

Tony Curtis (1925-2010), b. Manhattan, NY, of Slovak ancestry; film actor
Bio: "Tony Curtis,", in: Wikipedia. See - https://en.wikipedia.org/wiki/Tony_Curtis; Curtis, Tony, Barry Paris, *Tony Curtis: The Autobiography*. New York: William Morrow & Company, 1993; Curtis, Tony, Peter Golenbock, *Tony Curtis: American Prince: My Autobiography*. New York: Harmony Books, 2008.

Alexandra Anna Daddario (1986-), b. New York, NY, of Slovak ancestry; film actrees
Bio: Rechcigl, Miloslav, Jr., "Alexandra Anna Daddario," in: *Encyclopedia of Bohemian and Czech-American Biography*, Bloomington, IN: AuthorHouse, 2016, Vol. 2, p. 734; "Alexandra Daddario," in: Wikipedia. See - https://en.wikipedia.org/wiki/Alexandra Daddario; Woodhall, Alex, "Woman of the Week: Alexandra Daddario," *The Gentleman's Journal*, United Kingdom, February 21, 2016.

Matthew Daddario (1987-), b. New York, NY, of Slovak ancestry; actor
Bio; "Matthew Daddario," in: Wikipedia. See - https://en.wikipedia.org/wiki/Matthew_Daddario

Ernst Deutsch (1890-1969), b. Prague, Bohemia; actor
Bio: "Ernst Deutsch," in: Wikipedia. See - https://en.wikipedia.org/wiki/Ernst_Deutsch

Peter Falk (1927-2011), b. New York City, of Bohemian ancestry; actor
Bio: Falk, Peter, *Just One More Thing: Stories from My Life*. New York: Carroll & Graf Publishers, 2006; "Peter Falk," in: Wikipedia. See - https://en.wikipedia.org/wiki/Peter Falk

Hans Feher (1922-1958), b. Vienna, of Slovak ancestry; actor
Bio: Rechcigl, Miloslav, Jr., "Hans Ferher," in: *Encyclopedia of Bohemian and Czech-American Biography*, Bloomington, IN: AuthorHouse, 2016, Vol. 2, p. 736.

Tibor Feldman (1947-), b. Michalovce, Czech.; stage, film and TV actor
Bio: "Tibor Feldman," in: Wikipedia. See - https://en.wikipedia.org/wiki/Tibor Feldman

Rudolf Friml, Jr. (1910-1972), b. Long Angeles, CA, of Czech father; actor
Bio: Rechcigl, Miloslav, Jr., "Rudolf Friml, Jr.," in: *Encyclopedia of Bohemian and Czech-American Biography*, Bloomington, IN: AuthorHouse, 2016, Vol. 2, p. 737; "Rudolf Friml, Jr.," in: IMDb. See - http://www.imdb.com/name/nm1631530/?ref_=nmbio_trv_3

Sara Gilbert (née Sara Rebecca Abeles) (1975-), b. Santa Monica, CA, of Bohemian ancestry, actress, co-host and creator of CBS daytime show 'The Talk'
Bio: "Sara Gilbert," in: Wikipedia. See - https://en.wikipedia.org/wiki/Sara Gilbert; Rechcigl, Miloslav, Jr., "Sara Gilbert," in: *Encyclopedia of Bohemian and Czech-American Biography*, Bloomington, IN: AuthorHouse, 2016, Vol. 2, p. 737.

Hugo Haas (1901-1968), b. Brno, Moravia; film actor, director and writer
Bio: "Hugo Haas," in Wikipedia. See - https://en.wikipedia.org/wiki/Hugo HaasTeo

Teo Halm (1999-), b. Los Angeles, CA, of Czech ancestry; A, merica teenage actor;
Bio: "Teo Halm," in: Wikipedia. See - https://en.wikipedia.org/wiki/Teo Halm

Paul Henreid (1992-), b. Trieste, Italy, of Bohemian ancestry; actor and film director
Bio: "Paul Henreid," in: *Encyclopedia of Bohemian and Czech- American Biography*. Bloomington, IN: AuthorHouse, 2016, Vol. 2, pp. 740-741.

Oskar Homolka (1888-1978), b. Vienna, of Bohemian ancestry; actor, film and theatre actor
Bio: "Oscar Homolka, Actor, Dies at 79. The Uncle in 'I Remember Mama'," *The New York Times,* January 29, 1978; "Oskar Homolka," in: Wikipedia. See - https://en.wikipedia.org/wiki/Oskar Homolka

Matt Iseman (1971-), b. Denver, CO, of Bohemian ancestry; comedian, actor, TV host and physician
Bio: "Matt Iseman," in: Wikipedia. See - https://en.wikipedia.org/wiki/Matt_Iseman

Angelina Jolie (1975-), b. Los Angeles, CA, of Slovak and Czech ancestry; actress, filmmaker, humanitarian
Bio: "Angelina Jolie," in: Wikipedia. See -https://en.wikipedia.org/wiki/Angelina_Jolie

Werner Klemperer (1920-2000), b. Cologne, of Czech ancestry; stage, film and TV comedic and dramatic actor, singer/musician
Bio: "Werner Klemperer," in: Wikipedia. See - https://en.wikipedia.org/wiki/Werner_Klemperer

Susan Kohner (1936-), Los Angeles, CA, of Bohemian ancestry; actress, also in film and TV
Bio: Wikipedia. See: https://en.wikipedia.org/wiki/Susan Kohner

Leopoldine Konstantin (1886-1965), b. Brno, Moravia; stage and film actress
Bio: Rechcigl, Miloslav, Jr., "Leopoldine Konstantin," in: *Encyclopedia of Bohemian and Czech- American Biography*. Bloomington, IN: AuthorHouse, 2016, Vol. 2, p. 744-745; "Leopoldine Konstantin," in: Wikipedia. See - https://en.wikipedia.org/wiki/Leopoldine Konstantin

Christine Lakin (1979-), of Czech ancestry; actress
Bio: "Christine Lakin," in: Wikipedia. See - https://en.wikipedia.org/wiki/Christine_Lakin

Hedy Lamarr (née Kiesler) (1914-2000), b. Vienna, of Moravian ancestry; actrees and inventor
Bio: Rechcigl, Miloslav, Jr., "Heddy Lamarr," in: *Encyclopedia of Bohemian and Czech- American Biography*. Bloomington, IN: AuthorHouse, 2016, Vol. 2, pp. 746-747; "Hedy Lamarr," in: Wikipedia. See - https://en.wikipedia.org/wiki/Hedy_Lamarr

Charles D. Lederer (1906-1976), b. New York City, of Bohemian ancestry; screenwriter and film director
Bio: "Charles Lederer," in: Wikipedia. See - https://en.wikipedia.org/wiki/Charles Lederer; "Charles Lederer Dead at 65; The Stage and Screen Writer," *The New York Times,* March 7, 1976.

Francis Lederer (1899-2000), b. Prague, Bohemia; film and stage actor
Bio: "Francis Lederer," in: Wikipedia. See - https://en.wikipedia.org/wiki/Francis Lederer

Otto Lederer (1886-1965), b. Prague, Bohemia; actor
Bio: "Otto Lederer," in: Wikipedia. See - https://en.wikipedia.org/wiki/Otto_Lederer

Peter Lorre (orig. Löwenstein) (1904-1964), b. Ružomberok, Slovakia; actor
Bio: "Peter Lorre," in: Wikipedia. See - https://en.wikipedia.org/wiki/Peter Lorre; French, Philip, "Peter Lorre: a great screen actor remembered," *The Observer*, August 31, 2014; Youngkin, Stephen D., *The Lost One: A Life of Peter Lorre*. University Press of Kentucky, 2005.

Joshua 'Diosh' Dylan Meyers (1976-), b. Bedford, NH, of Czech ancestry; actor, comedian
Bio: Rechcigl, Miloslav. Jr., "Josh Meyers," in: *Encyclopedia of Bohemian and Czech-American Biography*. Bloomington, IN: AuthorHouse, 2016, Vol. 2, p. 751.

Seth Meyers (1973-), b. Evanston, IL, of Czech ancestry; actor, comedian, TV personality, producer, writer
Bio: "Seth Meyers," in: Wikipedia. See - https://en.wikipedia.org/wiki/Seth Meyers; Rechcigl, Miloslav, Jr., "Seth Adam Meyers," in: *Encyclopedia of Bohemian and Czech-American Biography*. Bloomington, IN: AuthorHouse, 2016, Vol. 2, p. 751.

Martin Miller (orig. Rudolph Műller) (1899-1969), b. Kroměříž, Moravia; character actor
Bio: "Martin Miller," in: Wikipedia. See - https://en.wikipedia.org/wiki/Martin Miller (actor); *International Biographical Dictionary of Central European Emigrés 1933-1945*. Műnchen: K. G. Saur, 1983, Vol. 2, p. 819.

Miroslava (orig. Miroslava Šternová) (1925-1955), b. Prague, Czech.; Mexican film actress
Bio: "Miroslava," in: Wikipedia. See - https://en.wikipedia.org/wiki/Miroslava (actress);

Elinor 'Nell' Teresa Newman (1959-), b. New York, NY, of Slovak ancestry; child actress, environmentalist, biologist

Bio: "Nell Newman," in: Wikipedia. See - https://en.wikipedia.org/wiki/Nell_Newman

Melissa Newman (1961-), b. Hollywood, CA, of Slovak ancestry; screen actress, artist, singer
Bio: "Melissa Newman," in: Wikipedia. See - https://en.wikipedia.org/wiki/Melissa_Newman

Paul Newman (1925-2008), b. Shaker Heights, OH, of Slovak ancestry; actor, film director, producer, activist, race car driver
Bio: "Paul Newman," in: Wikipedia. See - https://en.wikipedia.org/wiki/Paul Newman;
Godfrey, Lionel, *Paul Newman Superstar: A Critical Biography.* New York, NY: St. Martin's Press, 1979; O'Brien, Daniel, *Paul Newman.* London, UK: Faber, 2004; Landry, J. C., *Paul Newman.* New York, NY: McGraw-Hill, 1983; Lax, Eric, 6). *Paul Newman: A Biography.* Atlanta, GA: Turner Pub., 1996.

Scott Newman (1950-1978), b. Cleveand, OH, of Slovak ancestry; film and TV actor, stuntman
Bio: "Scott Newman," in: Wikipedia. See - https://en.wikipedia.org/wiki/Scott_Newman_(actor)

Catherine Reitman (1981-), b. Los Angeles, CA, of Slovak ancestry; actress, film critic
Bio: "Catherine Reitman," in: Wikipedia. See - https://en.wikipedia.org/wiki/Catherine_Reitman

Frederick Ritter (1896-1987), b. Vienna, of Moravian father; actor, writer
Bio: Rechcigl, Miloslav, Jr., "Frederick Ritter,", in: *Encyclopedia of Bohemian and Czech- American Biography.* Bloomington, IN: AuthorHouse, 2016, Vol. 2, p. 1246.

Antonio Sabato, Jr. (1972-), b. Rome, Italy, of Bohemian ancestry; actor and model
Bio: "Antonio Sabato, Jr.," in: Wikipedia. See - https://en.wikipedia.org/wiki/Antonio Sabàto Jr.

Joseph Schildkraut (1896-1964), b. Vienna, of Slovak ancestry; stage and film actor
Bio: "Joseph Schildkraut," in: Wikipedia. See - https://en.wikipedia.org/wiki/Joseph Schildkrauthttps://en.wikipedia.org/wiki/Joseph Schildkraut

Stefan Schnabel (1912-1999), b. Berlin, Germany, of Moravian ancestry, actor
Bio: Rechcigl, Miloslav, Jr. in: *Encyclopedia of Bohemian and Czech- American Biography*. Bloomington, IN: AuthorHouse, 2016, Vol. 2, p. 757.

Libby Skala, b. Englewood, NJ, of Czech ancestry; Canadian actress and writer
Bio: "Libby Skala," in Wikipedia. See - https://en.wikipedia.org/wiki/Libby Skala

Lilia Skala (née Sofer) (1896-1994); b. Vienna, of Bohemian mother; actress
Bio: Rechcigl, Miloslav, Jr., "Lilia Skala," in: Encyclopedia of Bohemian and Czech- American Biography. Bloomington, IN: AuthorHouse, 2016, Vol. 2, p. 758.

Erika Alena Slezak (1946-), b. Hollywood, CA, of Moravian ancestry; stage actress
Bio: "Biography for Erika Slezak," IMDb Website.

Walter Slezak (1902-1983), b. Vienna, of Moravian ancestry; character actor and singer
Bio: Walter Slezak's Obituary, *New York Times*, April 23, 1983; Biography of Walter Slezak, IMDb. See: http://www.imdb.com/name/nm0805790/bio; Wikipedia. See: https://en.wikipedia.org/wiki/Walter Slezak

Magda Sonja (1886-1974), b. Hradisko, Slovakia, silent movie actress
Bio: "Magda Sonja," in: Wikipedia. See - https://en.wikipedia.org/wiki/Magda_Sonja

Ruby Wax (orig. Wachs) (1953-), b. Evanston, IL, of Moravian ancestry; Amercan actress, mental health campaigner, author
Bio: "Ruby Wax," in: Wikipedia. See - https://en.wikipedia.org/wiki/Ruby_Wax

Matt Wayne (1986-), b. York, PA, of Slovak ancestry; illusionist, producer and TV personality
Bio: "Matt Wayne," in: Wikipedia. See - https://en.wikipedia.org/wiki/Matt Wayne (magician)Helene

Helene Weigel (1900-1971), b. Vienna, of Moravian parents; stage actress
Bio: "Helene Weigel," in: Wikipedia. See - https://en.wikipedia.org/wiki/Helene_Weigel

Chris Weitz (1969), b. New York city, of Bohemian ancestry; filmmaker, actor
Bio: Wikipedia. See: https://en.wikipedia.org/wiki/Chris_Weitz

Paul John Weitz (1965-), b. New York City, of Bohemian ancestry;
Bio: "Paul Weitz (filmmaker)," in: Wikipedia. See - https://en.wikipedia.org/wiki/Paul_Weitz_(filmmaker)

Cornel Wilde (1912-1989 Prievidza, Slovakia; actor and film director
Bio: "Cornell Wilde," in: Wikipedia. See - https://en.wikipedia.org/wiki/Cornel_Wilde

Roland Winters (1904-1989), b. Boaton, MA, of Bohemian ancestry; actor in films and TV
Bio: "Roland Winters," in: Wikipedia. See - https://en.wikipedia.org/wiki/Roland Winters; "Roland Winters, 84; Played Charlie Chan," *The New York Times*, October 25, 1989

Trevor Wright (1980-), b. San Diego, CA, of Czech ancestry; actor
Bio: "Trevor Wright,", in: Wikipedia. See - https://en.wikipedia.org/wiki/Trevor_Wright

Ed Wynn (1886-1966), b. Philadelphia, PA, of Bohemian ancestry; actor and comedian
Bio: "Ed Wynn," in: Wikipedia. See - https://en.wikipedia.org/wiki/Ed Wynn

Keenan Wynn (1916-1986), b. New York City, of Bohemian ancestry; character actor
Bio: "Keenan Wynn," in: Wikipedia. See - https://en.wikipedia.org/wiki/Keenan Wynn

Ned Wynn (1941-), b. New York, NY, of Bohemian ancestry; actor
Bio: "Rechcigl, Miloslav, Jr., "Ned Wynn," in: *Encyclopedia of Bohemian and Czech- American Biography*. Bloomington, IN: AuthorHouse, 2016, Vol. 2, p. 764.

3. Dancers

Adele Astaire (orig. Austerlitz) (1898-1981), b. Omaha, NE, of Bohemian ancestry; vaudeville and theatre dancer and actress
Bio: Rechcigl, Miloslav, Jr.., "Adele Astaire," in: *Encyclopedia of Bohemian and Czech- American Biography*. Bloomington, IN: AuthorHouse, 2016, Vol. 2, p. 765.

Fred Astaire (orig. Austerlitz) 1899-1987), b. Omaha, NE, of Bohemian ancestry; dancer, actor, singer, choreographer
Bio: Freeland, Michael. *Fred Astaire.* An Illustrated Biography. Grosset & Dunlap, 1976;
Billman, Larry. *Fred Astaire - A Bio-Bibliography*, Greenwood Press, 1997; Boyer, G. Bruce. Fred Astaire Style, Assouline, 2005; Epstein, Joseph, *Fred Astaire.* New Haven, CT: Yale University Press, 2009. 224 p.; Garofalo, Alessandra. *Austerlitz Sounded Too Much Like a Battle: The Roots of Fred Astaire Family in Europe.* Editrice UNI Service, 2009; "Fred Astaire," in: Wikipedia. See - https://en.wikipedia.org/wiki/Fred Astaire

Getrude Bunzel (née Goldschmied) (1910-d.), b. Vienna, of Moravian father; dancer, choreographer

Bio: Rechcigl, Miloslav, Jr., "Getrude Bunzel," in: *Encyclopedia of Bohemian and Czech- American Biography*. Bloomington, IN: AuthorHouse, 2016, Vol. 2, p. 767.

Getrude Prokosch Kurath (1903-1992), b. Chicago, IL, of Bohemian father; dancer, researcher, author, ethnomusicologist
Bio: Rechcigl, Miloslav, Jr., "Getrude Prokosch Kurath," in: *Encyclopedia of Bohemian and Czech- American Biography*. Bloomington, IN: AuthorHouse, 2016, Vol. 1, 703.

Maria Ley-Piscator (née Friederike Czada) (1898-1999), b. Vienna, of Bohemian ancestry, dancer and choreographer
Bio: "Maria Ley-Piscator," in: Wikipedia. See: https://en.wikipedia.org/wiki/Maria_Ley-Piscator; *International Biographical Dictionary of Central European Emigrés 1933-1945*. Műnchen: K. G. Saur, 1983, Vol. 2, p. 724.

Rebecca Nettl-Fiol (1953-), b. Indiana, of Czech father; dancer, choreographer, professor of modern dance, University of Illinois
Bio: Rechcigl, Miloslav, Jr., "Rebecca Nettl-Foil," in: *Encyclopedia of Bohemian and Czech- American Biography*. Bloomington, IN: AuthorHouse, 2016, Vol. 2, p. 769.

Ruth A. Sobotka (1925-1967), b. Vienna, of Bohemian ancestry; dancer, custom designer, art director, painter and actress
Bio: Rechcigl, Miloslav, Jr., "Ruth A. Sobotka," in: *Encyclopedia of Bohemian and Czech- American Biography*. Bloomington, IN: AuthorHouse, 2016, Vol. 2, pp. 770-771.

4. Directors, Producers

Norbert Auerbach (1924-2009), b. Vienna, of Bohemian mother; president of United Artists
Bio: Saperstein, Pat, "Studio executive Norbert Auerbach dies," Variety, December 16, 2009; Rechcigl, Miloslav, Jr., "Norbert Auerbach," in: *Encyclopedia of Bohemian and Czech- American Biography*. Bloomington, IN: AuthorHouse, 2016, Vol. 2, p. 772; "Norbert Auerbach," in: Wikipedia. See - https://cs.wikipedia.org/wiki/Norbert_Auerbach

Martin Beck (1867-1940), b. Liptovský Mikuláš, Slovakia; vaudeville theater manager, owner, and impresario
Bio: Downer, Alan S., "Beck, Martin," in: *Dictionary of American Biography*, Suppl. 2, pp. 32-33; "Martin Beck Dies, Theatre Veteran," *The New York Times*, November 17, 1940; "Martin Beck (vaudeville)," in: Wikipedia. See - https://en.wikipedia.org/wiki/Martin_Beck_(vaudeville)

Michael Bergmann, b. of Czech ancestry; American writer, director and producer
Bio: Rechcigl, Miloslav, Jr., "Michael Bergmann," in: *Encyclopedia of Bohemian and Czech- American Biography*. Bloomington, IN: AuthorHouse, 2016, Vol. 2, pp. 772-773; "Michael Bergmann," in: Wikipedia. See - https://en.wikipedia.org/wiki/Michael Bergmann

Breck Eisner (1970-), b. California, of Bohemian ancestry; TV and film director
Bio: "Breck Eisner," in: Wikipedia. See - https://en.wikipedia.org/wiki/Breck Eisner

Eric Eisner (ca. 1970), b. California, of Bohemian ancestry; film director and producer, founder of Double E. Pictures
"Eric Eisner," in: Wikipedia. See - https://en.wikipedia.org/wiki/Eric_Eisner

Miloš Forman (1932-), b. Čáslav, Bohemia; film director, screenwriter, actor, and professor
Bio: "Forman, Miloš," *Current Biography Yearbook* 1971 (1982), pp. 138-140; Slater, Thomas J., *Miloš Forman: A Bio-Bibliography*. Westport, CT: Greenwood Press, 1987. 208p.; "Miloš Forman," in: Wikipedia. See - https://en.wikipedia.org/wiki/Milo%C5%A1 Forman

Peter R. Gimbel (1927-1987), b. New York, NY, of Bohemian ancestry; film maker and underwater photojournalist
Bio: Rechcigl, Miloslav, Jr., "Peter R. Gimbel," in: *Encyclopedia of Bohemian and Czech- American Biography*. Bloomington, IN: AuthorHouse, 2016, Vol. 2, pp. 776-777.

Kate Guinzburg (19577-2017), b. New York, NY, of Bohemian ancestry; producer, Michelle Pfeiffer's producing partner
Bio: Rechcigl, Miloslav, Jr., "Kate Guinzburg," *Encyclopedia of Bohemian and Czech- American Biography.* Bloomington, IN: AuthorHouse, 2016, Vol. 2, p. 777; Barnes, Mike, "Kate Guinzburg, Producing Partner of Michelle Pfeiffer, Dies at 60," The Hollywood Reporter, September 19, 2017

Zuzana Justman (née Pick) (1931-) b. Prague, Czech.; documentary filmmaker and writer
Bio: "Zuzana Justman, in: Wikipedia. See - https://en.wikipedia.org/wiki/Zuzana Justman' Rechcigl, Miloslav, Jr. "Zuzana Justman," in: *Encyclopedia of Bohemian and Czech- American Biography.* Bloomington, IN: AuthorHouse, 2016, Vol. 2, p. 778.

Alexandra Kerry (1973-), b. Concord, MA, of Moravian ancestry; filmmaker, partner of Locomotive Films and co-founder of Fictional Pictures
Bio: "Alexandra Kerry," in: Wikipedia. See - https://en.wikipedia.org/wiki/Alexandra Kerry

Pancho (née Paul Julius) Kohner (1939-), b. Los Angeles, CA; producer and director
Bio: "Pancho Kohner: Film producing is not an easy job," in: UNITEDFilm. See - http://www.unitedfilm.cz/unitedvision/index.php/en/articles/item/393-pancho-kohner-film-producing-is-not-an-easy-job

Fritz Lang (1890-1976), b. Vienna, of Moravian ancestry; filmmaker, screenwriter, film producer and actor
Bio: "Fritz Lang," in: Wikipedia. See - https://en.wikipedia.org/wiki/Fritz Lang

George Lederer (1862-1938), b. Wilkes-Barre, PA, of Bohemian parents; producer and director on Broadway
Bio: "George Lederer," in: Wikipedia. See - https://en.wikipedia.org/wiki/George Lederer

Terry Hamlisch Liebling (1942-2001), b. New York, NY, of Moravian ancestry; a casting director
Bio: Rechcigl, Miloslav, Jr., "Terry Hamlisch Liebling," in: *Encyclopedia of Bohemian and Czech- American Biography.* Bloomington, IN: AuthorHouse, 2016, Vol. 2, pp. 779-780.

Ernst Lothar (1890-1974), b. Brno, Moravia; writer, theatre director/ manager, producer
Bio: Ernst Lothar," in: Wikipedia. See - https://en.wikipedia.org/wiki/ Ernst Lothar

Kyle Newacheck (1984-), b. Walnut Creek, CA, of Bohemian ancestry; TV writer, director, producer and actor
Bio: "Kyle Newacheck," in: Wikipedia. See - https://en.wikipedia.org/ wiki/Kyle Newacheck

Emil Radok (1918-1994), b. Koloděje nad Lužnicí, Czech., film director, co-inventor of the multimedia show Laterna magica, immigrated to Canada
Bio: "Emil Radok," in: Wikipedia. See - https://en.wikipedia.org/wiki/ Emil_Radok

Gottfried Reinhardt (1913-1994), b. Berlin, Ger., of Bohemian and Slovak ancestry; film director and producer
Bio: Grimes, William, "Gottfried Reinhardt, 81, Film Director and Producer," *The New York Times*, July 21, 1994; "Gottfried Reinhardt," in: Wikipedia. See - https://en.wikipedia.org/wiki/Gottfried_Reinhardt

Max Reinhardt (1873-1943), b. Baden, near Vienna, of Bohemian and Slovak ancestry; theatre and film director, intendant and theatrical producer
Bio: "Max Reinhardt," in: Wikipedia. See - https://en.wikipedia.org/wiki/ Max Reinhardt

Karel Reisz (1926-2002), b. Ostarva, Czech.; filmmaker

Bio: Rechcigl, Miloslav, Jr., "Karel Reisz," in: *Encyclopedia of Bohemian and Czech- American Biography*. Bloomington, IN: AuthorHouse, 2016, Vol. 2, p. 783.

Ivan Reitman (1946-), b. Komárno, Slovakia; Canadian film producer and director
Bio: "Ivan Reitman," in: Wikipedia. See - https://en.wikipedia.org/wiki/Ivan_Reitman

Jason Reitman (1977-), b. Montreal, Canada, of Slovak ancestry; Canadian-American film director, screenwriter and producer
Bio: "Jason Reitman," in: Wikipedia. See - https://en.wikipedia.org/wiki/Jason Reitma

Kurt Robitschek (later Ken Robey) (1890-1950), b. Prague, Bohemia; vaudeville, theatre director
Bio: *Osterreichisches biographisches Lexikon, 1815-1950*, Vol. 9 (1985), p. 190

Erich von Stroheim (1885-1957), b. Vienna, of Bohemia mother; director, producer and actor of the silent era
Bio: Rechcigl, Miloslav, Jr., "Erich von Stroheim," in: *Encyclopedia of Bohemian and Czech- American Biography*. Bloomington, IN: AuthorHouse, 2016, Vol. 2, p. 784; "Erich von Stroheim," in: Wikipedia. See - https://en.wikipedia.org/wiki/Erich_von_Stroheim

Edgar G. Ulmer (1904-1972), b. Olomouc, Moravia; film director who worked on Hollywood B movies and other low-budget productions
Bio: "Edgar G. Ulmer," in: Wikipedia. See - https://en.wikipedia.org/wiki/Edgar_G._Ulmer

Jiří Weiss (1913-2004), b. Prague, Bohemia; film director and screenwriter
Bio: 'Rechcigl, Miloslav, Jr., "Jiří Weiss," in: *Encyclopedia of Bohemian and Czech- American Biography*. Bloomington, IN: AuthorHouse, 2016, Vol. 2, p. 785; Jiří Weiss," in: Wikipedia. See – https://en.wikipedia.org/wiki/Jiří_Weiss; Koppel, Lily, "Jiri Weiss, 91, Czech Director Who Shaped Postwar Cinema," The New York Times, June 6, 2004

Chris Weitz (1969-), b. New York, NY, of Bohemian ancestry; filmmaker, author, actor
Bio: "Chris Weiz," in: Wikipedia. See - https://en.wikipedia.org/wiki/Chris Weitz

Paul Weitz (1965-), b. New York, NY, of Bohemian ancestry; film director, producer, screenwriter, actor
Bio: "Paul Weitz," in: Wikipedia. See - https://en.wikipedia.org/wiki/Paul_Weitz_(filmmaker)

Peter Zinner (1919-2007), b. Vienna, of Slovak ancestry; American filmmaker and producer
Bio: "Peter Zinner," in: Wikipedia. See - https://en.wikipedia.org/wiki/Peter_Zinner

5. Scenic Designers and Art Directors

Lisa Aronson (née Jalowetz), set designer, part of the Broadway theater design team, with her husband Boris Aronson, garnering six Tony awards
Bio: "Lisa Aronson (Jalowetz)," in: GENi. See - https://www.geni.com/people/Lisa-Aronson/6000000021036714587

Harry Horner (1910-1994), b. Holice, Bohemia; art director, film and television director
Bio: "Harry Horner," in: Wikipedia. See - https://en.wikipedia.org/wiki/Harry Horner; rechcigl, Miloslav, Jr., "Harry Horner," in: *Encyclopedia of Bohemian and Czech - American Biography.* Bloomington, IN: AuthorHouse, 2016, Vol. 2, p. 796.

James Horner (1955-), b. Los Angeles, CA, of Bohemian ancestry; set designer, with MGM
Bio: Rechcigl, Miloslav, Jr., "James Horner," in: *Encyclopedia of Bohemian and Czech- American Biography.* Bloomington, IN: AuthorHouse, 2016, Vol. 2, p. 796.
J. Michael Riva (1948-2012), b. Manhattan, NY, of Bohemian ancestry; production designer

Bio: "J. Michael Riva," in: Wikipedia. See - https://en.wikipedia.org/wiki/J. Michael Riva; Rechcigl, Miloslav, Jr., "J. Michael Riva," in: *Encyclopedia of Bohemian and Czech- American Biography*. Bloomington, IN: AuthorHouse, 2016, Vol. 2, p. 797; Reiss, Jon, "A Tribute to an Exceptional Man: Michael Riva, in the Details," *Filmmaker Magazine*, June 11, 2012.

6. Screenwriters

Hans Janowitz (1890-1954), b. Poděbrady, Czech.; film scriptwriter
Bio: "Hans Janowitz," in: Wikipedia. See - https://en.wikipedia.org/wiki/Hans Janowitz; Rechcigl, Miloslav, Jr., "Hans Janowitz," in: *Encyclopedia of Bohemian and Czech-American Biography*. Bloomington, IN: AuthorHouse, 2016, Vol. 2, p. 808.

Milena Jelinek (née Tobolová) (1935-), b. Czech.; screenwriter, playwright and teacher
Bio: "Milena Jelinek," in: Wikipedia. See - https://en.wikipedia.org/wiki/Milena Jelinek; Rechcigl, Miloslav, Jr., "Milena Jelinek," in: : *Encyclopedia of Bohemian and Czech-American Biography*. Bloomington, IN: AuthorHouse, 2016, Vol. 2, pp. 808-809

Charles Davies Lederer (1906-1976), b. New York, NY, of Bohemian ancestry; screenwriter and film director
Bio: "Charles Lederer," in: Wikipedia. See - https://en.wikipedia.org/wiki/Charles Lederer; Rechcigl, Miloslav, Jr., "Charles Davies Lederer," in: *Encyclopedia of Bohemian and Czech-American Biography*. Bloomington, IN: AuthorHouse, 2016, Vol. 2, p. 809.

Steve Stoliar (1954-), b. St. Louis, MO, of Bohemian ancestry; actor and scriptwriter for TV and film
Bio: Rechcigl, Miloslav, Jr., "Steve Stoliar,", in: *Encyclopedia of Bohemian and Czech-American Biography*. Bloomington, IN: AuthorHouse, 2016, Vol. 2, pp. 809-810.

Joseph Urban (1872-1933), b. Vienna, of Bohemian ancestry; architect, illustrator and scenic designer

Bio: "Joseph Urban," in: Wikipedia. See - https://en.wikipedia.org/wiki/Joseph Urban; Rechcigl, Miloslav, Jr., "Joseph Urban," in: *Encyclopedia of Bohemian and Czech-American Biography*. Bloomington, IN: AuthorHouse, 2016, Vol. 2, p. 798.

Tracy Keenan Wynn (1945-), b. Hollywood, CA, of Bohemian ancestry, screenwriter, producer
Bio: "Tracy Keenan Wynn," in: Wikipedia. See - https://en.wikipedia.org/wiki/Tracy_Keenan_Wynn

7. Talent Agents

Paul Kohner (1902-1988), b. Teplice-Šanov, Bohemia; talent agent and producer
Bio: "Paul Kohner," in: Wikipedia. See - https://en.wikipedia.org/wiki/Paul Kohner; Rechcigl, Miloslav, Jr., "Paul Kohner," in: *Encyclopedia of Bohemian and Czech-American Biography*. Bloomington, IN: AuthorHouse, 2016, Vol. 2, p. 799.

Walter Kohner (1914-1996), b. Teplice-Šanov, Bohemia; Hollywood talent agent
Bio: Rechcigl, Miloslav, Jr., "Walter Kohner,", in: *Encyclopedia of Bohemian and Czech-American Biography*. Bloomington, IN: AuthorHouse, 2016, Vol. 2, p. 799.

8. Performing Arts Educators and Historians

Stefan Brecht (1924-2009), b. Berlin, Ger., of Moravian ancestry; poet, critic and scholar of theater
Bio: "Stefan Brecht," in: Wikipedia. See - https://en.wikipedia.org/wiki/Stefan Brecht; Rechcigl, Miloslav, Jr., "Stefan Brecht," in: *Encyclopedia of Bohemian and Czech-American Biography*. Bloomington, IN: AuthorHouse, 2016, Vol. 2, p. 801; Hunt, Ken, "Stefan Brecht: Poet, philosopher and theatre historian who struggled to escape his father's shadow," Independent, May 21, 2009; "Stefan Brecht, Theater Historian, is dead at 84," *The New York Times*, April 22, 2009.

Joan Copjec (1946-), b. Hartford, CT, of Czech ancestry; specialist on cinema studies, professor of modern culture and media, Brown University, philosopher, feminist, political theorist
Bio: Rechcigl, Miloslav, Jr. "Joan Copjec," in: *Encyclopedia of Bohemian and Czech-American Biography*. Bloomington, IN: AuthorHouse, 2016, Vol. 2, p. 802; Nickel, Mark, "Joan Copjec," *News from Brown,* Brown University. See - https://news.brown.edu/new-faculty/humanities/joan-copjec

Marinka Gurewich (1902-1990), b. Bratislava, Slovakia, of Bohemian ancestry; voice teacher and mezzo-soprano
Bio: "Marinka Gurewich, A Voice Teacher, 88," *The New York Times,* December 25, 1990;
"Marinka Gurewich," in: Wikipedia. See - https://en.wikipedia.org/wiki/Marinka Gurewich;

Marketa Kimbrell (1928-2011), b. nr. Prague, Czech.; actress, professor of acting and film directing, co-founder of the New York Street Theater Caravan
Bio: Rechcigl, Miloslav, Jr., "Marketa Kimbrell," in: *Encyclopedia of Bohemian and Czech-American Biography*. Bloomington, IN: AuthorHouse, 2016, Vol. 2, p. 803; "Marketa Kimbrell," in: Wikipedia. See - https://en.wikipedia.org/wiki/Marketa_Kimbrell

Antonín Liehm (1924-), b. Prague, Czech.; journalist, cultural publicist, author of books on films
Bio: Rechcigl, Miloslav, Jr., "Antonín Liehm," in: *Encyclopedia of Bohemian and Czech-American Biography*. Bloomington, IN: AuthorHouse, 2016, Vol. 2, p. 804; "Antonín J. Liehm," in: Wikipedia. See - https://en.wikipedia.org/wiki/Anton%C3%ADn J. Liehm

Jennie Mannheimer (aka Jane Manner) (1872-1943), b. New York, of Bohemian ancestry; dramatist, founder of the Cincinnati School of Expression, director of drama department of the Cincinnati College of Music
Bio: Rechcigl, Miloslav, Jr., "Jane Manner," in: *Encyclopedia of Bohemian and Czech-American Biography*. Bloomington, IN: AuthorHouse, 2016, Vol. 2, p. 805; "Jennie Mannheimer," in: Wikipedia. See - https://en.wikipedia.org/wiki/Jennie_Mannheimer.

Lisa Peschel (1965-), b. Madison, WI, of Bohemian ancestry; theater historiographer
Bio: Rechcigl, Miloslav, Jr., "Lisa Peschel," in: *Encyclopedia of Bohemian and Czech-American Biography*. Bloomington, IN: AuthorHouse, 2016, Vol. 2, pp. 805-806; "Follow Dr. Lisa Peschel," in: US Holocaust Museum 2018, 25.

George E. Wellwarth (1932-), b. Vienna, of Bohemian mother; actor, professor of theater and comparative literature, State University of New York, Binghamton
Bio: Rechcigl, Miloslav, Jr., "George E. Wellwarth," in: *Encyclopedia of Bohemian and Czech-American Biography*. Bloomington, IN: AuthorHouse, 2016, Vol. 2, p. 808.

G. Visual Art

1. General

Kisch, Guido, "Painting and Graphic Arts," in: *In Search of Freedom*. A History of American Jews from Czechoslovakia 1592-1948. London: Edward Goldston, 1948, pp. 177-180.

2. Architects

David Adler (1882-1949), b. Milwaukee, WI, of Bohemian ancestry; architect, Chicago
Bio: "David Adler," in: Wikipedia. See - https://en.wikipedia.org/wiki/David_Adler_(architect)

Felix Augenfeld (1893-1984), b. Vienna, of Bohemian ancestry; architect, interior designer
Bio: "Felix Augenfeld," in: Wikipedia, See - https://de.wikipedia.org/wiki/Felix Augenfeld; "Felix Augenfeld," *The New York Times*, July 23, 1984; Rechcigl, Miloslav, Jr. "Felix Augenfeld," in: *Encyclopedia of Bohemian and Czech-American Biography*. Bloomington, IN: AuthorHouse, 2016, Vol. 2, p. 898.

John Jacob Desmond (1922-2008), b. Denver, CO, of Bohemian ancestry; architect in Baton Rouge, LA
Bio: "John Jacob Desmond," *Who's Who in America, 1997*, pp. 1045-1046; "John Desmond," in: Wikipedia. See - https://en.wikipedia.org/wiki/John Desmond; "John J. Desmond Obituary," *The Advocate*, March 29, 2008. See also - http://obits.theadvocate.com/obituaries/theadvocate/obituary.aspx?pid=106519855

John Michael Desmond (1953-), b. New Orleans, LA, of Bohemian ancestry; architect
professor of architecture, Louisiana State University
Bio: "John Michael Desmond," in: *Encyclopedia of Bohemian and Czech-American Biography*. Bloomington, IN: AuthorHouse, 2016, Vol. 2, p. 901.

Cyrus Lazelle Warner Eidlitz (1853-1921), b. New York, NY, of Bohemian father; architect, NYC
Bio: "Cyrus L. Eidlitz," in: *Encyclopedia of Bohemian and Czech-American Biography*. Bloomington, IN: AuthorHouse, 2016, Vol. 2, p. 902.

Leopold Eidlitz (1823-1908), b. Prague, Bohemia; prominent NYC architect
Bio: Holliday, Kathryn E., *Leopold Eidlitz: Architecture and Idealism in the Gilded Age*. New York, NY: W.W. Norton & Co., 2008. 200p.; Schuyler, Montgomery, "A Great American Architect: Leopold Eidlitz," *The Architectural Record*, 24 (July-December 1908), pp. 163-179, 277-292, 364-378.

Robert James Eidlitz (1863-1935), b. New York, NY, of Bohemian ancestry; architect, NYC
Bio: Recghcigl, Miloslav, Jr., "Robert James Eidlitz," in: *Encyclopedia of Bohemian and Czech-American Biography*. Bloomington, IN: AuthorHouse, 2016, Vol. 2, p. 902.

Martin Eisler (1913-1977), b. Vienna, of Bohemian ancestry; architect, furniture designer, founder of the iconic Brazilian furniture company Forma, Buenos Aires

Bio: Rechcigl, Miloslav, Jr., "Martin Eisler," in: *Encyclopedia of Bohemian and Czech-American Biography*. Bloomington, IN: AuthorHouse, 2016, Vol. 2, pp. 902-903.

Frances Adler Elkins (1888-1953), b. Milwaukee, WI, of Bohemian ancestry; interior designer
Bio: Rechcigl, Miloslav, Jr., "Frances Adler Elkins," in: *Encyclopedia of Bohemian and Czech-American Biography*. Bloomington, IN: AuthorHouse, 2016, Vol. 2, p. 920; "Decorator to Know: Frances Elkins," in: The Study. See - https://www.1stdibs.com/blogs/the-study/frances-elkins/

Victor Fűrth (1893-1984), b. Horažďovice, Bohemia; architect, professor of architecture, University of Miami
Bio: "Victor Furth," in: Wikipedia. See - https://en.wikipedia.org/wiki/Victor_Furth

Victor Gruen (1903-1980), b. Vienna, of Moravian ancestry; architect, pioneer of shopping centers
Bio: Hardwick, M. Jeffrey, Mall Maker, *Victor Gruen, Architect of an American Dream*. Philadelphia: University of Pennsylvania Press, 2003; *Current Biography Yearbook*,1959, pp. 162-63; and Who Was Who in America,1985, Vol. 8, pp. 240-41.

Kamil Stephen Gschwind (1931-2005), b. Plzeň, Czech.; architect, Richmond Heights, OH
Bio: Rechcigl, Miloslav, Jr., "Kamil Stephen Gschwind," in: *Encyclopedia of Bohemian and Czech-American Biography*. Bloomington, IN: AuthorHouse, 2016, Vol. 2, p. 904.

Albert Janowitz (1867-1936), b. London, of Bohemian parents; architect, Peoria, IL
Bio: Rechcigl, Miloslav, Jr., "Albert Janowitz," in: *Encyclopedia of Bohemian and Czech-American Biography*. Bloomington, IN: AuthorHouse, 2016, Vol. 2, p. 906.

Arnold Karplus (1877-1943), b. Vítkov, Moravia; architect, NYC

Bio: "Arnold Karplus," in: Wikipedia. See - https://en.wikipedia.org/wiki/Arnold_Karplus

Gerhard Emanuel Karplus (1909-1995), b. Vienna, of Moravian ancestry; architect, Florida
Bio: "Karplus, Gerhard Emanuel, Architect," in: Florida DBPR. See - https://www.myfloridalicense.com/LicenseDetail.asp?SID=&id=04F03A65CFE4FB8E45E272EE50DD3679

Robert Michael Kliment (1933-), b. Prague, Czech.; architect, NYC, professor in several universities
Bio: Rechcigl, Miloslav, Jr., "Robert Michael Kliment" in: *Encyclopedia of Bohemian and Czech-American Biography*. Bloomington, IN: AuthorHouse, 2016, Vol. 2, pp. 906-907; "Robert Kliment Obituary," *The New York Times*, June 6, 2017.

Stephen Alexander Kliment (1930-2008), b. Prague, Czech.; architect and editor
Bio: Rechcigl, Miloslav, Jr., "Stephen Alexander Kliment," in: *Encyclopedia of Bohemian and Czech-American Biography*. Bloomington, IN: AuthorHouse, 2016, Vol. 2, p. 907; "S. A. Kliment, 78, Architect and Editor, is Dead," *The New York Times,* September 18, 2008.

Karl Kohn (1894-1979), b. Prague, Bohemia; architect, Quito, Ecuador
Bio: "Karl Kohn," in: Wikipedia. See - https://en.wikipedia.org/wiki/Karl_Kohn

Otto Kohn (1887-1965), b. Libeznice, Bohemia; architect, NYC
Bio: Otto Kohn," in: Wikipedia. See - https://cs.wikipedia.org/wiki/Otto_Kohn

Otto Kollisch (1881-1951), b. Vienna, of Moravian ancestry; architect and master builder
Bio: "Otto Kollisch," in: *Architektenlexicon,* Wien 1770-1945. See - http://www.architektenlexikon.at/de/310.htm

Dion Neutra (1926), b. Los Angeles, CA, of Czech ancestry; architect, modernist
Bio: "Dion Neutra," in: Wikipedia. See - https://en.wikipedia.org/wiki/Dion_Neutra

Richard Neutra (1892-1970), b. Vienna, of Moravian ancestry; architect, introduced international style
Bio: Thomas S. Hines, "Neutra, Richard," *Dictionary of American Biography*, Suppl. 8 (1988), pp. 462-54; *Current Biography Yearbook* (1961), pp. 341-43.

Ernst Preisler (1855-1934), b. Prague, Bohemia; architect, St. Louis
Bio: Rechcigl, Miloslav, Jr., "Ernst Preisler," in: *Encyclopedia of Bohemian and Czech-American Biography*. Bloomington, IN: AuthorHouse, 2016, Vol. 2, p. 913.

Walther Prokosch (1911-1991), b. Madison, WI, of Bohemian ancestry, architect
Bio: "Walther Prokosch, 79, a Designer of Airports," The New York Times, January 9, 1991.

Emery Roth (1871-1948), b. Sečovce, Slovakia; architect
Bio: Ruttenbaum, Steven, *Mansions in the Cloud: The Skyscraper Palazzi of Emery Roth*. Balsam Press, 1986; "Emery Roth," in: Wikipedia. See - https://en.wikipedia.org/wiki/Emery Roth

Rudolph Michael Schindler (orig. Schlesinger) (1887-1953), b. Vienna, of Bohemian father; architect in or near Los Angeles
Bio: Rechcigl, Miloslav, Jr., "Rudolph Michael Schindler," in: *Encyclopedia of Bohemian and Czech-American Biography*. Bloomington, IN: AuthorHouse, 2016, Vol. 2, p. 915; "Rudolph Schindler," in: Wikipedia.See - https://en.wikipedia.org/wiki/Rudolph_Schindler_(architect)

Walter Sobotka (1888-1972), b. Vienna, of Bohemian father; architect, specializing in residential interiors and furniture design, professor of textile and applied arts, University of Pittsburgh
Bio: "Walter Sobotka," in: GENi. See - https://www.geni.com/people/Walter-Sobotka/6000000008155204724; Rechcigl, Miloslav, Jr., "Walter

S. Sobotka," in: *Encyclopedia of Bohemian and Czech-American Biography*. Bloomington, IN: AuthorHouse, 2016, Vol. 2, pp. 916-917.

Clarence Samuel Stein (1882-1975), b. Rochester, NY, of Bohemian ancestry; urban planner, architect, a major proponent of the Garden City movement in the US
Bio: Rechcigl, Miloslav, Jr., "Clarence Stein," in: *Encyclopedia of Bohemian and Czech-American Biography*. Bloomington, IN: AuthorHouse, 2016, Vol. 2, pp. 917-918; "Clarence Stein," in: Wikipedia. See - https://en.wikipedia.org/wiki/Clarence_Stein

Andrew Steiner (1908-2009), b. Dunajská Streda, Slovakia; architect
Bio: "Andrew Steiner," in: Wikipedia. See - https://en.wikipedia.org/wiki/Andrew_Steiner

Eugene Sternberg (1915-2005), b. Bratislava, Slovakia; architect, Colorado
Bio: "Eugene Sternberg," in: Wikipedia. See - https://en.wikipedia.org/wiki/Eugene_Sternberg

William G. Tachau (1875-1969), b. Louisville, KY, of Bohemian ancestry; architect
Bio: Rechcigl, Miloslav, Jr., "William Gabriel Tachau," in: *Encyclopedia of Bohemian and Czech-American Biography*. Bloomington, IN: AuthorHouse, 2016, Vol. 2, p. 918-919; "William G. Tachau," in: Wikipedia. See - https://en.wikipedia.org/wiki/William_G._Tachau

Norbert Troller (1896-1984), b. Brno, Moravia; architect
Bio: Rechcigl, Miloslav, Jr., "Norbert Troller," in: *Encyclopedia of Bohemian and Czech-American Biography*. Bloomington, IN: AuthorHouse, 2016, Vol. 2, p. 919; "Norbert Troller," in: Wikipedia. See - https://en.wikipedia.org/wiki/Norbert Troller

Liane Zimbler (née Juliana Fischer) (1892-1987); b. Přerov, Moravia; architect, interior designer; first European woman to obtain an architecture degree

Bio: "Liane Zimbler," in: Wikipedia. See - https://en.wikipedia.org/wiki/Liane Zimbler

3. Painters

Egon Adler (1892-1963), b. Karlovy Vary, Bohemia; painter, expressionist
Bio: "Egon Adler," in: askArt. See - http://www.askart.com/artist_bio/Egon_Adler/11155828/Egon_Adler.aspx

Dina Babbitt (née Gottliebová) (1923-2009), b. Brno, Czech.; artist, Holocaust survivor
Bio: "Dina Babbitt," in: Wikipedia. See - https://en.wikipedia.org/wiki/Dina Babbitt; Bruce Weber, Bruce, "Dina Babbitt, Artist at Auschwitz, Is Dead at 86," the New York Times, August 1, 2009;

Maurice Braun (1877-1941), b. Bytča, Slovakia; artist landscape impressionist
Bio; "Maurice Braun," in: Wikipedia. See - https://en.wikipedia.org/wiki/Maurice Braun

Jan De Ruth (1922-1991), b. Karlovy Vary, Czech.; Holocaust survivor, portraitist, one of best known painters of the nude female
Bio: Rechcigl, Miloslav, Jr., "Jan De Ruth," in: *Encyclopedia of Bohemian and Czech-American Biography*. Bloomington, IN: AuthorHouse, 2016, Vol. 2, p. 814; "Jann De Ruth (1922-191), in: RoGallery.com. See - http://rogallery.com/Deruth_Jan/DeRuth-biography.htm

Fred (Bedřich) Feigl (1884-1965), b. Prague, Bohemia; painter
Bio: Hodin, J.P., "Fred Feigl at Eighty," *Jewish Quarterly*, 12, No. 2 (1964), pp. 27-28; "Bedřich Feigl," in: Wikipedia. See - https://en.wikipedia.org/wiki/Bedřich_Feigl

David Friedmann (1892-1980), b. Moravská Ostrava, Moravia; painter, Holocaust survivor
Bio: Morris, Miriam Friedman, "Biography of David Friedman," in: Wall of the Historically Noteworthy, Austria-Czech SIG. See - https://www.jewishgen.org/austriaczech/wall-of-fame/friedmann.html; Rechcigl,

Miloslav, Jr. "David Friedmann," in: *Encyclopedia of Bohemian and Czech-American Biography*. Bloomington, IN: AuthorHouse, 2016, Vol. 2, p. 818.

Juliet Hartford (1965-), b. New York, NY, of Bohemian ancestry; artist, painter
Bio: Rechcigl, Miloslav, Jr., "Juliet Hartford," in: *Encyclopedia of Bohemian and Czech-American Biography*. Bloomington, IN: AuthorHouse, 2016, Vol. 2, p. 821.

Fritz Hirschberger (1912-), b. Dresden, Germany, of Czech mother; Holocaust painter
Bio: Feinstein, Stephen C., *Fritz Hirschberger: The Sur-Rational Holocaust Paintings*. Center for Holocaust and Genocide Studies, 2002; Rechcigl, Miloslav, Jr. "Fritz Hirschberger," in: *Encyclopedia of Bohemian and Czech-American Biography*. Bloomington, IN: AuthorHouse, 2016, Vol. 2, p. 821,

Alfred Kantor (1923-2002), Prague, Czech.; Holocaust artist, survivor
Bio: Rechcigl, Miloslav, Jr. "Alfred Kantor," in: *Encyclopedia of Bohemian and Czech-American Biography*. Bloomington, IN: AuthorHouse, 2016, Vol. 2, pp. 825-826; Lewis, Paul, "Alfred Kantor Dies at 79; Depicted Life in Nazi Camps," *The New York Times*, January 26, 2003

Leo Katz (1887-1982), b. Rožnov, Bohemia; painter, modernist, muralist
Bio: Rechcigl, Miloslav, Jr., "Leo Katz," 453-454in: *Beyond the Sea of Beer*. Bloomington, IN: AuthorHouse, 2017, p. 453-454; "Leo Katz Biography," in: The Annex Galleries. See - https://www.annexgalleries.com/artists/biography/1205/Katz/Leo

Enit Kaufman (1897-1961), b. Rosice, Moravia; portrait painter
Bio: Rechcigl, Miloslav, Jr., "Enit Kaufman," in: *Encyclopedia of Bohemian and Czech-American Biography*. Bloomington, IN: AuthorHouse, 2016, Vol. 2, pp. 826-827; "Enit Kaufman, 63, Portraitist, Dead; Impressionist Painted Four Presidents - also did Hull, Marshall, Leahy, Frost," *The New York Times*, January 20, 1961.

Charles H. Kellner (1890-1979), b. Košice, Slovakia; painter, Chicago

Bio: "Charles Kellner," in: askArt. See - http://www.askart.com/artist/Charles H Kellner/70727/Charles H Kellner.aspx

Tatana Kellner (1950-), b. Czech.; artist, photographer
Bio: "Tatana Kellner," in: Wikipedia. See - https://en.wikipedia.org/wiki/Tatana Kellner

Amy Salz Klauber (1872-1928), b. Stockton, CA, of Bohemian ancestry; painter
Bio: Rechcigl, Miloslav, Jr., "Amy Salz Klauber," in: *Encyclopedia of Bohemian and Czech-American Biography*. Bloomington, IN: AuthorHouse, 2016, Vol. 2, p. 828.

Alice Ellen Klauber (1871-1951), b. San Diego, CA, of Bohemian ancestry; painter
Bio: Rechcigl, Miloslav, Jr., "Alice Ellen Klauber," in: *Beyond the Sea of Beer*. Bloomington, IN: AuthorHouse, 2017, p. 683

Leda Josephine Klauber (1881-1981), b. San Diego, CA, of Bohemian ancestry; painter
Bio: Rechcigl, Miloslav, Jr., "Leda Josephine Klauber," in: *Beyond the Sea of Beer*. Bloomington, IN: AuthorHouse, 2017, p. 684

Leo Kober (1876-1931), b. Brno, Moravia; artist, portrait painter and lithographer
Bio: *Who's Who in American Jewry*. Vol. 1, p. 32; Rechcigl, Miloslav, Jr. "Leo Kober," in: *Encyclopedia of Bohemian and Czech-American Biography*. Bloomington, IN: AuthorHouse, 2016, Vol. 2, p. 828.

Henry L. Levy (1868-1940), b. Hartford, CT, of Bohemian ancestry; grandson of Samuel Kakeles of Prague; figure, interiors and still life painter
Bio: Rechcigl, Miloslav, Jr., "Henry L. Levy," in: *Encyclopedia of Bohemian and Czech-American Biography*. Bloomington, IN: AuthorHouse, 2016, Vol. 2, p. 833.

George Lowy (1926-2016), b. Ostrava, Czech.; corporation executive, later becoming a watercolor painter, Silver Spring, MD
Bio: Rechcigl, Miloslav, Jr., "George Lowy," in: *Encyclopedia of Bohemian and Czech-American Biography*. Bloomington, IN: AuthorHouse, 2016, Vol. 2, p. 833.

Gabriele Ella Margules (1927-2016), b. Tachov, Czech.; publishing companies' executive, but is known as an artist and painter.
Bio: Rechcigl, Miloslav, Jr., "Gabriele Ela Margules," in: *Encyclopedia of Bohemian and Czech-American Biography*. Bloomington, IN: AuthorHouse, 2016, Vol. 2, pp. 834-835; "Gabriele Ella Margules," in: Prabook. See - https://prabook.com/web/gabriele_ella.margules/577250

Paul Moschcowitz (1873-1942), b. Giraltovce, Slovakia; artist
Bio: *American Jewish Year Book*, Vol. 6, p. 158.

William Pachner (1915-2017), b. Brtnice, Moravia; abstract painter and illustrator
Bio: "William Pachner," in: Wikipedia. See - https://en.wikipedia.org/wiki/William Pachner; Rechcigl, Miloslav, Jr., "William Pachner," in: *Beyond the Sea of Beer*. Bloomington, IN: AuthorHouse, 2017, p. 589.

Max Pollak (1886-1970), b. Prague, Bohemia; painter
Bio: Rechcigl, Miloslav, Jr. "Max Pollak," in: *Encyclopedia of Bohemian and Czech-American Biography*. Bloomington, IN: AuthorHouse, 2016, Vol. 2, p. 840; "Max Pollak," in: The Annex Galleries. See - https://www.annexgalleries.com/artists/biography/1894/Pollak/Max

Helen A. Salz (1883-1957), b. San Francisco, CA, of Bohemian ancestry; painter in oil, and watercolor, later in pastels
Bio: "Helen Salz (1883-1978)," AskART Website

Frederick Serger (1889-1965), b. Ivančice, Moravia; painter
Bio: "Frederick Serger," in: askArt. See - http://www.askart.com/artist bio/Frederick B Serger/26603/Frederick B Serger.aspx;

Rechcigl, Miloslav, Jr. "Frederick B. Serger," in: *Encyclopedia of Bohemian and Czech-American Biography*. Bloomington, IN: AuthorHouse, 2016, Vol. 2, p. 841.

Melanie Kent Steinhardt (1899-1952), b. Bohemia; painter
Bio: *International Biographical Dictionary of Central European Émigrés 1933-1945*

Daniel Stein-Kubin (1958-), b. Czech.; painter, poet, philosopher
Bio: Rechcigl, Miloslav, Jr., "Daniel Stein-Kubin," in: *Encyclopedia of Bohemian and Czech-American Biography*. Bloomington, IN: AuthorHouse, 2016, Vol. 2, p. 843.

Amy Josephine Klauber Wormser (1903-1988), b. San Diego, CA, of Bohemian ancestry; painter
Bio: Rechcigl, Miloslav, Jr., "Amy Josephine Klauber Wormser," in: *Beyond the Sea of Beer*. Bloomington, IN: AuthorHouse, 2017, p. 685; "Amy Josephine Klauber Wormser (1903 – 1988)," AskART Website.

Ella Klauber Wormser (1863-1932), b. Carson City, NV, of Bohemian ancestry; painter, photographer
Bio: Rechcigl, Miloslav, Jr., "Ella Klauber Wormser," in: *Beyond the Sea of Beer*. Bloomington, IN: AuthorHouse, 2017, p. 683; "Ella Klauber Wormser (1863-1932)," AskART Website.

4. Illustrators

Albert Bloch (1882-1961), b. St. Louis, MO, of Bohemian father; painter, modernist, caricaturist, illustrator
Bio: "Albert Bloch," in: Wikipedia. See - https://en.wikipedia.org/wiki/Albert Bloch;
Rechcigl, Miloslav, Jr., "Albert Bloch," in: *Encyclopedia of Bohemian and Czech-American Biography*. Bloomington, IN: AuthorHouse, 2016, Vol. 2, p. 812.

René Robert Bouché (orig. Buchstein) (1905-1963), fashion and advertising illustrator and painter, with *Vogue* magazine

Bio: Rechcigl, Miloslav, Jr., "Rene Robert Bouché," in: *Encyclopedia of Bohemian and Czech-American Biography.* Bloomington, IN: AuthorHouse, 2016, Vol. 2, pp. 848-849.

William Pachner (1915-), b. Brtnice, Moravia; abstract painter and illustrator
Bio: "William Pachner," in: Wikipedia. See: https://en.wikipedia.org/wiki/William_Pachner ; *International Biographical Dictionary of Central European Emigrés 1933-1945.* Műnchen: K. G. Saur, 1983, Vol. 2, p. 882.

Hugo Steiner-Prag (1880-1945), b. Prague, Bohemia; graphic artist
Bio: Rechcigl, Miloslav, Jr., "Hugo Steiner-Prag," in: *Beyond the Sea of Beer.* Bloomington, IN: AuthorHouse, 2017, p. 456; *Ottův naučný slovník nové doby,* Vol. 6, No. 1, p. 357.

Walter Trier (1890-1951), b. Prague, Bohemia; Canadian illustrator
Bio: *Humorist Walter Trier: Selections from the Trier-Fodor Foundation Gift.* The Art Gallery of Ontario, 1981; Rechcigl, Miloslav, Jr., "Walter Trier," in: *Encyclopedia of Bohemian and Czech-American Biography.* Bloomington, IN: AuthorHouse, 2016, Vol. 2, p. 852; "Walter Trier," in: Wikipedia. See - https://en.wikipedia.org/wiki/Walter Trier

Emil Weiss (1896-1965), b. Moravia; illustrator
Bio: "Emil Weiss," in: *Encyclopedia of Bohemian and Czech-American Biography.* Bloomington, IN: AuthorHouse, 2016, Vol. 2, p. 852-853; "Emil Weiss," in: Wikipedia. See-https://en.wikipedia.org/wiki/Emil Weiss

5. Graphic Artists, Designers

Fritzi Brod (née Schermer) (1900-1952), b. Prague, Bohemia; textile designer, graphic designer
Bio: Rechcigl, Miloslav, Jr., "Fritzi Brod," in: *Encyclopedia of Bohemian and Czech-American Biography.* Bloomington, IN: AuthorHouse, 2016, Vol. 2, pp. 858-859; "Fritzi Brod," in: Modernism in the New City - Chicago Artists, 1920-1950. See - http://www.chicagomodern.org/artists/fritzi_brod/

Charles (Karl) Bruml (1912-1998), b. Prague, Bohemia; graphic artist

Bio: Rechcigl, Miloslav, Jr., "Charles Bruml," in: *Encyclopedia of Bohemian and Czech-American Biography*. Bloomington, IN: AuthorHouse, 2016, Vol. 2, p. 859.

Hans Jelinek (1910-1992), b. Vienna, of Bohemian ancestry; graphic artist, professor of art at City College, NYC
Bio: Rechcigl, Miloslav, Jr., "Hans Jelinek," in: *Encyclopedia of Bohemian and Czech-American Biography*. Bloomington, IN: AuthorHouse, 2016, Vol. 2, p. 824.

Ervine Metzl (1899-1963), b. Chicago, IL, of Bohemian ancestry; graphic artist and illustrator
Bio: "Ervine Metzl," in: Wikipedia. See - https://en.wikipedia.org/wiki/Ervine Metzl; Rechcigl, Miloslav, Jr., "Ervine Metzl," in: *Encyclopedia of Bohemian and Czech-American Biography*. Bloomington, IN: AuthorHouse, 2016, Vol. 2, p. 836.

George Sadek (1928-2007), b. Ústí nad Labem, Bohemia; graphic designer, professor, Dean, Cooper Union
Bio: Rechcigl, Miloslav, Jr., "George Sadek," in: *Encyclopedia of Bohemian and Czech-American Biography*. Bloomington, IN: AuthorHouse, 2016, Vol. 2, p. 861.

Henry Wolf ((1925-2005), b. Vienna, of Moravian ancestry; graphic designer, photographer, art director
Bio: "Henry Wolf," in: Wikipedia. See - https://en.wikipedia.org/wiki/Henry Wolf; Rechcigl, Miloslav, Jr., "Henry Wolf," in: *Encyclopedia of Bohemian and Czech-American Biography*. Bloomington, IN: AuthorHouse, 2016, Vol. 2, p. 863.

6. Cartoonists, Animators

Art Babbitt (orig. Arthur Harold Babitsky) (1907-1992), b. Omaha, NE, of Czech ancestry; animator, developer of the character 'Goofy.'
Bio: "Art Babbitt," in: Wikipedia. See - https://en.wikipedia.org/wiki/Art_Babbitt

Oscar Berger (1901-1997), Prešov, Slovakia; cartoonist in Prague, later in the US
Bio: Berger, Oscar, *Famous Faces; Caricaturist's Scrapbook*. London, Hutchinson. 1950; Berger, Oscar, *My Victims. How to Caricature*. Harper & Bros. NY. 1952; "Oscar Berger (Cartoonist), in: Wikipedia. See - https://en.wikipedia.org/wiki/Oscar Berger (cartoonist)

Albert Bloch (1882-1961), b. St. Louis, MO, of Bohemian father; cartoonist, associated with Der Blaue Reiter, professor of art, University of Kansas
Bio: "Albert Bloch," in: Wikipedia. See - https://en.wikipedia.org/wiki/Albert_Bloch

Gene Deitch (1924-), b. Chicago, based in Prague; illustrator, cartoonist, animator, film director
Bio: "Gene Deitch," in: Wikipedia. See - https://en.wikipedia.org/wiki/Gene Deitch; Rechcigl, Miloslav, Jr., "Gene Deitch," in: *Encyclopedia of Bohemian and Czech-American Biography*. Bloomington, IN: AuthorHouse, 2016, Vol. 2, p. 798.

Will Eisner (1917-2005), b. Brooklyn, NY, of Czech mother; cartoonist, writer and entrepreneur
Bio: Eisner, Will, *The Will Eisner Sketchbook*. Dark Horse, 2004. 200p.; Andelman, Bob, *Will Eisner: A Spirited Life*. An authorized biography, M Press, 2005.352p.; Eisner, Will, *Life, in Pictures: Autobiographical Stories*. W. W. Norton & Company, 2007. 496p.' Schumacher, Michael, *Will Eisner: A Dreamer's Life in Comics*. Bloomsbury Publishing, 2010; "Will Eisner," in: Wikipedia. See - https://en.wikipedia.org/wiki/Will Eisner

Leo Kober (1876-1931), b. Brno, Moravia; cartoonist, with the Sunday World
Bio: Rechcigl, Miloslav, Jr., "Leo Kober," in: *Encyclopedia of Bohemian and Czech-American Biography*. Bloomington, IN: AuthorHouse, 2016, Vol. 2, p. 856; "Kober, Leo," in: *Who's Who in American Jewry*, Vol. 1, p.323.

Paul Peter Porges (1927-2016), b. Vienna, of Bohemian ancestry; cartoonist, with *The New Yorker, Mad* magazine, *Harper's* and the *Saturday Evening Post*
Bio: "Paul Peter Porges," in: Wikipedia. See - https://en.wikipedia.org/wiki/Paul_Peter_Porges

7. Sculptors

Hana Geber (née Kraus) (1910-1990) b. Prague, Bohemia; Canadian sculptor
Bio: Rechcigl, Miloslav, Jr. "Hana Geber," in: *Encyclopedia of Bohemian and Czech-American Biography*. Bloomington, IN: AuthorHouse, 2016, Vol. 2, p. 882.

Frederick Victor Guinzburg (1897-1978), b. New York city, of Bohemian ancestry;
sculptor and draftsman
Bio: Rechcigl, Miloslav, Jr. "Frederick Victor Guinzburg," in: *Encyclopedia of Bohemian and Czech-American Biography*. Bloomington, IN: AuthorHouse, 2016, Vol. 2, p. 882.

Gyula Kosice (orig. Ferdiand Fallik) (1924-2016), b. Košice, Czech.; Argentine sculptor
Bio: "Gyula Kosice," in: Wikipedia. See - https://en.wikipedia.org/wiki/Gyula Kosice

Anna Justine Mahler (1904-1988), b. Vienna, of Bohemian father; sculptor
Bio: "Anna Mahler," in: Wikipedia. See - https://en.wikipedia.org/wiki/Anna_Mahler

Maria Porges (1954-), b. Oakland, CA, of Bohemian ancestry; artist, writer, sculptor, draftsman
Bio: Rechcigl, Miloslav, Jr. "Maria Porges," in: *Encyclopedia of Bohemian and Czech-American Biography*. Bloomington, IN: AuthorHouse, 2016, Vol. 2, p. 887; "Maria Porges," in: Wikipedia. See - https://en.wikipedia.org/wiki/Maria Porges

Victoria Thorson (1943-), b. NYC (?), of Moravian ancestry; daughter of painter Ruth Rogers-Altmann and the granddaughter of architect Arbnold Karplus; New York-based sculptor, editor, art historian
Bio: "Victoria Thorson," in: Wikipedia. See - https://en.wikipedia.org/wiki/Victoria Thorson; "Victoria Thorson," in: Gallery RIVAA. See - http://rivaa.com/artist/victoria-thorson

8. Photographers, Cinematographers

Sonja Bullaty (1923-2000), b. Prague, Czech.; photographer
Bio: "Sonja Bullaty," in: Wikipedia. See - ttps://en.wikipedia.org/wiki/Sonja_Bullaty; "Sonja Bullaty, 76, a Photographer of Lyricism," *The New York Times*, October 13, 2000.

Fred Fehl (1906-1995), b. Vienna, of Bohemian ancestry; photographer
Bio: "Fred Fehl," in: Wikipedia. See - https://en.wikipedia.org/wiki/Fred Fehl

Bedřich Grűnzweig (1910-2009), b. Prague, Bohemia; photographer
Bio: Rechcigl, Miloslav, Jr., "Bedřich Grűnzweig," in: *Encyclopedia of Bohemian and Czech-American Biography*. Bloomington, IN: AuthorHouse, 2016, Vol. 2, p. 869; "Bedřich Grűnzweig," in: Wikipedia. See - https://cs.wikipedia.org/wiki/Bed%C5%99ich_Gr%C3%BCnzweig

Alexandr Hackenschmied, a.k.a. Alexander Hamid (1907-2004), b. Linz, of Bohemian ancestry; photographer, film director, cinematographer
Bio: Shattuck, Kathryn L., "Alexander Hammid, 96, Filmmaker Known for Many Styles," *The New York Times,* Aug. 8, 2004; "Alexandr Hackenschmied," in: Wikipedia. See - https://en.wikipedia.org/wiki/Alexandr Hackenschmied

Robert Hupka (1919-2001), of Bohemian ancestry; recording enmgineer for RCA Victor, and then cameraman for CBS TV in New York
Bio: "Robert Hupka," in: Wikipedia. See - https://en.wikipedia.org/wiki/Robert_Hupka

Edward Klauber (1835-1918), b. Bohemia; professional photographer in Louisville, KY
Bio: Rechcigl, Miloslav, Jr., *Encyclopedia of Bohemian and Czech-American Biography*. Bloomington, IN: AuthorHouse, 2016, Vol. 2, p. 872.

Robert J. Kositchek, Jr. (1952-), b. Santa Monica, CA, of Bohemian ancestry; Director of photography, teacher of cinematography
Bio: Rechcigl, Miloslav, Jr., "Robert J. Kositchek," *Encyclopedia of Bohemian and Czech-American Biography*. Bloomington, IN: AuthorHouse, 2016, Vol. 2, pp. 794-795.

Sylvia Plachy (1943-), b. Budapest, of Bohemian mother; photographer, staff photographer for the *Village Voice*
Bio: "Sylvia Plachy," in: Wikipedia. See - https://en.wikipedia.org/wiki/Sylvia Plachy; Rechcigl, Miloslav, Jr., "Sylvia Plachy," in: *Encyclopedia of Bohemian and Czech-American Biography*. Bloomington, IN: AuthorHouse, 2016, Vol. 2, p. 874.

Johnny Rozsa (1949-), b. Nairobi, Kenya, of Czech ancestry; fashion, portrait, and celebrity photographer
Bio: "Johnny Rozsa," in: Wikipedia. See - https://en.wikipedia.org/wiki/Johnny Rozsa

William Schleisner (1912-1962), b. Baltimore, of Bohemian ancestry; photographer of architecture
Bio: Rechcigl, Miloslav, Jr., "William Schleisner," in: *Encyclopedia of Bohemian and Czech-American Biography*. Bloomington, IN: AuthorHouse, 2016, Vol. 2, p. 875.

Julian Henry Stein (1883-1937), b. Milwaukee, WI, of Bohemian father; photographer
Bio: Rechcigl, Miloslav, Jr., "Julian Henry Stein," in: *Encyclopedia of Bohemian and Czech-American Biography*. Bloomington, IN: AuthorHouse, 2016, Vol. 2, pp. 875-876.

Simon Leonard Stein (1854-1922), b. Mariánské Lázně, Bohemia; portrait photographer, Chicago, president of the Photographic Assn. of America
Bio: Rechcigl, Miloslav, Jr., "Simon Leonard Stein," in: *Encyclopedia of Bohemian and Czech-American Biography.* Bloomington, IN: AuthorHouse, 2016, Vol. 2, p. 876.

Ralph Steiner (1899-1986), b. Cleveland, OH, of Bohemian ancestry; photographer, pioneer documentarian, avant-garde film
Bio: "Ralph Steiner," in: Wikipedia. See - https://en.wikipedia.org/wiki/Ralph Steiner; Rechcigl, Miloslav, Jr., "Ralph Steiner," in: *Encyclopedia of Bohemian and Czech-American Biography.* Bloomington, IN: AuthorHouse, 2016, Vol. 2, p. 876.

Paul Strand (orig. Nathaniel Paul Stransky) (1890-1976), New York City, of Bohemian ancestry; photographer and filmmaker
Bio: Barberie, Peter, *Paul Strand: Aperture Master of Photography.* Hong Kong: Aperture;
Stange, Maren, Ed., *Paul Strand: Essays on His Life and Work*, New York: Aperture 1991; Szegedy-Maszak, Andrew and Paul Strand, *Toward a Deeper Understanding: Paul Strand at Work;* Steidl/Aperture Foundation/Pace/MacGill Gallery, 2007; "Paul Strand," in: Wikipedia. See - https://en.wikipedia.org/wiki/Paul_Strand

Arthur Taussig (aka Harry A. Taussig) (1941-), b. Los Angeles, of Bohemian ancestry; physicist, biophysicist, collage artist, photographer, film analyst, author and fingerstyle guitarist
Bio: Arthur Taussig Website. See - http://www.arthurtaussig.com/about-mr-taussig/; "Harry Taussig," in: Wikipedia. See - https://en.wikipedia.org/wiki/Harry Taussig

9. Decorative Artists and Craftsmen

Moritz Fuerst (1782-1840), b. Pezinok, Slovakia; US Mint engraver, medalist

Bio: "Moritz Fuerst," in: Wikipedia. See - https://en.wikipedia.org/wiki/Moritz_Fuerst

Trude Guermonprez (née Gertrud Jalowetz) (1910—1976), b. Danzig, Germany, of Moravian father; weaver, textile artist and designer, teacher at California College of Arts and Crafts
Bio: "Trude Guermonprez," *The New York Times*, May 11, 1976; "Trude Guermonprez," in: Wikipedia. See - https://en.wikipedia.org/wiki/Trude Guermonprez; "Trude Guermonprez," in: Collection of Cooper Hewitt." See - https://collection.cooperhewitt.org/people/18046169/bio#ch

Axel Jakob Salmson (1807-1876), b. Stockholm, Sweden, of Bohemian father; lithographer, pioneer of color printing,
Bio: Rechcigl, Miloslav, Jr., "Axel Jakob Salmson," in: *Encyclopedia of Bohemian and Czech-American Biography*. Bloomington, IN: AuthorHouse, 2016, Vol. 2, pp. 879-880; "Axel Salmson," in: Wikipedia. See - https://sv.wikipedia.org/wiki/Axel_Salmson

Melanie Kent Steinhardt (1899-1952), b. Lemberg, Poland, raised in Bohemia; Bohemian painter, printmaker and ceramist
Bio: Hill, Richard T., *Mela - The Life and Art of Melanie Kent Steinhardt*, Rabbit Hill Press, 2002; Rechcigl, Miloslav, Jr., "Melanie Kent Steinhardt," in: *Encyclopedia of Bohemian and Czech-American Biography*. Bloomington, IN: AuthorHouse, 2016, pp. 925-926; "Melanie Kent Steinhardt," in: Wikipedia. See - https://en.wikipedia.org/wiki/Melanie Kent Steinhardt

Zeisel, Eva Streiker (1906-2011), b. Budapest, Hungary, of Slovak ancestry; industrial designer, ceramist
Bio: "Eva Zeisel," in: Wikipedia. See - https://en.wikipedia.org/wiki/Eva Zeisel

10. Fashion Designers

Rudi Gernreich (1922-1985), b. Vienna, of Bohemian ancestry; fashion designer

Bio: "Rudi Gernreich," in: Wikipedia. See - https://en.wikipedia.org/wiki/Rudi Gernreich

Tori Praver (1987-), b. San diego, CA, of Czech ancestry; American model and swimwear fashion designer
Bio: "Tori Praver," in: Wikipedia. See - https://en.wikipedia.org/wiki/Tori_Praver

Ruth Rogers-Altmann (née Karplus) (1917-2015), b. Vienna, of Moravian ancestry; painter, fashion designer, NYC
Bio: "Ruth Rogers-Atmann," in: Wikipedia. See - https://en.wikipedia.org/wiki/Ruth_Rogers-Altmann

11. Multi-Genre Visual Artists

Ruth Francken (1924-2006), b. Prague, Czech.; Czech-American sculptor, painter, furniture designer, living mostly in Paris
Bio: "Ruth Francken," in: Wikipedia. See - https://en.wikipedia.org/wiki/Ruth Francken

Nicola Ginzel (ca 1970-), b. Hollywood, CA, of Bohemian ancestry; mixed-media artist
Bio: "Nicola Ginzel - Biography." See - http://www.nicolaginzel.com/biography; Rechcigl, Miloslav, Jr., "Nicola Ginzel," in: *Encyclopedia of Bohemian and Czech-American Biography*. Bloomington, IN: AuthorHouse, 2016, Vol. 2, pp. 929-930.

Anita H. Grosz (1955-), b. Warren, PA, of Czech father; trained as a lawyer, also a photographer and an artist, ceramist, scuptor
Bio: "Anita H. Grosz," in her Homepage. See - http://www.anitagrosz.co.uk/; Rechcigl, Miloslav, Jr., "Anita H. Grosz," in: *Encyclopedia of Bohemian and Czech-American Biography*. Bloomington, IN: AuthorHouse, 2016, Vol. 2, p. 922.

Susan E. Jahoda (1952-), b. Bolton, England, of Czech ancestry; artist in a range of genres, including video, sound, photography, text, performance, and installation

Bio: Rechcigl, Miloslav, Jr., "Susan E. Jahoda," in: *Encyclopedia of Bohemian and Czech-American Biography*. Bloomington, IN: AuthorHouse, 2016, Vol. 2, pp. 922-923.

Tatana Kellner (1950-), b. Prague, Czech.; visual artist, photographer, book artist
Bio: Rechcigl, Miloslav, Jr. "Tatana Kellner," in: *Encyclopedia of Bohemian and Czech-American Biography*. Bloomington, IN: AuthorHouse, 2016, Vol. 2, 879, and 924; "Tatana Kellner," in: Wikipedia. See - https://en.wikipedia.org/wiki/Tatana Kellner

John Michael Anthony Koerner (1913-2014), b. Nový Jičín, Moravia; painter, printmaker, etcher, muralist, educator, author, his mediums were oil, acrylic, watercolor, casein, crayon, ink, collage, lithograph and etching.
Bio: Rechcigl, Miloslav, Jr., "John Michael Anthony Koerner," in: *Encyclopedia of Bohemian and Czech-American Biography*. Bloomington, IN: AuthorHouse, 2016, Vol. 2, 828.

Maxim Kopf (1892-1958), b. Vienna, of Bohemian ancestry, raised in Prague; painter
Bio: Rechcigl, Miloslav, Jr., "Maxim Kopf," in: *Encyclopedia of Bohemian and Czech-American Biography*. Bloomington, IN: AuthorHouse, 2016, Vol. 2, 829; "Maxim Kopf," in: Wikipedia. See - https://de.wikipedia.org/wiki/Maxim_Kopf

Ann Pachner (1944-), b. New York, NY, of Bohemian father; artist in a range of genres, including drawings, archival digital prints and wood carvings
Bio: Rechcigl, Miloslav, Jr, "Ann Pachner," in: *Encyclopedia of Bohemian and Czech-American Biography*. Bloomington, IN: AuthorHouse, 2016, Vol. 2, pp. 924-925.

Edward Ruscha (1937-), b. Omaha, NE, of Czech ancestry; a Pop artist, proficient in many media, including photography, drawing, painting, and the creation of artist books
Bio: Rechcigl, Miloslav, Jr., Edward joseph Ruscha," in: *Encyclopedia of Bohemian and Czech-American Biography*. Bloomington, IN: AuthorHouse,

2016, Vol. 2, p. 925; "Ed Ruscha/Edward Ruscha," in: Widewalls. See - https://www.widewalls.ch/artist/ed-ruscha/

Gordon Samstag (1906-1990), b. New York, NY, of Bohemian ancestry; painter, sculptor illustrator, educator
Bio: "Gordo Samstag," in: askArt. See- http://www.askart.com/artist bio/ Gordon Samstag/61491/Gordon Samstag.aspx; Rechcigl, Miloslav, Jr., "Gordon Samstag," in: Bloomington, IN: AuthorHouse, 2016, Vol. 2, 840-841.

Tibor Spitz (1929-), b. Dolný Kubín, Slovakia; glass specialist, painter, also did sculpting, ceramics, woodcarvings and wood burnings
Bio: "Tibor Spitz," in: Wikipedia. See - https://en.wikipedia.org/wiki/ Tibor Spitz

Melanie Kent Steinhardt (1899-1952), b. Lemberg, Poland; a Bohemian-American painter, printmaker and ceramist
Bio: Rechcigl, Miloslav, Jr., "Melanie Kent Steinhardt," in: *Encyclopedia of Bohemian and Czech-American Biography.* Bloomington, IN: AuthorHouse, 2016, Vol. 2, pp. 925-926; "Melanie Kent Steinhardt," Wikipedia - ttps:// en.wikipedia.org/wiki/Melanie_Kent_Steinhardt

12. Art Dealers

Hugo Feigl (1889-1961); art dealer, owner of Feigl Gallery, NYC
Bio: "Hugo Feigl," in: Wikipedia. See - https://cs.wikipedia.org/wiki/ Hugo_Feigl

Hans Peter Kraus, Jr., b. of Bohemian, ancestry, photography dealer, owner of a gallery 'Fine Photographs,' historian and publisher, NYC
Bio: Rechcigl, Miloslav, Jr., "Hans Peter Kraus, Jr.," in: *Encyclopedia of Bohemian and Czech-American Biography.* Bloomington, IN: AuthorHouse, 2016, Vol. 2, pp. 942-943.

13 Art Historians

Adele Brandeis (1885-1975), b. Louisville, KY, of Bohemian ancestry; art historian and art administrator, with WPA Federal Art Project
Bio: "Adele Brandeis," in: Wikipedia. See - https://en.wikipedia.org/wiki/Adele Brandeis

Margaret Deutsch Carroll (ca 1943-), b. US, of Bohemian ancestry; art historian, professor of art, Wellesley College
Bio: Rechcigl, Miloslav, Jr., "Margaret Deutsch Carroll," in: *Encyclopedia of Bohemian and Czech-American Biography*. Bloomington, IN: AuthorHouse, 2016, Vol. 2, p. 928; "Margaret D. Carroll," in: Wellesley College. See - https://www.wellesley.edu/art/faculty/carroll

Lorenz C. Eitner (1919-2000), b. Brno, Czech.; art historian, museum director
Bio: "Eitner, Lorenz," in: *Dictionary of Art Historians*. Edited by Lee Sorensen, Online

Philipp Fehl (1920-2000), b. Vienna, of Czech ancestry; art historian
Bio: Marilyn Perry, "Philipp P. Fehl: Artist, Scholar, Humanist, Witness," *Artibus et Historiae. Istituto Internationale per le Ricerche di Storia dell'Arte,* 24, No. 48, 2003, pp. 13–15; *International Biographical Dictionary of Central European Emigrés 1933-1945*. Műnchen: K. G. Saur, 1983, Vol. 2, p. 283.

Raina Fehl (née Schweinburg) (1920-2009), b. Vienna, of Moravian father; art historian, classicist, author
Bio: "Raina Fehl,", in: Wikipedia. See - https://en.wikipedia.org/wiki/Raina_Fehl

Paul Frankl (1878-1962), b. Prague, Bohemia, art historian, historian of architecture
Bio: Frankl, Paul," in *Dictionary of Art Historians*. Edited by Lee Sorensen, Online; *International Biographical Dictionary of Central European Emigrés 1933-1945*. Műnchen: K. G. Saur, 1983, Vol. 2, p5. 321-322.

Stella Kramrisch (1896-1993), b. Mikulov, Moravia; art historian, professor of Indian art, New York University, curator
Bio: Rechcigl, Miloslav, Jr, "Stella Kramrisch," in: *Encyclopedia of Bohemian and Czech-American Biography*. Bloomington, IN: AuthorHouse, 2016, Vol. 2, p. 939.

Heinrich Schwarz (1894-1974), b. Prague, Bohemia; art historian, curator, historian of photography
Bio: "Schwarz, Heinrich," in *Dictionary of Art Historians*. Edited by Lee Sorensen, Online; *International Biographical Dictionary of Central European Emigrés 1933-1945*. Műnchen: K. G. Saur, 1983, Vol. 2, p.1062.

Erica Tietze-Conrat (1883-1958), b. Vienna, of Moravian ancestry; art historian
Bio: "Erica Tietze-Conrat), in: Wikipedia. See - https://en.wikipedia.org/wiki/Erica Tietze-Conrat

Hans Karl Tietze (orig. Taussig) (1880-1954), b. Prague, Bohemia; art historian
Bio: "Hans Tietze," in: Wikipedia. See - https://en.wikipedia.org/wiki/Hans Tietze

Hary Brandeis Wehle (1887-1969), b. Louisville, KY, of Bohemian ancestry; curator of the Metropoliutan Museum of Art, NYC
Bio: "Wehle, Harry B.," in: *Dictionary of Art Historians*. See - http://arthistorians.info/wehleh; Horsley, Carter B., "Harry Wehle, 82, Ex-curator, dead," *The New York Times*, December 15, 1969.

H. Allied Health and Social Services

1. Nurses

Naomi Deutsch (1890-1983), b. Brno, Moravia; leader in public health nursing

Bio: Rechcigl, Miloslav, Jr., "Naomi Deutsch," in: *Encyclopedia of Bohemian and Czech-American Biography*. Bloomington, IN: AuthorHouse, 2016, Vol. 3, pp. 2081-2082.

2. Public Health Specialists

Max Joseph Exner (1871-1943), b. Aust., of Bohemian ancestry; pioneer in sex education
Bio/; Rechcigl, Miloslav, Jr., "Max Joseph Exner," in: *Encyclopedia of Bohemian and Czech-American Biography*. Bloomington, IN: AuthorHouse, 2016, Vol. 3, p. 2088.

Sonia Ehrlich Sachs (1954-), b. Prague, Czech.; pediatrician and public health specialist
Bio: Rechcigl, Miloslav, Jr., "Sonia Ehrlich Sachs," in: *Encyclopedia of Bohemian and Czech-American Biography*. Bloomington, IN: AuthorHouse, 2016, Vol. 3, p. 2094.

Christopher Tietze (1908-1984), b. Vienna, of Bohemian ancestry; physician, advocate of pro-choice movement to permit abortion
Bio: "Christopher Tietze," in: Wikipedia. See - https://en.wikipedia.org/wiki/Christopher Tietze; Barron, James, "Christopher Tietze, Physician and Authority on Pregnancy," *The New York Times,* April 5, 1984

Nina Wallerstein (1953-), b. of Bohemian ancestry; professor, founding director of Public Health Program, at the University of New Mexico
Bio: Rechcigl, Miloslav, Jr., "Nina Wallerstein," in: *Encyclopedia of Bohemian and Czech-American Biography*. Bloomington, IN: AuthorHouse, 2016, Vol. 3, pp. 2095-2096.

Toni Weschler (1955-), b. US, of Moravian ancestry; women's health educator, author of the groundbreaking bestseller, *Taking Charge of your Fertility*
Bio: "Spotlight Interview with Toni Weschler," *WEGO Health,* December 11, 2008

3. Social Workers

Eleanor H. Adler (1884-d.), b. New York City, of Bohemian ancestry; social worker
Bio: Rechcigl, Miloslav, Jr., "Eleanor H. Adler," in: *Encyclopedia of Bohemian and Czech American Biography*. Bloomington, IN.: AuthorHouse, 2016, Vol. 3, p. 2132.

Helen Goldmark Adler (1859-1948), b. Brooklyn, NY; social worker
Bio: "Mrs. Felix Adler Dies at Age of 89," *New York Times*, March 21, 1948, 60:2; Rechcigl, Miloslav, Jr., "Helen Goldmark Adler," in: *Encyclopedia of Bohemian and Czech American Biography*. Bloomington, IN.: AuthorHouse, 2016, Vol. 3, p. 2133.

Caroline Flexner (1892-1958), b. Louisville, KY, of Bohemian ancestry; social worker with UNRRA
Bio: Rechcigl, Miloslav, Jr., "Caroline Flexner,", in: *Encyclopedia of Bohemian and Czech American Biography*. Bloomington, IN.: AuthorHouse, 2016, Vol. 3, p. 2133.

Peter Kollisch (1928-2015), b. Vienna, of Moravian ancestry; social worker, with New York Board of Education
Bio: "Peter Kollisch Obituary," *The New York Times*, July 31 to August 1, 2015.

Hertha Kraus (1897-1968), b. Prague, Bohemia; social worker, educator
Bio:_Schirrmacher, Gerd, *Hertha Kraus - Between the Worlds*. Biography of a Social Scientist and Quaker (1897-1968). Frankfurt a. M.: Lang, 2002.

Louis Lowy (1920-1991), b. Munich, Ger., of Bohemian ancestry; Holocaust survivor; professor of gerontology, Dean, Boston University
Bio: Rechcigl, Miloslav, Jr., "Louis Lowy," in: *Encyclopedia of Bohemian and Czech-American Biography*. Bloomington, IN: AuthorHouse, 2016, Vol. 3, pp. 2128; Gardella, Lorrie, *The Life and Thought of Louis Lowy: Social Work through the Holocaust.* Syracuse: Syracuse University Press, 2011.

Jean Brandeis Tachau (1894-1978); Louisville, KY, of Bohemian ancestry; social worker
Bio: Rechcigl, Miloslav, Jr., "Jean Brandeis Tachau," in: *Beyond the Sea of Beer*. Bloomington, IN: AuthorHouse, 2017, p. 223; "Tachau, Jean Brandeis," in: *The Encyclopedia of Louisville*. Louisville: The University Press of Kentucky, 2001, p. 866

Frances Taussig (1883-1981), b. Chicago, IL, of Bohemian ancestry; social worker
Bio: Rechcigl, Miloslav, Jr., "Frances Taussig," in: *Encyclopedia of Bohemian and Czech-American Biography*. Bloomington, IN, 2016, Vol. 2, p. 1433 and Vol. 3, p. 2134.

I. Sports

1. Baseball Players

David Abeles (1890-1932), b. Newark, NJ, of Bohemian ancestry; played in the Texas League for the US Army
Bio: Rechcigl, Miloslav, Jr., "David Abeles," in: *Encyclopedia of Bohemian and Czech-American Biography*. Bloomington, IN: AuthorHouse, 2016, Vol. 3, p. 2232.

2. Football Players

Charles A. Taussig (1881-1925), b. Annapolis, MD, of Bohemian ancestry; star end at Cornell University, later lawyer
Bio: Rechcigl, Miloslav, Jr., "Charles A. Taussig," in: *Encyclopedia of Bohemian and Czech-American Biography*. Bloomington, IN: AuthorHouse, 2016, Vol. 3, p. 2261.

John Hawley Taussig (1876-1925), b. Annapolis, MD, of Bohemian ancestry; All American, while at Cornell University
Bio: Rechcigl, Miloslav, Jr., "John Hawley Taussig," in: *Encyclopedia of Bohemian and Czech-American Biography*. Bloomington, IN: AuthorHouse, 2016, Vol. 3, p. 2261.

Joseph K. Taussig (1877-19470, b. Dresden, Ger., of Bohemian ancestry; starred as Navy's quarterback, winner of the Thompson Trophy, later became officer in US Navy
Bio: Rechcigl, Miloslav, Jr., "Joseph K. Taussig," in: *Encyclopedia of Bohemian and Czech-American Biography*. Bloomington, IN: AuthorHouse, 2016, Vol. 3, p. 2261.

3. Soccer Players

Pavel Mahrer (1900-198), b. Teplice, Bohemia; soccer player
Bio: Rechcigl, Miloslav, Jr., "Pavel Mahrer," *Encyclopedia of Bohemian and Czech-American Biography*. Bloomington, IN: AuthorHouse, 2016, Vol. 3, p. 2297; "Pavel Mahrer," in: Wikipedia. See - https://en.wikipedia.org/wiki/Pavel_Mahrer

4. Hockey Players

Ladislav Kohn (1975-), b. Uherské Hradiště, Czech.; NHL right winger
Bio: Rechcigl, Miloslav, Jr., "Joseph K. Taussig," in: *Encyclopedia of Bohemian and Czech-American Biography*. Bloomington, IN: AuthorHouse, 2016, Vol. 3, p. 2276.

5. Boxers

Buddy Baer ((1915-1986), b. Denver, CO; of Bohemian ancestry; boxer, later actor
Bio: Rechcigl, Miloslav, Jr., "Buddy Baer," in: *Encyclopedia of Bohemian and Czech-American Biography*. Bloomington, IN: AuthorHouse, 2016, Vol. 3, p. 2248; "Buddy Baer," in: Wikipedia. See - https://en.wikipedia.org/wiki/Buddy_Baer

Max Baer (1909-1959), b. Omaha, NE, of Bohemian ancestry; boxer
Bio: Rechcigl, Miloslav, Jr., "Max Baer," in: *Encyclopedia of Bohemian and Czech-American Biography*. Bloomington, IN: AuthorHouse, 2016, Vol. 3, p. 2248; "Max Baer," in: Wikipedia. See - https://en.wikipedia.org/wiki/Max_Baer_(boxer)

6. Swimmers

Katie Ledecky (1997-), b. Washington, DC, of Czech ancestry; competitive swimmer
Bio: "Katie Ledecky," in: Wikipedia. See - https://en.wikipedia.org/wiki/Katie Ledecky; Rechcigl, Miloslav, Jr., "Katie Ledecky," in: *Encyclopedia of Bohemian and Czech-American Biography*. Bloomington, IN: AuthorHouse, 2016, Vol. 3, p. 2302-2303.

Otto Wahle (1879-1963), b. Vienna, of Bohemian father; swimmer who competed in the late 19th and early 20th century
Bio: "Otto Wahle," in: Wikipedia. See - https://en.wikipedia.org/wiki/Otto_Wahle

7. Tennis and Table Tennis Players

Ladislav Hecht (1909-2004), b. Žilina, Slovakia; professional tennis player
Bio: "Ladislav Hecht," in: Wikipedia. See - https://en.wikipedia.org/wiki/Ladislav Hecht

Gertrude Kleinová (1918-1976), b. Brno, Czech.; world champion tennis player
Bio: "Gertrude Kleinová," in: Wikipedia. See - https://en.wikipedia.org/wiki/Gertrude_Kleinová

8. Track and Field Athletes

Istvan Barta (Berger) (1895-1948), b. Hungary, of Slovak ancestry; water polo player
Bio: "Istvan Barta," in: Wikipedia. See - https://en.wikipedia.org/wiki//István Barta

Kurt Epstein (1904-1975), b. Roudnice nad Labem, Bohemia; Olympic water polo player
Bio: "Kurt Epstein," in: Wikipedia. See - https://en.wikipedia.org/wiki/Kurt_Epstein

Hugo Friend (1882-1966), b. Prague, Bohemia; athlete in the long jump and hurdles, later lawyer and jurist
Bio: "Hugo Friend," in: Wikipedia. See - https://en.wikipedia.org/wiki/Hugo_Friend

Arie Gluck (1930-2016), b. Czech.; an Israeli Olympic runner
Bio: "Arie Gluck,", in: Wikipedia. See - https://en.wikipedia.org/wiki/Arie_Gluck

9. Sports Team Owners and Executives

Robert Hays Gries (1900-1966), b. Cleveland, OH, of Bohemian ancestry; collector, co-founder of Cleveland Rams, co-founder of Cleveland Browns
Bio: Rechcigl, Miloslav, Jr., "Robert Hays Gries," in: *Encyclopedia of Bohemian and Czech-American Biography*. Bloomington, IN: AuthorHouse, 2016, Vol. 1, p. 91; "Gries, Robert Hays," in *Encyclopedia of Cleveland History*. See - http://case.edu/ech/articles/g/gries-robert-hays/

Jon Ledecky (1958-), New York, NY, of Czech ancestry; businessman, majority owner of the NHL team of the New
York Islanders and the AHL team of Bridgeport Sound Tigers
Bio: Jon Ledecky," in: Wikipedia. See - https://en.wikipedia.org/wiki/Jon_Ledecky

Bob Lurie (1929-), b. San Francisco, CA, of Bohemian ancestry; former ownerof the SanbFrancisco Giants franchise of Major League Baseball
Bio: "Bob Lurie," in: Wikipedia. See - https://en.wikipedia.org/wiki/Bob_Lurie

Max Winter (1903-1996), b. Ostrava, Moravia; co-owner and manager of Minneapolis Lakers Basketball Team, founder of Minnesota Vikings
Bio: Rechcigl, Miloslav, Jr., "Max Winter," in: *Encyclopedia of Bohemian and Czech-American Biography*. Bloomington, IN: AuthorHouse, 2016, Vol. 1, pp. 94-95; "Max Winter," in: Wikipedia. See - https://en.wikipedia.org/wiki/Max_Winter

J. Recreation

1. Astrologists

Grant Lewi (1902-1951), b. Albany, NY., of Bohemian ancestry; astrologer and author, 'Father of Modern Astrology in America'
Bio: "Grant Lewi," in: Wikipedia. See - https://en.wikipedia.org/wiki/Grant Lewi

2. Card Players

George Michael Pisk (1932-2012), b. Vienna, of Moravian ancestry; known not only as English literature professor but also as noted bridge player
Bio: "George Pisk 1932-2012," in: SCORECARD - Bridge News Bulletin for the Texas Regional Conference, San Antonio, TX, Vol. 44, No. 3 (May-June 2012), p. 2; Rechcigl, Miloslav, Jr., "George Michael Pisk," in: *Encyclopedia of Bohemian and Czech-American Biography*. Bloomington, IN: AuthorHouse, 2016, Vol. 3, p. 2326.

3. Chess Players

Walter Korn (1908-1997), b. Prague, Bohemia; authority and author of books about chess
Bio: "Walter Korn," in: Wikipedia. See - https://en.wikipedia.org/wiki/Walter Korn

Herman Steiner (1905-1955), b. Dunajská Streda, Slovakia; US chess player, organizer, columnist
Bio: "Herman Steiner," in: Wikipedia. See -https://en.wikipedia.org/wiki/Herman_Steiner

Wilhelm Steinitz (1836-1900), b. Prague, Bohemia; chess Master, World Chess Champion
Bio: "Wilhelm Steinitz, "in; Wikipedia. See - https://en.wikipedia.org/wiki/Wilhelm Steinitz; Rechcigl, Miloslav, Jr., "Wilhelm Steinitz," in:

Encyclopedia of Bohemian and Czech-American Biography. Bloomington, IN: AuthorHouse, 2016, Vol. 3, p. 2326.

4. Magicians

Bernard M. L. Ernst (1879-1938), b. Uniontown, AL, of Bohemian ancestry; attorney, magician and associate of Harry Houdini
Bio: Rechcigl, Miloslav, Jr., "Bernard M. L. Ernst," in: *Encyclopedia of Bohemian and Czech-American Biography*. Bloomington, IN: AuthorHouse, 2016, Vol. 3, p. 2328; "Bernard M. L. Ernst," in: Wikipedia. See - https://en.wikipedia.org/wiki/Bernard_M._L._Ernst

5. Numismatists

Robert James Eidlitz (1864-1935), b. New York, NY, of Bohemian ancestry; architect by training, but also a noted numismatist
Bio: Rechcigl, Miloslav, Jr., "Robert James Eidlitz," in: *Encyclopedia of Bohemian and Czech-American Biography*. Bloomington, IN: AuthorHouse, 2016, Vol. 3, p. 2328.

Henry Philips, Jr. (1838-1895), b. Philadelphia, PA, of Bohemian ancestry; philologist and a noted numismatist
Bio: Kleeberg, John M., "Phillips, Henry, Jr.," in: *American National Biography*, Vol. 17 (1999), pp. 446-447; Rechcigl, Miloslav, Jr., "Henry Phillips,", in: *Encyclopedia of Bohemian and Czech-American Biography*. Bloomington, IN: AuthorHouse, 2016, Vol. 2, p. 1157.

6. Philatelists

Henry Hahn (1928-2007), b. Brno, Czech.; engineer, but also noted philatelist, specializing in Czechoslovak stamps.
Bio: NAPEX - In Memoriam: Henry Hahn. See - http://www.napex.org/memoriam.html; Rechcigl, Miloslav, Jr., "Henry Hahn," in: *Encyclopedia of Bohemian and Czech-American Biography*. Bloomington, IN: AuthorHouse, 2016, Vol. 3, p. 2327.

7. Puzzle Makers

Ben Taussig (1980-), b. Albany, NY, of Bohemian ancestry; American expert on puzzles
Bio: Rechcigl, Miloslav, Jr., "Ben Taussig," in: *Encyclopedia of Bohemian and Czech-American Biography*. Bloomington, IN: AuthorHouse, 2016, Vol. 3, p. 2328.

XI. Learning, Scholarship, Research

A. General

B. Humanities

1. Archeologists

Jacob Hoschander (1874-), b. Těšín, Silesia; Biblical archeologist
Bio: "Hoschander, Jacob," in: *Who's Who in American Jewry*, Vol. 1 p. 279

Benno Landsberger (1890-1958), b. Frýdek, Moravia; professor of Assyrian history, archeologist
Bio: Rechcigl, Miloslav, Jr., "Benno Landsberger," in: *Encyclopedia of Bohemian and Czech-American Biography*. Bloomington, IN: AuthorHouse, 2016, Vol. 2, p. 1157.

2. Historians

Harry Jindřich Benda (1919-1971), b. Liberec, Czech.; social and political historian, S.E. Asia
Bio: McVey, Ruth T., "Harry J. Benda – An Obituary," *Journal of Asian Studies* 31, No. 3 (May 1972), pp. 589-590; *International Biographical Dictionary of Central European Emigrés 1933-1945*. Műnchen: K. G. Saur, 1983, Vol. 2, p. 76.
Gotthard E. Deutsch (1859-1921), b. Dolní Kounice, Moravia; scholar of Jewish history
Bio: Lindgren, Carl Edwin, "Gotthard Deutsch," in: *American National Biography Online* Feb. 2000 (Oxford University Press); Raisin, Max, *Great Jews I Have Known* (1952), pp. 143–5; "Gotthard Deutsch," in: Wikipedia. See: https://en.wikipedia.org/wiki/Gotthard_Deutsch.

Eleanor Flexner (1908-1995), b. Georgetown, KY, of Bohemian ancestry; writer, historian

Bio: Flexner, Eleanor, 1908-1995. Papers of Eleanor Flexner, 1895? -1995. Arthur and Elizabeth Schlesinger Library on the History of Women in America, Radcliffe Institute for Advanced Study, Harvard University; "Eleanor Flexner," in: Wikipedia. See: https://en.wikipedia.org/wiki/Eleanor Flexner

JamesThomas Flexner (1908-2003), b. Manhattan, of Bohemian ancestry; historian and biographer
Bio: Marti, Douglas, "James Thomas Flexner, Washington Biographer, 95, Dies," in: *The New York Times,* February 16, 2003; "James Thomas Flexner," in: Wikipedia. See: https://en.wikipedia.org/wiki/James_Thomas_Flexner

Saul Friedländer (1932-), b. Prague, Czech.; historian
Bio: Rechcigl, Miloslav, Jr., "Saul Friedländer," in: *Encyclopedia of Bohemian and Czech-American Biography.* Bloomington, IN: AuthorHouse, 2016, Vol. 2, p. 1197.

Arthur Gustav Haas (1925-), b. Vienna, of Bohemian ancestry; historian
Bio: Rechcigl, Miloslav, Jr., "Arthur Gustav Hass," in: *Encyclopedia of Bohemian and Czech-American Biography.* Bloomington, IN: AuthorHouse, 2016, Vol. 2, p. 1197.

Fred Hahn (1906-2003), b. Staňkov, Bohemia, historian
Bio: Rechcigl, Miloslav, Jr., "Fred Hahn," in: *Encyclopedia of Bohemian and Czech-American Biography.* Bloomington, IN: AuthorHouse, 2016, Vol. 2, p. 1197.

George Huppert (1934-), b. Těšín, Czech; historian
Bio: Rechcigl, Miloslav, Jr., "George Huppert," in: *Encyclopedia of Bohemian and Czech-American Biography.* Bloomington, IN: AuthorHouse, 2016, Vol. 2, p. 111199.

Erich Kahler (1885-1970), b. Prague, Bohemia; historian and literary scholar
Bio: Rechcigl, Miloslav, Jr., "Erich Kahler," in: *Beyond the Sea of Beer. History* of Immigration of Bohemians and Czechs to the New World and their Contributions. Bloomington, IN: AuthorHouse, 2017, p. 584.

Alice Kessler-Harris (1941-), b. Leicester, England; historian
Bio: Rechcigl, Miloslav, Jr., "Alice Kessler-Harris," in: *Encyclopedia of Bohemian and Czech-American Biography*. Bloomington, IN: AuthorHouse, 2016, Vol. 2, p. 1201.

Bernard Klein (1928-), b. Czech., historian
Bio: Rechcigl, Miloslav, Jr., "Bernard Klein," *Encyclopedia of Bohemian and Czech-American Biography*. Bloomington, IN: AuthorHouse, 2016, Vol. 2, p. 1201.

Franz Kobler (1882-1965), b. Mladá Boleslav, Bohemia; attorney, historian
Bio: Rechcigl, Miloslav, Jr., "Franz Kobler," in: *Encyclopedia of Bohemian and Czech-American Biography*. Bloomington, IN: AuthorHouse, 2016, Vol. 2, pp. 985-986.

Hans Kohn (1891-1971), b. Prague, Bohemia; historian
Bio: Gordon, Adi, *Toward Nationalism's End: An Intellectual Biography of Hans Kohn*. Brandeis, 2017; Kohn, Hans. *Living in a World Revolution: My Encounters with History*. 1964; Maor, Zohar, "Hans Kohn and the Dialectics of Colonialism: Insights on Nationalism and Colonialism from Within," *Leo Baeck Institute Yearbook* 55 (1): 255–271; Wolf, Ken, "Hans Kohn's Liberal Nationalism: The Historian as Prophet," *Journal of the History of Ideas*, 37, No. 4 (1976), pp. 651-672.

Theodore K. Rabb (1937-), b. Teplice-Šanov, Czech.; historian
Bio: "Theodore K. Rabb," *Yale Books*, 13 April 2014; *International Biographical Dictionary of Central European Emigrés 1933-1945*. Műnchen: K. G. Saur, 1983, Vol. 2, pp. 933-934; Rechcigl, Miloslav, Jr., "Theodore K. Rabb," in: *Beyond the Sea of Beer. History* of Immigration of Bohemians and Czechs to the New World and their Contributions. Bloomington, IN: AuthorHouse, 2017, p. 579.

Oskar Rabinowicz (1902-1969), b. Vienna, of Bohemian ancestry; historian, Zionist
Bio: Bio: Rechcigl, Miloslav, Jr., "Oskar Rabinowicz," in: *Encyclopedia of Bohemian and Czech-American Biography*. Bloomington, IN: AuthorHouse, 2016, Vol. 2, p. 1211.

Katherine Tachau (1950-), b. Louisville, KY, of Bohemian ancestry; historian
Bio: Rechcigl, Miloslav, Jr., "Katherine Tachau," in: *Encyclopedia of Bohemian and Czech-American Biography*. Bloomington, IN: AuthorHouse, 2016, Vol. 2, p. 1215.

Walter P. Ullmann (1924-2011), b. České Budějovice, Czech.; historian
Bio: Bio: Rechcigl, Miloslav, Jr., "Walter P. Ullmann," in: *Encyclopedia of Bohemian and Czech-American Biography*. Bloomington, IN: AuthorHouse, 2016, Vol. 2, p. 1215.

3. Legal Scholars

Nina S. Appel (née Schick) (1936-), b. Prague, Czech.; lawyer, legal scholar, Dean
Bio: Haney, Thomas M., "Nina S. Appel: A Tribute to a Remarkable Dean," Loyola University Chicago Law Journal, 4, 4, 05. See - *https://www.luc.edu/media/lucedu/law/faculty/pdfs/haney_appel-dedication.pdf*

Nicholas Bala (1952-), b. Montreal, Canada, of Czech ancestry; legal scholar, educator
Bio: Rechcigl, Miloslav, Jr., "Nicholas Bala," in: *Encyclopedia of Bohemian and Czech-American Biography.* Bloomington, IN: AuthorHouse, 2016, Vol. 1, p. 514.

Fritz Braunfeld (1892-1971), b. Brno, Moravia; attorney, professor, legal scholar, Chicago
Bio: "Fritz Braunfeld," in: *Handbuch österreichischer Autorinnen und Autoren jüdischer Herkunft.* Munchen: S. G. Saur, 2002, p. 160.

Thomas Buergenthal (1939-), b. Lubochňa, Slovakia; jurist, legal scholar
Bio: "Thomas Buerghenthal," in: Wikipedia. See - https://en.wikipedia.org/wiki/Thomas_Buergenthal

Paul Abraham Freund (1908-1992), b. St. Louis, MO, of Bohemian ancestry; legal scholar

Bio: Kurland, Philip B., "Paul A. Freund," in: International Encyclopedia of the Social Sciences, Biographical Supplement, vol. 18, 202-205; Cox, Archibald, "Paul A. Freund (16 February 1908-5 February 1992)," *Proceedings of the American Philosophical Society*, Vol. 138, No. 2 (June 1994), pp. 325-26; Pace, Eric, "Paul A. Freund, Authority on Constitution, Dies at 83," *New York Times*, February 6, 1992.

Charles Fried (1935-), b. Prague, Czech.; lawyer, jurist
Bio: Rechcigl, Miloslav, Jr., "Charles Fried," in: *Encyclopedia of Bohemian and Czech-American Biography*. Bloomington, IN: AuthorHouse, 2016, Vol. 1, p. 517; "Charles Fried," in Wikipedia. See - https://en.wikipedia.org/wiki/Charles_Fried

Walter Gellhorn (1906-1995), b. St. Louis, MO, of Bohemian ancestry; legal scholar
Bio: Rechcigl, Miloslav, Jr., "Walter Gellhorn," in: *Encyclopedia of Bohemian and Czech-American Biography*. Bloomington, IN: AuthorHouse, 2016, Vol. 1, p. 518; "Walter Gellhorn, Law Scholar and Professor, dies at 89," *The New York Times*, December 11, 1995.

Ariela Gross (1965-), CA, of Czech ancestry; legal scholar
Bio: Rechcigl, Miloslav, Jr., "Ariela Gross," in: *Encyclopedia of Bohemian and Czech-American Biography*. Bloomington, IN: AuthorHouse, 2016, Vol. 1, p. 519.

Samuel R. Gross (1946-), attorney, educator, legal scholar
Bio: "Samuel R. Gross," in: Wikipedia. See - https://en.wikipedia.org/wiki/Samuel R. Gross; Faculty Profile: "Samuel R. Gross," University of Michigan Law School. See - http://www.law.umich.edu/FacultyBio/Pages/FacultyBio.aspx?FacID=srgross

Fred Herzog (1907-2008), b. Prague, Bohemia; legal scholar, Dean
Bio: Rechcigl, Miloslav, Jr., "Fred Herzog," in: *Encyclopedia of Bohemian and Czech-American Biography*. Bloomington, IN: AuthorHouse, 2016, Vol. 1, pp. 520-521.

Gerhart Husserl (1893-1973), b. Galle, Germany, of Moravian ancestry; legal scholar, philosopher

Bio: Rechcigl, Miloslav, Jr., "Gerhart Husserl," in: *Encyclopedia of Bohemian and Czech-American Biography*. Bloomington, IN: AuthorHouse, 2016, Vol. 1, p. 521; "Gerhart Husserl," in: Wikipedia. See - https://en.wikipedia.org/wiki/Gerhart_Husserl

Felix Kaufmann (1895-1949), b. Vienna, of Bohemia ancestry; philosopher of law

Bio: Rechcigl, Miloslav, Jr., "Felix Kaufmann," in: *Encyclopedia of Bohemian and Czech-American Biography*. Bloomington, IN: AuthorHouse, 2016, Vol. 1, p. 521; "Felix Kaufmann," in: Wikipedia. See - https://en.wikipedia.org/wiki/Felix_Kaufmann

Hans Kelsen (1881-1973)

Bio: "Kelsen Hans," *Current Biography* 1957 (1958), pp. 294-296; Ebenstein, William, "Kelsen, Hans," in: *International Encyclopedia of the Social Sciences*, Vol. 8, pp. 360-365; Rechcigl, Miloslav, Jr., "Tvůrce normativní teorie práva" (Creator of Normative Theory of Law), in: *Postavy naší Ameriky*. Praha: Pražská edice, 2000, pp. 271-273.

Guido Kisch (1889-1985), b. Prague, Bohemia; jurist, legal historian

Bio: "Guido Kisch," kin: Wikipedia. See - https://de.wikipedia.org/wiki/Guido Kisch;

Rechcigl, Miloslav, Jr., "Guido Kisch," in: *Encyclopedia of Bohemian and Czech-American Biography*. Bloomington, IN: AuthorHouse, 2016, Vol. 1, p. 522

Arthur Lenhoff (1885-1965), b. Teplice-Šanov, Bohemia; legal scholar

Bio: Rechcigl, Miloslav, Jr., "Arthur Lenhoff," in: *Encyclopedia of Bohemian and Czech-American Biography*. Bloomington, IN: AuthorHouse, 2016, Vol. 1, p. 523; "Arthur Lenhoff," in: Wikipedia. See - https://de.wikipedia.org/wiki/Arthur_Lenhoff

Marie Lenhoff Marcus (1933-), b. Vienna, of Bohemian ancestry; lawyer, educator

Bio: Rechcigl, Miloslav, Jr., "Marie Lenhoff Marcus," in: *Encyclopedia of Bohemian and Czech-American Biography*. Bloomington, IN: AuthorHouse, 2016, Vol. 1, pp. 523-524; "Maria Lenhoff Marcus," in: Prabook. See - https://prabook.com/web/maria_lenhoff.marcus/916510.

Nathan Levy, Jr. (1923-1994), b. Vicksburg, MS, of Bohemian ancestry; attorney, educator, legal scholar
Bio: Rechcigl, Miloslav, Jr., "Nathan Levy, Jr.," in: *Encyclopedia of Bohemian and Czech-American Biography*. Bloomington, IN: AuthorHouse, 2016, Vol. 1, p. 523.

George Petschek (1872-1947), b. Kolín, Bohemia; lawyer, legal scholar
Bio: Rechcigl, Miloslav, Jr., "George Petschek," in: *Encyclopedia of Bohemian and Czech-American Biography*. Bloomington, IN: AuthorHouse, 2016, Vol. 1, pp. 525-526.

Louis Heilprin Pollak (1922-2012), b. New York, NY, of Bohemian ancestry; attorney, jurist, educator, Dean, legal scholar
Bio: Rechcigl, Miloslav, Jr., "Louis Heilprin Pollak," in: *Encyclopedia of Bohemian and Czech-American Biography*. Bloomington, IN: AuthorHouse, 2016, Vol. 1, p. 526; "Louis H. Pollak," in: Wikipedia. See - https://en.wikipedia.org/wiki/Louis H. Pollak; Blumenthal, Jeff, "Longtime Philadelphia federal judge Pollak dies," *Philadelphia Business Journal*, May 9, 2012.

Walter Brandeis Raushenbush (1928-), b. Madison, WI, of Bohemian ancestry;
attorney, educator, legal scholar
Bio: Rechcigl, Miloslav, Jr., "Walter Brandeis Raushenbush," in: *Encyclopedia of Bohemian and Czech-American Biography*. Bloomington, IN: AuthorHouse, 2016, Vol. 1, pp. 526-527; "Walter Brandeis Raushenbush," in: Prabook. See - https://prabook.com/web/walter_brandeis.raushenbush/797631

Joseph Redlich (1869-1936), b. Hodonín, Moravia; jurist, politician, educator, legal scholar
Bio: Rechcigl, Miloslav, Jr., "Joseph Redlich," in: *Encyclopedia of Bohemian and Czech-American Biography*. Bloomington, IN: AuthorHouse, 2016, Vol.

1, p. 527; "Joseph Redlich," in: Wikipedia. See - https://de.wikipedia.org/wiki/Josef_Redlich

Eric Stein (1913- 22011), b. Holice, Bohemia; educator, legal scholar
Bio: Rechcigl, Miloslav, Jr., "Eric Stein," in: *Encyclopedia of Bohemian and Czech-American Biography*. Bloomington, IN: AuthorHouse, 2016, Vol. 1, p. 528; Faculty Profile: "Eric Stein," University of Michigan Law School. See - https://www.law.umich.edu/historyandtraditions/faculty/Faculty_Lists/Alpha_Faculty/Pages/EricStein.aspx

Hans Zeisel (1905-1992), b. Kadaň, Bohemia; educator, sociologist, legal scholar
Bio: Olen, Helaine, "Hans Zeisel, 86, U. of C. Professor," in: *Chicago Tribune*, March 10, 1992; Rechcigl, Miloslav, Jr., "Hans Zeisel," in: *Encyclopedia of Bohemian and Czech-American Biography*. Bloomington, IN: AuthorHouse, 2016, Vol. 1, p. 531; "Hans Zeisel," in: Wikipedia. See - https://en.wikipedia.org/wiki/Hans_Zeisel

4. Language and Literary Scholars

a. Classical Languages

Herbert Bloch (1911-2006), b. Berlin, Ger., of Bohemian ancestry; specialist on Greek and Latin
Bio: Christopher P. Jones, "Herbert Bloch," In: *Biographical Memoirs. Proc. Am. Philosophical Soc.*, 152, No. 4 (December 2008), pp. 533-540; *International Biographical Dictionary of Central European Emigrés 1933-1945*. Műnchen: K. G. Saur, 1983, Vol. 2, p. 119-120

b. English Language and Literature

Abraham Albert Avni (1921-1995), b. Brno, Czech.; professor of English and comparative literature, California State Long Beach
Bio: Rechcigl, Miloslav, Jr. "Abraham Albert Avni," in: *Encyclopedia of Bohemian and Czech-American Biography*. Bloomington, IN: AuthorHouse, 2016, Vol. 2, p. 1220.

Sigmund Eisner (1920-2012), b. Red Bank, NJ, of Bohemian ancestry; professor of English, University of Arizona
Bio: Rechcigl, Miloslav, Jr., "Sigmund Eisner," in: *Encyclopedia of Bohemian and Czech-American Biography*. Bloomington, IN: AuthorHouse, 2016, Vol. 2, p. 1223; "Sigmund Eisner," in: Wikipedia. See - https://en.wikipedia.org/wiki/Sigmund_Eisner_(academic)

Alexander Gelley (1933-), b. Czech.; professor of English and comparative literature, University of California, Irvine
Bio: Rechcigl, Miloslav, Jr., "Alexander Gelley," in: *Encyclopedia of Bohemian and Czech-American Biography*. Bloomington, IN: AuthorHouse, 2016, Vol. 2, p. 1224-1225.

Peter Gibian (1952-), b. Northampton, MA, professor of American literature, McGill University
Bio: Rechcigl, Miloslav, "Peter Gibian," in: *Encyclopedia of Bohemian and Czech-American Biography*. Bloomington, IN: AuthorHouse, 2016, Vol. 2, p. 1225.

Chaviva Milada Hosek (1946-), b. Bohemia; feminist, professor of English literature, University of Toronto
Bio: Rechcigl, Miloslav, Jr., "Chaviva Milada Hosek," in: *Encyclopedia of Bohemian and Czech-American Biography*. Bloomington, IN: AuthorHouse, 2016, Vol. 2, p. 1225.

Marjorie Perloff (née Gabriele Mintz) (1932-), b. Vienna, of Moravian ancestry; poetry scholar and critic, professor, Univ. of Southern California and Stanford
Bio: Rechcigl, Miloslav, Jr., "Marjorie Perloff," in: *Encyclopedia of Bohemian and Czech-American Biography*. Bloomington, IN: AuthorHouse, 2016, Vol. 2, p. 1231
; "Marjorie Perloff," in: Wikipedia. See - https://en.wikipedia.org/wiki/Marjorie_Perloff

George Michael Pisk (1932-2012), b. Vienna, of Moravian ancestry; professor of English, Southwest Texas University, San Marcos

Bio: "George Michael Pisk," *Austin American-Statesman*, April 5, 2012; Rechcigl, Miloslav, Jr., "George Michael Pisk," in: *Encyclopedia of Bohemian and Czech-American Biography*. Bloomington, IN: AuthorHouse, 2016, Vol. 2, p. 1231.

c. Germanic Languages and Literatures

Dorrit Claire Cohn (née Zucker-Halle) (1924-); b. Vienna, of Bohemian ancestry; literary scholar
Bio: "Cohn, Dorrit Claire," in: *International Biographical Dictionary of Central European Emigrés 1933-1945*. Műnchen: K. G. Saur, 1983, Vol. 2, pp. 190-191; "Dorrit Cohn. Memorial Minute…," The *Harvard Gazette*, June 3, 2013; "Dorrit Cohn," in: Wikipedia. See - https://en.wikipedia.org/wiki/Dorrit Cohn; Rechcigl, Miloslav, Jr., "Dorrit Cohn," in: *Encyclopedia of Bohemian and Czech-American Biography*. Bloomington, IN: AuthorHouse, 2016, Vol. 2, p. 1241.

Peter Demetz (1922-), b. Prague, Czech; literary scholar, Germanist
Bio: Demetz, Peter, *Prague in Danger: The Years of German Occupation, 1939-1945*. Memory and History, Terror and Resistance, Theater and Jazz, Film and Poetry, Politics and War. New York: Farrar, Straus & Giroux, 2008. 288p.

Ruth Deutsch (1912-2004), b. Prague, Bohemia; professor of German and German literature
Bio: Rechcigl, Miloslav, Jr., "Ruth Deutsch," in: *Encyclopedia of Bohemian and Czech-American Biography*. Bloomington, IN: AuthorHouse, 2016, Vol. 2, p. 1242.

Oscar Benjamin Frankl (1881-1955), b. Kroměříž, Moravia; Germanist, literary scholar, philosopher, free-lance writer and researcher, with Columbia University
Bio: Rechcigl, Miloslav, Jr., "Oscar Benjamin Frankl," in: *Encyclopedia of Bohemian and Czech-American Biography*. Bloomington, IN: AuthorHouse, 2016, Vol. 2, pp. 1175, 1242-1243.

Erich Heller (1911-1990), b. Chomutov, Bohemia; literary scholar

Bio: Peter B. Flint, "Dr. Erich Heller, Professor, 79; A Scholar of German Philosophy," *New York Times,* November 08, 1990; Erich Heller (1911-1990) Papers (1932-1990), Northwestern University Archives, Evanston, IL; Rechcigl, Miloslav, J., "Erich Heller," in: *Beyond the Sea of Beer.* History of Immigration of Bohemians and Czechs to the New World and their Contributions. Bloomington, IN: AuthorHouse, 2017, p. 585

Wilma Abeles Iggers (1921-), b. Miřkov, Czech.; professor of German, Canisius Coll., also specialist on Bohemian Jews and Czech literature
Bio: Rechcigl, Miloslav, Jr., "Wilma Abeles Iggers," in: *Encyclopedia of Bohemian and Czech-American Biography.* Bloomington, IN: AuthorHouse, 2016, Vol. 2, p. 1243.

Erich Kahler (1885-1990), b. Prague, Bohemia; literary scholar and essayist
Bio: Erich Kahler Papers, 1900-1989, Princeton University Manuscripts Division, Princeton, NJ;
Rechcigl, Miloslav, J., "Erich Kahler," in: *Beyond the Sea of Beer.* History of Immigration of Bohemians and Czechs to the New World and their Contributions. Bloomington, IN: AuthorHouse, 2017, p. 584; *International Biographical Dictionary of Central European Emigrés 1933-1945.* Műnchen: K. G. Saur, 1983, Vol. 2, p. 582; "Erich Kahler," in: Wikipedia. See: https://en.wikipedia.org/wiki/Erich Kahler.

Heinz Politzer (1910-1978), b. Vienna, of Moravian ancestry, educated in Prague; literary critic and historian, Germanist, professor at Bryn Mawr Coll., Oberlin Coll. and Univ. of California, Berkley
Bio: Rechcigl, Miloslav, Jr., "Heinz Politzer," in: *Encyclopedia of Bohemian and Czech-American Biography.* Bloomington, IN: AuthorHouse, 2016, Vol. 2, p. 1244-1245.

Rio Preisner (1925-2007), b. Mukačevo, Czech.; professor of German literature, Pennsylvania State Univ., Czech poet, translator
Bio: Rechcigl, Miloslav, Jr., "Rio Preisner," in: *Encyclopedia of Bohemian and Czech-American Biography.* Bloomington, IN: AuthorHouse, 2016, Vol. 2, p. 1245.

Frederick Ritter (1896-1987), b. Vienna, of Bohemian ancestry; originally actor, later Germanist, professor of German language and literature at the Illinois Inst. of Technology
Bio: Rechcigl, Miloslav, Jr., "Frederick Ritter," in: *Encyclopedia of Bohemian and Czech-American Biography*. Bloomington, IN: AuthorHouse, 2016, Vol. 2, p. 1246.

Barbara Zeisl Schoenberg (1940-), b. New York, NY, of Bohemian ancestry; professor of German language and literature at Pomona College
Bio: "Barbara Zeisl Schoenberg," in: Wikipedia. See - https://en.wikipedia.org/wiki/Barbara_Zeisl_Schoenberg

Hanna Spencer (née Fischl) (1913-2014), b. Kladno, Bohemia; Canadian literary scholar
Bio: "Dr. Hanna Spencer (née Fischl), December 16, 1913 - August 17, 2014," in: globeandmail.com, August 23, 2014.

Marketa Goetz-Stankiewicz (1927-), b. Liberec, Czech.; professor of German Studies, Univ. of British Columbia, also specialist on comparative literature
Bio: Rechcigl, Miloslav, Jr., "Marketa Goetz-Stankiewicz," in: *Encyclopedia of Bohemian and Czech-American Biography*. Bloomington, IN: AuthorHouse, 2016, Vol. 2, p. 1243; Jun, Dominik, "Czech-born author and publisher Marketa Goetz-Stankiewicz," in: Czech Radio - See- http://www.radio.cz/en/section/one-on-one/czech-born-author-and-publisher-marketa-goetz-stankiewicz

George Stefansky (1897-1957), b. Prague, Bohemia; Germanist, literary and intellectual historian, sociologist
Bio: Bio: Rechcigl, Miloslav, Jr., "George Stefansky," in: *Encyclopedia of Bohemian and Czech-American Biography*. Bloomington, IN: AuthorHouse, 2016, Vol. 2, p. 1247; "George Stefansky," in: Wikipedia. See - https://de.wikipedia.org/wiki/George Stefansky

Elizabeth Trahan (née Welt) (1924-2009), b. Berlin, of Moravian ancestry, raised in Ostrava; Germanist and specialist on comparative literature, professor at several US universities

Bio: Rechcigl, Miloslav, Jr., "Elizabeth Trahan," in: *Encyclopedia of Bohemian and Czech-American Biography*. Bloomington, IN: AuthorHouse, 2016, Vol. 2, p. 1247-1248.

d. Oriental Languages

Ruth Goldsmith Kunzer (1915-2005), b. Prague, Bohemia; professor of Jewish literature and history, Hebrew Union College, Los Angeles
Bio: Rechcigl, Miloslav, Jr., "Ruth Goldsmith Kunzer," in: *Encyclopedia of Bohemian and Czech-American Biography*. Bloomington, IN: AuthorHouse, 2016, Vol. 2, p. 1266.

Benno Landsberger (1890-1960), b. Frýdek, Moravia; specialist on Semitic languages
Bio: *International Biographical Dictionary of Central European Emigrés 1933-1945*. Műnchen: K. G. Saur, 1983, Vol. 2, p. 688; "Benno Landsberger," in: Wikipedia. See - https://en.wikipedia.org/wiki/Benno Landsberger.

Adolf Leo Oppenheim (1904-1974), b. Vienna, of Bohemian father; specialist on Near East
Bio: *International Biographical Dictionary of Central European Emigrés 1933-1945*. Műnchen: K. G. Saur, 1983, Vol. 2, p. 875; "A. Leo Oppenheim,' in: Wikipedia. See: https://en.wikipedia.org/wiki/A._Leo_Oppenheim

William Popper (1874-1963), b. St. Louis, MO, likely of Bohemian ancestry; professor of Semitic Languages, University of California, Berkley
Bio: Rechcigl, Miloslav Jr., 'William Popper," in: *Encyclopedia of Bohemian and Czech-American Biography*. Bloomington, IN: AuthorHouse, 2016, Vol. 2, p. 1267; "William Popper, Semitic Languages: Berkeley," in: California Digital Library.

Andreas Tietze (1914-2003), b. Vienna, of Bohemian ancestry; specialist on Turkish
Bio: William J. Griswold, "Andreas Tietze (1914-2003)," *Review of Middle East Studies*, 38, No. 1 (June 2004), pp. 142-144; *International Biographical Dictionary of Central European Emigrés 1933-1945*. Műnchen: K. G. Saur, 1983, Vol. 2, pp. 1164-1165.

e. Romance Languages and Literatures

Paul Amann (1884-1958), b. Prague, Bohemia; specialist on French, also a writer
Bio: "Amman, Paul," in: *International Biographical Dictionary of Central European Emigrés 1933-1945*. Műnchen: K. G. Saur, 1983, Vol. 2, p. 24.

Olga Bernal (1929-2002), b. Czech., Holocaust survivor; professor of French at Vassar and then at SUNY Buffalo
Bio: Rechcigl, Miloslav, Jr., "Olga Bernal," in: *Encyclopedia of Bohemian and Czech-American Biography*. Bloomington, IN: AuthorHouse, 2016, Vol. 2, p. 1249.

Alexander Fischler (1931-), b. Liberec, Czech.; professor of French and comparative literature, SUNY Binghamton
Bio: Rechcigl, Miloslav, Jr., "Alexander Fischler," in: *Encyclopedia of Bohemian and Czech-American Biography*. Bloomington, IN: AuthorHouse, 2016, Vol. 2, p. 1250; Wolfe, Sean, "Holocaust Witness," *Gazette-Times*, May 7, 2005.

John W. Kronik (1931-2006), b. Vienna, of Bohemian ancestry; Romanticist, specialist on Spanish literature
Bio: Cardona, Rodolfo, "John W. Kronik (1931-2006)," *Bulletin of Spanish Studies*, 83, No. 4 (2006), pp. 553-556; Crawford, Franklin, "John W. Kronik, Cornell professor emeritus of Spanish literature, dies at 74," *Cornell Chronicle*, February 1, 2006.

Eva Dubská Kushner (1929-), b. Prague, Czech.; professor of French and comparative literature, Univ. of Toronto
Bio: Rechcigl, Miloslav, Jr., "Eva Dubská Kushner," in: *Encyclopedia of Bohemian and Czech-American Biography*. Bloomington, IN: AuthorHouse, 2016, Vol. 2, p. 1251-1252.

Thomas Mermall (1937-2011), b. Užhorod, Czech.; professor of Spanish, Brooklyn College
Bio: Rechcigl, Miloslav,
Jr., "Thomas Mermall," in: *Encyclopedia of Bohemian and Czech-American Biography*. Bloomington, IN: AuthorHouse, 2016, Vol. 2, p. 1252.

Erika Ostrovsky (née Spielberg) (1926-2010), b. Vienna, of Bohemian ancestry; professor of French, New York University, author
Bio: Rechcigl, Miloslav, Jr., "Erika Ostrovsky," in: *Encyclopedia of Bohemian and Czech-American Biography*. Bloomington, IN: AuthorHouse, 2016, Vol. 2, pp. 987-988.

George Oswald Schanzer (1914-2011), b. Vienna, of Bohemian ancestry; specialist on Spanish
Bio: *International Biographical Dictionary of Central European Emigrés 1933-1945*. Műnchen: K. G. Saur, 1983, Vol. 2, p. 1023; "George E. Schanzer," in: Wikipedia. See - https://de.wikipedia.org/wiki/George O. Schanzer

Helen Waldstein Wilkes (1936-), b. Czech.; professor of French in Canada and the US
Bio: Rechcigl, Miloslav, Jr., "Helen Waldstein Wilkes," in: *Encyclopedia of Bohemian and Czech-American Biography*. Bloomington, IN: AuthorHouse, 2016, Vol. 2, p. 989.

f. Slavic Languages

George Gibian (1924-2000), b. Prague, Czech. professor of Russian and comparative literature, Cornell University
Bio: Rechcigl, Miloslav, Jr., "George Gibian," in: *Encyclopedia of Bohemian and Czech-American Biography*. Bloomington, IN: AuthorHouse, 2016, Vol. 2, pp. 1257-1258

Peter Kussi (1925-2012), b. Prague, Czech.; adj. professor of Slavic Languages and Literatures, Columbia University, translator
Bio: Rechcigl, Miloslav, Jr., "Peter Kussi," in: *Encyclopedia of Bohemian and Czech-American Biography*. Bloomington, IN: AuthorHouse, 2016, Vol. 2, p. 1258.

Peter Steiner (1956-), b. Prague, Czech.; professor of Slavic Languages and Literatures, University of Pennsylvania
Bio: Rechcigl, Miloslav, Jr., "Peter Steiner," in: *Encyclopedia of Bohemian and Czech-American Biography*. Bloomington, IN: AuthorHouse, 2016, Vol. 2, p. 1262.

Malynne Sternstein (1966-), b. Bangkok, Thailand, of Czech ancestry; professor of Slavic Studies, University of Chicago
Bio: Rechcigl, Miloslav, Jr., "Malynne Sternstein," in: *Encyclopedia of Bohemian and Czech-American Biography*. Bloomington, IN: AuthorHouse, 2016, Vol. 2, p. 1263.

Bronislava Volková (1946-), b. Děčín, Czech.; professor of Slavic languages, Indiana Univ., Czech poet
Bio: Rechcigl, Miloslav, Jr., "Bronislava Volková," in: *Encyclopedia of Bohemian and Czech-American Biography*. Bloomington, IN: AuthorHouse, 2016, Vol. 2, p. 1264.

5. Linguists

Isaac Bacon (1914-2007), b. Svinov, Moravia; linguist, Dean of Yeshiva College
Bio: Norman Adler, "Remembering Dean Isaac Bacon," *The Commentator* (Yeshiva College), May 6, 2007.

Leonard Bloomfield (1887-1949), b. Chicago, IL; nephew of Maurice Bloomfield; linguist, pioneer in structural linguistics
Bio: Hall, Robert A. Jr., *A life for Language: A biographical memoir of Leonard Bloomfield.* Philadelphia: John Benjamins, 1990; "Leonard Bloomfield," in: Wikipedia. See - https://en.wikipedia.org/wiki/Leonard_Bloomfield

Maurice Bloomfield (1855-1928), b. Bílsko, on Moravian-Silesian border; philologist and Sanskrit scholar, professor at University of Chicago and then at Yale.
Bio: "Maurice Bloomfield," in: Wikipedia. See - https://en.wikipedia.org/wiki/Maurice_Bloomfield

Paul Garvin (1919-1994), b. Karlovy Vary, Czech.; professor of linguistics, SUNY Buffalo
Bio: Rechcigl, Miloslav, Jr., "Paul Garvin," in: *Encyclopedia of Bohemian and Czech-American Biography*. Bloomington, IN: AuthorHouse, 2016, Vol. 2, p. 1272; Daneš, František, "Paul Garvin, 1919-1994: An obituary of

an excellent (socio)linguist and old good friend," *Journal of the Sociology of Language,* 118, No.1, pp. 205–208.

Ruth Weir Hirsch (1926-1965), b. Belovec, Czech.; professor of linguistics, Stanford University
Bio: Rechcigl, Miloslav, Jr., "Ruth Weir Hirsch," in: *Encyclopedia of Bohemian and Czech-American Biography.* Bloomington, IN: AuthorHouse, 2016, Vol. 2, p. 1273.

Roman Jakobson (1896-1982), b. Moscow, Russia, studied and resided in Prague, linguist
Bio: Caton, Steve C., "Contributions of Roman Jakobson," *Annual Review of Anthropology,* Vol 16 (1987), pp. 223–260; Holenstein, E., *Roman Jakobson's Approach to Language: Phenomenological Structuralism,* Bloomington and London: Indiana University Press, 1975; Rechcigl, Miloslav, Jr., "Roman Jakobson," in: *Encyclopedia of Bohemian and Czech-American Biography.* Bloomington, IN: AuthorHouse, 2016, Vol. 2, p. 1273; "Roman Jakobson," in: Wikipedia. See - https://en.wikipedia.org/wiki/Roman_Jakobson

Nathan Suskind (1907-1984), b. Slovakia; lexicologist, authority on Yiddish
Bio: Pace, Eric, "Nathan Suskind, College Teacher, 87; Was Yiddish Expert," *The New York Times,* July 20, 1994.

Thomas G. Winner (orig. Weiner) (1917-2004), b. Prague, Bohemia; linguist, educator, founder of first semiotic center in US
Bio: Zezima, Katie, "Thomas Winner, 86, Scholar Who Escaped from Nazi Europe," The New York Times, April 29, 2004; Rechcigl, Miloslav, Jr., "Thomas G. Winner," in: *Encyclopedia of Bohemian and Czech-American Biography.* Bloomington, IN: AuthorHouse, 2016, Vol. 2, p. 1265; "Thomas G. Winner," in: Wikipedia. See - https://en.wikipedia.org/wiki/Thomas_G._Winner

6. Philosophers

Maximilian Beck (1887-1950), b. Pilsen, Bohemia, philosopher
Bio: Rechcigl, Miloslav, Jr., "Maximilian Beck," in: *Encyclopedia of Bohemian and Czech-American Biography*. Bloomington, IN: AuthorHouse, 2016, Vol. 2, p. 1170.

Michael Bergmann, b. of Czech ancestry; philosopher, epistemologist, philosopher of religion, writer, director, producer
Bio: "Michael Bergmann," in: Wikipedia. See - https://en.wikipedia.org/wiki/Michael_Bergmann_(philosopher)

Herbert Feigl (1902-1988), b. Liberec, Bohemia; philosopher
Bio: "Herbert Feigl," in: Wikipedia. See - https://en.wikipedia.org/wiki/Herbert Feigl; Rechcigl, Miloslav, Jr., "Herbert Feigl," in: *Beyond the Sea of Beer.* History of Immigration of Bohemians and Czechs to the New World and their Contributions. Bloomington, IN: AuthorHouse, 2017, p. 583.

Vilém Flusser (1920-1991), b. Prague, Bohemia; philosopher, writer, journalist
Bio: Rechcigl, Miloslav, Jr., "Vilém Flusser," in: *Encyclopedia of Bohemian and Czech-American Biography*. Bloomington, IN: AuthorHouse, 2016, Vol. 2, pp. 1174-1175.

Erich Frank (1883-1949), b. Prague, Bohemia; philosopher
Bio: "Erich Frank," in: *Wikipedia.* See: https://de.wikipedia.org/wiki/Erich Frank (Philosoph); *International Biographical Dictionary of Central European Emigres 1933-1945.* Műnchen: K. G. Saur, 1983, Vol. 2, p. 317; Rechcigl, Miloslav, Jr., "Erich Frank," in: *Beyond the Sea of Beer.* History of Immigration of Bohemians and Czechs to the New World and their Contributions. Bloomington, IN: AuthorHouse, 2017, p. 583.

Philipp Frank (1884-1966), b. Vienna, professor at University of Prague; physicist and philosopher of science
Bio: "Philipp Frank," in: Wikipedia. See: https://en.wikipedia.org/wiki/Philipp Frank; *International Biographical Dictionary of Central European Émigrés 1933-1945.* Műnchen: K. G. Saur, 1983, Vol. 2, p. 318; Rechcigl, Miloslav,

Jr., "Philipp F. Frank," in: *Beyond the Sea of Beer.* History of Immigration of Bohemians and Czechs to the New World and their Contributions. Bloomington, IN: AuthorHouse, 2017, p. 583.

Lubomír Gleiman (1923-2006), b. Trnava, Slovakia; philosopher
Bio: Gleiman, Lubomir, From the Maelstrom. A Pilgrim's Story of Dissent and Survival in the Twentieth Century. Bloomington, IN: AuthorHouse, 2011.

Heinrich Gomperz (1873-1942), b. Vienna, of Moravian ancestry; philosopher
Bio: "Heinrich Gomperz," in: Wikipedia. See: https://en.wikipedia.org/wiki/Heinrich Gomperz; *International Biographical Dictionary of Central European Emigrés 1933-1945.* Műnchen: K. G. Saur, 1983, Vol. 2, p. 402; Rechcigl, Miloslav, Jr., "Heinrich Gomperz," in: *Beyond the Sea of Beer.* History of Immigration of Bohemians and Czechs to the New World and their Contributions. Bloomington, IN: AuthorHouse, 2017, p. 582.

Stephen Kőrner (1913-2000), b. Moravská Ostrava, Moravia; philosopher educator
Bio: Rechcigl, Miloslav, Jr., "Stephen Kőrner," in: *Encyclopedia of Bohemian and Czech-American Biography.* Bloomington, IN: AuthorHouse, 2016, Vol. 2, p. 1178.

Pavel Kovaly (1928-2006), b. Prague, Czech.; philosopher, librarian
Bio: Rechcigl, Miloslav, Jr., "Pavel Kovaly," in: *Encyclopedia of Bohemian and Czech-American Biography.* Bloomington, IN: AuthorHouse, 2016, Vol. 2, p. 1178.

Bernard Martin (1923-d.), b. Seklence, Czech.; Rabbi, philosopher, educator
Bio: Rechcigl, Miloslav, Jr., "Bernard Martin," in: *Encyclopedia of Bohemian and Czech-American Biography.* Bloomington, IN: AuthorHouse, 2016, Vol. 2, p. 1179.

Ernest Nagel (1901-1985), b. Nové Mesto nad Váhom, Slovakia; philosopher of science

Bio: Suppes, Patrick, "Nagel, Ernest," in: American National Biography Online, February 2000. Retrieved 10 April 2014; Suppes, Patrick (1994), "Ernest Nagel," in: *Biographical Memoirs of the National Academy of Sciences. National Academy of Sciences.* Retrieved 10 April 2014;
"Ernest Nagel," in: Wikipedia. See: https://en.wikipedia.org/wiki/Ernest Nagel

Tamar Schapiro (1965-), b. Chicago, IL, of Bohemian ancestry; philosopher
Bio: Rechcigl, Miloslav, Jr., "Tamar Schapiro," in: *Encyclopedia of Bohemian and Czech-American Biography*. Bloomington, IN: AuthorHouse, 2016, Vol. 2, p. 1184.

Alfred Schűtz (1899-1959), b. Vienna, of Bohemian mother; philosopher, social phenomenologist
Bio: Barber, M., *The Participating Citizen: A Biography of Alfred Schűtz*. New York, State University of New York Press, 2004; Wagner, H. R., *Alfred Schűtz: An Intellectual Biography*. Chicago and London, The University of Chicago Press, 1983.

7. Theologians

Leo Baeck (1873-1956), b. Lissa, Poland; of Moravian ancestry; Rabbi and religious thinker
Bio: Rechcigl, Miloslav, Jr., "Leo Baeck," in: *Encyclopedia of Bohemian and Czech-American Biography*. Bloomington, IN: AuthorHouse, 2016, Vol. 2, p. 1168.

Bernard J. Bettelheim (1811-1870), b. Bratislava, Slovakia; physician, Protestant missionary to Okinawa, Army physician during Civil War
Bio: "Bernard Jean Bettelheim," in: Wikipedia. See - https://en.wikipedia.org/wiki/Bernard Jean Bettelheim

Maximilian Heller (1860-1929), b. Prague, Bohemia; Reform Rabbi, Zionist
Bio: "Rabbi Maximilian Heller, Outstanding Leader and Educator, Dies," Jewish Telegraphic Agency, April 1, 1929; Rechcigl, Miloslav,

Jr., "Maximilian Heller," in: *Encyclopedia of Bohemian and Czech-American Biography*. Bloomington, IN: AuthorHouse, 2016, Vol. 1, p. 292.

Leo Jung (1892-1972), b. Uherský Brod, Moravia; Orthodox Rabbi, philosopher
Bio: "Leo Jung," in: Wikipedia. See - https://en.wikipedia.org/wiki/Leo_Jung; Konvitz, Milton R., "Leo Jung-Rabbi for All Jews," *Midstream* 39, No. 6 (Aug/Sept 1993).; Menachem, Mendel Kasher, Norman Lamm, Leonard Rosenfeld. *Leo Jung Jubilee Volume Essays in Honor on the Occasion of his Seventieth Birthday*. N.Y.: The Jewish Center Synagogue, 1962; Rechcigl, Miloslav, Jr., "Leo Jung," in: *Encyclopedia of Bohemian and Czech-American Biography*. Bloomington, IN: AuthorHouse, 2016, Vol. 1, p. 292 and Vol. 2, p. 1177.

Moses Jung (1891-1960), b. Uherský Brod, Moravia; theologian
Bio: Rechcigl, Miloslav, Jr., "Moses Jung," in: *Encyclopedia of Bohemian and Czech-American Biography*. Bloomington, IN: AuthorHouse, 2016, Vol. 2, p. 1168.

Eugene Kohn (1887-1977), b. Newark, NJ, of Bohemian ancestry; Reconstructionist Rabbi
Bio: Rechcigl, Miloslav, Jr., "Eugene Kohn," in: *Encyclopedia of Bohemian and Czech-American Biography*. Bloomington, IN: AuthorHouse, 2016, Vol. 1, p. 292.

Jacob Kohn (1881-1968), b. Newark, NJ, of Bohemian ancestry; conservative Rabbi, educator
Bio: "Jacob Kohn," kin" Prabook. See - https://prabook.com/web/jacob.kohn/283946; Rechcigl, Miloslav, Jr., "Jacob Kohn," in: *Encyclopedia of Bohemian and Czech-American Biography*. Bloomington, IN: AuthorHouse, 2016, Vol. 1, p. 292 and Vol. 2, p. 1088 and 1168.

John Maria Oesterreicher (1904-1993), b. Libava, Moravia; professor of sacred theology at Seton Hall University, South Orange, NJ
Bio: Rechcigl, Miloslav, Jr., "John Maria Oesterreicher," in: *Beyond the Sea of Beer*. History of Immigration of Bohemians and Czechs to the New World and their Contributions. Bloomington, IN: AuthorHouse, 2017,

p. 58; "John M. Oesterreicher," in: Wikipedia. See: https://en.wikipedia.org/wiki/John M. Oesterreicher; Saxon, Wolfgang, "J.M. Oesterreicher, Monsignor Who Wrote on Jews, Dies at 89," *New York Times*, April 20, 1993; *International Biographical Dictionary of Central European Emigrés 1933-1945*. Műnchen: K. G. Saur, 1983, Vol. 2, p. 872.

Isaac Mayer Wise (1819-1900), b. Lomnička, Bohemia: American Reform Rabbi, editor, and college president
Bio:_Max B. May, *Isaac Mayer Wise, The Founder of American Judaism*. New York and London: G. P. Putnam's Sons, 1916; James G. Heller, M. *Wise, His Life, Work and Thought*. The Union of American Hebrew Congregations, 1965; "Isaac Mayer Wise," in: Wikipedia. See - https://en.wikipedia.org/wiki/Isaac Mayer Wise;

C. Social Sciences

1. Anthropologists

Melville J. Herskovits (1895-1963), b. Bellefontaine, OH, of Slovak ancestry"; anthropologist
Bio: Gershenhorn, Jerry, *Melville J. Herskovits and the Racial Politics of Knowledge. Lincoln, NE:*
University of Nebraska Press, 2004; Merriam, Alan P., "Melville Jean Herskovits, 1895-1963," *American Anthropologist*, Vol. 66, No. 1 (1964), pp. 83-109; "Melville J. Herskovits," in: Wikipedia. See - https://en.wikipedia.org/wiki/Melville J. Herskovits

Ivan Kalmar (1948-), b. Prague, Czech.; Canadian anthropologist, educator
Bio: "Ivan Kalmar," in: Wikipedia. See - https://en.wikipedia.org/wiki/Ivan_Kalmar

Beate Salz (1913-2006), b. Heidelberg, Ger., of Bohemian father; anthropologist, sociologist

Bio: Rechcigl, Miloslav, Jr., "Beate Salz," in: *Encyclopedia of Bohemian and Czech-American Biography.* Bloomington, IN: AuthorHouse, 2016, Vol. 2, 1285.

Michael Taussig (1940-), b. Sydney, Australia, of Bohemian ancestry; anthropologist, professor
Bio: "Michael Taussig," in: Wikipedia. See - https://en.wikipedia.org/wiki/Michael Taussig

2. Economists

John Hans Adler (1912-1980), b. Tachov, Bohemia; economist
Bio: Rechcigl, Miloslav, J., "John Hans Adler," in: *Beyond the Sea of Beer.* History of Immigration of Bohemians and Czechs to the New World and their Contributions. Bloomington, IN: AuthorHouse, 2017, p. 575; Schudel, Matt, "World Bank Economist Hans Adler, 83," *Washington Post,* February 2005, p. B06.

Antonín Basch (1896-1971), b. Německý Brod, Czech., economist
Bio: Rechcigl, Miloslav, J., "Antonín Basch," in: *Beyond the Sea of Beer.* History of Immigration of Bohemians and Czechs to the New World and their Contributions. Bloomington, IN: AuthorHouse, 2017, p. 572; "Antonín Basch," in: Wikipedia. See - https://cs.wikipedia.org/wiki/Antonín Basch

Alfred Viktor Berger-Vesendorf (1901-1980), b. Vienna, of Moravian, father; economist
Bio: Rechcigl, Miloslav, Jr., "Alfred Viktor Berger-Vesendorf," in: *Encyclopedia of Bohemian and Czech-American Biography.* Bloomington, IN: AuthorHouse, 2016, Vol. 2, 1292.

Rudolf Carl Blitz (1919-), b. Vienna, of Moravian, father; economist
Bio: "Blitz, Rudolph Carl," in: *International Biographical Dictionary of Central European Emigrés 1933-1945.* Műnchen: K. G. Saur, 1983, Vol. 2, p. 117.

Otto Hld Ehrlich (1892-1979), b. Vienna, of Moravian father; economist

Bio: Rechcigl, Miloslav, Jr., "Otto Hild Ehrlich," in: *Encyclopedia of Bohemian and Czech-American Biography*. Bloomington, IN: AuthorHouse, 2016, Vol. 2, pp. 1297-1298;

Marianne A. Ferber (**née Abeles (1923-)** b. Miřkov, Bohemia; economist
Bio: "Ferber, Marianne A.," in: *International Biographical Dictionary of Central European Emigrés 1933-1945.*Műnchen: K. G. Saur, 1983, Vol. 2, p. 293; Rechcigl, Miloslav, Jr., "Marianne A. Ferber," in: *Beyond the Sea of Beer.* History of Immigration of Bohemians and Czechs to the New World and their Contributions. Bloomington, IN: AuthorHouse, 2017, p. 576.

Herbert Furth (1899-1995), b. Vienna, of Bohemian ancestry; jurist and economist
Bio: "Herbert Furth," in: Wikipedia. See - https://en.wikipedia.org/wiki/Herbert_Furth

Werner Hochwald (1910-1989), b. Berlin, Ger., of Bohemian father; economist
Bio: Rechcigl, Miloslav, Jr., "Werner Hochwald," in: *Encyclopedia of Bohemian and Czech-American Biography*. Bloomington, IN: AuthorHouse, 2016, Vol. 2, p. 1306.

Berthold Frank Hoselitz (1913-1995), b. Vienna, of Czech ancestry; senior economist at Rand Corporation
Bio: "Bert F. Hoselitz," in: Wikipedia. See - https://en.wikipedia.org/wiki/Bert F. Hoselitz; Rechcigl, Miloslav, Jr., "Berthold Frank Hoselitz," in: *Encyclopedia of Bohemian and Czech-American Biography*. Bloomington, IN: AuthorHouse, 2016, Vol. 2, pp. 1304-1305.

Alexandre Kafka (1917-2007); b. Prague, Bohemia;
Bio: "Alexandre Kafka," in: Wikipedia. See - https://en.wikipedia.org/wiki/Alexandre Kafka;
Lamb, Yvonne Shinhoster, "Alexandre Kafka, IMF Executive Director," *Washington Post,* January 5, 2008; Rechcigl, Miloslav, J., "Alexandre Kafka," in: *Beyond the Sea of Beer.* History of Immigration of Bohemians and Czechs to the New World and their Contributions. Bloomington, IN: AuthorHouse, 2017, p. 576.

Emil Kauder (1901-1982), b. Berlin, Ger., of Bohemian father; economist
Bio: Rechcigl, Miloslav, Jr., "Emil Kauder," in: *Encyclopedia of Bohemian and Czech-American Biography*. Bloomington, IN: AuthorHouse, 2016, Vol. 2, p. 1386.

Herbert Kisch (1924-1978), b. Prague, Bohemia; professor of economics, Michigan State University
Bio: Rechcigl, Miloslav, Jr., "Herbert Kisch," in: *Encyclopedia of Bohemian and Czech-American Biography*. Bloomington, IN: AuthorHouse, 2016, Vol. 2, p. 1306.

Meir Gregory Kohn (1946-), b. Kamenice-Šenov, Czech.; economist, professor of economics at Dartmouth University
Bio: Rechcigl, Miloslav, Jr., "Meir Gregory Kohn," in: *Encyclopedia of Bohemian and Czech-American Biography*. Bloomington, IN: AuthorHouse, 2016, Vol. 2, p. 1307.

Emil Lederer (1882-1939), b. Plzeň, Bohemia; economist
Bio: Rechcigl, Miloslav, J., "Alexandre Kafka," in: *Beyond the Sea of Beer.* History of Immigration of Bohemians and Czechs to the New World and their Contributions. Bloomington, IN: AuthorHouse, 2017, pp. 571-572; Strauss, Herbert A., and Werner Roder, eds., *International Biographical Dictionary of Central European Émigrés 1933-1945*. München-New York – London – Paris: K. G. Saur, 1983, Part 12: L-Z, pp. 699-700; "Emil Lederer," in: Wikipedia. See - https://en.wikipedia.org/wiki/Emil Lederer

Kari Polanyi Levitt (1923-), b. Vienna, of Slovak ancestry; Canadian economist, professor, Mcgill University
Bio: "Biography," in: Kari Polanyi Levitt website. See http://www.karipolanyilevitt.com/biography/ "Kari Polanyi Levitt," in: Wikipedia. See - https://en.wikipedia.org/wiki/Kari_Polanyi_Levitt

Eugen Lőbl (1907-1987), b. Holíč, Slovakia; economist, politician
Bio: "Eugen Lőbl," in: Wikipedia. See - https://cs.wikipedia.org/wiki/Eugen Löbl

Frank Meissner (1923-1990), b. Třešť, Czech.; agricultural economist
Bio: Rechcigl, Miloslav, Jr., "Frank Meissner," in: *Encyclopedia of Bohemian and Czech-American Biography*. Bloomington, IN: AuthorHouse, 2016, Vol. 2, p. 1376.

Ilse S. Mintz (née Schuller), (1904-1978), b. Vienna, of Moravian father, economist
Bio: Rechcigl, Miloslav, Jr., "Ilse S. Mintz," in: *Encyclopedia of Bohemian and Czech-American Biography*. Bloomington, IN: AuthorHouse, 2016, Vol. 2, p. 1312.

Franz Herman Muller (1900-1994), b. Berlin, Ger., of Bohemian father; economist
Bio: Mueller Franz Herman Joseph," in: *Encyclopedia of Religion and Society*. By William H. Swatos, Jr. Walnut creek-London-New Delhi: AltaMira Press, 1998, p. 314.

Karl H. Niebyl (1906-1985), b. Karlín, Bohemia, economist
Bio: Rechcigl, Miloslav, J., "Karl H. Niebyl," in: *Beyond the Sea of Beer*. History of Immigration of Bohemians and Czechs to the New World and their Contributions. Bloomington, IN: AuthorHouse, 2017, pp. 574-575.

Franz Pick (1898-1985), b. Česká Lípa, Bohemia; economist
Bio: Rechcigl, Miloslav, J., "Franz Pick," in: *Beyond the Sea of Beer*. History of Immigration of Bohemians and Czechs to the New World and their Contributions. Bloomington, IN: AuthorHouse, 2017, p. 572-573; "Franz Pick," *The New York Times*, December 3, 1985;

Karl Paul Polanyi (1886-1964), b. Vienna, of Slovak ancestry; economic historian, anthropologist and sociologist, political economist, social philosopher
Bio: "Karl Polanyi," in: Wikipedia. See - https://en.wikipedia.org/wiki/Karl_Polanyi

Karl Gabriel Pribram (1877-1973), b. Prague, Bohemia; economist, also social philosopher and sociologist

Bio: Mark Perlman, "An Essay on Karl Pribram's, A History of Economic Reasoning," *Revue économique*, Vol. 38, No. 1 (January 1987), pp. 171–6; Karl Pribram's Papers,1877-1973, M. E. Grenander Department of Special Collections & Archives, University Libraries, University at Albany, State University of New York, Albany, NY.

Alan Rabinowitz (1927-2017), b. NYC, of Bohemian ancestry; urban economist, professor of urban planning, University of Washington, Seattle
Bio: "Alan Rabinowitz 1927-2017 Obituary," *The Seattle Times,* December 1-Dec. 2, 2017.

Elizabeth Brandeis Raushenbush (1896-1980), b. Boston, MA, of Bohemian ancestry; economist
Bio: Rechcigl, Miloslav, Jr. "Elizabeth Brandeis Raushenbush," in: *Encyclopedia of Bohemian and Czech-American Biography.* Bloomington, IN: AuthorHouse, 2016, Vol. 2, p. 1318.

George Friedrich Rohrlich (1914-1995), b. Vienna, of Bohemian ancestry; economist
Bio: Rechcigl, Miloslav, Jr., "George Friedrich Rohrlich," in: *Encyclopedia of Bohemian and Czech-American Biography.* Bloomington, IN: AuthorHouse, 2016, Vol. 2, p. 1318.

Gideon Rosenbluth (1921-2007), b. Berlin, Germany, of Bohemian mother; economist
Bio: "Rosenbluth, Gideon," in: *International Biographical Dictionary of Central European Émigrés 1933-1945.*Műnchen: K. G. Saur, 1983, Vol. 2, p. 985; Rechcigl, Miloslav, Jr., "Gideon Rosenbluth," in: *Beyond the Sea of Beer.* History of Immigration of Bohemians and Czechs to the New World and their Contributions. Bloomington, IN: AuthorHouse, 2017, p. 576.

Arthur Salz (1881-1963), b. Stod, Bohemia; economist
Bio: Rechcigl, Miloslav, J., "Arthur Salz," in: *Beyond the Sea of Beer.* History of Immigration of Bohemians and Czechs to the New World and their Contributions. Bloomington, IN: AuthorHouse, 2017, p. 573; "Salz, Arthur," in: *International Biographical Dictionary of Central European Emigrés 1933-1945.* Műnchen: K. G. Saur, 1983, Vol. 2, p. 1015.

Richard Schűller (1870-1972), b. Brno, Moravia; economist
Bio: Rechcigl, Miloslav, Jr., "Richard Schueller," in: *Encyclopedia of Bohemian and Czech-American Biography*. Bloomington, IN: AuthorHouse, 2016, Vol. 2, p. 1319.

Joseph Alois Schumpeter (1883-1950), b. Třešť, Moravia; economist
Bio: Harris, Seymour E., *Schumpeter, Social Scientist*. Cambridge: Harvard University Press, 1951; Rechcigl, Miloslav, Jr., "Ekonomický myslitel z Třešti" (Economic scholar from Třesť), in: *Postavy naší Ameriky*. Praha: Pražská edice, 2000, pp. 268-270; Schneider, Erich, *Schumpeter. Life and Work of a Great Social Scientist*. Bureau of Business Research, University of Nebraska, 1975; Wikipedia. See: https://en.wikipedia.org/wiki/Joseph_Schumpeter

Herbert A. Simon (1916-2001), b. Milwaukee, WI, of Bohemian ancestry; professor of computer science and psychology, Nobel Prize recipient in economics
Bio: "Herbert Simon's Autobiography," in: *Nobel Lectures, Economics 1969-1980*, Edited by Assar Lindbeck, Singapore: World Scientific Publishing Co., 1992; *Models of a Man: Essays in Memory of Herbert A. Simon*. Eds. Mie Augier and James G. March. MIT Press, 2004

Josef Soudek (1905-1992), b. Podmokly, Bohemia; economist
Bio: Rechcigl, Miloslav, Jr., "Josef Soudek," in: *Encyclopedia of Bohemian and Czech-American Biography*. Bloomington, IN: AuthorHouse, 2016, Vol. 2, p.1322.

Frank William Taussig (1859-1940), b. St. Louis, MO, of Bohemian ancestry; professor of economics at Harvard
Bio: Frank, A. H. and E. S. Mason, "Frank William Taussig," in: *Ten Great Economists from Marx to Keynes*. Edited by Joseph A. Schumpeter. New York: Oxford University Press, 1951, pp. 191-221; Opie, Redveras, "Frank William Taussig," *Economic Journal*, 51 (1941), pp. 347-368; *Who's Who in America*, 1905; Schumpeter, Joseph A., A. A. Cole and E. S. Mason, "Frank William Taussig," in: *The Great Economists from Marx to Keynes*. Ed. Joseph A. Schumpeter. New York: Oxford University Press, 1951, pp. 191-221; Rechcigl, Miloslav, Jr., "Otec moderního ekonomického myšlení" (Father

of the New Economic Thinking), in: *Postavy naší Ameriky*. Praha: Pražská edice, 2000, pp. 265-267.

Michael K. Taussig (1938-2010), b. Prague, Czech.; professor of economics, Rutgers University
Bio: "Michael K. Taussig," *Home News Tribune*, February 28, 2010.; Rechcigl, Miloslav, Jr., "Michael K. Taussig," in: *Encyclopedia of Bohemian and Czech-American Biography*. Bloomington, IN: AuthorHouse, 2016, Vol. 2, pp. 1325-1326.

Thomas E. Weisskopf (1940-), b. NYC, of Bohemian ancestry; economist
Bio: Rechcigl, Miloslav, Jr., "Thomas E. Weisskopf," in: *Encyclopedia of Bohemian and Czech-American Biography*. Bloomington, IN: AuthorHouse, 2016, Vol. 2, p. 1328.

Walter Albert Weisskopf (1898-1943), b. Liberec, Bohemia; economist, professor, Roosevelt Univ.
Bio: Rechcigl, Miloslav, Jr., "Walter Albert Weiskopf," in: *Encyclopedia of Bohemian and Czech-American Biography*. Bloomington, IN: AuthorHouse, 2016, Vol. 2, p. 1328.

3. Geographers and Area Specialists

Thomas. A. Reiner (1931-2009), b. Teplice-Šanov, Bohemia; professor of regional science
Bio: Rechcigl, Miloslav, Jr., "Thomas Andrew Reiner," in: *Encyclopedia of Bohemian and Czech-American Biography*. Bloomington, IN: AuthorHouse, 2016, Vol. 2, 1342.

4. Management Specialists

Lotte Bailyn (née Lazarsfeld) (1930-), b. Vienna, of Moravian ancestry; social psychologist, pressor of management, MIT
Bio: Rechcigl, Miloslav, Jr., "Lotte Bailyn," in: *Encyclopedia of Bohemian and Czech-American Biography*. Bloomington, IN: AuthorHouse, 2016, Vol. 2, p. 1362.

Peter Frederick Drucker (1909-2005), b. Vienna, of Bohemian ancestry, management expert

Bio: "Petr Drucker," in: Wikipedia. See - https://en.wikipedia.org/wiki/Peter Drucker; Flaherty, John E., *Peter Drucker: Shaping the Managerial Mind*, 1999.

Frank William Kolmin (1915-2002), b. Vienna, of Bohemuan father; professor of accounting, Dean, Ithaca Coll.

Bio: Rechcigl, Miloslav, Jr., "Frank William Kolmin," in: *Encyclopedia of Bohemian and Czech-American Biography*. Bloomington, IN: AuthorHouse, 2016, Vol. 2, p. 1335.

Tom A. Nohel (1960-), b. Atlanta, GA, of Czech parents; professor of finance, Loyola Univ., Chicago

Bio: Rechcigl, Miloslav, Jr., "Tom A. Nohel," in: *Encyclopedia of Bohemian and Czech-American Biography*. Bloomington, IN: AuthorHouse, 2016, Vol. 2, p. 1336.

5. Political Scientists

Frederick Mechner Barnard (1921-2011), b. Ostrava, Moravia; political scientist

Bio: Rechcigl, Miloslav, Jr., "Frederick Mechner Barnard," in: *Encyclopedia of Bohemian and Czech-American Biography*. Bloomington, IN: AuthorHouse, 2016, Vol. 2, 1386.

Karl W. Deutsch (1912-1992), b. Prague, Bohemia; social and political scientist

Bio: *From National Development to Global Community*. Essays in Honor of Karl W. Deutsch. Ed. by Richard I. Merritt and Bruce M. Russett. London: Allen & Unwin, 1981; Rechcigl, Miloslav, Jr., "Inovačni politolog," (Innovative Political Scientist), in: *Postavy naší Ameriky*. Praha: Pražská edice, 2000, pp. 279-281; "Karl W. Deutsch," in: Wikipedia, See - https://en.wikipedia.org/wiki/Karl Deutsch

Frederick Charles Engelsmann (1921-2008), b. Vienna, of Moravian ancestry; political scientist, Canada

Bio: Rechcigl, Miloslav, Jr., "Frederick Charles Engelsmann," in: *Encyclopedia of Bohemian and Czech-American Biography*. Bloomington, IN: AuthorHouse, 2016, Vol. 2, 1390.

Erich Hula (1900-1987), b. Vienna, of Bohemian father; political scientist
Bio: "Erich Hula," in: Wikipedia. See - https://de.wikipedia.org/wiki/Erich_Hula; Rechcigl, Miloslav, Jr., "Erich Hula," in: *Encyclopedia of Bohemian and Czech-American Biography*. Bloomington, IN: AuthorHouse, 2016, Vol. 2, 1393-1394.

John H. Kautsky (1922-), b. Vienna, of Bohemian ancestry; political scientist
Bio: "Kautsky, John H.," in: *International Biographical Dictionary of Central European Émigrés 1933-1945*. Műnchen: K. G. Saur, 1983, Vol. 2, pp. 607-608; Rechcigl, Miloslav, J., "John H. Kautsky," in: in: *Beyond the Sea of Beer.* History of Immigration of Bohemians and Czechs to the New World and their Contributions. Bloomington, IN: AuthorHouse, 2017, p. 570.

Josef Korbel (1909-1977), b. Kyšperk, Bohemia; diplomat, political scientist
Bio: Josef Tomeš et al, *Český biografický slovník XX. století.* Praha: Paseka, 1999, p.125; Josef Korbel, Wikipedia: http://en.wikipedia.org/wiki/Josef Korbel; Rechcigl, Miloslav, J., "Josef Korbel," in: *Beyond the Sea of Beer.* History of Immigration of Bohemians and Czechs to the New World and their Contributions. Bloomington, IN: AuthorHouse, 2017, pp. 568-569.

Michael Kraus (1949-), b. Prague, Czech.; political scientist
Bio: Rechcigl, Miloslav, Jr., "Michael Kraus," in: *Encyclopedia of Bohemian and Czech-American Biography*. Bloomington, IN: AuthorHouse, 2016, Vol. 2, pp. 1397.

Wolfgang Herbert Kraus (1905-1977), b. Frankfurt a. M., of Bohemian father; political scientist
Bio: Rechcigl, Miloslav, Jr, "Wolfgang Herbert Kraus (1905-1977), in: *Encyclopedia of Bohemian and Czech-American Biography*. Bloomington, IN: AuthorHouse, 2016, Vol. 2, pp. 1396-1397.

Frank Munk (1901-1999), b. Kutná Hora, Bohemia; political scientist and economist
Bio: Frank Munk, *My Century and My Many Lives. Memoirs*, 1993; Rechcigl, Miloslav, J., "Frank Munk," in: *Beyond the Sea of Beer.* History of Immigration of Bohemians and Czechs to the New World and their Contributions. Bloomington, IN: AuthorHouse, 2017, p. 568; Rechcigl, Miloslav, Jr., "Frank Munk," in: *Encyclopedia of Bohemian and Czech-American Biography.* Bloomington, IN: AuthorHouse, 2016, Vol. 2, p. 1400.

Michael Munk (1934-), b. Prague, Czech.; political scientist
Bio: Rechcigl, Miloslav, Jr., "Michael Munk," in: *Encyclopedia of Bohemian and Czech-American Biography.* Bloomington, IN: AuthorHouse, 2016, Vol. 2, pp. 1400-1401

Richard Elliot Neustadt (1919-2003), b. Philadelphia, PA, of Czech ancestry; political scientist
Bio: Rechcigl, Miloslav, Jr., "Richard Elliot Neustadt," in: *Beyond the Sea of Beer.* History of Immigration of Bohemians and Czechs to the New World and their Contributions. Bloomington, IN: AuthorHouse, 2017, p. 499; "Richard Neustadt," in: Wikipedia. See - https://en.wikipedia.org/wiki/ Richard Neustadt.

Frank J. Popper (1944-), b. of Bohemian ancestry; political scientist
Bio: Rechcigl, Miloslav, Jr., "Frank J. Popper," in: *Encyclopedia of Bohemian and Czech-American Biography.* Bloomington, IN: AuthorHouse, 2016, Vol. 2, p. 1403.

Kurt Steiner (1912-2003), b. Vienna, of Bohemian mother; political scientist
Bio: Rechcigl, Miloslav, Jr., "Kurt Steiner," in: *Beyond the Sea of Beer.* History of Immigration of Bohemians and Czechs to the New World and their Contributions. Bloomington, IN: AuthorHouse, 2017, p. 570.

Michael Wallerstein (1951-2006), b. Topeka, KS, of Bohemian ancestry; political scientist, Northwestern University
Bio: Cohen, Jodi, "Michael Wallerstein 1951-2006), Leading Political Scientist…," *Chicago Tribune*, January 2, 20006; Rechcigl, Miloslav, Jr.,

"Michael Wallerstein," in: *Encyclopedia of Bohemian and Czech-American Biography*. Bloomington, IN: AuthorHouse, 2016, Vol. 2, p. 1409.

6. Psychologists (Social)

Edward Louis Bernays (1891-1995), of Moravian ancestry; 'Father of Public Relations.'
Bio: Bernays, Edward, *Biography of an Idea: Memoirs of Public Relations Counsel*. New York: Simon & Schuster, 1965; Rechcigl, Miloslav, Jr., "Muž, který ovlivnil americké veřejné mínění" (Man who Influenced American Public Opinion), in: *Postavy naší Ameriky*. Praha: Pražská edice, 2000, pp. 277-278; Tye, Larry, *The Father of Spin: Edward L. Bernays and the Birth of Public Relations*. Picador, 2002, 320p.

Curt W. Bondy (1894-1972), b. Hamburg, Ger., of Bohemian ancestry; psychologist, educator
Bio: Rechcigl, Miloslav, Jr., "Curt W. Bondy," in: *Encyclopedia of Bohemian and Czech-American Biography*. Bloomington, IN: AuthorHouse, 2016, Vol. 2, p. 1411.

Erna Furman (née Popper) (1926-2002), b. Vienna, of Bohemian ancestry; psychologist, child psychoanalyst, teacher
Bio: "Erna Furman," in: Wikipedia. See - https://en.wikipedia.org/wiki/Erna_Furman; Rechcigl, Miloslav, Jr., "Erna Furman," in: *Encyclopedia of Bohemian and Czech-American Biography*. Bloomington, IN: AuthorHouse, 2016, Vol. 2, pp. 1413-1414.

Maria Jahoda (1907-2001), b. Vienna, of Bohemian ancestry; psychologist
Bio: Cook, Stuart W., "Marie Jahoda," in: *Women in Psychology: A Bio-Bibliographic Sourcebook*. Edited by Agnes N. O'Connell and Nancy F. Russo. New York: 1990, pp. 207–219; Rechcigl, Miloslav, Jr., "Marie Jahoda," in: *Beyond the Sea of Beer*. History of Immigration of Bohemians and Czechs to the New World and their Contributions. Bloomington, IN: AuthorHouse, 2017, p. 565-566.

Charles J. Ksir (1945-), b. Albuquerque, NM, of Bohemian ancestry; psychologist, University of Wyoming

Bio: Rechcigl, Miloslav, Jr., “Charles J. Ksir,” in: *Encyclopedia of Bohemian and Czech-American Biography*. Bloomington, IN: AuthorHouse, 2016, Vol. 2, p. 1417.

Rudolf George Mortimer (orig. Mautner) (1931-), b. Trutnov, Bohemia; industrial psychologist, specialist in human factors in vehicle safety
Bio: Rechcigl, Miloslav, Jr., “Rudolf George Mortimer,” in: *Encyclopedia of Bohemian and Czech-American Biography*. Bloomington, IN: AuthorHouse, 2016, Vol. 2, p. 1421.

William R. Perl (1906-1998), b. Prague, Bohemia; lawyer and psychologist
Bio: “William R. Perl,” in: Wikipedia. See - https://en.wikipedia.org/wiki/William R. Perl; Rechcigl, Miloslav, Jr., “William R. Perl,” in: *Encyclopedia of Bohemian and Czech-American Biography*. Bloomington, IN: AuthorHouse, 2016, Vol. 2, p. 1422.

Marcel Isaac Perlman (1934-), b. Prague, Czech.; psychologist, Yeshiva University
Bio: “Celebrating the Career of a University Legend,” *Yeshiva University News*, October 16, 2017; Rechcigl, Miloslav, Jr., “Marcel Isaac Perlman,” in: *Encyclopedia of Bohemian and Czech-American Biography*. Bloomington, IN: AuthorHouse, 2016, Vol. 2, pp. 1422-1423.

Emma Nuschi Plank (née Spira) (1905-1990), b. Vienna, of Czech ancestry; developmental and educational psychologist, Case Wstrern Reserve Univ. School of Medicine
Bio: “Emma Nuschi Plank,” in: Jewish Women’s Archive. See - https://jwa.org/people/plank-emma; Rechcigl, Miloslav, Jr., “Emma Nuschi Plank,” in: *Encyclopedia of Bohemian and Czech-American Biography*. Bloomington, IN: AuthorHouse, 2016, Vol. 2, p. 1423.

Edgar Schein (1928-), b. Zurich, Switzerland, of Slovak ancestry; social psychologist, professor, MIT
Bio: “Edgar Schein,” in: Wikipedia. See - https://en.wikipedia.org/wiki/Edgar_Schein

Max Wertheimer (1880-1943), b. Prague, Bohemia; psychologist, founder of Gestalt psychology
Bio: Watson, Robert, "Wertheimer: Gestalt Psychology," in: *The Great Psychologists.* From Aristotle to Freud. Philadelphia: Lippincott, 1953, pp. 403-422; Rechcigl, Miloslav, Jr., "Zakladatel pysychologie gestaltismu" (Founder of Gestalt Psychology), in: *Postavy naší Ameriky.* Praha: Pražská edice, 2000, pp. 274-276; King, D. and Michael Wertheimer, *Max Wertheimer and Gestalt Theory.* Transaction Publishers, 2007.

Michael Matthew Wertheimer (1927-), b. Berlin, Ger., of Bohemian father; psychologist, educator
Bio: Rechcigl, Miloslav, Jr., "Michael Matthew Wertheimer," in: *Encyclopedia of Bohemian and Czech-American Biography.* Bloomington, IN: AuthorHouse, 2016, Vol. 2, p. 1428.

Marha Wolfenstein (1911-1976), b. Cleveland, OH, of Moravian ancestry; child psychologist,
Bio: "Prof. Martha Wolfenstein Is Dead; A Specialist in Child Psychology," *The New York Times.* December 1, 1976; Rechcigl, Miloslav, Jr., "Martha Wolfenstein," in:
Encyclopedia of Bohemian and Czech-American Biography. Bloomington, IN: AuthorHouse, 2016, Vol. 2, pp. 1428-1429; Spitz, Ellen Handler, "Martha Wolfenstein: Toward the Severance of Memory from Hope," *Psychoanalytic Review,* 85 (1998), pp. 105-115; Nellie Thompson, "American Women Psychoanalysts, 1911-1941," *Annual of Psychoanalysis,* 29 (2001), pp. 161-177; Martha Wolfenstein, *Children's Humor: A Psychological Analysis. Glencoe,* IL: Free Press, 1954.

7. Sociologists

Joseph Hans Bunzel (1907-1975), b. Graz, Austria, of Bohemian father; sociologist
Bio: Rechcigl, Miloslav, Jr., "Joseph Hans Bunzel," in: *Encyclopedia of Bohemian and Czech-American Biography.* Bloomington, IN: AuthorHouse, 2016, Vol. 2, 1434.

Julius Drachsler (1889-1927), b. Bella, Slovakia; sociologist, social service expert, author
Bio: "Prof. Drachsler, Noted Educator and Jewish Social Service Expert, Dies," Jewish Telegraphic Agency, July 25, 1927. See - https://www.jta.org/1927/07/25/archive/prof-drachsler-noted-educator-and-jewish-social-service-expert-dies

Emerich K. Francis (1906-1994), b. Jablonec, Bohemia; Canadian sociologist
Bio: Rechcigl, Miloslav, Jr., "Emerich K. Francis," in: *Encyclopedia of Bohemian and Czech-American Biography*. Bloomington, IN: AuthorHouse, 2016, Vol. 2, pp. 1435-1436; "Emerich K. Francis," in: Wikipedia. See - https://de.wikipedia.org/wiki/Emerich_K._Francis

Paul Lazersfeld (1901-1976), b. of Moravian ancestry; pioneering sociologist
Bio: Jerábek, Hynek, "Paul Lazarsfeld - The Founder of Modern Empirical Sociology: A Research Biography." *International Journal of Public Opinion Research* 13 (2001), pp. 229-244.

Egon Mayer (1944-2004), b. Caux, Switzerland, of Slovak father; sociologist, professor at Brooklyn College
Bio: "Egon Mayer," in: Wikipedia. See - https://en.wikipedia.org/wiki/Egon_Mayer_(sociologist)

Alfred Schűtz (1899-1959), of_Bohemian ancestry; noted philosopher and sociologist
Bio: Wagner, H. R., Alfred Schutz: An Intellectual Biography. Chicago and London: The University of Chicago Press, 1983; Barber, M., *The Participating Citizen: A Biography of Alfred Schutz*. New York: State University of New York Press, 2004.

Edward Alfred Steiner (1866-1956), b. Senica, Slovakia; Congregational Church minister, educator, professor of applied Christianity, writer on immigration
Bio: Steiner, Edward Alfred, *From Alien to Citizen: The story of my Life in America*. Boston: Pilgrim Press, 1914.

Werner Stark (1909-1985), b. Mariánské Lázně, Bohemia; sociologist, economist, social science theorist and historian
Bio: "Werner Stark," in: Wikipedia. See - https://en.wikipedia.org/wiki/Werner Stark; Rechcigl, Miloslav, Jr., "Werner Stark," in: *Encyclopedia of Bohemian and Czech-American Biography*. Bloomington, IN: AuthorHouse, 2016, Vol. 2, p. 1441.

Ilse Williams (née Zeisl (1909-1999), b. Nový Harcov, Bohemia; social scientist, specialist on opinion research
Bio: "Ilse Zesisel (Williams) (1909-1999), Sociakl scientist, market and opinion researcher," in: *Transatlantic Perspectives*, May 20, 2011

D. Biological Sciences

1. Agriculturists

Paul Griminger (1920-2009), b. of Moravian mother; poultry nutritionist
Bio: "Paul Griminger," *Home News Tribune*, March 3, 2009; "Paul Griminger," in: Prabook. See - https://prabook.com/web/paul.griminger/86722

2. Anatomists

Rudof Altschul (1901-1963), b. Praague, Bohemia; Canadian "Rudolf Altschul,", in: Wikipedia. See - anatomist
Bio: "Rudolf Altschul," in: Wikipedia. See - https://de.wikipedia.org/wiki/Rudolf Altschul

Louis Barkhouse Flexner (1902-1996), b. Louisville, KY, of Bohemian ancestry; anatomist, professor
Bio: Rechcigl, Miloslav, Jr., "Louis Barkhouse Flexner," in: *Encyclopedia of Bohemian and Czech-American Biography*. Bloomington, IN: AuthorHouse, 2016, Vol. 2, p. 1447.

3. Biochemists

Oskar Baudisch (1881-1950), b. Vratislavice nad Nisou, Bohemia; biochemist, radiographer
Bio: "Oskar Baudisch," in: Wikipedia. See - https://en.wikipedia.org/wiki/Oskar_Baudisch

Gerty R. Cori (1896-1957), b. Prague, Bohemia; biochemist, recipient of Nobel Prize
Bio: *Nobel Lectures, Physiology or Medicine 1942-1962*, Elsevier Publishing Company, Amsterdam, 1964; Bio: Houssay, B. A., "Carl F. and Gerty R. Cori" *Biochimica et Biophysica Acta,* 20 (1956), pp. 11-16; Rechcigl, Miloslav, Jr. "Gerty Theresa Radnitz Cori," in: *Beyond the Sea of* Beer. History of Immigration of Bohemians and Czechs to the New World and their Contributions. Bloomington, IN: AuthorHouse, 2017, p. 481 and 719.

John Hans Fessler (1928-), b. Vienna, of Moravian mother; molecular biologist
Bio: "Fessler, John Hans," in: *International Biographical Dictionary of Central European Emigrés 1933-1945.*Műnchen: K. G. Saur, 1983, Vol. 2, p. 293.

George Hauser (1922-2012), b. Vienna, whose father was from Miroslav, Moravia, biochemist, neurochemist
Bio: "Hauser, George," in: *International Biographical Dictionary of Central European Emigrés 1933-1945*. Műnchen: K. G. Saur, 1983, Vol. 2, p. 467.

Felix Haurowitz (1896—1987), b. Prague, Bohemia; biochemist
Bio: Putnam, Frank W., *Felix Haurowitz, 1896-1987.*A Biographical Memoir. Washington, DC: National Academy of Sciences, 1994.

Charles Heidelberger (1920-1983), b. NYC, of Bohemian ancestry; organic chemist, biochemist
Bio: "Charles Heidelberger,", in: *Encyclopedia of Bohemian and Czech-American Biography*. Bloomington, IN: AuthorHouse, 2016, Vol. 2, p. 1456.

Ralph Heimer (1921-2001), b. Vienna, of Moravian father; whose father was native of Moravské Budějovice, Moravia

Bio: "Heimer, Ralph," in: *International Biographical Dictionary of Central European Emigrés 1933-1945*. Műnchen: K. G. Saur, 1983, Vol. 2, p. 478.

Arnošt Kleinzeller (1914-1997), b. Moravská Ostrava, Moravia; biochemist, physiologist, professor, Philadelphia
Bio: "Arnost Kleinzeller, a Physiologist, 82, Dies," *The New York Times*, February 16, 1997; Zadunaisky, J.A., "Arnost Kleinzeller: A Man of all Seasons," *J. Exp. Zoology*, 279 (1997), pp. 393-397.

Gertrude Erika Perlmann (1912-1974), b. Liberec, Bohemia; biochemist
See: "Gertrude E. Perlmann," *Nature*, 251, Issue 5473 (1974), p. 363; *International Biographical Dictionary of Central European Emigrés 1933-1945*. Műnchen: K. G. Saur, 1983, Vol. 2, p. 897.

Manfred Eliezer Reichmann (1925-2012), b. Trenčín, Czech., biochemist, microbiologist
Bio: Herbert A. Strauss and Werner Roder, eds., *International Biographical Dictionary of Central European Emigrés 1933-1945*. München-New York – London – Paris: K. G. Saur, 1983, Part 12: L-Z, p. 952.

Frieda Reischsman (1957-), b. US, of Moravian ancestry; molecular and cellular biologist
Bio: Rechcigl, Miloslav, Jr., "Frieda Reichsman," in: *Encyclopedia of Bohemian and Czech-American Biography*. Bloomington, IN: AuthorHouse, 2016, Vol. 2, pp. 1520-1521; "Frieda Reischman," in: The Concord Consortium. See - https://concord.org/about/staff/frieda-reichsman/

DeWitt Stetten (1909-1990), b. New York, NY, of Bohemian ancestry; biochemist
Bio: Rechcigl, Miloslav, Jr., "DeWitt Stetten," in: *Encyclopedia of Bohemian and Czech-American Biography*. Bloomington, IN: AuthorHouse, 2016, Vol. 2, p. 1468-1469.

Rudolf Vrba (orig. Walter Rosenberg) (1924-2006), b. Topoľčany, Slovakia; Canadian biochemist, pharmacologist
Bio: "Rudolf Vrba," in: Wikipedia. See - https://en.wikipedia.org/wiki/Rudolf_Vrba

Heinrich Benedict Waelsch (1904-1986), b. Brno, Moravia, biochemist
Bio: Rechcigl, Miloslav, Jr., "Heinrich Benedict Waelsch," in: *Encyclopedia of Bohemian and Czech-American Biography*. Bloomington, IN: AuthorHouse, 2016, Vol. 2, p. 1471; Weil-Malherbe, H., "Heinrich Waelsch," *Experimental Brain Res.*, 2, No.1 (1966); Sperry, Warren M., "Heinrich H. Waelsch," *Journal of Neurochemistry*, 13, No. 11 (1966), pp. 1261–1263; *International Biographical Dictionary of Central European Emigrés 1933-1945*. Műnchen: K. G. Saur, 1983, Vol. 2, pp. 1198-1199.

Jan Wiener (1920-2010), b. Hamburg, of Bohemian ancestry; historian, RAF pilot, political prisoner
Bio: "Obituary: Jan Wiener, Czech Jew who served with RAF in Scotland," *The Scotsman,* 19:15.

4. Biologists

Gert Kreibich (1939-), b. Chomutov, Bohemia; cell biologist, professor, New York University
Bio: Rechcigl, Miloslav, Jr., "Gert Kreibich," in: *Encyclopedia of Bohemian and Czech-America Biography*. Bloomington, IN: AuthorHouse, 2016, Vol. 2, p. 1481.

Rosi Kuerti (née Jahoda) (1905-2004), b. Vienna, of Moravian ancestry; biologist, peace activist, Cleveland
Bio: Rechcigl, Miloslav, Jr., "Rosi Kuerti," in *Encyclopedia of Bohemian and Czech-America Biography*. Bloomington, IN: AuthorHouse, 2016, Vol. 2, p. 1481.

Lisa Amelia Steiner (1933-), b. Vienna, of Czech ancestry; biologist, immunologist
Bio: "Lisa Steiner," in: Wikipedia. See - https://en.wikipedia.org/wiki/Lisa Steiner; Rechcigl, Miloslav, Jr., "Lisa Amelia Steiner," in: *Encyclopedia of Bohemian and Czech-America Biography*. Bloomington, IN: AuthorHouse, 2016, Vol. 2, p. 1506

William B. Terzaghi (ca 1957-, b. New Zealand, of Bohemian ancestry; biologist, professor, Utah

Bio: Will Terzaghi's Home Page. See - http://staffweb.wilkes.edu/william.terzaghi/

5. Biophysicists

Hans Hoch (1909-2004), b. Vienna, of Bohemian parents; biophysicist, Martinsburg, VA
Bio: Rechcigl, Miloslav, Jr., "Hans Hoch," in: *Encyclopedia of Bohemian and Czech-America Biography*. Bloomington, IN: AuthorHouse, 2016, Vol. 2, p. 1473.

Michael Pollak (1926-), b. Ostrava, Czech.; biophysicist, professor, Riverside, CA
Bio: Rechcigl, Miloslav, Jr., "Michael Pollak," in: *Encyclopedia of Bohemian and Czech-America Biography*. Bloomington, IN: AuthorHouse, 2016, Vol. 2, pp. 1472-1473.

6. Botanists

Michael Robert Blatt (1953-), b. Illinois, of Moravian ancestry; botanist
Bio: Rechcigl, Miloslav, Jr., "Michael Robert Blatt," in: *Encyclopedia of Bohemian and Czech-America Biography*. Bloomington, IN: AuthorHouse, 2016, Vol. 2, p. 1474.

Hugo Iltis (1882-1950), b. Brno, Moravia; botanist
Bio: "Hugo Iltis," in: Wikipedia. See - https://en.wikipedia.org/wiki/Hugo Iltis; Dunn, L.C., "Hugo Iltis: 1882-1952), *Science*, 117 (January 2, 1953), pp. 3-4.

Hugh Helmut Iltis (1925-), b. Brno, Czech.; botanist
Bio: "Hugh Iltis," in: Wikipedia: http://en.wikipedia.org/wiki/Hugh Iltis; *International Biographical Dictionary of Central European Emigrés 1933-1945.* Műnchen: K. G. Saur, 1983, Vol. 2, p. 550.

7. Epidemiologists

Joseph Goldberger (1874-1929), b. Giraltovce, Slovakia; physician, epidemiologist
Bio: Parsons, Robert P., *Trail to Light: A Biography of Joseph Goldberger.* New York: The Bobbs-Merrill Corp., 1943; "Joseph Goldberger," in: Wikipedia. See - https://en.wikipedia.org/wiki/Joseph_Goldberger

8. Geneticists

Martin Frank Gellert (1929-), b. Prague, Czech.; molecular geneticist
Bio: Rechcigl, Miloslav, Jr., "Martin Frank Gellert," in: *Encyclopedia of Bohemian and Czech-America Biography.* Bloomington, IN: AuthorHouse, 2016, Vol. 2, p. 1495

Hans Kalmus (1906-1988), b. Prague, Czech.; geneticist, biologist
Bio: *Odyssey of a Scientist: An Autobiography.* By Hans Kalmus and David Benedictus.London: Weidenfeld and Nicolson, va 1991.

Renata Laxova (1931-), b. Brno, Czech.; pediatric geneticist
Bio: "Renata Lexova," in: Wikipedia. See - https://en.wikipedia.org/wiki/Renata Laxova; Ravenna, Daniele, Felix Humm, *Fred Iltis. Biologist, Photographer and Friend*, Milano, DR&C Editore, 2009.

Helen Salz (1955-), b. CA, opf Czech ancestry; geneticist, professor, Case Western Reserve Univ, Cleveland
Bio: Rechcigl, Miloslav, Jr., "Helen Salz," in: *Encyclopedia of Bohemian and Czech-American Biography.* Bloomington, IN: AuthorHouse, 2016, Vol. 2, p. 1498.

9. Immunologists

Karl Frank Austen (orig. Arnstein) (1928-), b. Akron, OH, of Bohemian ancestry; immunologist
Bio: Rechcigl, Miloslav, Jr., "Karl Frank Austen," in: *Encyclopedia of Bohemian and Czech-American Biography.* Bloomington, IN: AuthorHouse, 2016, Vol. 3, p. 1964.

Karl Landsteiner (1868-1943), b. Vienna, of Bohemian ancestry; immunologist
Bio: Michael Heidelberger, *Karl Landsteiner: June 14, 1868-June 26, 1943.* Biographical Memoir. National Academy of Sciences. Columbia University Press, 1969; Speiser, Paul and Ferdinand G. Smekal, *Karl Landsteiner: The Discoverer of the Blood-groups and a Pioneer in the Field of Immunology.* Biography of a Nobel Prize winner of the Vienna Medical School. Wien, Hollinek, 1975. 198p.

David Walter Weiss (1927-), b. Vienna, of Czech ancestry; immunologist
Bio: Rechcigl, Miloslav, Jr., "David Walter Weiss," in: *Encyclopedia of Bohemian and Czech-American Biography.* Bloomington, IN: AuthorHouse, 2016, Vol. 2, p. 1518; "David Walter Weiss," in: Prabook. See - https://prabook.com/web/david_walter.weiss/552257

10. Microbiologists

Maria Kirber (née Wiener) (1917-2010), b. Prague, Bohemia; bacteriologist, virologist
Bio: Her obituary: http://chestnuthilllocal.com/issues/2010.03.18/obituaries.html; "Kirber, Maria, in: *International Biographical Dictionary of Central European Emigrés 1933-1945.* Műnchen: K. G. Saur, 1983, Vol. 2, p. 620.

Frederick Wiener Kraus (1910-2002), b. Prague, Bohemia; physician, bacteriologist, professor, University of Alabama
Bio: Rechcigl, Miloslav, Jr., "Frederick Wiener Kraus," in: *Encyclopedia of Bohemian and Czech-American Biography.* Bloomington, IN: AuthorHouse, 2016, Vol. 2, p. 1512.

Ernst Loewenstein (1878-1950), b. Karlovy Vary, Bohemia; physician, bacteriologist, San Francisco
Bio: "Loewenstein, Ernst," in: *Universal Jewish Encyclopedia.* New York, 1942., Vol. 7, p. 164.

Vladimír Munk (1925-), b. Pardubice, Czech.; microbiologist, professor, SUNY, Platsburgh

Bio: "Vladimir Munk," in: Prabook. See - https://prabook.com/web/vladimir.munk/645772

Ernst August Pribrem (1879-2015), b. Prague, Bohemia; physician, bacteriologist, Chicago
Bio: Rechcigl, Miloslav, Jr., "Ernest Auguist Pribram," in: *Encyclopedia of Bohemian and Czech-American Biography*. Bloomington, IN: AuthorHouse, 2016, Vol. 2, p. 1515-1516;
"Ernst August Pribram," in: Wikipedia. See - https://de.wikipedia.org/wiki/Ernst August Pribram

Fritz Schiff (1899-1940), b. Berlon, Ger., of Bohemian ancestry; physician, bacteriologist
Bio: "Fritz Schiff," in: Wikipedia. See - https://de.wikipedia.org/wiki/Fritz Schiff

Frederick B. Traub (1911-1974), b. Plzen, Bohemia; physician, bacteriologist, NYC
Bio: Rechcigl, Miloslav, Jr., "Frederick Bedřich Traub," in: *Encyclopedia of Bohemian and Czech-American Biography*. Bloomington, IN: AuthorHouse, 2016, Vol. 2, p. 1517.

11. Pathologists

Kurt Aternman (1913-2002), b. Bielsko on Moravian-Silesian border; pathologist
Bio: Herbert A. Strauss and Werner Roder, eds., *International Biographical Dictionary of Central European Emigrés 1933-1945*. München-New York – London – Paris: K. G. Saur, 1983, Part 12: L-Z, p. 38; Kurt Aterman Obituary: http://www.spponline.org/kurt-aterman.asp

William Hans Bauer (1886-1956), b. Prague, Bohemia; pathologist, St. Louis, MO
Bio: "Bauer, Wilhelm," in: *Handbuch österreichischer Autorinnen und Autoren jüdischer Herkunft*. Munchen: K. G. Saur, 2002, p.78.

George Brecher (1913-2004), b. Olomouc, Moravia; pathologist

Bio: "Brecher, George," in: *International Biographical Dictionary of Central European Emigrés 1933-1945*. Műnchen: K. G. Saur, 1983, Vol. 2, p. 148; Levin, Jack, "George Brecher, MD, 1913–2004," *Experimental Hematology*, 32, No. 11 (November 2004), pp. 1126–1127.

Simon Flexner (1865-1946), b. Louisville, KY, of Bohemian ancestry; pathologist, educator, director of the Rockefeller Institute for Medical Research

Bio: Flexner, James Thomas, *An American Saga. The Story of Helen Thomas and Simon Flexner.* Boston - Toronto: Little, Brown and Co., 1983. 494p.; Rechcigl, Miloslav, Jr., "Budovatel Rockefellerovy university" (Builder of Rockefeller University), in: *Postavy naší Ameriky*. Praha: Pražská edice, 2000, pp. 283-285.

Otakar Jaroslav Pollak (1906-2000), b. Brno, Moravia; pathologist

Bio: Herbert A. Strauss and Werner Roder, eds., *International Biographical Dictionary of Central European Emigrés 1933-1945*. München- New York – London – Paris: K. G. Saur, 1983, Part 12: L-Z, pp. 916-17.

Hans Popper (1903-1988), b. Vienna, of Bohemian ancestry; pathologist, Dean

Bio: Gerber, Michael A. and Swan N. Thung, "Hans Popper, M.D., Ph.D.," *Am. Pathology* 133, No. 1 (October 1986), pp. 13-14; Lueck, Thomas J., "Dr. Hans Popper, an Authority on Liver Diseases, Is Dead at 84," *The New York Times*, May 08, 1988; Schmid, Rudi, "Hans Popper, Nov. 4, 1903-May 6, 1988)," *Biographical Memoirs of the National Academy of Sciences,* 65 (1994), pp. 290-309.

Philipp Raphael Rezek (1894-1953), b. Vienna, of Bohemian ancestry; pathologist

Bio: "Rezek, Philipp Raphael," in: *International Biographical Dictionary of Central European Emigrés 1933-1945.*Műnchen: K. G. Saur, 1983, Vol. 2, pp. 964-965; Levinson, S.A., "Philipp Rezek, M.D., 1894-1963," *American Journal of Clinical Pathology*, 41, No. 2 (February 1964), pp. 209-210; Rechcigl, Miloslav, Jr., "Philipp Rafael Rezek," in: *Encyclopedia of Bohemian and Czech-American Biography*. Bloomington, IN: AuthorHouse, 2016, Vol. 2. P. 1544.

Walter Schiller (1887-1960), b. Vienna, of Bohemian ancestry; pathologist
Bio: "Walter Schiller." In: Wikipedia. See - https://en.wikipedia.org/wiki/Walter Schiller; "Walter Schiller," in: *Gedenkbuch für die Opfer des Nationlsozialismus and der Universität Wien 1938.*

Max Wachstein (1905-1965), b. Vienna, of Czech mother; histologist, pathologist
Bio: Novikoff, A. B., "In Memoriam: Max Wachstein," *Journal of Histochemistry and Cytochemistry,* 13, No. 8 (1965), p. 699.

Nathan Weidenthal (1855-1931), b. Cleveland, OH, of Bohemian ancestry; pathologist
Bio: "Weidenthal, Nathan," in: *Who's Who in American Jewry.* New York, 1926, Vol. 1, p. 637.

Milton C. Winternitz (1885-1959), b. Baltimore, MD, of Bohemian ancestry, pathologist, Dean
Bio: Spiro, Howard M. and Priscilla Waters Norton, "Dean Milton C. Winternitz at Yale," *Perspectives in Biology and Medicine,* 46, No. 3 (Summer 2003), pp. 403-412.

Frederick Gerald Zak (1915-2005), b. Vienna, of Moravian father; pathologist
Bio: "Death: Frederick G. Zak, M.D." *The New York Times,* February 13, 2005

12. Pharmacologists

Frank Milan Berger (1913-2008), b. Pilsen, Bohemia; pharmacologist
Bio: "Frank Berger, 94, Miltown Creator," *The New York Times,* May 21, 2008

Charles William Flexner (ca 1956-), b. US, of Bohemian ancestry; clinical pharmacologist, infectious disease specialist
Bio: Rechcigl, Miloslav, Jr., "Charles William Flexner," in: *Encyclopedia of Bohemian and Czech-American Biography.* Bloomington, IN: AuthorHouse, 2016, Vol. 2, p. 1549.

Karl Heinz Ginzel (1921-2013), b. Liberec, Czech.; pharmacologist, toxicologist
Bio: "Dr. Karl Heinz Ginzel Obituary," *Las Cruces Sun-News*, July 3, 2013 team

Hans (Sigmund) Heller (1905-1944), b. Brno, Moravia; pharmacologist
Bio: "Hans (Sigmund Heller), in: *Encyclopedia of Bohemian and Czech-American Biography*. Bloomington, IN: AuthorHouse, 2016, Vol. 2, p. 1551.

Henry George Mautner (1925-1995), b. Prague, Czech; pharmacologist, biochemist, professor, Harvard and then Tufts Univ.
Bio: "Henry Mautner, 70, Expert on Selenium," *The New York Times*, April 15, 1995; "Henry G. Mautner, 70, Research chemist, professor," *The Boston Globe*, April 19, 1995.

Ernst Peter Pick (1872-1960), b. Jaroměř, Bohemia; pharmacologist
Bio: Antopol, W., "In Memoriam Ernst Peter Pick 1872-1960," *J. Mt. Sinai Hosp.* N Y., 27 (1960), pp. 485-87.

Wolfgang Adolf Ritschel (1933-), b. Trutnov, Bohemia; pharmacologist, professor, Univ. of Cincinnati, painter
Bio: "Wolfgang Ritschel: Learned in Science, Explored in Art," in: UNC Libraries, Chapel Hill. See - https://hsl.lib.unc.edu/events/ritschel

13. Physical Anthropologists

William Sprott Pollitzer (1923-2002), b. Charleston, SC, of Bohemian ancestry; physical anthropologist, anatomist, professor
Bio: "William Sprott Pollitzer," *The Greenville News*. March 17, 2002.

14. Physiologists

Walter Ehrlich (1915-2016), b. Karlovy Vary, Bohemia; physician, physiologist
Bio: "Dr. Walter Ehrlich, retired Hopkins professor, dies," *The Baltimore Sun,* February 18, 2018; American Physiological Society, "Walter

Ehrlich,1915-2016." See - http://www.the-aps.org/mm/Membership/Living-History/Ehrlich

Frank Gollan (1910-1988), b. Brno, Moravia; physiologist
Bio: "Dr. Frank Gollan, 78; Isolated the Polio Virus," *The New York Times*, October
10, 1988; Rechcigl, Miloslav, Jr., "Frank Gollan," in: *Encyclopedia of Bohemian and Czech-America Biography*. Bloomington, IN: AuthorHouse, 2016, Vol. 2, p. 1562; "Polio Virus Pioneer Dr. Frank Gollan, Wife, Suicide Victims," Los Angeles Times, October 11, 1988.

Petr Hahn 1923-2007), b. Berlin of Czech parents; physiologist, nutritionist biochemist, professor, British Columbia, Canada
Bio: Rechcigl, Miloslav, Jr., "Petr Hahn," in: *Encyclopedia of Bohemian and Czech-America Biography*. Bloomington, IN: AuthorHouse, 2016, Vol. 2, p. 1562-1563.

E. Morton Jellinek (1890-1963), b. New York, NY, of Moravian ancestry; physiologist, alcoholism researcher, biostatistician
Bio: "E Morton Jellinek," in: Wikipedia. See - https://en.wikipedia.org/wiki/E. Morton Jellinek;
Archibald, H.D., "Dr. Elwin [sic] Morton Jellinek: (1891–1964)," *American Journal of Psychiatry,* Vol.120, (June 1964), pp. 1217–1218

Robert L. Ney (1933-1986), b. Brno, Czech.; internist, physiologist, professor, Baltimore
Bio: Rechcigl, Miloslav, Jr., "Robert Lee Nay," in: *Encyclopedia of Bohemian and Czech-America Biography*. Bloomington, IN: AuthorHouse, 2016, Vol. 2, p. 1569.

Aaron M. Rappaport (1904-1992), b. Bukovina; physiologist, professor, Toronto
Bio: Rechcigl, Miloslav, Jr., "Aaron M. Rappaport," in: *Encyclopedia of Bohemian and Czech-America Biography*. Bloomington, IN: AuthorHouse, 2016, Vol. 2, p. 1572.

15. Psychologists (Clinical)

Alfred Adler (1870-1937), b. Vienna, of Bohemian ancestry; physician, psychotherapist, founder of the school of individual psychology
Bio: *The Individual Psychology of Alfred Adler.* A Systematic Presentation in Selections from his Writings. Edited and annotated by Heinz L. Ansbacher and Rowena R. Ansbacher. New York: Harper & Row, 1965; Hoffman, Edward, *The Drive for Self: Alfred Adler and the Founding of Individual Psychology.* Perseus Books, 1997. 416p.

Martin S. Bergmann (1913-2014), b. Prague, Bohemia;_clinical psychologist
Bio: Rechcigl, Miloslav, Jr., "Martin S. Bergmann," in: *Encyclopedia of Bohemian and Czech-American Biography.* Bloomington, IN: AuthorHouse, 2016, Vol. 3, p. 2097; "Martin S. Bergmann," in: Wikipedia. See - https://en.wikipedia.org/wiki/Martin S. Bergmann

Bruno Bettelheim (1903-1990), b. Vienna, of Slovak ancestry; clinical psychologist, psychoanalyst
Bio: "Bruno Bettelheim," in: Wikipedia. See - https://en.wikipedia.org/wiki/Bruno Bettelheim; Pollak, Richard, *The Creation of Doctor B: A Biography of Bruno Bettelheim.* New York: Simon & Schuster, 1997.

Eva Fishell Blatt (1933-), b. Liberec, Czech.; clinical psychologist, Mount Sinai Hospital, Chicago
Bio: Rechcigl, Miloslav, Jr., "Eva Fishell Blatt," in: *Encyclopedia of Bohemian and Czech-American Biography.* Bloomington, IN: AuthorHouse, 2016, Vol. 3, p. 2097.

Fred Brown (1905-2005), b. of Czech ancestry; clinical psychologist, Col. US Army, later with Mount Sinai School of Medicine
Bio: "Death: Brown, Fred, Ph.D.," *The New York Times,* July 22, 2005; Rechcigl, Miloslav, Jr., "Fred Brown," in: *Encyclopedia of Bohemian and Czech-American Biography.* Bloomington, IN: AuthorHouse, 2016, Vol. 3, p. 2099.

Hana Bruml (1922-2000), b. Prague, Czech; clinical psychologist
Bio: Rechcigl, Miloslav, Jr., "Hana Bruml," in: *Encyclopedia of Bohemian and Czech-American Biography*. Bloomington, IN: AuthorHouse, 2016, Vol. 3, pp. 1411-1412.

František Engelsmann (1922-), b. Nové Mesto nad Váhom, of Moravian ancestry; clinical psychologist, professor, McGill University
Bio: Rechcigl, Miloslav, Jr., "František Engelsmann," in: *Encyclopedia of Bohemian and Czech-American Biography*. Bloomington, IN: AuthorHouse, 2016, Vol. 3, p. 2099.

Ernst Walter Kris (1900-1957), b. Vienna, of Bohemian ancestry;
Bio: Rechcigl, Miloslav, Jr., "Ernst Walter Kris," in: *Encyclopedia of Bohemian and Czech-American Biography*. Bloomington, IN: AuthorHouse, 2016, Vol. 3, p. 2105; "Ernst Kris," in: Wikipedia. See - https://de.wikipedia.org/wiki/Ernst Kris

Sophie Lazarsfeld (née Munk) (1881-1976), b. Opava, Moravia; psychotherapist, student of Alfred Adler
Bio: Rechcigl, Miloslav, Jr., "Sophie Lazarsfeld," in: *Encyclopedia of Bohemian and Czech-American Biography*. Bloomington, IN: AuthorHouse, 2016, Vol. 3, p. 2106-2017;
"Sophie Lazarsfeld," in: Wikipedia. See - https://en.wikipedia.org/wiki/Sophie Lazarsfeld

Eva Fischell Lichtenberg (1933-), b. Liberec, Czech; clinical psychologist, Northwestern University School of Medicine
Bio: Rechcigl, Miloslav, Jr., "Eva Fischell Lichtenberg," in: *Encyclopedia of Bohemian and Czech-American Biography*. Bloomington, IN: AuthorHouse, 2016, Vol. 3, p. 2107.

Erving Polster (1922-), b. Czech.; clinical psychologist, Gestalt therapist and teacher
Bio: Rechcigl, Miloslav, Jr., "Erving Polster," in: *Encyclopedia of Bohemian and Czech-American Biography*. Bloomington, IN: AuthorHouse, 2016, Vol. 3, pp. 2110-2111;

Stephen Porges (1945-), b. Chicago, of Bohemian ancestry; psychologist, neuroscientist
Bio: "Stephen Porges," in: Wikipedia. See - https://en.wikipedia.org/wiki/Stephen Porges; Rechcigl, Miloslav, Jr., "Stephen Porges," in: *Encyclopedia of Bohemian and Czech-American Biography*. Bloomington, IN: AuthorHouse, 2016, Vol. 3, p. 2038.

Herbert Emanuel Rie (1931-1982), b. Prague, Czech.; clinical psychologist, professor, Western Reserve University
Bio: Rechcigl, Miloslav, Jr., "Herbert Emanuel Rie," in: *Encyclopedia of Bohemian and Czech-American Biography*. Bloomington, IN: AuthorHouse, 2016, Vol. 3, p. 2111.

Thomas Roth (1942-), b. Czech.; clinical professor, director of the Sleep Disorders and Research Center, and professor, Wayne State University School of Medicine, Detroit, MI
Bio: Rechcigl, Miloslav, Jr. "Thomas Roth," in: *Encyclopedia of Bohemian and Czech-American Biography*. Bloomington, IN: AuthorHouse, 2016, Vol. 3, p. 2112.

Eva Marie Rosenfeld (1892-1977), b. New York, NY, of Moravian father; psychoanalyst and teacher
Bio: Rechcigl, Miloslav, Jr., "Eva Marie Rosenfeld," in: *Encyclopedia of Bohemian and Czech-American Biography*. Bloomington, IN: AuthorHouse, 2016, Vol. 3, p. 2112.

Melitta Schmideberg (née Klein) (1904-1983), b. Ružomberok, Slovakia; psychiatrist, psychoanalyst and author
Bio: Rechcigl, Miloslav, Jr., "Melitta (Klein) Schmideberg," in: *Encyclopedia of Bohemian and Czech-American Biography*. Bloomington, IN: AuthorHouse, 2016, Vol. 3, p. 2114-2115.

Doris Schwarz-Lisenbee (1946-), b. US, of Moravian ancestry; clinical psychologist
Bio: Rechcigl, Miloslav, Jr., "Doris Schwarz," in: *Encyclopedia of Bohemian and Czech-American Biography*. Bloomington, IN: AuthorHouse, 2016, Vol. 3, p. 2115.

Eva Marie Spitz-Blum (1919-2009), b. Budapest, of Bohemian ancestry; clinical psychologist
Bio: Rechcigl, Miloslav, Jr., in: *Encyclopedia of Bohemian and Czech-American Biography*. Bloomington, IN: AuthorHouse, 2016, Vol. 3, p. 2116.

Emanuel Windholz (1903-1986), b. Hronec, Slovakia; psychologist
Bio: Rechcigl, Miloslav, Jr., "Emanuel Windholz," in: *Beyond the Sea of Beer.* History of Immigration of Bohemians and Czechs to the New World and their Contributions. Bloomington, IN: AuthorHouse, 2017, pp. 567-568.

16. Zoologists

Wilfred Gregor Iltis (1923-2008), b. Brno, Czech.; entomologist
Bio: "Fred Iltis," in: Wikipedia. See - https://en.wikipedia.org/wiki/Fred_Iltis

Laurence Monroe Klauber (1883-1968), b. San Diego, CA; herpetologist, foremost authority on rattlesnakes, also businessman and inventor
Bio: Shaw, Charles E., "Laurence Monroe Klauaber, 1883-1968," *Copeia,* Vol. 1969, No. 2 (Jun. 3, 1969), pp. 417-419; "Laurence Monroe Klauber," in: Wikipedia. See - https://en.wikipedia.org/wiki/Laurence_Monroe_Klauber

E. Medical Sciences

1. General

Kisch, Guido, "Medicine," in: *In Search for Freedom.* A History of American Jews from Czechoslovakia 1592-1948. London: Edward Goldston, 1948, pp. 135-145.

2. Anesthesiologists

Peter Safar (1924-2003), b. Vienna, of Czech ancestry; anesthesiologist, pioneer in cardio-pulmonary resuscitation
Bio: "Peter Safar," in: Wikipedia. See - https://en.wikipedia.org/wiki/Peter Safar; Rechcigl, Miloslav, Jr., "Peter Safar," in: *Encyclopedia of Bohemian and Czech-American Biography*. Bloomington, IN: AuthorHouse, 2016, Vol. 3, p. 1904.

Karl Frederick Urbach (1917-), b. Vienna, of Bohemian father; anesthesiologist
Bio: "Karl Urbach," in: *Memorial Book for the Victims of National Socialism at the University of Vienna in 1938.*

3. Cardiologists

William Ganz (1919-2009), b. Košice, Czech.; cardiologist, inventor of the Swan-Ganz catheter and co-innovator of catheter technology
Bio: "Pioneering cardiologist William Ganz, MD, passes at age 90," *Cardiology Today*, December 2009.

Eva E. Hausner (1953-), b. Prague, Czech; cardiologist
Bio: Rechcigl, Miloslav, Jr., "Eva Engelsmannová Hausner," in: *Encyclopedia of Bohemian and Czech-American Biography*. Bloomington, IN: AuthorHouse, 2016, Vol. 3, p. 1907.

Bruno Zacharias Kisch (1890-1966), b. Prague, Bohemia; cardiologist
Bio: "Bruno Kisch," in: Wikipedia. See - https://de.wikipedia.org/wiki/Bruno Kisch; Reichert, Philip, "Bruno Z. Kisch 1890–1966. A Tribute," *American Journal of Cardiology*,18, No. 6 p. 967.

Richard Langendorf (1908-1987), b. Prague, Bohemia; cardiologist, Chicago
Bio: Heise, Kenan, "Richard Langendorf, A Leader in Cardiology," *Chicago Tribune*, July 9, 1987; Rechcigl, Miloslav, Jr., "Richard Langendorf," in: *Encyclopedia of Bohemian and Czech-American Biography*. Bloomington, IN: AuthorHouse, 2016, Vol. 3, 1975.

Alfred Pick (1907-1982), b. Prague, Bohemia; cardiologist, Chicago
Bio: Rechcigl, Miloslav, Jr., "Alfred Pick," in: *Encyclopedia of Bohemian and Czech-American Biography*. Bloomington, IN: AuthorHouse, 2016, Vol. 3, 1911.

Ruth Pick (1913-2003), b. Karlovy Vary, Bohemia; cardiologist, Chicago
Bio: Rechcigl, Miloslav, Jr., "Ruth Pick," in: *Encyclopedia of Bohemian and Czech-American Biography*. Bloomington, IN: AuthorHouse, 2016, Vol. 3, 1911.

Helen Brooke Taussig (1898-1986), b. Cambridge, MA, of Bohemian ancestry, pediatric cardiologist
Bio: Neill, C A; Clark, E B (1999), "The Paediatric Cardiology Hall of Fame: Helen Brooke Taussig MD. May 24, 1898 to May 21, 1986," *Cardiology in the Young,* 9, No. 1 (1999), pp. 104–108; Rechcigl, Miloslav, Jr., "Žena, která zachránila na tisíce dětských životu" (Woman who Saved Thousands of Children's Lives" in: *Postavy naší Ameriky*. Praha: Pražská edice, 2000, pp. 332-333.

4. Dermatologists

Sigmund Pollitzer (1859-1937), b. Richmond Co., NY, of Czech ancestry; dermatologist
Bio: Rechcigl, Miloslav, Jr., "Sigmund Politzer," in: *Encyclopedia of Bohemian and Czech-American Biography*. Bloomington, IN: AuthorHouse, 2016, Vol. 3, p. 1927.

Erich Urbach (1893-1946), b. Prague, Bohemia; dermatologist
Bio: "Erich Urbach," in: Wikipedia. See - https://en.wikipedia.org/wiki/Erich_Urbach

Frederick Urbach (1922-2004), b. Vienna, of Bohemian father; dermatologist, Roswell Park Memorial Institute, Buffalo
Bio: "Frederick Urbach," in: Prabook. See - https://prabook.com/web/frederick.urbach/791040

Laurence R Taussig (1893-1940), b. San Francisco, CA, of Bohemian ancestry; dermatologist
Bio: Rechcigl, Miloslav, Jr., "Laurence R. Taussig," in: *Encyclopedia of Bohemian and Czech-American Biography*. Bloomington, IN: AuthorHouse, 2016, Vol. 3, p. 1928.

Joseph Zeisler (1858-1919), b. Bilsko, on Silesian-Moravian border; dermatologist
Bio: "Joseph Zeisler, M.D., 1858-1919), *Arch. Derm. Syphilol.*, 1, No. 1 (January 1920), pp. 61-62.

5. Family Physicians

Eduard Bloch (1872-1945), b. Hluboká nad Vltavou, Bohemia; physician of Hitler's family until 1907, then practicing in Linz, unable to practice after immigrating to NYC
Bio: Rechcigl, Miloslav, Jr., "Eduard Bloch," in: *Encyclopedia of Bohemian and Czech-American Biography*. Bloomington, IN: AuthorHouse, 2016, Vol. 3, p. 1933.

Bruno Ebel Hammerschlag (1904-1974), b. Vítkovice, Moravia; physician, Panama
Bio: Rechcigl, Miloslav, Jr., "Bruno Ebel Hammerschlag," in: *Encyclopedia of Bohemian and Czech-American Biography*. Bloomington, IN: AuthorHouse, 2016, Vol. 3, p. 1937.

Oswald Alois Holzer (1911-2000), b. Benešov, Bohemia; physician, Melbourne, FL
Bio: Rechcigl, Miloslav, Jr., "Oswald A. Holzer," in: *Encyclopedia of Bohemian and Czech-American Biography*. Bloomington, IN: AuthorHouse, 2016, Vol. 3, p. 1938.

Leopold 'Leo' Karpeles (1920-2016), b. Washington, DC, of Bohemian ancestry; professor of medicine at University of Maryland School of Medicine and then country doctor, with practice in Blue Ridge Summit, PA
Bio: Rasmussen, Frederick N., "Dr. Leopold M. 'Leo' Karpeles, longtime physician, dies," *The Baltimore Sun,* May 2, 2016.

William Grant Lewi (1870-1956), b. Albany, NY, of Bohemian ancestry; physician, Albany, NY
Bio: "William Grant Lewi," in: *Encyclopedia of Bohemian and Czech-American Biography*. Bloomington, IN: AuthorHouse, 2016, Vol. 3, p. 1940.

Julian Endreich Meyer (1894-1956), b. Selma, AL, of Bohemian mother; physician, NE
Bio: "Julian Endreich Meyer," in: *The History of Platte County, Nebraska*. By Margaret Curry. Culver City, CA: Murray & Gee, Inc., 1950, pp. 816-817; Rechcigl, Miloslav, Jr., "Julian Endreich Meyer," in: *Encyclopedia of Bohemian and Czech-American Biography*. Bloomington, IN: AuthorHouse, 2016, Vol. 3, p. 1942.

Kamil J. Neuman (1911-1978), b. Czech.; family physician, Schenectady, NY
Bio; "Kamil. Neuman," in: *SVU Directory*. 2nd ed. New York, NY: SVU Press, 1969.

Alexander Pollak (1899-1966), b. Michalovce, Slovakia; Holocaust survivor, physician in general practice, Cleveland, OH
Bio: Rechcigl, Miloslav, Jr., "Alexander Pollak," in: *Encyclopedia of Bohemian and Czech-American Biography*. Bloomington, IN: AuthorHouse, 2016, Vol. 3, p. 1944.
Wied

Anna Rezek (née Bunzl) (1895-1974), b. Vienna, of both Czech and Slovak ancestry; physician, Miami, Florida
Bio: Rechcigl, Miloslav, Jr., "Anna Rezek," in: *Encyclopedia of Bohemian and Czech-American Biography*. Bloomington, IN: AuthorHouse, 2016, Vol. 3, p. 1945.

6. Gastroenterologists

James Lee Flexner (1906-1964), b. Memphis, TN, of Bohemian ancestry; physician, gastroenterology, NYC

Bio: Rechcigl, Miloslav, Jr., "James Lee Flexner," in: *Encyclopedia of Bohemian and Czech-American Biography*. Bloomington, IN: AuthorHouse, 2016, Vol. 3, p. 1968-1969.

Norton J. Greenberger (1933—), b. Cleveland, OH, of Czech ancestry; gastroenterologist
Bio: Lewis, Myron, "Biography of Norton J. Greenberger, MD," *Journal of Clinical Gastroenterology*, 50, no. 4 (April 2016), pp. 269-270; Rechcigl, Miloslav, Jr., "Norton J. Greenberger," in: *Encyclopedia of Bohemian and Czech-American Biography*. Bloomington, IN: AuthorHouse, 2016, Vol. 3, p. 1970.

Otto Porges (1879-1967), b. Brandýs nad Labem, Bohemia; gastroenterologist
Bio: "Otto Porges," in: *Memorial Book for the Victims of National Socialism at the University of Vienna in 1938.*

Jonathan D. Wirtschafter (1935-2004), b. Cleveland, OH, of Slovak ancestry; ophthalmologist n KY and then MN, professor
Bio: "In Memoriam: Jonathan D. Wirtschafter '56," *Reed Magazine*, February 2005.

7. Gynecologists

Salo Marcus Boltuch (1906-d.), b. Plzeň, Bohemia; gynecologist, obstetrician, NYC
Bio: Rechcigl, Miloslav, Jr., "Salo Marcus Boltuch," in: *Encyclopedia of Bohemian and Czech-American Biography*. Bloomington, IN: AuthorHouse, 2016, Vol. 3, p. 1952.

Egon Walter Fischmann (1884-d.), b. Prague; gynecologist
Bio: Rechcigl, Miloslav, Jr., "Egon Walter Fischmann," in: *Encyclopedia of Bohemian and Czech-American Biography*. Bloomington, IN: AuthorHouse, 2016, Vol. 3, p. 1953.

Robert Frank Porges (1930-2012), b. Vienna, of Bohemian ancestry; obstetrician, gynecologist

Bio: "Robert Frank Porges," in: *Encyclopedia of Bohemian and Czech-American Biography*. Bloomington, IN: AuthorHouse, 2016, Vol. 3, p. 1957.

Heliodor Schiller (1871-d.), b. Luka, Bohemia; physician, gynecologist
Bio: "Schiller, Heliodor," *Who's Who in American Jewry*, Vol. 1, p. 546

Irving Freiler Stein (1887-1976), b. Chicago, of Bohemian ancestry; obstetrician, gynecologist
Bio: Rechcigl, Miloslav, Jr., "Irving Freiler Stein," in: *Encyclopedia of Bohemian and Czech-American Biography*. Bloomington, IN: AuthorHouse, 2016, Vol. 3, pp. 1959-1960; *Who's Who in American Jewry*. New York: Jewish Biographical Bureau, 1926, Vol. 1, p. 592.

Karel Steinbach (1894-1990), b. Třebsko, Bohemia; physician, gynecologist
Bio: "Karel Steinbach," in: Wikipedia. See - https://cs.wikipedia.org/wiki/Karel Steinbach; Rechcigl, Miloslav, Jr., "Karel Steinbach," in: *Encyclopedia of Bohemian and Czech-American Biography*. Bloomington, IN: AuthorHouse, 2016, Vol. 3, p. 1960.

Frederick Joseph Taussig (1872-1943), b. Brooklyn, NY, of Bohemian ancestry; obstetrician, gynecologist, St. Louis
Bio: Rechcigl, Miloslav, Jr., "Frederick Joseph Taussig," in: *Encyclopedia of Bohemian and Czech-American Biography*. Bloomington, IN: AuthorHouse, 2016, Vol. 3, pp. 1960-1961.

8. Internists

Franz Karl Bauer (1917-1976), b. Vienna, of Bohemian ancestry; internist, professor of medicine and radiology at University of California, Los Angeles
Bio: "Franz Bauer," in: *Memorial Book for the Victims of National Socialism at the University of Vienna in 1938*. See - http://gedenkbuch.univie.ac.at/index.php?L=2&person single id=10112; Rechcigl, Miloslav, Jr., "Franz Karl Bauer," in: *Encyclopedia of Bohemian and Czech-American Biography*. Bloomington, IN: AuthorHouse, 2016, Vol. 3, p. 1965.

Julius Bauer (1887-1979), b. Náchod, Bohemia; internist, professor of medicine at Loma Linda University, CA
Bio: "Julius Bauer," in: *Memorial Book for the Victims of National Socialism at the University of Vienna in 1938*. See - http://gedenkbuch.univie.ac.at/index.php?L=2&person single id=32769

Simon R. Blatteis (1876-1968), b. Těšín, Silesia; internist, pathologist, Brooklyn, NY
Bio: "Blatteis, Simon R.," in: *Who's Who in American Jewry*. New York: Jewish Biographical Bureau, 1926, Vol. 1, p. 61.

Arthur L. Bloomfield (1888-1962), b. Baltimore of Silesian acestry; internist, medical historian, educator, Dean
Bio: Cox, Alvin J. et al., "Arthur L. Bloomfield 1888-1962," *Calif. Med.*, 97, no. 3 (September 1962), pp. 191-192; Rechcigl, Miloslav, Jr., "Arthur Leonard Bloomfield," in: *Encyclopedia of Bohemian and Czech-American Biography*. Bloomington, IN: AuthorHouse, 2016, Vol. 3, p. 1966.

Jesse Bullowa (1879-1943), b. NYC, of Bohemian ancestry; internist, pofessor of pulmonary medicine, NY University College of Medine
Bio: "Jesse Bullowa," in: Wikipedia. See - https://en.wikipedia.org/wiki/Jesse Bullowa; Rechcigl, Miloslav, Jr., "Jesse G. M. Bullowa," in: *Encyclopedia of Bohemian and Czech-American Biography*. Bloomington, IN: AuthorHouse, 2016, Vol. 3, p. 1966.

Bertold Feldman (1904-1992), b. Spůle, Bohemia; internist, NYC
Bio: Rechcigl, Miloslav, Jr., "Bertold Feldman," in: *Encyclopedia of Bohemian and Czech-American Biography*. Bloomington, IN: AuthorHouse, 2016, Vol. 3, p. 1968.

John M. Flexner (1928-2011), b. Louisville, KY, of Bohemian ancestry; internist, specializing in hematology
Bio: Rechcigl, Miloslav, Jr., "John M. Flexner," in: *Encyclopedia of Bohemian and Czech-American Biography*. Bloomington, IN: AuthorHouse, 2016, Vol. 3, p. 1969; "Obituary: John M. Flexner M.D.," the Tennessean, December 301, 2011.

Morris Flexner (1890-1969), b. Louisville, KY, of Bohemian ancestry; internist, Louisville, KY
Bio: Rechcigl, Miloslasv, Jr., "Morris Flexner," in: *Encyclopedia of Bohemian and Czech-American Biography*. Bloomington, IN: AuthorHouse, 2016, Vol. 3, p. 1969.

Paul Heller (1914-2001), b. Chomutov, Bohemia; internist, hematologist
Bio: Rechcigl, Miloslav, Jr., "Paul Heller," in: *Encyclopedia of Bohemian and Czech-American Biography*. Bloomington, IN: AuthorHouse, 2016, Vol. 3, p. 1953; "Dr. Paul Heller, 87. Physician, concentration camp survivor," *Chicago Tribune*, September 29, 2001.

Alexander L. Kisch (ca 1928-), of Bohemian parents, internist, New York, NY
Bio: Rechcigl, Miloslav, Jr., "Alexander L. Kisch," in: *Encyclopedia of Bohemian and Czech-American Biography*. Bloomington, IN: AuthorHouse, 2016, Vol. 3, pp. 1973-1974.

Robert Kositchek (1913-2009), b. of Bohemian ancestry; physician, practiced in Beverly Hills and Los Angeles, founder of St. John's Retired Doctors Assn., past president of the Beverly Hills Medical Assn.
Bio: "Obituary: Robert J. Kositchek, MD," *Los Angeles Times*, November 24, 2009.

Lewis Benjamin Lefkowitz (1930-), b. Dallas, TX, of Slovak ancestry; internist, professor of preventive medicine at Vanderbilt University
Bio: Humphrey, Nancy, "Clinic Dedicated in Honor of Lefkowitz," *Reporter*, Vanderbilt University Medical' Center's weekly newspaper, March 9, 2001.

Arthur Jackson Patek, Jr. (1904-1991), b. Milwaukee, WI, of Bohemian ancestry; internist
Bio: Rechcigl, Miloslav, Jr., "Otto Porges," in: *Encyclopedia of Bohemian and Czech-American Biography*. Bloomington, IN: AuthorHouse, 2016, Vol. 3, p. 1977.

Otto Porges (1879-1967), b. Brandýs nad Labem, Bohemia; internist, Chicago
Bio: Rechcigl, Miloslav, Jr., "Otto Porges," in: *Encyclopedia of Bohemian and Czech-American Biography*. Bloomington, IN: AuthorHouse, 2016, Vol. 3, p. 1978.

Walter Redisch (1899-1993), b. Prague, Bohemia; internist, professor, NY Medical Coll
Bio: Rechcigl, Miloslav, Jr., "Walter Redisch," in: *Encyclopedia of Bohemian and Czech-American Biography*. Bloomington, IN: AuthorHouse, 2016, Vol. 3, p. 1979.

Gustav Schonfeld (1934-2011), b. Mukačevo, Czech.; internist, specializing in lipid metabolism, professor, St. Louis
Bio: Cohn, Robert A., "Gustav Schonfeld, 77; Shoah survivor, physician, professor," in: STL=Jewisih Light. See - http://www.stljewishlight.com/obituaries/article 9ace141e-86e7-11e0-909c-001cc4c002e0.html; Gotto, Antonio M., Jr., "Gustav Schonfeld, M.d.," *Trans. Am. Clin. Climatol. Assoc.*, 123 (2012), pp. xcviii–cii; "Gustav Schonfeld, 77; Shoah survivor, physician, professor," in: STL - Jewish Light. See - http://www.stljewishlight.com/obituaries/article_9ace141e-86e7-11e0-909c-001cc4c002e0.html

Kamil Schulhof (1888-1962), b. Prague, Bohemia; internist, Chicago
Bio: Rechcigl, Miloslav, Jr., "Kamil Schulhof," in: *Encyclopedia of Bohemian and Czech-American Biography*. Bloomington, IN: AuthorHouse, 2016, Vol. 3, p. 1981

Albert Ernest Taussig (1871-1944), b. St. Louis, of Bohemian ancestry; internist, professor, St. Louis
Bio: Rechcigl, Miloslav, Jr., "Albert Ernest Taussig," in: *Encyclopedia of Bohemian and Czech-American Biography*. Bloomington, IN: AuthorHouse, 2016, Vol. 3, p. 1982.

Austin Stanley Weisberger (1913-1970), b. Cleveland, OH, of Slovak ancestry; internist, hematologist, professor, Cleveland

Bio: "Austin S. Weinberger," *Blood,* 37, No. 1 (January 1971), pp.113-114; "Austin Weisberger, 56, Cleveland Medical Leader," *The New York Times*, June 22, 1970.

William W. Winternitz (1920-2015), b. New Haven, CT, of Bohemian ancestry; internist, professor, University of Alabama
Bio: "Late University of Alabama faculty member William Winternitz remembered as 'pioneer'," Tuscaloosanews.com. See - http://www.tuscaloosanews.com/article/DA/20160430/News/605159383/TL/

Zoltan Tilson Wirtschafter (1899-1967), b. Košice, Slovakia; internist
Bio: "Dr. Zoltan T. Wirtschafter," in: Find A Grave. See - https://www.findagrave.com/memorial/107790700/zolton-t.-wirtschafter

9. Neurologists

Otto Marburg (1874-1948), b. Rýmařov, Moravia; neurologist, neurooncologist
Bio: "Otto Marburg," in: Wikipedia. See - https://en.wikipedia.org/wiki/Otto_Marburg

Karl H. Pribram (1919-2015), b. Vienna, of Bohemian ancestry; neurologist, neurosurgeon
Bio: "Karl H. Pribram," in: Wikipedia. See - https://en.wikipedia.org/wiki/Karl H. Pribram; Rechcigl, Miloslav, Jr., "Karl H. Pribram," in: *Beyond the Sea of Beer. History of Immigration of Bohemians and Czechs to the New World and their Contri*butions. Bloomington, IN: AuthorHouse, 2017, p. 763.

10. Oncologists

Ellis Fischel (1883-1938), b. St. Louis, MO, of Bohemian ancestry; oncologist, St. Louis
Bio: "Ellis Fischel Cancer Center," in: Wikipedia. See - https://en.wikipedia.org/wiki/Ellis_Fischel_Cancer_Center

Alfred Gellhorn (1913-2008), b. St. Louis, MO, of Bohemian ancestry; oncologist, Dean

b. Rechcigl, Miloslav, Jr., "Alfred Gellhorn," in: *Encyclopedia of Bohemian and Czech-American Biography*. Bloomington, IN: AuthorHouse, 2016, Vol. 3, pp. 1992-1993; "Alfred Gellhorn M.D., Obituary," *The New York Times*, February 16, 2018.

Petr F. Hausner (1948-), b. Prague, Czech.; oncologist
Bio: "Peter F. Hausner," in: *Encyclopedia of Bohemian and Czech-American Biography*. Bloomington, IN: AuthorHouse, 2016, Vol. 3, p. 1993.

11. Ophthalmologists

Karl Wolfgang Ascher (1887-1971), b. Prague, Bohemia; ophthalmologist, professor, Cincinnati
Bio: "Karl Wolfgang Ascher," in: H*andbuch österreichischer Autorinnen und Autoren jüdischer Herkunft*. München: K. G. Saur, 2002, p. 41; Rechcigl, Miloslav, Jr., "Karl Wolfgang Ascher," in: *Encyclopedia of Bohemian and Czech-American Biography*. Bloomington, IN: AuthorHouse, 2016, Vol.3, p. 1996.

Thomas Czerner (1938-), b. Prague, Czech.; ophthalmologist, univ. professor, San Francisco
Bio: Rechcigl, Miloslav, Jr., "Thomas Czerner," in: *Encyclopedia of Bohemian and Czech-American Biography*. Bloomington, IN: AuthorHouse, 2016, Vol. 3, p. 1997; "Czerner, Thomas B. 1938-" in: encyclopedia.com. See: https://www.encyclopedia.com/arts/educational-magazines/czerner-thomas-b-1938

Frederick John Hoitash (1883-1952), b. Sušice, Bohemia; ophthalmologist
Bio: Rechcigl, Miloslav, Jr., "Frederick John Hoitash," in: *Encyclopedia of Bohemian and Czech-American Biography*. Bloomington, IN: AuthorHouse, 2016, Vol. 3, p. 1997.

Karl Koller (1857-1944), b. Sušice, Bohemia; ophthalmologist
Bio: Becker, Hortense Koller, "Carl Koller and Cocaine," *Psychoanalyt. Quart.*, July 1963;
Diamant, H (November 1996). "Should they have got the Nobel Prize?" *Adler Museum Bulletin* (South Africa) 22 (3), pp, 18–20; Leonard, M., "Carl Koller: Mankind's Greatest Benefactor? The Story of Local Anesthesia,"

J. Dent. Res., 77, No. 4 (April 1998, pp. 535-538; Rechcigl, Miloslav, Jr., "Objevitel lokální anestezie" (Discoverer of Local Anesthesia) in: *Postavy naší Ameriky*. Praha: Pražská edice, 2000, pp. 322-323.

Arthur Linksz (1900-1988), b. Hlohovec, Slovakia; ophthalmologist, NYC
Bio: Rechcigl, Miloslav, Jr., "Arthur Linksz," in: *Encyclopedia of Bohemian and Czech-American Biography*. Bloomington, IN: AuthorHouse, 2016, Vol. 3, p. 1999.

Ernst Saxl (1868-1914), b. Strakonice, Bohemia; ophthalmologist, St. Louis, MO
Bio: Rechcigl, Miloslav, Jr., "Ernst Saxl," in: *Encyclopedia of Bohemian and Czech-American Biography*. Bloomington, IN: AuthorHouse, 2016, Vol. 3, p. 2000' "Ernst Saxl, M.D.," *Journal of the Missouri State Medical Assn.*, Vol. 11 (October 1914), p. 194.

Daniel T. Weidenthal (1932-), b. Cleveland, OH, of Bohemian ancestry; ophthalmologist, Beachwood, Ohio
Bio: Rechcigl, Miloslav, Jr., "Daniel T. Weidenthal," in: *Encyclopedia of Bohemian and Czech-American Biography*. Bloomington, IN: AuthorHouse, 2016, Vol. 3, pp. 2001-2002.

Henry L. Wofner (1860-1935), b. Chicago, IL, of Bohemian ancestry; ophthalmologist, St. Louis, MO
Bio: Rechcigl, Miloslav, Jr., "Henry L. Wolfner," in: *Encyclopedia of Bohemian and Czech-American Biography*. Bloomington, IN: AuthorHouse, 2016, Vol. 3, p. 2002.

12. Orthopedists

Joseph Ivan Krajbich (1947-), b. Prague, Czech.; orthopedic surgeon, Portland, OR
Bio: Rechcigl, Miloslav, Jr., "J. Ivan Krajbich," in: *Encyclopedia of Bohemian and Czech-American Biography*. Bloomington, IN: AuthorHouse, 2016, Vol. 3, p. 2004.

Maurice J. Lewi (1857-1957), b. Albany, NY, of Bohemian ancestry; podiatrist, Albany and New York City
Bio: Rechcigl, Miloslav, Jr., "Maurice J. Lewi," in: *Encyclopedia of Bohemian and Czech-American Biography*. Bloomington, IN: AuthorHouse, 2016, Vol. 3, p. 2004.

Arthur Steindler (1878-1959), b. Kraslice, Bohemia; orthopedic surgeon
Bio: Rechcigl, Miloslav, Jr., "Artghui0 Steindler," in: *Encyclopedia of Bohemian and Czech-American Biography*. Bloomington, IN: AuthorHouse, 2016, Vol. 3, p. 2006.

William W. Winternitz, Jr. (ca 1949-), b. of Bohemian ancestry; orthopedist, professor, Davis, CA
Bio: "William W. Winternitz, Jr., MD," in: WebMD Physician directory. See - https://doctor.webmd.com/doctor/william-winternitz-jr-md-558d58b0-defe-4ce9-8850-8e8d2f692d62-overview

13. Otolaryngologists

Joseph Carl Beck (1870-1942), b. Bohemia; otologist and laryngologist, Chicago
Bio: *Who's Who in Chicago*. Chicago: A. N. Marquis & Co., 1917, p.42; Rechcigl, Miloslav, Jr., "Joseph Carl Beck," in: *Encyclopedia of Bohemian and Czech-American Biography*. Bloomington, IN: AuthorHouse, 2016, vol. 3, p. 2008.

Arthur J. Herzig (1881-1954), b. New York, NY, of Bohemian ancestry; otolaryngologist, also eye doctor
Bio: Rechcigl, Miloslav, Jr. "Arthur J. Herzig," in: *Encyclopedia of Bohemian and Czech-American Biography*. Bloomington, IN: AuthorHouse, 2016, Vol. 3, p. 2009.

Francis Loeffler Lederer (1898-1973), b. Chicago, IL, of Bohemian ancestry; otolaryngologist, Chicago
Bio: Rechcigl, Miloslav, Jr., "Francis Loeffler Lederer," in: *Encyclopedia of Bohemian and Czech-American Biography*. Bloomington, IN: AuthorHouse, 2016, Vol. 3, p. 2010.

Karl Löwy (1904-1978), b. Vienna, of Bohemian ancestry; otolaryngologist, professor, Rochester
Bio: "Löwy, Karl," in: *Handbuch österrechischer Autorinnen und Autoren jűdischer Herkunft.*
Műnchen: K. G. Saur, 2002, Band 1, A-I, p. 870.

Robert Sonnenschein (1879-1939), b. Chicago, IL, of Bohemian ancestry; otolaryngologist, Chicago
Bio: Rechcigl, Miloslav, Jr., "Robert Sonneschein," in: *Encyclopedia of Bohemian and Czech-American Biography.* Bloomington, IN: AuthorHouse, 2016, Vol. 3, p. 2012.

14. Pediatricians

Victor Eisner (1921-2002), b. Red Bank, NJ, of Bohemian ancestry; professor of maternal and child health, San Francisco
Bio: Rechcigl, Miloslav, Jr., "Victor Eisner," in: *Encyclopedia of Bohemian and Czech-American Biography.* Bloomington, IN: AuthorHouse, 2016, Vol. 3, p. 2013.

Gaston Jacob Greil (1878-1932), b. Montgomery, AL, of Bohemian father; pediatrician, Montgomery, AL
Bio: Rechcigl, Miloslav, Jr., "Gaston J. Greil," in: *Encyclopedia of Bohemian and Czech-American Biography.* Bloomington, IN: AuthorHouse, 2016, Vol. 3, p. 1937.

Hans Mautner (1886-d.); b. České Budějovice, Bohemia; pediatrician
Bio: Rechcigl, Miloslav, Jr., "Hans Mautner," in: *Encyclopedia of Bohemian and Czech-American Biography.* Bloomington, IN: AuthorHouse, 2016, Vol. 3, p. 2017.

Daniel N. Neuspiel (1952-), b. Haifa, Israel, of Czech father; pediatrician
Bio: Rechcigl, Miloslav, Jr., "Daniel N. Neuspiel," in: *Encyclopedia of Bohemian and Czech-American Biography.* Bloomington, IN: AuthorHouse, 2016, Vol. 3, p. 2018.

15. Physiatrists

Robert Anthony Muller (1895-1959), b. Karlovy Vary, Bohemia; physiatrist, med. director of Jewish Inst. of Physiotherapy
Bio: Rechcigl, Miloslav, Jr., in: *Encyclopedia of Bohemian and Czech-American Biography*. Bloomington, IN: AuthorHouse, 2016, Vol. 3, p. 2024.

Andor A. Weiss (1906-1986), b. Čop, Slovakia; professor of rehabilitation medicine
Bio: Rechcigl, Miloslav, Jr., "Andor A. Weiss," in: *Encyclopedia of Bohemian and Czech-American Biography*. Bloomington, IN: AuthorHouse, 2016, Vol. 3, p. 2025-2026.

16. Psychiatrists

Jan Ehrenwald (1900-1988), b. Bratislava, Slovakia; psychiatrist
Bio: "Jan Ehrenwald," in: Wikipedia. See - https://en.wikipedia.org/wiki/Jan_Ehrenwald

Ladislav V. Fischmeister (1923-2003), b. Humpolec, Czech.; psychiatrist
Bio: Rechcigl, Miloslav, Jr., "Ladislav Fischmeister," in: *Encyclopedia of Bohemian and Czech-American Biography*. Bloomington, IN: AuthorHouse, 2016, Vol. 3, p. 2028.

Marie Franziska Fleischl (1911-1997), b. Vienna, of Bohemian ancestry; psychiatrist
Bio: *Handbuch österreichische Autorinnen und Autoren jüdischer Herkunft 18. bis 20. Jahrhundert,* Band 1, A-I, p. 535.

Viktor Emil Frankl (1905-1997), b. Vienna, of Czech ancestry; neurologist and psychiatrist
Bio: Frankl, Viktor, *Recollections: An Autobiography*. Basic Books, 2008; "Viktor Frankl," in: Wikipedia. See - https://en.wikipedia.org/wiki/Viktor_Frankl

Kurt Freund (1914-1996), b. Chrudim. Bohemia; Canadian physician, sexologist

Bio: "Kurt Freund," in Wikipedia. See - https://en.wikipedia.org/wiki/Kurt_Freund

Hanuš J. Grosz (1924-2001), b. Brno, Czech.; psychiatrist
Bio: Rechcigl, Miloslav, Jr., "Hanuš Jiří Grosz," in: *Encyclopedia of Bohemian and Czech-American Biography.* Bloomington, IN: AuthorHouse, 2016, Vol. 3, pp. 2029-2030.

Edward Hitschmann (1871-1957), b. Vienna, of Moravian ancestry; psychoanalyst
Bio: Becker, Philip P., "Edward Hitschmann," in: *Psychoanalytic Pioneers.* New Brunswick - London: Transaction Publishers, 1995, pp. 160-161.

Irene Hitschmann (née Link) (1908-1986), b. Hohenems, Aust., of Slovak ancestry; psychiatrist
Bio: Rechcigl, Miloslav, Jr., "Irene Hitschmann," in: *Encyclopedia of Bohemian and Czech-American Biography.* Bloomington, IN: AuthorHouse, 2016, Vol. 3, p. 2031.

Julius Hoenig (1916-2009.), b. Prague, Bohemia; Canadian psychiatrist
Bio: *International Biographical Dictionary of Central European Emigrés 1933-1945.* New York: R. G. Sauer, 1983; Rechcigl, Miloslav, Jr., "Julius Hoenig," in: *Encyclopedia of Bohemian and Czech-American Biography.* Bloomington, IN: AuthorHouse, 2016, Vol. 3, pp. 2029-2030.

Ferdinand Knobloch (1916-), b. Prague, Bohemia; psychiatrist, professor, University of British Columbia, Canada
Bio: Rechcigl, Miloslav, Jr. "Ferdinand Knobloch," in: *Encyclopedia of Bohemian and Czech-American Biography.* Bloomington, IN: AuthorHouse, 2016, Vol. 3, p. 2034

Lida Morawetz Jeck (1952-), b. of Bohemian ancestry; psychiatrist, psychoanalyst
Bio: Rechcigl, Miloslav, Jr., "Lida Morawetz Jeck," in: *Encyclopedia of Bohemian and Czech-American Biography.* Bloomington, IN: AuthorHouse, 2016, Vol. 3, pp. 2032.

Robert Kellner (1922-1992), b. Budapest, of Czech ancestry; psychiatrist
Bio: "Robert Kellner, M.D., Ph.D., 1922-1992," *Psychosomatics*, 34 (July-August 1993), pp. 287-289; Rechcigl, Miloslav, Jr., "Robert Kellner," in: *Encyclopedia of Bohemian and Czech-American Biography*. Bloomington, IN: AuthorHouse, 2016, Vol. 3, pp. 2033-2034.

Marianne Kriss (née Rie) (1900-1980), b. Vienna, of Bohemian ancestry; physician, psychoanalyst, NYC
Bio: Rechcigl, Miloslav, Jr., "Marianne Kris," in: *Encyclopedia of Bohemian and Czech-American Biography*. Bloomington, IN: AuthorHouse, 2016, Vol. 3, pp. 2105-2106.

Wilhelm Neutra (1876-1947), b. Vienna, of Moravian ancestry, psychiatrist, NYC
Bio: Rechcigl, Miloslav, Jr., "Wilhelm Neutra," in: *Encyclopedia of Bohemian and Czech-American Biography*. Bloomington, IN: AuthorHouse, 2016, Vol. 3, pp. 2036.

George O. Papanek (1931-2004), b. Vienna, of Moravian ancestry; psychiatrist
Bio: Rechcigl, Miloslav, Jr., "George O. Papanek," in: *Encyclopedia of Bohemian and Czech-American Biography*. Bloomington, IN: AuthorHouse, 2016, Vol. 3, pp. 2036.

Charles W. Popper (1946-), b. of Bohemian ancestry; child and adolescent psychiatrist, psychopharmacologist, Belmont, MA
Bio: Rechcigl, Miloslav, Jr., "Charles W. Popper," in: *Encyclopedia of Bohemian and Czech-American Biography*. Bloomington, IN: AuthorHouse, 2016, Vol. 3, pp. 2038.

Franz Karl Reichsman (1913-1996), b. of Moravian mother; psychiatrist, specializing in psychosomatic medicine, professor, Brooklyn, NY
Bio: "Franz Reichsman, 82, Medical Professor," *The New York Times*, February 11, 1996; Rechcigl, Miloslav, Jr., "Franz Karl Reichsman," in: *Encyclopedia of Bohemian and Czech-American Biography*. Bloomington, IN: AuthorHouse, 2016, Vol. 3, p. 1979.

Raya Czerner Schapiro (1934-2007), b. Prague, Bohemia; psychiatrist
Bio: Rechcigl, Miloslav, Jr., "T Raya Czerner Schapiro," in: *Encyclopedia of Bohemian and Czech-American Biography.* Bloomington, IN: AuthorHouse, 2016, Vol. 3, p. 2039.

Adolph Stern (1878-1958), b. Cheb, Bohemia; psychiatrist, psychoanalyst
Bio: Shoenfeld, Dudley D., "In Memoriam: Adolph Stern, M.D. 1878-1958)," *Journal of American Psychoanalytic Association*, 7, No. 2 (April 1959), pp. 381-382.

Robert S. Wallerstein (1921-2014), b. Berlin, Germany, of Bohemian ancestry; psychiatrist, psychoanalyst
Bio: Rechcigl, Miloslav, Jr., "Robert S. Wallerstein," in: *Encyclopedia of Bohemian and Czech-American Biography.* Bloomington, IN: AuthorHouse, 2016, Vol. 3, pp. 2041-2042.

Robert Weil (1909-2002), b. Vimperk, Bohemia; psychiatrist
Bio: Rechcigl, Miloslav, Jr., "Robert Weil," in: *Encyclopedia of Bohemian and Czech-American Biography.* Bloomington, IN: AuthorHouse, 2016, Vol. 3, pp. 2042.

Joseph A. Winn (orig. Wiener) (1901-1983), b. Poděbrady, Bohemia; psychiatrist, neurologist, also a poet, New York, NY
Bio: "Dr. Joseph Winn, Psychiatrist and Ex-Head of 2 V.A. Clinics," *The New York Times,* February 11, 1983; Rechcigl, Miloslav, Jr., "Joseph Alcantara Winn," in: *Encyclopedia of Bohemian and Czech-American Biography.* Bloomington, IN: AuthorHouse, 2016, Vol. 3, 1992.

17. Radiologists

Philip Braunstein (1930-2004), b. Karlovy Vary, Czech.; radiologist
Bio: Rechcigl, Miloslav, Jr., "Philip Braunstein," in: *Encyclopedia of Bohemian and Czech-American Biography.* Bloomington, IN: AuthorHouse, 2016, Vol. 3, pp. 2043; "In Memoriam: Philip Braunstein," in: University of California, the Academic Senate. See - https://senate.universityofcalifornia.edu/_files/inmemoriam/html/philipbraunstein.htm

Felix G. Fleischner (1893-1969), b. Vienna, of Bohemian ancestry; radiologist, Boston
Bio: Rechcigl, Miloslav, Jr., "Felix G. Fleischner," in: *Encyclopedia of Bohemian and Czech-American Biography*. Bloomington, IN: AuthorHouse, 2016, Vol. 3, pp. 2044-2045.

Anna Goldfeder (1898-1993), b. Poland, raised and educated in Prague; radiologist
Bio: Rechcigl, Miloslav, Jr., "Anna Goldfeder,", in: *Encyclopedia of Bohemian and Czech-American Biography*. Bloomington, IN: AuthorHouse, 2016, Vol. 3, p. 2045.

Igor Laufer (1944-2010), b. Czech.; radiologist
Bio: Rechcigl, Miloslav, Jr., "Igor Laufer," in: *Encyclopedia of Bohemian and Czech-American Biography*. Bloomington, IN: AuthorHouse, 2016, Vol. 3, p. 2047.

Bertram V. A. Low-Beer (1900-1955), b. Topoľčany, Slovakia; radiologist
Bio: Rechcigl, Miloslav, Jr., "Bertram V. A. Low-Beer," in: *Encyclopedia of Bohemian and Czech-American Biography*. Bloomington, IN: AuthorHouse, 2016, Vol. 3, pp. 2047-2048.

Max Sgalitzer (1884-1973), b. Prague, Bohemia; radiologist
Bio: Rechcigl, Miloslav, Jr., "Max Sgalitzer," in: *Encyclopedia of Bohemian and Czech-American Biography*. Bloomington, IN: AuthorHouse, 2016, Vol. 3, pp. 2049-2050.

Julian O. Salik (1909-1999), b. Slavonice, Moravia; radiologist
Bio: Rechcigl, Miloslav, Jr., "Julian O. Salik," in: *Encyclopedia of Bohemian and Czech-American Biography*. Bloomington, IN: AuthorHouse, 2016, Vol. 3, p. 2049.

Gerhart Steven Schwarz (1912-1982), b. Vienna, of Moravian ancestry; radiologist
Bio: Rechcigl, Miloslav, JR., "Gerhard Steven Schwarz," in: *Encyclopedia of Bohemian and Czech-American Biography*. Bloomington, IN: AuthorHouse, 2016, Vol. 3, p. 2049.

18. Rheumatologists

Andrew J. Porges (1960-), b. New York, NY, of Bohemian ancestry; rheumatologist, New Hyde Park, NY
Bio: Rechcigl, Miloslav, Jr., "Andrew J. Porges" in: *Encyclopedia of Bohemian and Czech-American Biography*. Bloomington, IN: AuthorHouse, 2016, Vol. 3, p. 1978.

Peter H. Schur (1933-), b. Vienna, of Bohemian mother; rheumatologist, professor at Harvard
Bio: Stobo, John D., "Introducing the New Editor: Peter H. Schur, MD," *Arthritis & Rheumatism,* 33, No. 7 (December 2005).

19. Surgeons

Carl Beck (1864-1911), b. Milin, Bohemia; surgeon, Chicago
Bio: *Who's Who in Chicago*. Chicago: A. N. Marquis & Co., 1917, p.42; Rechcigl, Miloslav, Jr., "Carl Beck," in: *Encyclopedia of Bohemian and Czech-American Biography*. Bloomington, IN: AuthorHouse, 2016, Vol. 3, p.2052.

Emil George Beck (1866-1932), b. Bohemia; physician, surgeon, Chicago
Bio: *Who's Who in Chicago*. Chicago: A. N. Marquis & Co., 1917, p.42; Rechcigl, Miloslav, Jr., "Emil G. Beck," in: *Encyclopedia of Bohemian and Czech-American Biography*. Bloomington, IN: AuthorHouse, 2016, Vol. 3, p. 2052.

William Carl Beck (1907-1994), b. Chicago, of Bohemian ancestry; surgeon
Bio: Rechcigl, Miloslav, Jr., "William Carl Beck," in: *Encyclopedia of Bohemian and Czech-American Biography*. Bloomington, IN: AuthorHouse, 2016, Vol. 3, p. 2053.

Felix Albert Bettelheim (1861-1890), physician and surgeon of Panama
Bio: "Felix Albert Bettelheim," in: Jewish Encyclopedia.com. See - http://www.jewishencyclopedia.com/articles/3230-bettelheim

Oscar Edgeworth Bloch (1871-1951), b. Cromwell, KY, of Bohemian ancestry; surgeon
Bio: Rechcigl, Miloslav, Jr., "Oscar Edgeworth Bloch," in: *Encyclopedia of Bohemian and Czech-American Biography*. Bloomington, IN: AuthorHouse, 2016, Vol. 3, p. 2053.

Jacob Richter Buchbinder (1887-1947), b. Chicago, IL, of Bohemian ancestry; surgeon, Chicago
Bio: Rechcigl, Miloslav, Jr., "Jacob Richter Buchbinder," in: *Encyclopedia of Bohemian and Czech-American Biography*. Bloomington, IN: AuthorHouse, 2016, Vol. 3, p. 2053.

John Lewi Donhauser (1883-1964), b. Washington, DC, of Bohemian ancestry; surgeon
Bio: Rechcigl, Miloslav, Jr., "John Lewi Donhauser," in: *Encyclopedia of Bohemian and Czech-American Biography*. Bloomington, IN: AuthorHouse, 2016, Vol. 3, p. 2054.

Richard Heller (1907-1998), b. Chicago, IL, of Bohemian ancestry; surgeon
Bio: Rechcigl, Miloslav, Jr., "Richard Heller," in: *Encyclopedia of Bohemian and Czech-American Biography*. Bloomington, IN: AuthorHouse, 2016, Vol. 3, p. 205; "Richard Heller, 90, Longtime Surgeon," *Chicago Tribune*, June 1, 1998.

Alexis Victor Moschcowitz (1865-1933), b. Giraltovce, Slovakia; surgeon
Bio: Lilienthal, Howard, "Alexis Victor Moschcowitz," *Annals of Surgery*, 99, No. 3 (1934), pp. 557-558; "Moschcowitz, Alexis Victor," in: *Who's Who in American Jewry*, Vol. 1., p. 445.

Emil C. Robitschek (1880-d.), b. Milevsko, Bohemia; surgeon
Bio: "Robitschek, Emil C." in: *Who's Who in American Jewry*, Vol. 1., p. 502.

Irving F. Stein, Jr. (1918-1997), b. of Bohemian ancestry; surgeon, Chicago, professor, Northwestern Univ. Medical School
Bio: Heise, Kenan, "Dr. Irving F. Stein, Surgeon, Professor," *Chicago Tribune*, September 20, 1997.

David Henry Winternitz (1891-1952), b. Hoxie, KS, of Bohemian ancestry; surgeon
Bio: Rechcigl, Miloslav, Jr., "David Henry Winternitz," in: *Encyclopedia of Bohemian and Czech-American Biography*. Bloomington, IN: AuthorHouse, 2016, Vol. 3, p. 2066.

Philip Yosowitz (ca 1950-), b. Cleveland, OH, of Czech immigrant father; plastic surgeon, Houston, TX - a surgeon by day, a composer by night
Bio: Rechcigl, Miloslav, Jr., "Philip Yosowitz," in: *Encyclopedia of Bohemian and Czech-American Biography*. Bloomington, IN: AuthorHouse, 2016, Vol. 1, p. 565.

20. Urologists

Benjamin Berger (1884-1968), b. Hrabovec, Slovakia; physician, dermatologist, urologist, NYC
Bio: *Who's Who in American Jewry*. New York: Jewish Biographical Bureau, 1926, Vol. 1., p. 45.

F. Physical Sciences

1. Astronomers

Charles D. Bailyn (1959-), b. Cambridge, MA, of Bohemian ancestry; astronomer
Bio: "Charles Bailyn," in: Wikipedia. See - https://en.wikipedia.org/wiki/Charles Bailyn; Rechcigl, Miloslav, Jr., "Charles d. Bailyn," in: *Encyclopedia of Bohemian and Czech-American Biography*. Bloomington, IN: AuthorHouse, 2016, Vol. 2, p. 1586.

Guido Beck (1903-1988), b, Liberec, Bohemia; theoretical physicist, astrophysicist, Brazil, Argentina
Bio: Rechcigl, Miloslav, Jr., "Guido Beck", in: *Encyclopedia of Bohemian and Czech-American Biography*. Bloomington, IN: AuthorHouse, 2016, Vol. 2, p. 1680.

Martin Otto Harwit (orig. Haurowitz) (1931-), b. Prague, Czech.; astronomer
Bio: Oral History Transcript – Martin Otto Harwit, Niels Bohr Library and Archives, April 19, 1983; Rechcigl, Miloslav, Jr., "Martin Harwit," in: *Encyclopedia of Bohemian and Czech-American Biography*. Bloomington, IN: AuthorHouse, 2016, Vol. 2, pp. 1587-1588.

2. Chemists

Alfred Bader (1924-), b. Vienna, of bohemian ancestry; chemist, fine art collector, philanthropist
Bio: "Alfred Bader,", in: Wikipedia. See - https://en.wikipedia.org/wiki/Alfred Bader; Rechcigl, Miloslav, Jr., "Alfred Bader," in: *Beyond the Sea of Beer. History of Immigration of Bohemians and Czechs to the New World and their Contri*butions. Bloomington, IN: AuthorHouse, 2017, pp. 550-551.

Ernst Berl (1877-1946), b. Bruntál, Moravia; chemist
Bio: "Ernst Berl," in: Wikipedia. See- https://de.wikipedia.org/wiki/Ernst Berl; Rechcigl, Miloslav, Jr., "Ernst Berl," in: *Encyclopedia of Bohemian and Czech-American Biography*. Bloomington, IN: AuthorHouse, 2016, Vol. 2, pp. 1596-1597.

Erwin Buncel (1931-), b. Prešov, Czech; physical organic chemist, professor, Queens Univ., Canada
Bio: Rechcigl, Miloslav, Jr., "Erwin Buncel," in: *Encyclopedia of Bohemian and Czech-American Biography*. Bloomington, IN: AuthorHouse, 2016, Vol. 2, p. 1685.

Thomas Joseph Katz (1936-), b. Prague, Czech.; organic chemist
Bio: Rechcigl, Miloslav, Jr., "Thomas Joseph Katz," in: *Encyclopedia of Bohemian and Czech-American Biography*. Bloomington, IN: AuthorHouse, 2016, Vol. 2, p. 1616.

Martin Karplus (1930-), b. Vienna, of Moravian ancestry; theoretical chemist, recipient of Nobel Prize in chemistry
Bio: "Martin Karplus," in: Wikipedia. See - https://en.wikipedia.org/wiki/Martin Karplus;

Rechcigl, Miloslav, Jr., Martin Karplus," in: *Encyclopedia of Bohemian and Czech-American Biography*. Bloomington, IN: AuthorHouse, 2016, Vol. 2, pp. 1615-1616.

Gerard Kraus (1920-ca 1990), b. Prague, Czech.; physical chemist
Bio: Rechcigl, Miloslav, Jr., "Gerard Kraus," in: *Encyclopedia of Bohemian and Czech-America Biography*. Bloomington, IN: AuthorHouse, 2016, Vol. 2, p. 1622.

Ernst Mahler (1887-1967), b. Vienna, of Bohemian ancestry; paper chemist
Bio: Rechcigl, Miloslav, Jr., "Ernst Mahler," in: *Encyclopedia of Bohemian and Czech-American Biography*. Bloomington, IN: AuthorHouse, 2016, Vol. 2, pp. 1627.

Herbert Morawetz (1915-2017), b. Prague, Bohemia; polymer chemist
Bio: "Herbert Morawetz Obituary," *The New York Times*, October 31, 2017; Rechcigl, Miloslav, Jr., "Herbert Morawetz," in: *Encyclopedia of Bohemian and Czech-American Biography*. Bloomington, IN: AuthorHouse, 2016, Vol. 2, pp. 1630.

John C. Polanyi (orig. Pollacsek) (1929-), b. Berlin, Ger., of Slovak ancestry, Canadian chemist, recipient of the Nobel Prize in chemistry
Bio: "John Polanyi," in: Wikipedia. See - https://en.wikipedia.org/wiki/John_Polanyi

Otto Redlich (1896-1978), b. Vienna, of Bohemian ancestry; physical chemist, chemical engineer
Bio: "Otto Redlich," in: Wikipedia. See - https://en.wikipedia.org/wiki/Otto_Redlich

Arnold E. Reif (1924-), b. Vienna, of Moravian ancestry; physical chemist, cancer researcher
Bio: Rechcigl, Miloslav, Jr., "Arnold E. Reif," in: *Encyclopedia of Bohemian and Czech-American Biography*. Bloomington, IN: AuthorHouse, 2016, Vol. 2, p. 1504.

Jan Roček (1924-), b. Prague, Czech.; organic chemist, Dean
Bio: Rechcigl, Miloslav, Jr., "Jan Roček," in: *Encyclopedia of Bohemian and Czech-American Biography*. Bloomington, IN: AuthorHouse, 2016, Vol. 2, pp. 1639.

Arnold Weissberger (1898-1984), b. Chemnitz, Saxony, of Bohemian ancestry; chemist
Bio: Fowler, Glenn, "Dr. Arnold Weissberger Dies; Chemist for Eastman Kodak," *The New York Times,* September 7, 1984; Rechcigl, Miloslav, Jr., "Arnold Weissberger," in: *Beyond the Sea of Beer. History of Immigration of Bohemians and Czechs to the New World and their Contri*butions. Bloomington, IN: AuthorHouse, 2017, p. 551.

Stephen S. Winter (1926-), B. Vienna, of Bohemian father; physical chemist
Bio: "Stephen Winter," in: The Chemical Institute of Canada. See - http://www.cheminst.ca/awards/ccucc-chemistry-doctoral-award/stephen-winter

John Henry Wotiz (1919-2000), b. Ostrava, Czech.; chemist
Bio: "John H. Wotiz," in: Wikipedia. See - https://de.wikipedia.org/wiki/John_H._Wotiz;
Rechcigl, Miloslav, Jr., "John Henry Wotiz," in: *Beyond the Sea of Beer. History of Immigration of Bohemians and Czechs to the New World and their Contri*butions. Bloomington, IN: AuthorHouse, 2017, p. 551; "John H. Wotiz," in: School of Chemical Sciences. See - http://www.scs.illinois.edu/~mainzv/HIST/awards/Dexter%20Papers/WotizDexterBioJJB.pdf

3. Geologists

Ernst Robert Deutsch (1924-), b. Frankfurt / Main, of Moravian father from Opava
Bio: Deutsch, Ernst Robert," in: *International Biographical Dictionary of Central European*
Emigrés 1933-1945. Műnchen: K. G. Saur, 1983, Vol. 2, p. 212.

Irene Kaminka Fischer (1907-2009), b. Vienna, of Bohemian mother; geodesist
Bio: Irene Kaminka Fischer, Wikipedia: http://en.wikipedia.org/wiki/Irene Fischer; Lawrence, J. M., "Irene K. Fischer; measured earth; at 102," *The Boston Globe,* October 28, 2009; "Irene K. Fischer," in: *Memorial Tributes.*National Academy of Sciences, 2011, Vol. 14, pp. 78-85.

Otto Henry Haas (1887-1976), b. Brno, Moravia, lawyer, geologist, paleontologist, curator
Bio: "Haas, Otto Henry," in: *International Biographical Dictionary of Central European Emigrés 1933-1945.* Műnchen: K. G. Saur, 1983, Vol. 2, p. 445.

Eric B. Kraus (1913-2003), b. Liberec, Bohemia; geophysicist, meteorologist, professor, Univ. of Miami
Bio: Rechcigl, Miloslav, Jr., "Eric B. Kraus," in: *Encyclopedia of Bohemian and Czech-American Biography.* Bloomington, IN: AuthorHouse, 2016, Vol. 2, pp. 1661.

Ivo Lucchita (1937-), b. České Budějovice, Czech.; geologist, astrogeologist
Bio: Rechcigl, Miloslav, Jr. "Ivo Lucchita," in: *Encyclopedia of Bohemian and Czech-American Biography.* Bloomington, IN: AuthorHouse, 2016, Vol. 2, p. 1663.

4. Mathematicians

Peter George Braunfeld (1930-), b. Vienna, of Moravian father, mathematical educator
Bio: "Braunfeld, Peter George," in: *International Biographical Dictionary of Central European Emigrés 1933-1945.* Műnchen: K. G. Saur, 1983, Vol. 2, p. 147.

William Welch Flexner (1904-1998), b. New York, NY, of Bohemian ancestry; mathematician, professor, Cooper Union
Bio: Rechcigl, Miloslav, Jr., "William Welch Flexner," in: *Encyclopedia of Bohemian and Czech-American Biography.* Bloomington, IN: AuthorHouse, 2016, Vol. 2, p. 1734

Hilda Geiringer (1893-1973), b. Vienna, of Slovak ancestry; mathematician, professor, Wheaton College
Bio: "Hilda Geiringer," in: Wikipedia. See - https://en.wikipedia.org/wiki/Hilda_Geiringer

Heini Halberstam (1926-2014), b. Most, Bohemia; mathematician
Bio: "Heini Halberstam,", in: Wikipedia. See - https://en.wikipedia.org/wiki/Heini_Halberstam

Joseph J. Kohn (1932-), b. Prague, Bohemia; mathematician, professor, Princeton Univ.
Bio: Wikipedia. See: https://en.wikipedia.org/wiki/Joseph J. Kohn; "Joseph John Kohn," Office of the Dean of the Faculty. See: https://dof.princeton.edu/about/clerk-faculty/emeritus/joseph-john-kohn

Robert Kendall Lazarsfeld (1953-), b. New York, NY, of Moravian ancestry; mathematician, Professor, Stony Brook University
Bio: Rechcigl, Miloslav, Jr., "Robert Kendall Lazarsfeld," in: *Encyclopedia of Bohemian and Czech-American Biography*. Bloomington, IN: AuthorHouse, 2016, Vol. 2, p. 1742.

Charles Loewner (1893-1968), b. Prague, Bohemia; mathematician
Bio: Loewner, Charles," in: *International Biographical Dictionary of Central European Emigrés 1933-1945*. Műnchen: K. G. Saur, 1983, Vol. 2, p. 745.

Henry J. Lowig (1904-1995), b. Královské Vinohrady, Prague, Bohemia; mathematician
Bio: Martina Bečvářová et al., *The Forgotten Mathematician Henry Lowig (1904-1995)*. Praha: Matfyzpress, 2012.

Paul Mandl (1917-2010), b. Slavkov, Moravia; Canadian mathematician
Bio: "Mandl, Paul," in: *International Biographical Dictionary of Central European Emigrés 1933-1945*. Műnchen: K. G. Saur, 1983, Vol. 2, p. 767.

Henry Berthold Mann (1905-2000), b. Vienna, of Bohemian ancestry; mathematician, professor

Bio: Rechcigl, Miloslav, Jr., "Henry Berthold Mann," in: *Encyclopedia of Bohemian and Czech-American Biography*. Bloomington, IN: AuthorHouse, 2016, Vol. 2, p. 1743.

Peter E. Ney (1930-), b. Brno, Czech., mathematician
Bio: "Ney, Peter E.," in: *International Biographical Dictionary of Central European Emigrés 1933-1945*. Műnchen: K. G. Saur, 1983, Vol. 2, p. 862; "Peter E. Ney," in: Wikipedia. See - https://de.wikipedia.org/wiki/Peter E. Ney

John Adolph Nohel (1924-1999), b. Prague, Czech.; mathematician, Univ. of Wisconsin, Madison
Bio: Rechcigl, Miloslav, Jr., "John Adolph Nohel," in: *Encyclopedia of Bohemian and Czech-American Biography*. Bloomington, IN: AuthorHouse, 2016, Vol. 2, p. 1744.

Hans Schneider (1927-2014), b. Vienna, of Bohemian ancestry; mathematician
Bio: "Schneider, Hans," in: *International Biographical Dictionary of Central European Emigrés 1933-1945*. Műnchen: K. G. Saur, 1983, Vol. 2, pp. 1042-1043.

Emil Schoenbaum (1882-1967), b. Prague, Bohemia; insurance mathematician and mathematical statistician
Bio: Rechcigl, Miloslav, Jr., "Emil Schoenbaum," in: *Encyclopedia of Bohemian and Czech-America Biography*. Bloomington, IN: AuthorHouse, 2016, Vol. 2, p. 1756.

Olga Taussky-Todd (1906-1995), b. Olomouc, Czech.; mathematician
Bio: Luchins, Edith H., "Olga Taussky-Todd," in: *Women of Mathematics: A Biobibliographic Sourcebook*. Edited by Louise Grinstein and Paul Campbell. Westport, CT: Greenwood Press, 1987; Taylor, Lyn, "Olga Taussky-Todd," in: *Notable Women in Mathematics: A Biographical Dictionary*. Edited by Charlene Morrow and Teri Perl. Westport, CT: Greenwood Press, 1998, pp. 246-252

Hans Felix Weinberger (1928-), b. Vienna, of Bohemian father; mathematician

Bio: Weinberger, Hans Felix," in: *International Biographical Dictionary of Central European Emigrés 1933-1945*. Műnchen: K. G. Saur, 1983, Vol. 2, p. 1222.

František Wolf (1904-1989), b. Prostějov, Moravia, was a Czech mathematician
Bio: František Wolf Bade, William G., Bade, Murray H. Protter and Angus E. Taylor, Angus E., "František Wolf, Mathematics: Berkeley," University of California: In Memoriam, 1991, Academic Senate, University of California.

5. Physicists

Benjamin Abeles (1925-), b. Vienna, of Bohemian ancestry; developer of germanium-silicon alloys used to power space probes
Bio: "Benjamin Abeles," in: Wikipedia. See - https://en.wikipedia.org/wiki/Benjamin Abeles

Guido Beck (1903-1988), b. Liberec, Bohemia; physicist, Argentina
Bio: "Guido Beck," in: Wikipedia. See - https://en.wikipedia.org/wiki/Guido_Beck

George Bekefi (1925-1995), b. Prague, Czech., plasma physicist, inventor, educator
Bio: "George Bekefi," in: Wikipedia. See - https://en.wikipedia.org/wiki/George Bekefi; "George Bekefi, 70, Physics Researcher," *The New York Times*, August 22, 1995.

Peter Gabriel Bergmann (1915-2002), b. Berlin, Ger.; physicist
Bio: "Peter Bergmann," in: Wikipedia. See - https://en.wikipedia.org/wiki/Peter Bergmann; Overbye, Dennis," Peter G. Bergmann, 87; Worked with Einstein," *The New York Times*, October 23, 2002

Frank Joachim Blatt (1924-), b. Vienna, of Bohemian ancestry; physicist
Bio: Rechcigl, Miloslav, Jr., "Frank Joachim Blatt," in: *Encyclopedia of Bohemian and Czech-American Biography*. Bloomington, IN: AuthorHouse, 2016, Vol. 2, p. 1682.

John M. Blatt (1921-1990), b. Vienna, of Moravian mother; physicist, applied mathematician
Bio: Franklin, James, "Profile of a Mathematician: John Blatt," *Parabola,* 37, No. 2 (2001), pp. 15-17; "John Blatt," in: Wikipedia. See - https://de.wikipedia.org/wiki/John_Blatt

Felix Bloch (1905-1983, b. Zürich, Switzerland; physicist; recipient of Nobel Prize in physics
Bio: Shampo, M. A. and R. A. Kyle, "Felix Bloch—developer of magnetic resonance imaging," *Mayo Clin. Proc.* 70 (9) (1995), p. 889ff.; Rechcigl, Miloslav, Jr., "Objevitel nukleární magnetické resonance" (Discoverer of Nuclear Magnetic Resonance), in: *Postavy naší Ameriky.* Praha: Pražská edice, 2000, pp. 298-300.

Ingram Bloch (1920-1995), b. Louisville, KY; of Bohemian ancestry; theoretical physicist, professor, Vanderbilt Univ.
Bio: "Ingram Bloch," *Physics Today*, 49, No. 9 (1996), p. 112.

Otto Blűh (1902-11981), b. Ostrava, Moravia; physicist
Bio: "Otto Bluh," in: *Encyclopedia of Bohemian and Czech-American Biography.* Bloomington, IN: AuthorHouse, 2016, Vol. 2, p. 1683.

Henry Victor Bohm (1929-2011), b. Vienna, of Moravian ancestry; physicist, professor, Wayne State Univ.
Bio: Rechcigl, Miloslav, Jr., "Henry Victor Bohm," in: *Encyclopedia of Bohemian and Czech-American Biography.* Bloomington, IN: AuthorHouse, 2016, Vol. 2, p. 1684.

Otto Brill (1881-1954), b. Pardubice, Bohemia; atomic physicist, ezpert on radioactivity, director of Vanadium Corp. in US, the largest producer of radium and uranium
Bio: "Otto Brill, Dr.," in: GENi.

Leo Diesendruck (1920-2011), b. České Budějovice, Czech.; physicist, professor, Queens Coll., NY

Bio: Rechcigl, Miloslav, Jr., "Leo Diesendruck," in: *Encyclopedia of Bohemian and Czech-American Biography*. Bloomington, IN: AuthorHouse, 2016, Vol. 2, p. 1687.

George Feher (1924-2017), b. Bratislava, Czech.; physicist and biophysicist
Bio: "George Feher," in: Wikipedia. See: https://en.wikipedia.org/wiki/George_Feher; "George G Feher 1924-2017," in: LaJolla Light Obituaries. See: http://www.legacy.com/obituaries/lajollalight/obituary.aspx?n=&pid=187592684&referrer=0&preview=True

Leslie Lawrence Foldy (1919-2001), b. Sabinov, Czech.; theoretical physicist
Bio: "Obituaries: Leslie Lawrence Foldy," *Physics Today*, 52, No. 12 (2001), p. 75; Leslie Lawrence Foldy," in: Wikipedia. See- https://en.wikipedia.org/wiki/Leslie_Lawrance_Foldy

Philipp Frank (1884-1966), b. Vienna, physicist, mathematician, philosopher, held professorship at Prague University
Bio: Rechcigl, Miloslav, Jr., "Philipp G. Frank," in: *Encyclopedia of Bohemian and Czech-American Biography*. Bloomington, IN: AuthorHouse, 2016, Vol. 2, p. 1175; Wikipedia. See: https://en.wikipedia.org/wiki/Philipp Frank

David Jonathan Gross (1941-), b. Washington, DC., of Czechoslovak ancestry; physicist, recipient of the Nobel Prize
Bio: Rechcigl, Miloslav, Jr., "David Jonathan Gross," in: *Encyclopedia of Bohemian and Czech-American Biography*. Bloomington, IN: AuthorHouse, 2016, Vol. 2, p. 1691.

Peter Andreas Grűnberg (1839-), b. Pilsen, Bohemia; physicist, recipient of Nobel Prize in physics
Bio: "Peter Grűnberg," in: Wikipedia. See - https://en.wikipedia.org/wiki/Peter Greenberg;
Rechcigl, Miloslav, Jr., "Peter Andreas Grűnberg," in: *Encyclopedia of Bohemian and Czech-American Biography*. Bloomington, IN: AuthorHouse, 2016, Vol. 2, p. 1691.

Arthur Erich Haas (1884-1941), b. Brno, Moravia; physicist

Bio: "Haas, Arthur Erich," in: *International Biographical Dictionary of Central European Emigrés 1933-1945*. Műnchen: K. G. Saur, 1983, Vol. 2, p. 443-444.

George Arthur Haas (1926-), b. Vienna, of Moravian ancestry; physicist
Bio: Rechcigl, Miloslav, Jr., "George Arthur Haas," in: *Encyclopedia of Bohemian and Czech-American Biography*. Bloomington, IN: AuthorHouse, 2016, Vol. 2, p. 1692.

Alex Harwit (ca. 1960), b. US, of Czech ancestry; applied and engineering physicist,
Bio: Rechcigl, Miloslav, Jr., "Alex Harwit," in: *Encyclopedia of Bohemian and Czech-American Biography*. Bloomington, IN: AuthorHouse, 2016, Vol. 2, p. 1692.

Heinz Kurt Heinisch (1922-2006), b. Nejdek, Czech.; physicist, historian of photography
Bio: Rechcigl, Miloslav, Jr., "Heinz Kurt Heinisch," in: *Encyclopedia of Bohemian and Czech-America Biography*. Bloomington, IN: AuthorHouse, 2016, Vol. 2, p. 1692-1693; Smeltz, Adam, "Heinz K. Heinisch; physicist & photographic historian," *Centre Daily Times* (Pennsylvania), March 24, 2006.

Karl Ferdinand Herzfeld (1892-1978), b. Vienna, of Moravian mother, physicist, professor, Catholic Univ.
Bio: "Karl Herzfeld," in: Wikipedia. See - https://en.wikipedia.org/wiki/Karl Herzfeld; Rechcigl, Miloslav, Jr., "Karl Ferdinand Herzfeld," in: *Encyclopedia of Bohemian and Czech-America Biography*. Bloomington, IN: AuthorHouse, 2016, Vol. 2, p. 1693-1694.

Frederick de Hoffmann (1924-1989), b. Vienna, raised in Czechoslovakia; nuclear physicist, with Manhattan Projet, president, Salk Inst.
Bio: Rechcigl, Miloslav, Jr., "Frederick de Hoffmann," in: *Encyclopedia of Bohemian and Czech-America Biography*. Bloomington, IN: AuthorHouse, 2016, Vol. 2, p. 1687; "Frederick de Hoffman," in: WikiVisually. See - https://wikivisually.com/wiki/Frederic_de_Hoffmann

Robert Karplus (1927-1990), b. Vienna, of Bohemian ancestry; theoretical physicist
Bio: "Robert Karplus," in Wikipedia. See - https://en.wikipedia.org/wiki/Robert Karplus;
"Robert Karplus, 63; Professor Improved Teaching of Science," *The New York Times*, March 24, 1990

Walter Kohn (1923-), Vienna, of Moravian ancestry; physicist, recipient of Nobel Prize in chemistry
Bio: "Walter Kohn," in: *National Cyclopaedia of American Biography*. James T. White & Co. 1984, Vol. 61, pp. 310–312; Kohn, Walter, "Autobiography," in: *Les Prix Nobel. The Nobel Prizes 1998.* Edited by Tore Frängsmyr, Stockholm: Nobel Foundation, 1999; Rechcigl, Miloslav, Jr., "Walter Kohn," in: *Beyond the Sea of Beer. History of Immigration of Bohemians and Czechs to the New World and their Contri*butions. Bloomington, IN: AuthorHouse, 2017, pp. 495-486.

Herta Regina Leng (1903-1997)), b. Vienna, of Bohemian mother; physicist
Bio: "Herta Regina Leng," in: Wikipedia. See - https://en.wikipedia.org/wiki/Herta Regina Leng; Rechcigl, Miloslav Jr., "Herta Regina Leng," in: *Encyclopedia of Bohemian and Czech-America Biography*. Bloomington, IN: AuthorHouse, 2016, Vol. 2, p. 1703.

Ralph Pokorny Levey, Jr. (1923-1965), b. New Orleans, LA, of Moravian ancestry; nuclear physicist, inventor, with the Manhattan Project
Bio: "Levey, 42, Took Part in A-Bomb Project," *New Orleans Times-Picayune*, October 19, 1965.

Douglas Osheroff (1945-), b. Aberdeen, WA, of Slovak ancestry; physicist, recipient of the Nobel Prize
Bio: "Douglas Osheroff," in Wikipedia. See - https://en.wikipedia.org/wiki/Douglas_Osheroff

Wolfgang Pauli (1900-1958), b. Vienna, of Bohemian ancestry; theoretical physicist

Bio: Enz, Charles P., *No Time to be Brief, A scientific biography of Wolfgang Pauli.* Oxford Univ. Press, 2002; Laurikainen, K. V., *Beyond the Atom – The Philosophical Thought of Wolfgang Pauli.* Berlin: Springer Verlag, 1988; Lindorff, David, *Pauli and Jung: The Meeting of Two Great Minds.* Quest Books, 1994.

Albert G. Peschek (1928-2004), b. Prague, Czech.; theoretical physicist, Los Alamos
Bio: *Bulletin of Am. Astronomical Society*, 37, No. 4, pp. 1554-15555.

Harry E. Petschek (1930-2005), b. Prague, Czech.; physicist
Bio: Rechcigl, Miloslav, Jr., "Harry E. Petschek," in: *Encyclopedia of Bohemian and Czech-American Biography.* Bloomington, IN: AuthorHouse, 2016, Vol. 2, p. 1710.

Rolfe George Petschek (1954-), b. Los Alamos, NM, of Bohemian ancestry; physicist, professor, Case Western Reserve Univ.
Bio: Rechcigl, Miloslav, Jr., "Rolfe George Petrschek," in: *Encyclopedia of Bohemian and Czech-American Biography.* Bloomington, IN: AuthorHouse, 2016, Vol. 2, pp. 1710-1711.

George Placzek (1905-1955), b. Brno, Moravia; physicist
Bio: Cassidy, David C., "Placzek, George," in: *Dictionary of Scientific Biography*, Suppl. 2, Vol. 18, pp. 714-715._Fischer, J. "George Placzek - an Unsung Hero of Physics," *Cern Courier*, 45, No. 7 (2005), pp. 25-27; Gottvald, A., "Kdo byl Georg Placzek (1905-1955," *Čs. čas. fyz.*, 55, No. 3 (2005), pp. 275-287; Van Hove, Leon, "George Placzek, 1905-1955," *Nuclear Physics* 1 (1956), pp. 623-626.

Michael Pollak (1926-), b. Ostrava-Vítkovice, Czech.; physicist, professor, University of California, Riverside
Bio: Rechcigl, Miloslav, Jr., "Michael Pollak," in: *Encyclopedia of Bohemian and Czech-American Biography.* Bloomington, IN: AuthorHouse, 2016, Vol. 2, p. 1713.

Karl Gustav Porges (1920-), b. Vienna, of Bohemian ancestry; physicist, Argonne Nat. Lab.

Bio: Rechcigl, Miloslav, Jr., "Karl Gustav Porges," in: *Encyclopedia of Bohemian and Czech-American Biography*. Bloomington, IN: AuthorHouse, 2016, Vol. 2, p. 1713.

John Karl Pribram (1941-), b. Chicago, IL, of Bohemian ancestry; physicist, professor, Bates College, Lewiston, MA
Bio: Rechcigl, Miloslav, Jr., "John Karl Pribram," in: *Encyclopedia of Bohemian and Czech-American Biography*. Bloomington, IN: AuthorHouse, 2016, Vol. 2, p. 1713.

Martin Roček (1954-), b. Prague, Czech.; theoretical physicist, professor, SUNY, Stony Brook
Bio: "Martin Roček," in: Wikipedia. See - https://en.wikipedia.org/wiki/Martin_Roček

Fritz Rohrlich (1921-), b. Vienna, of Bohemian mother; physicist
Bio: "Fritz Rohrlich," in: Wikipedia. See - https://en.wikipedia.org/wiki/Fritz Rohrlich; Rechcigl, Miloslav, JR., "Fritz Rohrlich," in: *Encyclopedia of Bohemian and Czech-American Biography*. Bloomington, IN: AuthorHouse, 2016, Vol. 2, p. 1715.

Marcel Schein (1902-1960), b. Trstená, Slovakia; physicist
Bio: "Marcel Schein," in Wikipedia. See - https://en.wikipedia.org/wiki/Marcel Schein; "Obituary: Prof. Marcel Schein," Nature 186 (1960), pp. 355-356.

William Taussig Scott (1916-1999), b. Yonkers, NY, of Bohemian ancestry; physicist
Bio: Rechcigl, Miloslav, Jr., "William Taussig Scott," in: *Encyclopedia of Bohemian and Czech-American Biography*. Bloomington, IN: AuthorHouse, 2016, Vol. 2, pp. 1716.

David P. Stern (1931-), b. Podmokly nad Labem, Bohemia; physicist, Goddard Space Flight Center, Greenbelt, MD
Bio: Rechcigl, Miloslav, Jr., "David P. Stern," in: *Encyclopedia of Bohemian and Czech-American Biography*. Bloomington, IN: AuthorHouse, 2016, Vol. 2, pp. 1718-1719.

Leo Szilard (orig. Spitz) (1898-1964), b. Budapest, Hungary, of Slovak father; physicist
Bio: "Leo Szilard," in: Wikipedia. See - https://en.wikipedia.org/wiki/Leo Szilard; "Leo Szilard," in: Atomic Heritage Foundation. See - https://www.atomicheritage.org/profile/leo-szilard

Gerald Erich Tauber (1922-1989), b. Vienna, of Moravia ancestry; physicist
Bio: Rechcigl, Miloslav, Jr., "Gerard Erich Tauber," in: *Encyclopedia of Bohemian and Czech-American Biography.* Bloomington, IN: AuthorHouse, 2016, Vol. 2, p. 1720.

Edward Teller (1908-2003), b. Budapest, of Slovak ancestry; theoretical physicist, father of the hydrogen bomb
Bio: "Edward Teller," in: Wikipedia. See - https://en.wikipedia.org/wiki/Edward Teller; Blumberg, Stanley A., and Louis G. Panos, *Edward Teller: Giant of the Golden Age of Physics; a Biography. New York:* Scribner's, 1990; Hargittai, Istvan, *Judging Edward Teller: A Closer Look at One of the Most Influential Scientists of the Twentieth Century.* Amherst, NY: Prometheus, 2010.

Georges Maxime Temmer (1922-1997), b. Vienna, of Bohemian ancestry; physicist
Bio: Rechcigl, Miloslav, Jr., "Georges Maxime Temmer," in: *Encyclopedia of Bohemian and Czech-American Biography.* Bloomington, IN: AuthorHouse, 2016, Vol. 2, pp. 1721.

Harold Ticho (1921-), b. Brno, Czech; physicist
Bio: Rechcigl, Miloslav, Jr., "Harold Ticho," in: *Encyclopedia of Bohemian and Czech-American Biography.* Bloomington, IN: AuthorHouse, 2016, Vol. 2, p. 1721.

Victor F. Weisskopf (1909-2002), b. Vienna, of Bohemian father; physicist
Bio: Jackson, J. David and Kurt Gottfried, *Victor F. Weisskopf, 1908-2003. A Biographical Memoir.* Washington, DC: National Academy of Sciences, 2003; *Physics and Society*, Essays in Honor of Victor Frederick Weisskopf by the International Community of Physicists, Ed. by V. Stefan. New

York: Springer Verlag, 1998. 236p.; "Weisskopf Dies at 93; was protégé of physicist Niels Bohr," *MIT News*, April 24, 2002.

Emil Wolf (1922-), b. Prague, Czech; physicist, specializing in physical optics
Bio: "Emil Wolf,", in: Jew Age. See - http://www.jewage.org/wiki/en/Article:Emil Wolf - Biography; Emil Wolf," in: Wikipedia. See - https://en.wikipedia.org/wiki/Emil Wolf

Lincoln Wolfenstein (1923-), b. Cleveland, OH, of Moravin ancestry; physicist, professor, Carnegie-Mellon Univ.
Bio: Rechcigl, Miloslav, Jr., "Lincoln Wolfenstein," in: *Encyclopedia of Bohemian and Czech-American Biography*. Bloomington, IN: AuthorHouse, 2016, Vol. 2, p. 1729.

G. Engineering

1. Acoustical Engineers

Gerhard Reethof (1922-2002), b. Teplice-Šanov, Bohemia; mechanical and acoustical engineer
Bio: Rechcigl, Miloslav, Jr., "Gerhard Reethof," in: *Encyclopedia of Bohemian and Czech-American Biography*. Bloomington, IN: AuthorHouse, 2016, Vol. 2, pp. 1785.

2. Aeronautical Engineers

Karl Arnstein (1887-1974), b. Prague, Bohemia; airship engineer and designer
Bio: *When Giants Roared the Sky. Karl Arnstein and the Rise of Airships from Zeppelin to Goodyear.* Edited by Eric Brothers. Akron, OH: Akron University Press, 2007. 276p.; "Karl Arnstein," in: Wikipedia. See - https://en.wikipedia.org/wiki/Karl_Arnstein

Peter Glaser (1923-2014), b. Žatec, Czech; mechanical and aerospace engineer

Bio: Rechcigl, Miloslav, Jr., "Peter Glaser," in: *Encyclopedia of Bohemian and Czech-America Biography*. Bloomington, IN: AuthorHouse, 2016, Vol. 2, p. 1788.

Theodore von Karman (1881-1963), b. Budapest, of Bohemian ancestry; aerospace engineer, physicist
Bio: Gorn, M. H., The Universal Man: Theodore von Kármán's Life in Aeronautics. Washington, DC: Smithsonian Institution Press, 1992; Hall, R.C., "Shaping the course of aeronautics, rocketry, and astronautics: Theodore von Kármán, 1881–1963," *J. Astronaut. Sci.*, 26, No. 4 (1978), pp. 369–386; Wattendorf, F. L., Malina, F. J., "Theodore von Kármán, 1881–1963," *Astronautica Acta,* 10 (1964), p. 81.

Wolfgang Klemperer (1893-1965), b. Dresden, Ger., of Bohemian father; aviation and aerospace engineer
Bio: Rechcigl, Miloslav, Jr., "Wolfgang Benjamin Klemperer," in: *Encyclopedia of Bohemian and Czech-America Biography*. Bloomington, IN: AuthorHouse, 2016, Vol. 2, p. 1790;
"Wolfgang Klemperer," in: Wikipedia. See - https://en.wikipedia.org/wiki/Wolfgang Klemperer

Arnold Polak (1927-), b. Michalovce, Czech.; aerospace engineer
Bio: "Rechcigl, mloslav, Jr., "Arnold Polak," in: *Encyclopedia of Bohemian and Czech-America Biography*. Bloomington, IN: AuthorHouse, 2016, Vol. 2, p. 1791

3. Bioengineers

Samuel Meerbaum (1919-2008), b. Brno, Czech.; bioengineer
Bio: Rechcigl, Miloslav, Jr., "Samuel Meerbaum," in: *Encyclopedia of Bohemian and Czech-America Biography*. Bloomington, IN: AuthorHouse, 2016, Vol. 2, p. 1796.

Charles Susskind (1919-2004), b. Prague, Czech.; electrical engineer, co-founder of bioengineering at Univ. ofCalifornia, Berkeley

Bio: Rechcigl, Miloslav, Jr., "Charles Susskind," in: *Encyclopedia of Bohemian and Czech-America Biography*. Bloomington, IN: AuthorHouse, 2016, Vol. 2, pp. 1797-1798.

4. Chemical Engineers

Zola Gotthard Deutsch (1899-1965), b. Cincinnati, OH, of Moravian father; chemical engineer
Bio: Rechcigl, Miloslav, Jr., "Zola Gotthard Deutsch,", in: *Encyclopedia of Bohemian and Czech-America Biography*. Bloomington, IN: AuthorHouse, 2016, Vol. 2, p. 1799.

Harry G. Drickammer (orig. Weidenthal) (1918-2002), b. Cleveland, OH; chemical engineer and physical chemist
Bio: Rechcigl, Miloslav, Jr., "Harry G. Drickammer," in: *Beyond the Sea of Beer. History of Immigration of Bohemians and Czechs to the New World and their Contri*butions. Bloomington, IN: AuthorHouse, 2017, p. 766.

Frank C. Steiner (1922-2000), b. Prague, Czech.; chemical engineer, General Electric Co.
Bio: Rechcigl, Miloslav, Jr., "Frank C. Steiner," in: *Encyclopedia of Bohemian and Czech-America Biography*. Bloomington, IN: AuthorHouse, 2016, Vol. 2, p. 1808.

Paul Burg Weisz (1919-2012), b. Pilsen, Czech.; elecronics engineer
Bio: Degnan, Thomas F., Jr., "Paul B. Weisz," in: *Memorial Tributes*. Washington, DC: National Academies Press, 2015, Vol. 19, pp. 311-315; "Paul Burg Weisz," in: Prabook. See - https://prabook.com/web/paul_burg.weisz/1451211

Paul F. Winternitz (1891-1983), b. Vienna, of Bohemian ancestry; chemical engineer
Bio: Rechcigl, Miloslav, Jr., "Paul Winternitz," in: *Encyclopedia of Bohemian and Czech-America Biography*. Bloomington, IN: AuthorHouse, 2016, Vol. 2, p. 1810.

5. Civil Engineers

Paul William Abeles (18897-d.), b. Mistebach, Aust., of Moravian father; civil engineer
Bio: "Abeles, Paul William," in: *Handbuch österreichischer Autorinnen und Autoren jüdischer Herkunft: 18. bis 20. Jahrhundert,* Band 1, A-I, p. 2.

Oliver Freud (18911-1969), b. Vienna, of Moravian ancestry; son of Sigmund Freud; chemical enf gineer
Bio: Rechcigl, Miloslav, Jr., "Oliver Freud," in: *Encyclopedia of Bohemian and Czech-America Biography.* Bloomington, IN: AuthorHouse, 2016, Vol. 2, p. 1814.

Alfred M. Freudenthal (1906-1977), b. Poland, trained in Prague; civil engineer, materials science engineer, professor, George Washington Univ.
Bio: Hailey, Jean R., "Alfred M. Freudenthal, 71, GW Engineering Professor," *The Washington Post,* October 1, 1977.

Henry Goldmark (1857-1941), b. New York, NY, of Bohemian ancestry; civil engineer, designer and installer of the Panama Canal lock
Bio: Rechcigl, Miloslav, Jr., "Henry Goldmark," in: *Encyclopedia of Bohemian and Czech-America Biography.* Bloomington, IN: AuthorHouse, 2016, Vol. 2, p. 1815; "Henry C. Goldmark," in: Wikipedia. See - https://en.wikipedia.org/wiki/Henry_C._Goldmark

Abraham Gottlieb (1837-1894), b. Domažlice, Bohemia; civil engineer, materials science engineer
Bio: JewishEncyclopedia. Com. See: http://www.jewishencyclopedia.com/articles/6829-gottlieb-abraham

Gustav Lindenthal (1850-1935), b. Brno, Moravia; civil engineer, master bridge builder
Bio: Cross, Hardy, "Lindenthal, Gustav," in: *Dictionary of American Biography* 8, Suppl. 1, pp. 498-49; Rechcigl, Miloslav, Jr., "Mistrný stavitel mostů v Americe" (Master Builder of Bridges in America), in: *Postavy naší Ameriky.* Praha: Pražská edice, 2000, pp. 335-336.

Hubert Primm Taussig (1854-), b. St. Louis, MO, of Bohemian ancestry; civil engineer, St. Louis, MO
Bio: "Taussig, Hubert Primm," in: *The Book of St. Louisans.* 2nd ed. Chicago: A. N. Marquis & Co., 1912, p. 587.

6. Computer Scientists

Franz Leopold Alt (1910-2011), b. of Moravian parents; computer scientist
Bio: "Alt, Franz Leopold," in: *International Biographical Dictionary of Central European Emigrés 1933-1945.* Műnchen: K. G. Saur, 1983, Vol. 2, pp. 20-21.

Růžena Bajcsy (1933-), b. Bratislava, Slovakia; computer scientist, specializing in robotics
Bio: "Růžena Bajcsy," in: Wikipedia. See - https://en.wikipedia.org/wiki/Ruzena Bajcsy

Frederick Jelinek (1932-2010), b. Kladno, Czech.; information-theoretic linguist
Bio: "Frederick Jelinek (1932-2010)," in: *Memorial Tributes.* Washington, DC: The National Academies Press, 2011, Vol. 15, pp. 215-217.

Kevin Karplus (1954-), b. Chicago, IL, of Moravian ancestry; computer scientist, electrical engineer
Bio: Rechcigl, Miloslav, Jr., "Kevin Karplus," in: *Encyclopedia of Bohemian and Czech-American Biography.* Bloomington, IN: AuthorHouse, 2016, Vol. 2, pp. 1765.

Raymond 'Ray' Kurzweil (1948-), b. Queens, NYC, of Moravian ancestry; computer scientist, inventor, futurist
Bio: "Ray Kurzweil," in: Wikipedia. See - https://en.wikipedia.org/wiki/Ray_Kurzweil

7. Electrical Engineers

Fred Alt (1912-1967), b. Vienna, of Moravian parents; electrical engineer

Bio: Rechcigl, Miloslav, Jr., "Fred Alt," in: *Encyclopedia of Bohemian and Czech-America Biography*. Bloomington, IN: AuthorHouse, 2016, Vol. 2, p. 1825-1826.

Charles Leo Eidlitz (1866-1951), b. New York, NY, of Bohemian ancestry; electrical engineer
Bio: Rechcigl, Miloslav, Jr., "Charles Leo Eidlitz," in: *Encyclopedia of Bohemian and Czech-America Biography*. Bloomington, IN: AuthorHouse, 2016, Vol. 2, p. 1831.

Paul Eisler (1907-1992), b. Vienna, of Bohemian ancestry; electrical engineer, inventor, pioneer of printed circuit
Bio: "Paul Eisler," in: Wikipedia. See - https://en.wikipedia.org/wiki/Paul Eisler; "Obitaury: Paul Eisler," *The Independent*, October 29, 1992.

Gustav Frederick Haas (1927-), b. Vienna, of Moravian ancestry; electrical engineer, audiologist
Bio: Rechcigl, Miloslav, Jr., "Gustav Frederick Haas," in: *Encyclopedia of Bohemian and Czech-America Biography*. Bloomington, IN: AuthorHouse, 2016, Vol. 2, p. 1832.

Arthur Aron Hamerschlag (1872-1927), b. New York City, of Bohemian ancestry; electrical and mechanical engineer, first president of Carnegie Mellon University, Pittsburgh
Bio: Fenton, Edwin, *Carnegie Mellon 1900-2000: A Centennial History*. Pittsburgh: Carnegie Mellon University Press, 2000; "Arthur Hamerschlag," in: Wikipedia. See: https://en.wikipedia.org/wiki/Arthur Hamerschlag

Frederick Jelinek (1932-2010), b. nr. Prague, Bohemia; computer scientist, pioneer in speech recognition
Bio: "Fred Jelinek," in: Wikipedia. See: https://en.wikiquote.org/wiki/Fred Jelinek ; Loh, Steve, "Frederick Jelinek, Who Gave Machines the Key to Human Speech, Dies at 77," *The New York Times*, September 24, 2010; Young, Steven, "Frederick Jelinek 1932–2010: The Pioneer of Speech Recognition Technology," *Speech and Language Processing Technical Committee Newsletter*, 2010

Charles Susskind (1919-2004), b. Prague, Czech.; electrical engineer, co-founder of bioengineering studies
Bio: Rechcigl, Miloslav, Jr., "Charles Susskind," in: *Encyclopedia of Bohemian and Czech-America Biography*. Bloomington, IN: AuthorHouse, 2016, Vol. 2, p. 1797-1798; Eskenazi, Joe, "Charles Susskind, professor and author, dies at 82," *The Jewish News of Northern California*, June 25, 2004.

8. Geotechnical Engineers

Karl Terzaghi (1883-1963), b. Prague, Bohemia; civil and geotechnical engineer, geologist
Bio: Goodman, Richard E., *Karl Terzaghi: The Engineer as Artist*. ASCE Press, 1998. 355p.;
Goodman, Richard E., "Karl Terzaghi's Legacy in Geotechnical Engineering," *Geo-Strata Magazine of the ASCE*, October 2002; Terzaghi, Karl, *From Theory to Practice in Soil Mechanics: Selections from the writings of Karl Terzaghi*, with bibliography and contributions on his life and achievements. New York: Wiley, 1967. 425p.

9. Industrial Engineers

John Emanuel Ullmann (1923-2010), b. Vienna, of Moravian father; industrial engineer, professor, Hofstra Coll.
Bio: Rechcigl, Miloslav, Jr., "John Emanuel Ullmann," in: *Encyclopedia of Bohemian and Czech-America Biography*. Bloomington, IN: AuthorHouse, 2016, Vol. 2, p. 1855.

10. Material Science Engineers

Norbert J. Kreidl (1904-1994), b. Vienna, of Bohemian ancestry; materials science expert specializing in glass and ceramics
Bio: Rechcigl, Miloslav, Jr., "Norbert Joachim Kreidl," in: *Encyclopedia of Bohemian and Czech-America Biography*. Bloomington, IN: AuthorHouse, 2016, Vol. 2, p. 1087

11. Mechanical Engineers

Alfred Basch (1882-1958), b. Prague, Bohemia; mechanical engineer, mathematician
Bio: "Alfred Basch," in: Wikipedia. See - https://de.wikipedia.org/wiki/Alfred Basch

Itzhak Bentov (1923-1979), b. Humenné, Slovakia; amateur inventor, mystic, author
Bio: "Itzhak Bentov," in:
Wikipedia. See - https://en.wikipedia.org/wiki/Itzhak_Bentov

Herbert Deresiewicz (1925-2008), b. Brno, Czech.; mechanical engineer, professor, Columbia University
Bio: Rechcigl, Miloslav, Jr., "Herbert Deresiewicz," in: *Encyclopedia of Bohemian and Czech-America Biography.* Bloomington, IN: AuthorHouse, 2016, Vol. 2, p. 1862.

Adolph G. Hochbaum (1889-), b. Ozarov, Czech.; mechanical engineer, with Baldwin Locomotive Works, Philadelphia
Bio: Rechcigl, Miloslav, Jr., "Adolph G. Hochman," in: *Encyclopedia of Bohemian and Czech-America Biography.* Bloomington, IN: AuthorHouse, 2016, Vol. 2, p. 1865.

Harry Kraus (1932-1983), b. Ústí nad Labem, Czech.; mechanical engineer, professor, Rensselaer Polytechnic Inst., Dean
Bio: Rechcigl, Miloslav, Jr., "Harry Kraus," in: *Encyclopedia of Bohemian and Czech-America Biography.* Bloomington, IN: AuthorHouse, 2016, Vol. 2, p. 1868.

Erwin Loewy (1897-1959), b. Pilsen, Bohemia; mechanical engineer, hydraulic engineer
Bio: Records of Ludwig and Erwin Loewy, Lehigh University, Linderman Library, Special Collections. Bethlehem, PA

Ludwig Loewy (1887-1942), b. Pilsen, Bohemia; mechanical engineer, hydraulic engineer

Bio: Records of Ludwig and Erwin Loewy, Lehigh University, Linderman Library, Special Collections. Bethlehem, PA

Mathias Paul Leopold Siebel (1924-2006); b. Witten, Ger., of Bohemian father; mechanical engineer
Bio: "Mathias Paul Sieibel," in: Prabook. See - https://prabook.com/web/mathias_paul.siebel/462692

William Marcus Rosewater (1870-1935), b. Cleveland, OH, of Bohemian ancestry; mechanical engineer
Bio: Rechcigl, Miloslav, Jr., "William Marcus Rosewater," in: *Encyclopedia of Bohemian and Czech-America Biography*. Bloomington, IN: AuthorHouse, 2016, Vol. 2, p. 1875.

Lewis Weiner (1910-2003), b. Klatovy, Bohemia; mechanical engineer, with Walt Disney Productions, Los Angeles
Bio: Rechcigl, Miloslav, Jr., "Lewis Weiner," in: *Encyclopedia of Bohemian and Czech-America Biography*. Bloomington, IN: AuthorHouse, 2016, Vol. 2, p. 1882.

12. Metallurgical Engineers

Henry Hahn (1928-2007), b. Brno, Czech.; metallurgist, philatelist
Bio: Rechcigl, Miloslav, Jr., "Henry Hahn," in: *Encyclopedia of Bohemian and Czech-America Biography*. Bloomington, IN: AuthorHouse, 2016, Vol. 2, p. 1884.

13. Sanitary Engineers

Andrew Rosewater (1848-1909), b. Bukovany, Bohemia; civil and sanitary engineer
Bio: Rechcigl, Miloslav, Jr., "Andrew Rosewater," in: *Encyclopedia of Bohemian and Czech American Biography*. Bloomington, IN: AuthorHouse, 2016, Vol. 2, p. 1823; "Rosewater, Andrew," in: JewishEncyclopedia.com - http://www.jewishencyclopedia.com/articles/12884-rosewater-andrew

I. Exploration, Adventure, Espionage

1. Astronauts

Michael Fincke (1967-), b. Pittsburgh, PA, of Slovak ancestry; astronaut
Bio: "Michael Fincke," in: Wikipedia. See - https://en.wikipedia.org/wiki/Michael Fincke

George David Low (1956-2008), b. Berea, OH, of Czech ancestry; aeronautical engineer, aerospace executive and a NASA astronaut
Bio: Rechcigl, Miloslav, Jr., "George David Low," in: *Encyclopedia of Bohemian and Czech American Biography*. Bloomington, IN: AuthorHouse, 2016, Vol. 3, pp. 2207-2208; "G. David Low," in: Wikipedia. See - https://en.wikipedia.org/wiki/G. David Low; "G. David Low Nasa Astronaut (Deceased)," in: NASA Lyndon B. Johnson Space Center - Biographical Data. See - https://www.jsc.nasa.gov/Bios/htmlbios/low.html

2. Aviators and Navigators

Karl Arnstein (1887-1974), b. Prague, Bohemia; airship engineer, first who crossed the Atlantic with his famous airship 'Los Angeles'
Bio: Rechcigl, Miloslav, Jr., "Karl Arnstein," in: *Encyclopedia of Bohemian and Czech American Biography*. Bloomington, IN: AuthorHouse, 2016, Vol. 3, p. 2208.

3. Other Explorers and Adventurers

August Bondi (1833-1907), b. Vienna, of Bohemian parents; abolitionist, member of John Brown's military group against terrorism of 'Border Ruffians' in Kansas
Bio: Rechcigl, Miloslav, Jr., "August Bondi," in: *Encyclopedia of Bohemian and Czech American Biography*. Bloomington, IN: AuthorHouse, 2016, Vol. 3, p. 2210.

Alexander Eisenschiml (1838-1879), b. Měčín, Bohemia; veteran of US Civil War, Indian Scout

Bio: Rechcigl, Miloslav, Jr., "Alexander Eisenschiml," in: *Encyclopedia of Bohemian and Czech-American Biography*. Bloomington, IN: AuthorHouse, 2016, Vol. 2, p. 2181.

4. Forty-Eighter Revolutionaries

Isidor Bush (1822-1898), b. Prague, Bohemia; publisher of revolutionary papers in Vienna, had to escape to NYC in January 1849, where he published the first Jewish papers in US
Bio: Rechcigl, Miloslav, Jr., "Isidor Bush," in: *Encyclopedia of Bohemian and Czech-American Biography*. Bloomington, IN: AuthorHouse, 2016, Vol. 1, Vol. 1, pp. 42-43.

Adolph Huebsch (1830-1884), b. Liptovský Svätý Mikuláš, Slovakia; officer in in the Hungarian Revolutionary Army
Bio: Rechcigl, Miloslav, Jr., "Adolph Huebsch," in: *Beyond the Sea of Beer.* History of Immigration of Bohemians and Czechs to the New World and their Contributions. Bloomington, IN: AuthorHouse, 2017, p. 45.

Philip Korn, bookseller from Bratislava; Captain in the Hungarian Revolutionary Army, managed escaped to US
Bio: Rechcigl, Miloslav, Jr., "Adolph Huebsch," in: *Beyond the Sea of Beer.* History of Immigration of Bohemians and Czechs to the New World and their Contributions. Bloomington, IN: AuthorHouse, 2017, p. 46.

Josef Lewi (1820-1897), b. Radnice, Bohemia; one of the intellectuals who inspired the Revolution of 1848, future physician in Albany, NY
Bio: Rechcigl, Miloslav, Jr., "Joseph Lewi," in: *Encyclopedia of Bohemian and Czech American Biography*. Bloomington, IN: AuthorHouse, 2016, Vol. 1, p. 46.

Oswald Ottendorfer (1826-1900), b. Svitavy, Moravia; a member of Student Legion, fought at Schleswick-Holstein, Dresden and in Prague, future newspaper editor and publisher in NYC
Bio: Rechcigl, Miloslav, Jr., "Oswald Ottendorfer," in: *Encyclopedia of Bohemian and Czech American Biography*. Bloomington, IN: AuthorHouse, 2016, Vol. 1, p. 48.

James Taussig (1827-1916), b. Prague, Bohemia; member of student revolutionary bands until occupation of Prague by Austrian troops, had to flee and immigrate to the US, then practiced law in St. Louis
Bio: Rechcigl, Miloslav, Jr. "James Taussig," in: *Encyclopedia of Bohemian and Czech American Biography*. Bloomington, IN: AuthorHouse, 2016, Vol. 1, pp. 51-52

Benjamin Szold (1829-1902); b. Zemianske Sady, Slovakia; future Rabbi, for his participation in the Revolution of 1848 was expelled from Vienna where he studied
Bio: "Benjamin Szold," in: Wikipedia. See - https://en.wikipedia.org/wiki/Benjamin_Szold

Charles Wehle (1827-1900), b. Hungary, of Bohemian ancestry; officer in Kossuth's Army, sentenced to death but succeeded in escaping to the US, practiced law in NYC
Bio: Rechcigl, Miloslav, Jr., "Charles Wehle," in: *Encyclopedia of Bohemian and Czech American Biography*. Bloomington, IN: AuthorHouse, 2016, Vol. 1, p. 52.

5. Spies

Ruth Fischer (orig. Elfriede Eisler) (1898-1962), b. Leipzig, of Bohemian ancestry; co-founder of the Austrian Communist Party; later becoming a staunch anti-Communist activist and served as a key-agent of the American intelligence service, known as 'The Pond.'
Bio: "Ruth Fischer, in: Wikipedia. See - https://en.wikipedia.org/wiki/Ruth_Fischer

Kurt Singer (orig. Deutsch) (1911-2005), b. Vienna, of Bohemian ancestry; publicist, novelist, biographer, spy
Bio: Rechcigl, Miloslav, Jr., "Kurt Singer," in: *Encyclopedia of Bohemian and Czech-American Biography*. Bloomington, IN: AuthorHouse, 2016, Vol. 2, pp. 966-967; "Kurt D. Singer," in: Wikipedia. See - https://de.wikipedia.org/wiki/Kurt_D._Singer

John Leopold (1890-1958), b. Bohemia; spy for the Royal Canadian Mounted Police
Bio: "Leopold, John," in: *Encyclopedia of Cold War Espionage, Spies, and Secret Operations.* By Richard S. Trahair. Westport, CT: Greenwood Publishing Group, 2004, pp. 215-216.

XII. Organizations

Society for the History of Czechoslovak Jews, Inc. New York.

XIII. Genealogy and Family History

A. Genealogy

Austria-Czech SIG's Page of Links - See: https://www.jewishgen.org/austriaczech/all link.html

Czech and Slovak Republics: Jewish Family History Research Guide. July 2007. Courtesy of the Ackman & Ziff Family Genealogy Institute. See: https://www.cjh.org/pdfs/Czech-Slovak07.pdf

Gemeinde View (Gemeinde - Community) The Web Encyclopedia of Jewish Communities

in Bohemia and Moravia - See: https://www.jewishgen.org/austriaczech/gemeinde.htm

Czech Republic Jewish Records - See: https://www.familysearch.org/wiki/en/Czech Republic Jewish Records

Gundacker, Felix. Matrikenverzeichnis der Juedischen Matriken Boehmens (Register of Jewish Vital Statistics in the Czech State Archives pertaining to Bohemia). Felix Gundacker, 2000. In German and English. LBI q HB 1001 G83.

Gundacker, Felix. Matrikenverzeichnis der Juedischen Matriken Maehrens (Register of Jewish Vital Statistics in the Czech State Archives pertaining to Moravia). Felix Gundacker, 2000. In German and English. LBI q 69.

Jewish Genealogy in the Czech Republic - See: http://genguideswiki.com/wiki/index.php?title=Jewish Genealogy in the Czech Republic

Rechcigl, Miloslav, Jr., Czech Genealogy Sources. A Bibliography of Publications and Guide to Information Resources in the United States and the Czech Republic. Rockville, MD: Author, 1999.

Rechcigl, Miloslav, Jr., Czechoslovak Genealogy Sites on the Internet. 2nd Revised edition. Rockville, MD, 2001 (SVU Information Resources. Internet Guides, No. 3).

Schoenberg, E. Randol, Beginner's Guide to Austrian-Jewish Genealogy. OnLine:

http://www.jewishgen.org/austriaczech/ausguide.htm

Schoenberg, E. Randol and Julius Mueller, Getting Started with Czech-Jewish Genealogy. Updated 2013. OnLine: http://www.jewishgen.org/austriaczech/czechguide.html
Czech and Slovak Republics: Jewish Family History Research Guide. July 2007. Courtesy of the Ackman & Ziff Family Genealogy Institute. See: https://www.cjh.org/pdfs/Czech-Slovak07.pdf

B. FAMILY HISTORIES

1. Sources

Jewish Families from Prague - GENi. See: https://www.geni.com/projects/Jewish-Families-from-Prague/7995
Czech (Bohemian) American Jews - GENi. See: https://www.geni.com/projects/Czech-Bohemian-American-Jews/14626
Rechcigl, Miloslav, Jr., "Family Histories and Genealogies," in: *Czech It Out. Czech American Biography Sourcebook*. Bloomington, IN: AuthorHouse, 2015, pp. 782-843

2. Individual Families

ABELES

House on the Hill: The Story of the Abeles Family of Leavenworth, KS. By Julia Wood Kramer. Chicago: Author, 1990. 199p. Includes: Baer, Bailey, Bloch, Block, Friedberg, Harris, Hartman, Hess, Isaacs, Kohn, Kramer, Krevitz, Lasker, Lipsitz, Marcus, Palan, Pollak, Rothschild, Vorhaus and related families.

ADLER - see HONIG

ARNSTEIN - see BRUML

ASCHER - see KOHN

AUFRICHTIG

Roberts, Charlie and Ronny, "The Aufrichtig Family," in: Family Links. Web Sites by Members of Austria-Czech SIG. See: http://www.aufrichtigs.com/

BARTH - see GLAZIER

BAUM - see also GREENFIELD

Begats a History of the Baum - Simon Families. By Rudy Baum. North Bay Village, FL: Author, 1978. 186p. Includes: Heller.

BLOCH

Descendants of Salomon Bloch of Janowitz, Bohemia, and Baruch Wollman of Kempen-in-Posen, Prussia. By Joan Ferris Curran. Baltimore, MD: Gateway Press, 1996. 264 p.

BLOCK

Block II" – [Simon Block of Švihov Bohemia], in: First American Jewish Families. Compiled by Malcolm H. Stern. Cincinnati, OH: American Jewish Archives, 1991, p. 25 and p. 32.
Descendants of Abraham Block of Washington, Hemstead County, Arkansas, 1782-1857. By Pauline Booker Carter. A typescript. Monroe, LA: The Author, 1972.
A Family Migration. By Abraham J. Block. n.p., 1971. 42 l. LC

BOHM

Our Family through the Generations. By Aline Bohm Greif. August 1982, 55 p.

BONDI

The Family Bondi and their Ancestors. By Reiner J. Auman. Jamaica, NY, 1966. 100 p.

BRANDEIS

Brandeis: Family History. Salt Lake City, Utah: Filmed by the Genealogical Society of Utah, 1982.

BRUCKMAN

Ancestors, descendants and allied lines of Dr. Jacob George Bruckman, 1800-1885, and Dr. Philip Bruckman, 1797-1874: German Jewish immigrant physicians and brothers from Böhmen, Austria (now Czech Republic). Compiled and edited by Raymond C. Lantz. Berwyn Heights, MD: Heritage Books, 2015.

BRUML

Belonging. The Family "Bruml" 1968-1977. By Heel-Rose Klausner. N.p.: The Author, 1977.

BUSH

"Bush" – [Mathias Bush f. Prague, Bohemia], in: First American Jewish Families. Compiled by Malcolm H. Sern. Cincinnati, OH: American Jewish Archives, 1991, p. 25.

CAPPE - see also HŐNIG

"Descendants of Simon Aaron Cappe," in: GENi. See - - https://www.geni.com/list/descendants/6000000020035150307#8

CZERNER

Schapiro, Raya Czerner and Helga Czerner Weinberg, Letters from Prague: 1939-1941. Chicago: Academy Chicago Publishers, 1996. 254p.

EISNER - see also BRUML

Reminiscences of A Native of Prague. By Paul J. Edwards (Dr. Pavel Eisner). Rockville, MD: The Author, 1993. 127 p.; 5 gen. charts. Includes Auer, Edwards, Eisner, Steiner, Taussig.

Raw Carrots for Breakfast. By Helen Steiner. Schenectady, NY: Author, 1998. 145p. Includes: Edwards, Eisner, Steiner, Taussig

EPSTEIN

Epstein, H., Where She Came from: A Daughter's Search for Her Mother's History. New York: Little, Brown & Co., 1997. Includes: Epstein, Furcht, Rabinek, Sachsel

FISCHER - see HONIG

FREUND

A Bygone Yesterday: A Family Story. By Lawrence J. Freund. Bloomington, IN, 2014. 198p.

GLAZIER

Glazier Family Papers, 1852-1957, Judah L. Magnes Museum, Western Jewish Historical Center, Berkeley, CA. The collection consists of Glazier family genealogy; family history materials, including materials on the history of J. Barth and Co.

GOLD

The German Golds in America. By J. Stephen Gold. Bethlehem, PA: ABC Printing and Photo Offset, 1971.

The Gold Family History: Eleven Generations from Moravia. By O. David Gold. GreaterSpace Independent Publishing Platform, 2014. 224p.

GREENFIELD

Six Generations from Bohemia. A Chronicle of the Greenfield-Baum Family. By Robert David Baum. Arlington, VA: The Author, 1977. 140 p. LC

HACHENBURG

The Hachenburg Family of Prague, Bohemia. The Lucky and the Unlucky - Two Important Family Profiles. N.p.: The Author, 2015. 54p.

HELLER - see also HONIG

Prague: My Long Journey Home A Memoir of Survival, Denial, and Redemption. By Charles Otta Heller, Bloomington, IN: Abbott Press, 2011.

HOLZER

Adventurers against their Will. By Joanie Holzer Schirm. Sarasota, FL: PeliPress, 2003. 351p

HONIG

Descendants of the Honig / Hoenig Family of Kirchenbirk, Falkenau and Karlsbad, Bohemia, including the Lov and Adler Families of Falkenau, the Heller Family of Mies, the Fischer Family of Alt-Rohlau / Karslbad and the Spiegl Family of Eger. By Leopold Hoenig. New York: The Author, 1981. 53 leaves

Hönig/Hoenig family of Kircherbirk, Falkenau, and Karlsbad, Bohemia: including the related families: Adler (Falkenau), Heller (Miles), Blaustern (Tachau and Vienna) and Aschner (Vienna), Fischer (Alt-Rohlau/ Karlsbad), Loewy (Budau near Saaz), Holzner. By Leopold Hoenig. New York, NY, 1998. 259p.

"Descendants of Lőbl Henoch Hőnig," in GENi. See - https://www.geni.com/list/descendants/6000000010220765644#4.

KLEIN

The Klein Family History. By Simon Friedman and Harrold Weinberger. Los Angeles, CA: Harrold A. Weinberger, 1980.
Klein Klippings. Updates of the Klein Family History. Yonkers, NY: M K Crasson, 1982.

KOHN

Illustrated Family Tree of the Kohn, Barnett and Other Related Families of Albany. By Walter A. Kohn., NY. Philadelphia: Author, 1946.
The Descendants of Isaak Kohn of Deutschrust (Saaz District), Czechoslovakia. By John Henry Richter. Ann Arbor, MI: The Author, 1980.
Two Hundred Years of Family History. The Story of Joseph Kohn and his Descendants. 1744-1945. By Sidney C. Singer. A typescript. Glendale, CA: Author, 1945. 52p., 22 charts. Includes: Ascher, Kohn, Rosenwasser, Rosewater, Ruzicka, Sampliner, Saphir, Singer, Steiner, Wodicka, Woditzka.

KORNFELD

A Genealogical History of an Extended Family with Rabbinical Ancestry. The Kornfeld Family Tree, with the Erteschik, Klein and Schubin Families, the Racker and Weil Connection. By Naomi Schubin Greenberg. West Hempstead, NY: The Author, 1981. 159 p.

KUSSY

The Story of Gustav and Bella Kussy of Newark, N.J. A Family Chronicle. By Sarah Kussy. Newark, NJ: The Author, 1945. 28 p.

LOTH

Bernard and Pauline Loth of Austria and their American Descendants. By Marie Loth Harris. AJA

LOW - see - HONIG

NEUBERG

Generations Past, but not Forgotten. A History of the Neuberg Family from Plzen Region in Bohemia. By Dennis D. Naiberg. Mesa, AZ: The Author, 2015.

PORGES

Porges Biographies and Family Trees. See: http://www.porges.net/HomeGeneral.html epstein

RAYMOND

Antonín Raymond a Reimannové: osud židovské rodiny ve XX. století. By Irena Veverková. Kladno: Patria, 2006. 46p.

ROSENWASSER - see also KOHN

The Rosenwasser Family Tree. By Sidney C. Singer. A typescript. Aug. 1, 1942. Cleveland, OH: Western Reserve Historical Society.

SCHOENBAUM - see HOLZER

SCHOENBERG

Schoenberg, E. Randol, "My Family Tree," in: Family Links. Web Sites by Members of Austria-Czech SIG. See: http://www.schoenberglaw.com/randols/private/family/WC_TOC.HTM

SCHWARTZ

The History of the Joseph and Sophie Schwartz Family 1789-1977. By Bryner Schwartz.
The Schwartz Family of el Paso. The Story of a Pioneer Jewish Family in the Southwest. By Floyd S. Fierman. El Paso, TX: Western Press, 1980. 64 p.
Our Kin, Past and Present. The Schwarts Family. By Martha Dee Guthrie. Dallas, TX: The Author, 1983. 388 p.

STEINER – see also KOHN
Steiner, Frank, Tales of Two Continents. Schenectady, NY: Author, ca. 1999. 85p. Family chart. Includes: Edwards, Steiner, Steinbach
Steiner, Helen, Raw Carrots for Breakfast. Schenectady, NY: Author, 1998. 145p. Includes: Edwards, Taussig

TAUSSIG - see - EISNER

The Taussig Genealogy and Family Tree Page. See: https://www.genealogytoday.com/surname/finder.mv?Surname=Taussig

THIEBEN

Thieben Family: Rousinov, Bohemia and Beyond. By Vera Fineberg. 2008. 74p.

UTITZ

The Utitz Legacy. A Personalized History of Central European Jewry. By Gerda Hoffer. Jerusalem: Posner & Sons, 1988. 187 p.

VODICKA - see - KOHN

WANDER

The Wanderer - Wander Family of Bohemia, Germany and America, 1450-1951. By Alvin J. Wanderer. Ann Arbor, MI: Edwards Bros., 1951.e

WASSERSTROM

The Old Country and the New: A Wasserstrom Family History. By Randy Wasserstrom. Baltimore, MD: Gateway Press, 1997.

WEHLE

Genealogy of the Wehle Family of Prague. By Theodore Wehle. New York: Author, 1898.

WINTERNITZ - see - HOLZER

WISE

Schoenberg, E. Randol, "A New Genealogy for Rabbi Isaac Mayer Wise." - See: http://schoenblog.com/?p=1140

C. Family Trees on GENi

Search at: https://www.geni.com/projects/Czech-Bohemian-American-Jews/people/14626
Note: The family trees frequently contain extensive biographical information

Abeles, Adolph, merchant, first Jew to be elected to the Missouri State legislature
Adler, Alfred, M.D., psychotherapist, founder of the school of individual psychology
Adler, David, wholesale clothing merchant, Milwaukee
Adler, David, architect, Chicago
Adler, Kurt, Chorus master and conductor
Adler, Margot Susanna, journalist, New York correspondent for National Public Radio (NPR)
Adler, Peter Herman, conductor
Albright, Madeleine, educator, politician, US Secretary of State
Allers, Franz Ludwig, conductor of ballet, opera, Broadway musicals, film scores, and symphony orchestras.
Altmann, Maria Victoria (Bloch-Bauer), Jewish refugee, businesswoman, known for her legal battle to recover family portraits painted by Gustav Klimt
Altmann, Siegfried, director of Institute, NYC
Altschul, Rudolf, Canadian anatomist, educator
Aragón, Angélica, Mexican stage, fil and TV actress and singer
Aronson, Lisa (née Jalowetz), set designer, part of the Broadway theater design team, with her husband Boris Aronson, garnering six Tony awards
Ascher, Leo, composer
Ascher-Nash, Franziska (Franzi), free-lance writer, poet lecturer
Astaire, Fred, film and stage dancer, choreographer, singer, actor
Arnstein, Karl, engineer, airship designer
Aterman, Kurt, M.D., physician, pathologist
Auerbach, Norbert, president of United Artists
Augenfeld, Felix, architect, interior designer
Babbitt, Dina, activist, Holocaust survivor

Bader Franz, art gallery and bookstore owner
Baeck, Leo, Rabbi, Jewish historian
Baer, Alan A. Brandeis, heir to J. l. Brandeis Department stores chain
Baer, Buddy, boxer, but later an actor
Baer, Max, boxer
Baer, Max, Jr., actor, screenwriter, producer and director
Barnard, Frederick (Bedřich), political scientist, educator
Barta, István (Berger), water polo player
Basch, Samuel Siegfried Karl Ritter von, personal physician of Emperor Maximilian of Mexico
Baum, Hedwig (Vicky), famous novelist
Beck, Carl, physician, Chicago
Beck, Emil G., physician, Chicago
Beck, Joseph G., physician, otologist, laryngologist, Chicago
Beckmann, Petr, electrical engineer, educator
Beer-Hofmann, Richard, author of novels, dramas, and poems
Bentley, Leopold Lionel Garrick (Bloch-Bauer), Canadian manufacturer
Bentley, Robert (Bloch-Bauer), Canadian manufacturer
Berger, Oscar, caricaturist, cartoonist
Berger-Vosendorf, Alfred Viktor, economist
Bergmann, Martin, clinical psychologist
Bernays, Edward Louis James, pioneer in the field of public relations and propaganda
Beth, Marianne (Weisl), lawyer and feminist, first woman to earn doctorate in law in Austria
Bettelheim, Aaron Siegfried, Rabbi, Hebraist
Bettelheim, Bruno, clinical psychologist, psychoanalyst
Bettelheim, Cyd, resident directress of Emanu El Sisterhood, NYC
Bettelheim, Felix Albert, physician and surgeon of Panama
Blatt, John Markus, applied mathematician, physicist
Bloch, Claude C., Admiral, US Navy
Bloch, Eduard, physician of Hitler's family
Bloch, Edward H., founder of the oldest Jewish publishing company in the US
Bloch, Felix, physicist, recipient of the Nobel Prize in physics

Bloch, Henry W., co-founder of H&R Block tax preparation co., philanthropist

Bloch, Herbert, professor of Latin

Bloch, Ingram, physicist, professor, Vanderbilt Univ., Nashville

Bloch, Leon Edwin, attorney, Minneapolis

Bloch, Leon Edwin, Jr., attorney, Kansas City

Bloch, Richard Adolf, founder of H&R Block tax preparation co., philanthropist

Bloch-Bauer, Karl David, associated with his brother Leopold's Canadian firm Pacific Veneer and Plywood Co.

Block, Abraham: pioneer Jewish settler in Arkansas, merchant

Block, Daniel, founder of the B'nai B'rith Synagogue, St. Louis

Block, Eleazer, pioneer lawyer, St. Louis, MO

Block, Simon, Sr., early settler

Bloomfield, Fannie, pianist

Blűh, Otto, physicist

Bluh, Pamela, librarian

Bodanzky, Artur, conductor

Bohm. Henry Victor, physicist, professor, Wayne State University

Bondi, August Mendel, abolitionist, member of John Brown's group

Bondi, Jonas, Rabbi, editor, founder and proprietor of a Jewish periodical *The Hebrew Leader*

Bories, Emil, pioneer physician, Portland, OR

Bories, Herman, Rabbi, Portland, OR

Brady, George, Holocaust survivor, founder of plumbing business, Toronto, Canada

Brandeis, Adele, art historian and art administrator, with WPA Federal art Project

Brandeis, Adolph, merchant

Brandeis, Arthur, businessman

Brandeis, Alice (née Goldmark), activist, on behalf of woman suffrage, industrial reform, organized labor, the legal rights of children

Brandeis, George Bohumil Gottlieb, president of J. L. Brandeis & Sons, retail dry goods, Omaha, NE

Brandeis, E. John, merchant, president of Brandeis Department Store, Omaha, civic leader

Brandeis, Frederick, pianist and accompanist, composer
Brandeis, Jonas Leopold, founder of the Department store, J. L. Brandeis & Son, Omaha, NE
Brandeis, Samuel, M.D., physician
Brecher, George, M.D., physician, pathologist
Brecht, Stefan, poet, critic and scholar of theater
Brill, Otto, physicist, expert on radioactivity
Brod, Fritzi, textile designer
Brody, Adrien, actor
Bruckman (née Kahn), Henrietta, founder of the first Jewish women's lodge in America
Bruckman, Jacob George, M.D., physician, PA
Bruckman, Philip, M.D., physician, NYC
Bruml, Hana (née Műller), clinical psychologist
Bruml, Karl (Charles), graphic artist
Buchbinder, Jacob Richter, surgeon
Budín, Stanislav, leftist journalist
Bulova, Arde Adolf, innovative watchmaker
Bulova, Joseph, jeweler, watchmaker, founder of J. Bulova Co., NYC
Bullowa, Alfred. L. M., attorney, NYC
Bullowa, Emilie M., attorney, NYC
Bullowa, Jesse G. M., physician, NYC
Bullowa, Ralph James, attorney, NYC
Bunzel, Joseph Hans, lawyer, sociologist, educator
Bunzl, Julius, wholesale tobacco merchant, NYC
Bunzl, Rudolph Hans, manufacturer, founder of American Filtrona Corp.
Bunzl, Walter Henry, paper manufacturer, Atlanta, GA
Bush, Isidor, pioneer journalist, businessman, civic leader, abolitionist, St. Louis, MO
Bush, Mathias, pioneer settler, merchant, activist, Philadelphia
Bush, Solomon, Lt. Col., highest ranking Jewish officer in the Continental Army
Cappé, Simon Aaron (orig. Benjamin Mozes Hönig), pioneer settler, US Virgin Islands

Collmus (Kalmus), Levi, pioneer settler, Baltimore, MD, veteran of 1812 War
Cori, Gerty Therese (née Radnitz), biochemist, recipient of the Nobel Prize in physiology and medicine
Curtis, Tony Bernard Herschel (Schwartz), actor
Daddario, Alexandra Anna, film actress
Dembitz, Lewis Naphtali, attorney, legal scholar, politician
Deresiewicz, Herbert, mechanical engineer, professor, Columbia Univ.
Derschowitz, Zvi, Rabbi
Deutsch, Eberhard Paul, attorney, authority on international law
Deutsch, Ernst, actor
Deutsch, Gotthard, Rabbi, historian, philosopher
Deutsch, Hermann Bacher, journalist
Deutsch, Naomi, leader in public health nursing
Deutsch, Ruth, professor of German and German literature
Dormitzer, Joachim Heinrich, wholesale tobacco merchant, NYC
Drickamer, Harry George chemist
Eidlitz, Charles Leo, electrical engineer, New York, NY
Eidlitz, Cyrus Lazelle Warner, architect, New York, NY
Eidlitz, Leopold, architect, New York, NY
Eidlitz, Marc, builder, New York, NY
Eidlitz, Otto Marc, building contractor, New York, NY
Eidlitz, Robert James, architect, New York, NY
Eisenschiml, Alexander, adventurer, soldier, merchant
Eisenschiml, Otto, chemist, inventor, controversial author
Eisler, Elfriede, co-founder of the Autrsian Communist Party, later becoming a staunch anti-Communist activist
Eisler, Hanns, composer
Eisner, J. Lester, v.p. of Sigmund Eisner Co. and director of other corporations
Eisner, J. Lester, Jr., attorney, regional administrator of the Federal Housing and Home Finance Agency
Eisner, Michael Dammann, businessman, CEO of the Walt Disney Corp.
Eisner, Monroe, president of Sigmund Eisner Co., Red Bank, NJ
Eisner, Sigmund, manufacturer of uniforms for the armed forces

Eitner, Lorenz, art historian, educator
Elbogen, Paul, writer, Canada
Elkins, Frances (Adler), interior designer
Epstein, Julius, journalist and scholar, anti-communist researcher and critic of the Soviet Union
Ernst, Bernard, attorney
Ernst, Morris Leopold, attorney, advocate of civil rights, author
Ernst, Richard Charles, founder of Atheneum Publishers, director of Scribner Book Companies
Ernst, Roger, diplomat, director of USAID in Ethiopia and Thailand
Falk, Peter Michael, actor
Fall, Richard, composer of operettas and popular songs
Feher, George, biophysicist
Fehl, Fred, photographer
Fehl, Maria Raina Leonora (Schweinburg), art historian, classicist, author
Fehl, Philipp P., artist, art historian
Feigl, Herbert, philosopher
Feigl, Hugo, art dealer, owner of Feigl Gallery, NYC
Firkušný, Leopold 'Leo', musicologist, Buenos Aires, Argentina
Firkušný, Rudolf, pianist
Fischel, Ellis, oncologist
Fischel, Washington Emil, physician, St. Louis, MO
Fischer, Irene Nekhama (née Kaminka), mathematician, geodesist
Fleischl, Marie Franziska, psychiatrist
Fleischmann, Charles Louis, innovative manufacturer of yeast
Fleischner, Isaac Newton, merchant, Portland, OR
Fleischner, Jacob, merchant, Albany, then Portland, OR
Fleischner, Louis, wholesale dry foods merchant, Portland, OR
Flexner, Abraham Flexner, educator, reformer of medical education
Flexner, Barnard, attorney
Flexner, Carline, social worker, with UNRRA
Flexner, Eleanor, historian, feminist
Flexner, Hortense, writer, playwright, poet
Flexner, Jacob Aaron, physician, Louisville, KY
Flexner, Jean Atherton, economist

Flexner, James Thomas, historian, biographer
Flexner, Louis Barkhouse, M.D., biochemist, neurochemist
Flexner, Simon, pathologist, educator, director of Rockefeller Institute for Medical Research
Flexner, William Welch, mathematician
Forman, Miloš, film director, screenwriter, actor, and professor
Francken, Ruth (Steinreich), sculptor, painter, furniture designer
Frank, Erich, philosopher
Frank, Philipp, physicist, mathematician, philosopher of science
Frankfurter, Felix, Associate Justice of the US Supreme Court
Frankl, Paul, art historian
Freschl, Carl, pioneer manufacturer of knit goods, Milwaukee
Freschl, Edward, manufacturer, president of Holeproof Hosiery Co., Milwaukee
Freund, Arthur Jerome, attorney, St. Louis
Freund, Harry, president of S. E. Freund's Sons Shoe and Clothing Co., St. Louis
Freund, Karl, cinematographer, film director
Freund, Moritz, together with his wife **Jetta**, pioneer bakers in St. Lous, famous for rye bread
Freund, Paul Abraham, educator, legal scholar
Friedländer, Saul, historian
Friend, Emil, journalist, with *Chicago News*, finance editor for *Chicago Examiner*, then *Herald Examiner*
Friend, Hugo, athlete, jurist
Friesleben, Daniel Nathan, merchant, rancher, CA
Friml, Rudolf, composer of operettas, musicals, songs and piano pieces, as well as a pianist
Friml, Rudolf, Jr., actor
Friml, William, composer and writer
Fűrth, Ernestine activist, founder and leader of suffrage movement in Austria
Furth, Jacob, merchant, entrepreneur, banker, communal worker
Furth, Viktor (Fűrth), architect, professor of architecture, University of Miami
Gellhorn, Alfred, oncologist

Gellhorn, Edna, suffragist, reformer, founder of National League of Women Voters

Gellhorn, Martha, novelist, travel writer, journalist

Gellhorn, Walter Fischel, educator, legal scholar

Gibian, George, literary scholar, professor at Cornell University

Gibian, Thomas, chemist

Gilbert, Sara, actress, co-host and creator of CBS daytime show 'The Talk'

Gilbert, Susan (née Brandeis), LL.B., attorney

Gilinsky, Jack, singer, part of the pop-rap duo Jack & Jack, along with Jack Johnson

Gimbel, Bruce A., head of the Gimbel's department-store chain

Ginsburg, Zdeněk, co-owner of the Leader Stores, Chicago

Glaser, Sigmund, merchant in laces and embroideries, St. Louis

Goldberger, Henry R., Rabbi, Erie, PA

Goldberger, Joseph, physician, epidemiologist

Goldberger, Leo Leib, Rabbi

Goldmark, Henry, civil engineer, designer of the Panama Canal locks

Goldmark, Josephine Clara, labor law reformer

Goldmark, Pauline Dorotha, social worker and activist

Gomperz, Heinrich Harry, philosopher

Gottlieb, Abraham, engineer

Graf, Herbert, opera producer

Graf, Max, musicologist, music critic

Gratz, Barnard, merchant, Philadelphia

Gratz, Hyman, merchant, philanthropist, Philadelphia

Gratz, Jacob, merchant, PA State legislator

Gratz, Michael, trader and merchant, Philadelphia

Gratz, Rebecca, educator, founder of Hebrew Benevolent Society, philanthropist

Greenhut, Benedict J., merchant, owner of Greenhut-Siegel-Cooper Department Store in Manhattan, director of Tudor Foundation

Greenhut, Clara G., social activist, philanthropist

Greenhut, Joseph B., businessman, founder of the largest distillery, Peoria, IL

Greil, Gaston Jacob, M.D., physician

Greil, Jacob, wholesale merchant
Gries, Moses Jacob, Rabbi
Gries, Robert Hay, collector, co-founder of Cleveland Rams, co-founder of Cleveland Browns
Gross, David Jonathan, physicist, recipient of the Nobel Prize
Gruen, Victor David, architect
Grűnberg, Peter Andreas, physicist, p recipient of the Nobel Prize in physics
Greenfield, Martin, master tailor, Brooklyn, NY
Grund, Francis Joseph, journalist, diplomat, Consul
Guermonprez Elsesser, Gertrud, textile artist and designer
Guinzburg, Aaron, Rabbi
Guinzburg, Adolph, pioneer merchant, Annapolis, MD
Guinzburg, Frank, merchant, PA
Guinzburg, Frederick Victor, sculptor
Guinzburg, Harold K., publisher, founder of Viking Press
Guinzburg, Henry Aaron, rubber manufacturer, Jewish communal worker
Guinzburg, Ralph Kleinert, rubber ware manufacturer
Guinzburg, Thomas H., editor, publisher
Guizburg, Victor, rubber manufacturer, inventor
Gurewich, Marinka, voice teacher, mezzo-soprano
Gutwillig, Emil, jobber and importer of woolens, owner of E. Gutwillig & Co., Chicago
Haas, Arthur Erich, physicist
Haas, Hugo, film actor, director, writer
Hahn, Aaron, Orthodox Rabbi
Hahn, Edgar Aaron, attorney, Cleveland
Halberstam, Heini, mathematician
Hamerschlag, Arthur Anton, electrical and mechanical engineer, first President of Carnegie Mellon University
Hamlisch, Marvin Moshe, composer
Hammid (orig. Hackenschmidt), Alexander, photographer, film director, cinematographer
Hartford, Huntington, businessman, philanthropist, stage and film producer and art collector, heir to A&P supermarket chain

Haurowitz, Felix Michael, immunochemist
Hecht, Ladislav, professional tennis player
Heidelberger, Charles, organic chemist, biochemist
Heitler, Emmett, innovative manufacturer, executive wih Schwader Bros., Inc., a manufacturer of Samsonite Luggaagge
Heller, James Gutheim, Rabbi, leader of Reform Judaism, Zionist, composer
Heller, Max, Rabbi, New Orleans, leader in Reform Judaism, Zionist
Henshel, Harry B., chairman and chief executive officer of the Bulova Corp.
Herzfeld, Karl Ferdinand physicist, physical chemist
Herzig, Arthur J., otolaryngologist
Herzog, Fred, educator, legal scholar, Dean
Hitschmanova, Lotta, Canadian humanitarian
Hoch, Hans, biophysicist
Hochwald, Adolf, M.D., physician
Hochwald, Werner, economist
Holmberg, Ruth Rachel (Sulzberger), publisher of The Chattanooga Times
Holzer, Oswald Alois, M.D., physician
Horner, Christopher, set designer
Horner, Harry, art director, film and TV director
Horner, Henry, pioneer Jewish settler in Chicago, merchant
Horner, Henry (orig. Levy), attorney, jurist, Governor of Illinois
Horner, James, set designer, with MGM
Horner, James Roy, composer, conductor, orchestrator of film scores
Hostovský, Egon, writer
Huebsch, Adolph, Rabbi
Huebsch, Benjamin W., publisher, NYC
Hula, Erich, legal scholar, political scientist
Hupka, Robert, recording engineer for RCA Victor, then cameraman for CBS TV in New York
Husserl, Gerhart Adolf, legal scholar, educator
Illoway, Henry, M.D., pioneer physician, NYC
Illowy, Bernard, Orthodox Rabbi, Cincinnati
Iltis, Fred, entomologist

Iltis Hugh Helmut, botanist
Iltis, Hugo, biologist
Jahoda, Fritz Friedrich, conductor, pianist, educator
Jakobson, Roman, linguist
Jalowetz, Heinrch, musicologist, conductor
Janowitz, Hans, film scriptwriter
Jelinek, Hans, graphic artist, professor of art at City College, NYC
Jellinek, Elvin Morton, physiologist, biostatician, alcoholism researcher
Jellinek, Oskar, free-lance writer, short story teller
Jonas, Benjamin Franklin, US Senator, LA
Joseph, Martha J., leader of the Greater Cleveland cultural community
Joseph, William Ralph, attorney, community activist, Cleveland
Jung, Leo, Rabbi
Jungk, Peter S., free-lance writer, novelist
Jungk, Robert, writer, journalist
Kafka, Alexandre Franz, economist, executive director of the International Monetary Fund
Kahler, Erich, literary scholar, essayist
Kaiser, Alois, chazzan and composer
Kalmus, Hans, geneticist, biologist
Karman, Theodore von, aerospace engineer, physicist
Karpeles, Leopold, Color Sgt., recipient of Congressional Medal of Honor
Karpeles, Leopold 'Leo', professor at University of Maryland School of Medicine and then country doctor, Blue Ridge Summit, PA
Karpeles, Maurice J, merchant with precious stones, Providence, RI
Karpeles, Simon R., physician, Washington, DC
Karplus, Martin, theoretical chemist, recipient of Nobel Prize in chemistry
Karplus, Robert, theoretical physicist
Kauder, Emil, economist
Kauder, Hugo, composer, pedagogue, and music theorist
Kauders, Erich, resident of Caig Machine, Inc., Lawrence, MA, Craig Vending Machine Co., **Kaufman, Enit Zerner,** portrait painter
Kaufmann, Felix, philosopher of law
Kaus, Gina Kranz Frischauer (née Wiener), novelist, screenwriter

Kaus, Otto Michael, judge of California Supreme Court
Kaus, Robert Michael, journalist, pundit, author
Kautsky, Hans 'John', political scientist, educator
Kelsen, Hans, jurist, legal philosopher
Kern, Jerome David, composer of popular music, songs
Kerry, Cameron Forbes, attorney
Kerry, John Forbes, US Senator, US Secretary of State
Kerry, Richard John, lawyer, US Foreign Service officer
Khuner, Felix, second violinist of the Kolisch Qaurtet
Kisch, Bruno Zacharias, M.D., physician, physiologist
Kisch, Egon, journalist,
Kisch, Herbert, economist, Michigan State University
Kisch, Guido, lawyer, legal scholar, historian
Klauber, Abraham, pioneer merchant in CA and NV
Klauber, Adolph, drama critic and theatrical producer
Klauber, Alice Ellen, painter
Klauber, Amy Josephine, painter
Klauber, Amy Josephine (Salz), painter
Klauber, Elvira 'Ella', painter, photographer
Klauber, Laurence, herpetologist
Klauber, Leda, painter
Klemperer, Otto, conductor composer
Klemperer, Werner, stage, film and TV comedic and dramatic actor, singer/musician
Klemperer, Wolfgang, aviation and aerospace engineer
Klímová, Rita, economist, politician, dissident, Czechoslovak Ambassador to the US
Kohn, Carl, banker, financier, New Orleans
Kohn, Eugene, Rabbi
Kohn, Jacob, Rabbi, theologian
Kohn, Joachim financier, New Orleans, LA
Kohn, Joseph John, mathematician
Kohn, Otto, architect, NYC
Kohn, Samuel: pioneer financier, New Orleans, LA
Kohn, Walter, theoretical physicist and chemist, recipient in of the Nobel Prize in chemistry

Kohner, Frederick, novelist, screenwriter
Kohner, Susan, film and TV actress
Kohner, Walter, Hollywood talent agent
Kohut, Rebekah (Bettelheim), communal worker
Kolisch, Rudolf, violinist, founder of the Kolisch String Quartet, teacher
Kollisch, Margarethe (née Moller), writer and poet
Kollisch, Otto, architect and master builder
Koller, Carl, ophthalmologist, discoverer of local anesthesia
Kopf, Maxim, painter
Kopperl, Moritz O., banker, Galveston, TX
Korbel, Josef, diplomat, educator, political scientist, Dean
Korn, Walter, authority and author on chess
Körner, Leon Joseph, Canadian businessman and philanthropist
Körner, Stephan, philosopher
Körner, Walter, Canadian businessman and philanthropist
Korngold, Erich Wolfgang, music composer
Korngold, George W., record producer
Korngold, Julius Leopold, noted music critic
Körper, Adolph, postmaster, South Wellington, CT, town's first selectman, reelected 10 times
Kramrisch, Stella (Nemenyi), art historian and curator
Kraus, Adolf, lawyer, Jewish leader
Kraus, Hans Peter, antiquarian bookseller
Kraus, Hans Peter, Jr., photographs dealer, historian, publisher
Kraus, Hertha, social worker, educator
Kraus, Lili, a noted pianist
Kreisler, Georg Franz, cabaretist, satirist, composer, songwriter
Kris, Ernest Walter, art historian, psychoanalyst
Kris, Marianne (née Rie), physician, psychoanalyst
Kuh, Anton, journalist, essayist
Kuh, Charles S., SC State Legislator
Kurzweil, Raymond Ray, computer scientist, inventor, futurist
Kussy, Nathan, journalist, attorney, writer
Kussy, Sarah, educator, communal worker, Zionist
Lakin, Christine, actress
Lamarr, Heddy, film actress, inventor

Landsberger, Benno, Assyriologist

Landsteiner, Karl, M.D., immunologist, discoverer of the blood groups, recipient of the Nobel Prize in physiology and medicine

Lang, Friedrich Christian Anton, filmmaker, screenwriter, film producer and actor

Langendorf, Richard, cardiologist, Chicago

Lauder, Estée, founder of Estee Lauder Companies, her eponymous cosmetics co.

Lauder Leonard, billionaire businessman, art collector, humanitarian

Lauder, Ronald, billionaire businessman, art collector, philanthropist, US Ambassador to Austria

Lazarsfeld, Marie (née Jahoda), social psychologist

Lazarsfeld, Paul Felix, sociologist

Lazarsfeld, Sophie, psychoanalyst, student of Alfred Adler

Ledecky, Jonathan Joseph 'Jon', businessman, founder of US Office Products

Ledecky, Katie, competition swimmer

Lederer, Charles Davies, film writer and director

Lederer, David Able, manufacturer of soap and cosmetics in New Jersey, then moved to New Haven, CT

Lederer, Emil, chemist, Dean

Lederer, Julius Yehuda, merchant and manufacturer, New Haven, CT

Lederer, Max, M., dealer in leather, hide and fertilizer, New Brunswick, NJ

Lederer, Samuel, pioneer merchant and manufacturer in New Jersey

Lefkowitz, David, Rabbi, Dallas, TX

Lekowitz, David, Jr., Rabbi, LA

Lefkowitz, Lewis Benjamin, Jr., internist, professor of preventive medicine, Vanderbilt University

Leichter, Henry O., attorney

Leichter, Otto, left-wing activist, journalist, author

Levey, Douglas Pokorny, merchant, New Orleans

Levey, Harold Alvin, chemical engineer, manufacturer, pioneer in the field of plastics, New Orleans, LA

Levey, Ralph Pokorny, merchant, New Orleans

Levy, Louis Edward, inventor

Lilienthal, David Eli, attorney, head of TVA and then of Atomic Energy Commission

Lindenthal, Gustav, civil engineer, master bridge builder

Lőbl, Eugen, economist, politician

Loewenstein, Ernst, bacteriologist

Loewner, Charles, mathematician

Lorre, Peter Laszlo (Löwenstein), actor

Loth, Moritz, communal worker

Lothar, Ernst Sigismund (orig. Műller), writer, theatre director/ manager, producer

Low, G. David, astronautical engineer, aerospace executive and NASA astronaut

Low, George Michael, NASA administrator and President of Rensselaer Polytechnic Institute.

Lowenbach, Jan Johann, musicologist, music critic

Lowy, Louis, gerontologist, Dean, Boston University

Lurie, Louis Robert, businessman, developer of downtown area of San Francisco

Lurie, Robert Alfred, real estate magnate, philanthropist, San Francisco

Lustig, Arnošt, author of novels, short stories, plays, and screenplays whose works often involved the Holocaust

Mackay, Lottie Elizabeth (Bohm), organic chemist

Mahler, Anna Justine, sculptor

Mahler, Fritz, conductor, composer

Mahler, Gustav, composer, conductor

Mahrer, Paul, soccer player

Mandl, Friedrich Alexander Maria, founder of a new airplane manufacturing plant, Industria Metalúrgica y Plástica Argentina

Mandl, Herbert Thomas, concert violinist, professor of music, philosopher, writer

Manner, Jennie (née Mannheimer), elocutionist, acting coach, and teacher of speech and drama

Maretzek, Max, composer, conductor, impresario

Marshall, Lenore Guinzburg, writer, co-founder of Committee for Nuclear Responsibility

Massary, Fritze (Friederike) (née Massarik), actress, soprano singer

May, Max Benjamin, attorney, Cincinnati, OH
Mayer, Egon, sociologist, professor at Brooklyn College
Metzl, Ervine, graphic artist and illustrator
Meyers, Joshua 'Josh' Dylan, actor, copmedian
Meyers, Seth Adam, actor, comedian, TV personality, producer, writer
Mintz, Ilse (née Schűller), economist, educator
Mintz, Walter, investor, co-founder of one of the first hedge-funds
Moll, Wilhelm, librarian
Morawetz, Albert Richard, career diplomat, judge
Morawetz, Leopold F., M.D., pioneer physician, Baltimore
Morawetz, Victor, attorney, Baltimore
Munk, Vladimír, microbiologist
Natonek, Hans (Hanuš), novelist, poet, publicist
Naumburg, Walter Wehle, commercial banker, NYC
Nettl, Bruno, musicologist, ethnomusicologist
Nettl, Paul, musicologist
Neumann, Ignatz, brewer, with Best Brewing Company, Chicago
Neustadt, Richard Elliot, political scientist, educator, Presidential advisor
Neustadtl, Isaac, first Bohemian Jew in Milwaukee, WI, grocer and insurance agent
Neutra, Richard Joseph, architect
Neutra, Wilhelm, psychiatrist, NYC
Newfield, Morris, Rabbi
Newman, Melissa, screen actress, artist, singer
Newman, Paul, actor, film director, producer,
Oplatka, Edward, merchant, founder of the Leader Department Store, Chicago
Oppenheim, Adolf Leo, archeologist, Assyriologist
Osheroff, Douglas Dean, physicist, Nobel Prize recipient in physics
Papanek, George Otto, psychiatrist
Patek, Arthur J., Jr., internist, Milwaukee, WI
Pauli, Wolfgang, physicist, recipient of the Nobel Prize in physics
Pereles, Nathan, pioneer Jewish grocery merchant in Milwaukee, attorney
Pereles, Thomas Jefferson, attorney, Milwaukee

Perl, William R., activist, Zionist, rescuer of Jews from annihilation by Nazis
Perlman, Ann S., poet, newspaper reporter
Perlmann, Gertrude Erika, biochemist
Perloff, Gabriele Marjorie, poetry scholar and critic, professor of English, CA
Phillips, Barnet, journalist, *New York Times*
Phillips, Henry Mayer, lawyer, US Congressman, and financier
Pick, Albert, merchant, Chicago
Pick, Albert, Jr., hotel magnate
Pick, Albert, philanthropist, investment executive
Pick, Alfred, cardiologist
Pick, Ernst, M.D., pharmacologist
Pick, Ruth, cardiologist
Pisk, Paul Amadeus, composer, musicologist
Placzek, Adolf Kurt, architectural librarian
Placzek, George, theoretical physicist
Plank, Emma Nuschi (née Spira), developmental and educational psychologist
Pokorny, Michael, shoemaker, merchant, New Orleans
Polanyi (orig. Pollacsek), John C., Canadian chemist, recipient of the Nobel Prize in chemistry
Polier, Justine Wise, Judge of the Domestic Relations Court, NY
Pollak, Otakar Jaroslav, MD, pathologist
Polier, Justine (née Wise), jurist
Politzer, Hugh David, theoretical physicist, recipient of the Nobel Prize in physics
Pollaczek -von Mises (Geiringer), mathematician, professor at Wheaton College
Pollak, Francis Deak, attorney, NYC
Pollak, Louis Heilprin, jurist
Pollak, Otakar Jaroslav, M.D., physician, pathologist
Pollak, Simon, M.D., pioneer physician, St. Louis
Pollak, Walter Heilprin, attorney, NYC
Pollitzer, Anita Lily, photographer, social activist, feminist, suffragette
Pollitzer, Carrie Teller, innovative teacher, advocate for women's rights

Pollitzer, Mabel Louise, innovative teacher
Pollitzer, Moritz, cotton merchant, Beaufort, SC
Pollitzer, Richard M., M.D., pioneer pediatrician, SC
Pollitzer, Sigmund, dermatologist
Pollitzer, William Sprott, anatomist, physical anthropologist
Popper, Frank, J., political scientist, urbanist
Popper, Hans, Dr. med., pathologist, Dean
Popper, Herbert Jan, opera conductor
Popper, Leo, manufacturer of glass beads, NYC
Porges, Otto, physician
Porges, Robert Frank, obstetrician, gynecologist
Pozarnik, Flora, Argentine poet
Prentice, John Hans (orig. Pick), lawyer, co-founder of Pacific Veneer manufacturing company, Canada
Pribram, Karl Gabriel, economist
Pribram, Karl H., neurosurgeon, educator
Prokosch, Eduard, historical linguist
Prokosch, Frederic, writer, novelist, poet, translator
Pulitzer, Joseph, newspaper publisher
Rabb, Theodore K., historian
Rabinowicz, Oskar K., historian, Zionist
Radok, Emil, film director, co-inventor of Laterna Magika, immigrated to Canada
Raushenbush, Elizabeth (née Brandeis), Ph.D., labor economist, social researcher
Redlich, Otto, physical chemist, chemical engineer
Reich, Morris, Rabbi
Reif, Arnold E., physical chemist, cancer researcher
Reiner, Thomas A., professor of regional science
Reinhardt, Max, stage and film actor and director
Reinhardt, Stephen Roy, attorney, Federal judge
Reisz, Karel, filmmaker
Reitman, Jason, Canadian film director, screenwriter, and producer
Rezek, Anna (née Bunzl), physician, Miami, FL
Rezek, Philipp Rafael, pathologist

Rich, Morris (Mauritius Reich), the founder of the Rich's Department Store chain, Atlanta, GA
Richman, Julia, educator, school district superintendent
Robi, Adolph, communal worker
Robitschek, Kurt, popular cabaret and theatre director
Roček (orig. Robitschek), Jan, chemist, Dean
Rohrlich, George F., economist, educator
Rosenbaum, Hulda (Lashanska), opera singer, soprano
Rosenblatt, Samuel, Rabbi
Rosenbluth, Gideon, economist
Rosenfeld, Eva Marie, psychoanalyst, teacher
Rosenwasser, Marcus, physician, Cleveland, OH
Rosewater, Charles Coleman, manager, organizer and publisher of newspapers and magazines in NE, CA, KS, WA and NYC
Rosewater, Edward, newspaper editor and publisher, founder of the *Omaha Bee,* politician
Rosewater, Victor S., newspaper managing editor, politician
Sadler, Bernard, Rabbi
Sabath, Adolph Joachim, attorney, US Congressman
Sabath, Joseph, attorney, jurist
Salz, Arthur, sociologist, economist
Salz, Beate Rosa, anthropologist, sociologist
Salzer, Felix, music theorist, musicologist
Schapiro, Andy, attorney, diplomat, US Ambassador to the Czech Republic
Schapiro, Raya Czerner, psychiatrist, Chicago
Schapiro, Tamar, educator, philosopher
Schein, Edgar, social psychologist, professor
Schein, Marcel, physicist
Schiff, Friedrich 'Fritz,' physician, bacteriologist
Schildkraut, Joseph, screen and film actor
Schiller, Walter, physician, pathologist
Schnabel, Artur, classical pianist, composer
Schnabel, Karl Urlich, pianist
Schnabel, Stefan, actor
Schoenbaum, Emil, mathematical statistician, insurance mathematician

Schoenberg, Arnold, classical composer and conductor

Schoenberg, Randol, attorney, grandsn of composer Arnold Schoenberg

Schreiber, Emanuel, Rabbi, editor, essayist

Schűller, Richard, political economist

Schumann-Heink, Ernestine, operatic contralto

Schur, Peter H., rheumatologist, professor

Schűtz, Alfred, sociologist, philosopher

Schweinburg, Erich Fritz, attorney, writer of novels and short stories

Senor, Daniel Samuel, columnist, writer, and political adviser.

Serkin, Peter, pianist

Serkin, Rudolf, pianist

Sgalitzer, Max, radiologist

Sherman, Carl, lawyer

Sicher, David E., pioneer merchant, NYC

Sichl, Jacob, merchant, Nebraska City

Simon, Herbert Alexander, political scientist, economist, sociologist, psychologist, recipient of the Nobel Prize in economics

Singer, Isidor Israel, encyclopedist, editor

Skala, Lilia, actress

Slezak, Leo, famous tenor

Slezak, Walter, character actor and singer

Sobotka, Ruth, dancer, costume designer, art director, painter, and actress

Sobotka, Walter, architect, specializing in residential interiors and furniture design

Solomon, Ezekiel, pioneer trader, Canada

Sonneschein, Rosa (née Fassel), founder and editor of *The American Jewess* magazine, first English periodical targeted to American Jewish women

Soudek, Josef, economist

Stark, Werner, sociologist, educator

Steele, Henry Bernard, merchant, Chicago

Stein, Adolf, businessman, in liquor business, Chicago

Stein, Irving Freiler, obstetrician, gynecologist

Stein, Irving F., Jr., surgeon, professor, Northwestern Univ. Medical School

Stein, S. Sidney, attorney, Chicago
Steinbach, Karel, physician, gynecologist
Steinbach, Lewis Weisskopf, M.D., physician, educator
Steiner, Kurt, lawyer, political scientist
Steiner, Robert Eugene, attorney, AL State Representative and Senator
Steiner-Prag, Hugo, painter, etcher, book illustrator
Steinitz, Wilhelm, chess master, World Chess Champion
Steinkopf, Maitland B., politician, legislator, Canada
Sternberg, Eugene, architect
Stetten, DeWitt, biochemist
Stiedry, Fritz, conductor and composer
Stőhr, Richard, composer, music author, teacher
Stolz, Robert, songwriter and conductor, composer of operettas and film music
Stonier Tom Ted, professor of futurology, humanist
Strakosch, Maurice, opera impresario
Strand, Mark, poet, essayist, translator
Strand, Paul, photographer, filmmaker
Stránský, Josef, conductor and composer
Stroheim, Erich Oswald von, director, producer, actor of the silent era
Sulzberger, Arthur Gregg, journalist, publisher, *The New York Times*
Sulzberger, Arthur Ochs, publisher, *The New York Times*
Sulzberger, Arthur Ochs, Jr., publisher, *The New York Times*
Sulzberger, Iphigene Ochs, heiress of *The New York Times*
Susskind, Walter Jan, conductor
Szell, George, conductor, composer
Szilard (orig. Spitz), Leo, physicist, inventor
Szold, Benjamin, Rabbi and scholar
Szold, Henrietta, Zionist leader and founder of Hadassah
Tachau, Eric S., civil rights activist
Tachau, Jean Brandeis, social activist, advocate of birth control
Tanzer, Lawrence A., attorney, NYC
Tanzer, Helen, archeologist
Taussig, Charles William, manufacturer, president of American Molasses Co.
Taussig, Edward D., Rear Admiral of US Navy

Taussig, Edward Holmes, corporate executive
Taussig, Frank William, economist, educator, Harvard University
Taussig, Joseph Knefler, Vice Admiral of US Navy
Taussig, Joseph Seligman, banker, broker, St. Louis
Taussig, William, physician, businessman, St. Louis, MO
Taussky-Todd, Olga, mathematician
Teller, Edward, theoretical physicist, father of the hydrogen bomb
Temmer, George, physicist
Tietze, Christopher, physician, advocate of pro-choice movement to permit abortion
Tietze, Erica (née Conrat), art historian
Tietze, Hans Karl, art historian
Tintner, Moritz, Rabbi
Toch, Ernst, composer of classical music and film scores
Treichlinger, David, owner of brokerage, communal worker, St. Louis
Trier, Walter, illustrator, Canada
Troller, Norbert, architect
Ullmann, John Hans Emanuel, industrial engineer
Urbach, Frederick, M.D., dermatologist
Urich, Robert Michael, film, television and stage actor and television produce
Urzidil, Johannes, writer, poet, historian, and journalist
Vogelstein, Hermann, Rabbi
Vogelstein, Ludwig, industrialist, philanthropist
Vogl-Garrett, Edith, musicologist
Voight, Angelina Jolie, actress, filmmaker, humanitarian
Vrba, Rudolf Walter (Rosenberg), biochemist, professor, Canada
Wachstein, Max, histologist, pathologist
Wachstein, Sonia (Sophie) Wachstein, teacher, social worker, psychotherapist
Waelsch, Heinrich Benedict, M.D., biochemist
Waeltsch, Samuel, cantor
Wahle, Otto, swimmer who competed in the late 19th and early 20th century
Waldes, Henry, industrialist, manufacturer of snap fasteners
Wallerstein, Lothar, M.D., physician, pianist, opera director

Wallerstein, Robert S., psychiatrist
Wax (orig. Wachs), Ruby, American actress, mental health campaigner, author
Wechsberg, Joseph, writer, journalist, musician, and gourmet
Wedeles, Emil, tobacco merchant, Chicago
Wedeles, Leopold, physician, Chicago
Wedeles, Max, tobacco packer and dealer, owner of Max Wedeles Tobacco Co., Gadson County, Florida
Wehle, Gottlieb, pioneer merchant, Madison, IN, then in NYC
Weidenthal, Henry J., journalist, with *Cleveland World, the Leader, Plain Dealer*; publisher-editor of the *Jewish Independent*
Weidenthal, Leopold, newspaper editor, founder of the Cleveland Cultural Gardens
Weidenthal, Maurice, founder of *Jewish Independent Weekly,* editor of the *Plain Dealer,* Cleveland
Weidenthal, Nathan, physician, Cleveland, OH
Weigel, Helene, stage actress
Weigl, Valerie (née Pick), composer, music therapist
Weil, Solomon, first Bohemian Jew in Michigan, owner of tannery, Ann Arbor
Weinberg, Zvi, Canadian politician
Weinberger, Caspar, attorney, US Secretary of HEW, US Secretary of Defense
Weinberger, Jaromír, composer
Weiner, Charles, tape manufacturer, owner of the Chicago Printed String
Weisgall, Hugo, composer, conductor
Weissberger, Arnold, chemist
Weisskopf, Victor Frederick, theoretical physicist, educator
Weisskopf, Walter, economist
Weitz, Chris, film producer, screenwriter, author, actor, and film director.
Weitz, Paul, film producer, screenwriter, playwright, actor, and film director
Weltsch, Ruben, librarian
Werfel, Franz, novelist, playwright, and poet
Wertheimer, Max, psychologist, founder of Gestalt psychology
Williams, Ilse (Zeisl), social scientist, specialist on opinion research

Winn, Joseph A., psychiatrist, writer
Winternitz, Milton Charles, pathologist, educator, Dean
Winters, Max, co-owner and manager of Minneapolis Lakers Basketball Team, founder of Minnesota Vikings
Wise, Aaron, Rabbi
Wise, Isaac Mayer, Rabbi, founder of Reform Judaism
Wise, Jonah Bondi, Rabbi
Wise, Leo, publisher and editor, American Israelite
Wise, Otto Irving, attorney, editor
Wise, Stephen Samuel, ReformRabbi, Zionist
Wittgenstein, Paul, concert pianist
Wohl, David Philip, shoe manufacturer
Wolfenstein, Lincoln, physicist, professor
Wolfenstein, Martha, essayist, story teller and publicist
Wolfenstein, Samuel, Rabbi, superintendent of Jewish Orphan Asylum, Cleveland
Worh, Karen (Weisskopf), specialist on science education
Wotiz, John Henry, chemist
Wymetal, Wilhelm, stage director, opera director
Wymetal, William, Jr., stage director, director of operas
Wynn, Ed, actor, comedian
Wynn, Keenan, actor
Wynn, Tracy Keenan, screenwriter, producer
Zeisel, Eva Amalia (Striker), industrial designer, ceramist
Zeisl (aka Zeisel), Eric, composer
Zeisler, Joseph, dermatologist, professor, Northwestern University
Zeisler, Sigmund, attorney, Chicago
Zimbler, Liane Juliane Angela, architect, interior designer
Zinner, Peter, American filmmaker and producer
Zoff, Otto, novelist, poet, correspondent
Zweig, Fridericke Maria (Fritzi) von Winternitz (née Burger), writer
Zweig, Fritz Frederick, conductor
Zweig, Stefan, novelist, playwright, journalist and biographer

Epilogue

This book about Czech Jewish people and their contribution to American history has been missing in society and perhaps for a good reason. As hard as it is to define who is Jewish, it is also extremely complicated to define who is a true Czech.

Jewish identity used to be determined through one's history on the grounds of blood and religion, later on nationality. At the end of the road, one might find a Jewish-born Buddhist with an American passport and anti-Israeli views. One might ask himself: "Could I perceive such a personality as a Jew? Does he perceive himself as a Jew? Based on what parameters? Who is he perceived to be and by whom?

Being Czech then represents the same challenge. The national determination of European nations is largely a question of the 18th and 19th centuries. Future nations of various lands of the Czech/Bohemian crown originally did not define themselves on the basis of their latter national identity.

Neither was it the language they spoke, be it Czech or German, which would provide a clue for a person's identity. Their religion might have been another point of identity they had claimed for themselves, complicating their final identity by today's perspective. In the end, who then was the son from a Czech/German mixed marriage, speaking German as the mother tongue, feeling himself to be Czech but being as Roman Catholic as a good Austrian? And if he married a Jewish girl, where does his identity fall? No wonder a book about Czech Jewish people in America was a missing item.

It is not surprising that some personalities of this book might have been astonished to be called Czechs from today's perspective. Many left their Austro-Hungarian state to become Americans, which superseded all of their previous identities. Nevertheless, today they would carry a passport from the Czech Republic, but maybe it would not be the only one they carry in their pocket.

Because the question of one's ancestral roots can be difficult to decipher, Mila Rechcigl, in writing this book, selected and organized personalities on the basis of their achievements and respective fields of operation.

Let us take this book as the first attempt to put together the first list of Czech Jews in American history. Let us be surprised by their Czech roots, however deep they are in individual cases. Let us be reminded by this book of an important fact: it doesn't matter who you think you are, what matters is what you have done with your life that matters.

Hynek Kmoníček

Ambassador of the Czech Republic to the US

Printed in the United States
By Bookmasters